RITCHIE YORKE has been at the cutting edge of music journalism
for over two decades. Internationally renowned, he has
contributed to all the world's major music journals including
Rolling Stone, *Billboard* and the *New Musical Express*. He was
the first journalist to recognise the potential of Led Zeppelin in
the late sixties and as a result gained unprecedented access to the
band. Apart from writing, he has been a peace envoy for John
Lennon and Yoko Ono, served on the Committee of Honour at
the Montreux International Jazz and Blues Festival, and produced
radio documentaries on Van Morrison, Simply Red and Pink
Floyd, to name but a few. He is currently based in Brisbane.

Led Zeppelin: The Definitive Biography has been researched and produced with the co-operation of Led Zeppelin members and close associates.

LED ZEPPELIN

The Definitive
Biography by
RITCHIE
YORKE

UNDERWOOD-MILLER
Novato, California
Lancaster, Pennsylvania

LED ZEPPELIN: The Definitive Biography
ISBN 0-88733-177-7

Previous version published in Great Britain in 1974 as *The Led Zeppelin Biography* by Sphere Books Ltd.

For Christine

who has remained pristine
in the slip-stream
since I don't know when . . .

Library of Congress Cataloging-in-Publication Data
Yorke, Ritchie
    Led Zeppelin, the definitive biography / by Ritchie Yorke.
    p. cm.
    Rev. ed. of: The Led Zeppelin biography. 1974.
    Discography: p.
    ISBN 0-88733-177-7 : $14.95
    1. Led Zeppelin (Musical group) 2. Rock musicians—England—
Biography. I. Yorke, Ritchie. Led Zeppelin biography. II. Title.
ML421.L4Y6 1993
782.42166'092'2—dc20
[B]   93-11561
                                                              MN

'There is nothing stable in the world; uproar's your only music.'
John Keats

'The rest may reason and welcome; 'tis we musicians know.'
Robert Browning

'Do What Thou Wilt Shall Be the Whole of the Law.'
Aleister Crowley

'We are the music makers,
We are the dreamers of dreams . . .
. . . We are the movers and shakers
Of the world for ever, it seems.'
Arthur O'Shaughnessy

'He makes a swan-like end,
Fading in music.'
Act III, *The Merchant of Venice*,
William Shakespeare

Contents

Acknowledgements

First and foremost, the author would like to extend very special thanks to the late John Bonham, Peter Grant, John Paul Jones, Jimmy Page and Robert Plant for the many, many hours they've made available so graciously over the past 24 years. Their early interest and encouragement in the instigation of this project was profoundly powerful.

Special thanks of a different ilk to Christine, Emily and Ian for their prolific patience and oceans of understanding, and of course, a whole lotta love, without which . . . As Mr. Dynamite likes to proclaim, I'll love you tomorrow, just like I love you today.

To Mr. Terrific, Tony Secunda, a vinyl veteran who remains a visionary, for putting the parts into place. Top stuff, Tony.

To many past and present staff members of Atlantic Records and Warner Music, in particular Phil Carson (Atlantic's chief European executive during the 1970s, and ultimately, personal manager of Jimmy Page, Jason Bonham and Robert Plant in the 1980s), Kim Cooke, Ahmet Ertegun, the late Nesuhi Ertegun, Linda Farenden, Harry Geran, Steve Hands, Stan Kulin, Bo Martin, Peter Mitchell, Mike Thies and Jerry Wexler. Take a bow, boys and girls.

This lengthy project was boosted enormously and immeasurably by the support and encouragement of many wonderful human beings, including Alf Annable, Joy Annable, Roy Annable, Anna our goanna, Vic Bailey, the Banks family, the Boyle family, Bob and Sue Braiden, Kenneth Cancellara, Brett Connell, Tom and Glynis Crowley, Frank Davies, Herbert and Irma Ditchburn, Ann, Don, Lee and Tim Ditchburn, Elizabeth and Kenneth Easton, Bob Elrick, Dyke Garratt, Goob, Walt Grealis, Alan Griffith, Bob Hart, Ronnie and Wanda Hawkins, Jim Holt, Richard Hutchison, John Kenny, Shooichi Kusano, Little Guy, Greg and Kate Lane, Arthur MacColl, John and Erin McElroy, Greg and Deb McIvor, Martin Melhuish, Hart Melvin, Van Morrison, Mother Nature, Artie Mull, Mungo, Kel and Trish Naughton, Claude Nobs, Rozo Ono,

Led Zeppelin

Yoko Ono, John Page, John Phillips III, Charlie and Prue Sparks, Scott Sanderson, Tom Steen, Peter Steinmetz, John Stokes, Barry Wheeler, Eve Wahn, Patrick White, and Chris and Samantha Yorke. Thank you one and all. Thanks, of course, in three-part harmony to my publishers, Underwood-Miller, Inc, in particular Tim Underwood.

The author also gratefully acknowledges the various music publications which proved to be a source of additional background research material over the past two decades, including *Billboard, Cashbox, Circus, Disc, Guitar Player, International Times, Melody Maker, Musician, Music Life, Music Week, New Musical Express, Oz, Q, Radio and Records, Rainbow, Record Mirror, Record World, Rolling Stone, She, Sounds, Time Off, Zigzag* and *Zoo World.*

And to many others around the world who must remain nameless but continue to inspire and influence the author through good times and bad.

What a grim existence it would be in a world without music, the ultimate instinct repellent.

Ritche Yorke
July 1993
Brisbane, Australia

Introduction

SOMETIMES IT FEELS LIKE it was only yesterday, the imprint remains so vividly electric to me. An absolutely unforgettable night in September 1971, the closest I ever came to experiencing what it must have been like to be an actual performing member of the live Led Zeppelin, to feel that supreme thrill of standing on stage in the face of the awesome molten energy of 18,000 ecstatically elevated souls.

Over the years I had the substantial pleasure of standing out there and introducing all five Zeppelin concert performances in Toronto, but this particular gig was to be extraordinarily special.

For Toronto audiences, it would be the performing zenith of the band's live career; the fiercely contested itineraries of future tours would for no particular reason preclude Toronto, one of the earliest North American markets to take the band to heart early in 1969.

Of course nobody was aware that night that this would be their final local appearance, but the capacity crowd *did* know they were soon to be on the receiving end of a very special event. Few, if any acts of the early 1970s delivered in concert the power or sparkle or potency – and resulting intense levels of audience enjoyment – that Led Zeppelin routinely mustered. Being the greatest live band in the world was their unwritten credo, and the punters revelled in an excess of expectations. They wouldn't be disappointed.

Backstage you could hear the muffled swarm of 18,000 excited voices, and you could feel the growing expression of that sea of expectation. When tour manager Richard Cole asked me – at the last possible moment with band members already gathered behind the back-stage curtain – if I'd 'do the honours, me old mate, and introduce the lads', I was both thrilled and terrified all at once. But there'd be no time to ponder the deep and meaningless.

The lights went down and there was a sudden hush. A hearty shove in the back from Richard Cole, the jerk of a jocular verbal insult from Bonzo Bonham, and I stumbled past the drum kit towards the front mike stand, illuminated by a pencil-thin white spotlight. Grasping the steel stand for reassurance, I gazed for an infinitely long second into the blackness of that ocean of anticipation. The surge of energy flowing from the audience towards the stage was mesmerising – words fail to capture the profound power of the force which confronted your reporter as he groped for those magic statements that the mass of blackness wanted so desperately to hear.

'Ladies and gentlemen, the greatest rock and roll band in the world, LED ZEPPELIN' finally gushed out past the croaking frog in my parched throat. The immediate roar from the blackness almost bowled me over as I retreated through a grinning Jimmy, Robert and John Paul and another shouted insult from Bonzo as he plonked his rear end on the drumstool. I was still stunned hours later from that first-hand, unadulterated exposure to the incredible intensity of Led Zeppelin's association with their audience.

Much has been churned out about how Led Zeppelin made the people feel, but not a lot has been written about how the people made the band members feel. I suspect I might have got a tiny taste of it that stunning evening in the venerable old hockey palace, the Toronto Gardens. It was eerily exhilarating, and not merely from an ego point of view; there was a unique awareness of something beyond the well-documented realms of rational reason, a connection perhaps with another level of consciousness.

For the players, it obviously must have represented an awesome buzz, likely something a tad too sacred to talk about. It was just a feeling. But what a bountiful artistic reward – the culmination of a lifetime of dreams and aspirations. A supremely special exchange of emotion and admiration, and something that took Led Zeppelin far beyond the course of their contemporaries – a relationship that set them apart from other music makers.

Count Ferdinand von Zeppelin, the visionary German aeronautical inventor, dreamed up the novel idea for the Zeppelin airship in 1874. It took a quarter of a century for his unusual concept to gain official support, and even then its purpose was grossly distorted.

From all reports, the Count was a peaceful man who had non-aggressive intentions for his flying machine. Eventually he reluctantly watched his invention utilised as a weapon in World War I.

After a subsequent disastrous commercial flight accident, the Zeppelin airship fell from favour and for another 25 years, it was nothing but the butt of a bad joke. Stating that a new idea or concept would go over like a lead Zeppelin meant that it was invariably bound to tumble down in flames.

Only recently, with the intensifying of environmental awareness, have air traffic experts re-evaluated the Count's proposals and begun to realise that his concept might be a far-from-laughable solution to one of mankind's insidious pollution problems. Our skies as yet may be streaked by the cigar-like shapes of Zeppelin passenger aircraft.

The comparison between the Count and the unique rock band which united to send its ferocious, blues-based music into the stratosphere under the Zeppelin name 94 years later is a trifle murky, but there are similarities.

Formed in late 1968, Led Zeppelin's historic battle for acceptance by the music establishment has been much shorter in duration, but it too has been overshadowed along the way by misunderstanding and misinterpretation.

Even though Jimmy Page, John Paul Jones, Robert Plant and John Bonham originally banded together with undoubtedly sincere musical motives, the band was savaged all too frequently by uninformed observers, who accused them of manipulation of the music scene, of pandering to gross commerciality, of ripping off the masses – all allegations unworthy of comment.

But this cacophony of resentment at Led Zeppelin's pervasive popularity took its toll on the lives of band members, and at one point they withdrew completely from all music industry activities, other than recording and live performances.

Near disasters at crammed concerts and anonymous threats of violence during later American tours more than once made them contemplate quitting altogether. But unlike many of their contemporaries, Led Zeppelin weren't in the business merely to make money, and somehow they found the fortitude to withstand the often overpowering pressures of rock world domination for a dozen dynamic years, producing some of the finest, timeless moments that rock music can boast in its first four decades.

From the outset in late 1968 Led Zeppelin was accorded incredible popular support from all quarters. From London to Tokyo, from Copenhagen to Los Angeles, from Istanbul to Melbourne, from Singapore to Sao Paulo, praise poured in. The band consistently baffled observers and detractors alike by constantly coming up with surprises on each album and in every tour. This key element of never-ending change, evolving out of the individual and unified talents of four remarkably skilled musicians always open to chance and circumstance, lies behind Zeppelin's enormous and unprecedented success.

Through the years, in between the unforgettable concert tours and albums and the inevitable swarm of rumours, Led Zeppelin has acquired an incredible mystique that was more intense than that of any other act in rock history, even including the Beatles, whose lives were daily grist for the tabloid mill. Led Zeppelin arose out of the late 1960s with all the raw potent power of the British blues boom, and they dominated the cutting edge of popular music through the 1970s and the early 1980s. For a dozen years, they were the frontrunners of the rock mainstream, constantly reinventing themselves and leading the field in a manner which was ultimately beyond imitation.

Their influence has lingered through the present time in the musical aspirations of countless bands, good and bad, all profoundly moved by the Zeppelin legacy. That Led Zeppelin have been able to deliver such notable achievements from within a group policy and philosophy of minimum artistic compromise is a stunning feat.

This was a band that steadfastly adhered to a policy of integrity. In the aftermath of the tragic accidental death of John Bonham in September 1980, the survivors' decision to disband Led Zeppelin wouldn't have come as any real surprise to the informed and compassionate enthusiast. John Bonham couldn't have been replaced, as more so than any drummer of a typical group, his was the essential base on which each song's structure was crafted. Whereas the almighty dollar would have dominated a decision to continue in most other camps, Led Zeppelin members wouldn't entertain the possibility of seeking another drummer. The money didn't matter – their integrity and their respect for what they had all created together were the deciding factors.

The emergence in recent times of John Bonham's son, Jason, as a powerful drummer in his own right (and his two appearances with Page, Plant and Jones at Led Zeppelin reunions in the late 1980s) has given rise to widely reported prospects of a full-scale reunion tour involving gigantic guarantees. While remaining doubtful that money will be the final arbiter in any decision to undertake a reunion tour, I believe the lure of proving sustained relevance in the music scene of the 1990s will – more likely sooner than later – see the lads hit the road one more time. Jason Bonham obviously can't be John Bonham, but he's as close as we're ever going to get to the master himself.

In the meantime, the Led Zeppelin musical legacy will live on, maturing and improving with each passing year, an outstanding testament to the brilliance of the four musicians who tore from their muse so many stirring anthems of the 1970s, such gems of style and often elegance, never lacking in soul and substance. The long-awaited 1990 release of the four-CD box set of quintessential Led Zeppelin, with its sharply focused clarity and the ingenuity of the new running order of familiar songs, underlines their artistic dominance of the hard rock genre, the unparallelled inventiveness and the inevitable risk-taking.

The risks they took are ours to enjoy in appreciating their art. It appears certain that it will be a long, long time before any rock act constructs a song to dethrone 'Stairway to Heaven' from its pre-eminent status as the world's most popular rock song.

The evolution of Led Zeppelin in itself is a classic story of the building of a stairway to nirvana heaven beyond the constraints of conventional rock music.

It has been an honour and a privilege to have observed at first hand – and at times participated in – the exciting evolution of Led Zeppelin's illustrious career. The band's contribution to our lives has been profoundly enriching and enlightening. They truly were the greatest rock and roll band in the world. And probably still are.

In closing, I can only hope that this book will be a door through which you will gain a keener and more acute perception of what this phenomenal, once-in-a-lifetime union of superb musical personalities was all about.

1 The Early Days – Personal Roots and Reasons

John Bonham (1948–1980)

BORN IN THE LUSH MIDLANDS COUNTRYSIDE of Worcestershire on 31 May 1948, drummer John Bonham felt the pull towards percussion at an early age. 'I'd wanted to be a drummer since I was about five years old,' he recalled. 'I used to play on a bath-salts container with wires on the bottom, and on a round coffee tin with a loose wire attached to it to give a snare drum effect. Plus there were always my mum's pots and pans.' The first child of Jack and Joan Bonham, John had a brother, Michael, three years his junior, and a sister, Debbie, fourteen years younger.

John's parents predictably tried hard to ignore their first-born's nerve-annihilating preoccupation, but as the years passed and he kept thumping away, they realised how serious he was. 'When I was ten,' he remembered with the adolescent pride of the kid he was then, 'my mum bought me a snare drum. I've always been fascinated by drums – I felt nothing for any other instrument.

'Later I played a bit of acoustic guitar, but it was always drums, first and foremost. I don't reckon on that jack-of-all-trades thing.'

In 1964, with British charts dominated by the Beatles, Cilla Black, the Dave Clark Five, the Searchers and the Merseybeats, the sixteen-year-old Bonham joined his first band, Terry Webb and the Spiders. 'My dad had bought me my first drum kit the year before. It was almost prehistoric – most of the metal had rusted. Later I learned how to properly look after my drums. People who don't care for their drums really annoy me.

'As soon as I left school, I decided I was definitely going to be a drummer. I was very determined. In Terry Webb and the Spiders, we used to wear purple jackets with velvet lapels. The singer wore a gold lamé jacket, and we all had greased hair and string ties.'

Bonham stayed with the Spiders for a year, and during that time he met his future wife, Pat Phillips, at a dance near his home in

Kidderminster. Just after he moved on to his second group, A Way of Life, at age seventeen, John and Pat were married. Most of the others did the same, and the group became inactive for a while.

'I swore to Pat that I'd give up drumming when we got married. But every night I'd come home and just sit down at the drums and play. I'd be miserable if I didn't.' Living in a fifteen-foot trailer, so desperate for funds that he had to quit smoking in order to pay the rent, John knew that his time had come. He had to take the plunge and drum professionally and make a go of it – or cast off his dreams and find another career.

A couple of years earlier, Bonham had met a young singer named Robert Plant who lived nearby. Now was the moment to renew acquaintances. As it turned out, Plant was a member of a group called the Crawling King Snakes and they needed a drummer.

As Plant remembered the episode, 'It was pretty debatable at first whether John would join us. It was a fairly long way to go and pick him up for a gig, and we never knew whether we'd have the petrol money to get over there.'

They maintained the arrangement for a few months while the band landed a steady supply of gigs. Unusually for that period, they wrote some of their own material, but their performance mainstays were fairly distinctive versions of songs like 'Plastic Fantastic Lover' and 'She Has Funny Cars'. But eventually the transportation problems became too much to handle and Bonham decided to rejoin A Way of Live. But he and Robert Plant by then had laid the groundwork for what would prove to be a fruitful musical relationship.

Bonham's musical reputation was growing rapidly in the Midlands. One Bonham-booster from that era was Birmingham-born Ed Pilling, who later achieved a measure of fame on the Canadian rock scene. Pilling recalled, 'A friend of mind, Tony Clarkson, was the bass player with A Way of Life and he took me to see the band in action.

'Bonham was just great – he was the strongest, loudest drummer I'd ever seen. He was the first local drummer to line his bass drum with aluminium to give it a cannon-like sound. The sound he got was just unreal.

'I went down to see the band play in London, and John broke his bass drumhead during the gig. Band members said that was typical. Actually several other groups told me that certain clubs wouldn't book bands in which John Bonham played drums, because he was too loud. Of course *we* all thought he was great, but some of the club managers felt he was too loud. In those days, bands weren't as loud as they are now.'

'Well yeah,' an ebullient Bonham admitted with a beaming grin when I raised the subject of power hitting in the early days of Led Zeppelin. 'I was *always* breaking drumheads when I first started playing. Later on I learned how to play louder but without hitting the drums so hard. It has all to do with the swing of the stick.'

Bonham was rightfully proud of his self-taught status in drumming. 'When I first started playing, I was interested in music and I was able to read it. But when I moved into playing with groups, I did a silly thing and dropped it. I do think it's great to be able to write down ideas in music form.

'But I also think that feeling is a lot more important in drumming than mere technique. It's all very well to be playing a triple paradiddle – but who's going to know you're actually doing it? If you pay too much attention to technique, you start to sound like every other drummer does. I think that being original is what counts. When I listen to other drummers, I like to be able to say, "Oh, that's nice, I haven't heard that before." I think that being yourself as a drummer is so much better than just sounding like anyone else.'

Bonham always claimed that he was exposed to the same rock percussion influences as other young British drummers emerging in the early 1960s. But he took his own style very seriously and he worked diligently and relentlessly at mastering a natural individual sound.

'I've never considered that I was particularly influenced by anyone or anything. When I started playing, I was most impressed by those early soul records. I liked the feel and the sound they achieved . . . and I suppose I just said to myself, "I'll get that sound too." I've always liked drums to be big and powerful. I've never been into using cymbals overmuch. I use them to crash into a solo and out of it, but basically I prefer the actual drum sound. To me drums sound better than cymbals.'

His passionate preference for the unique uncompromised tone of tight, taut pigskin ultimately led Bonham to perform Led Zeppelin solos with his bare hands. 'I've been doing that for an awfully long time,' he admitted. 'It goes back to when I first joined up with Robert Plant. Years ago I saw a group on a jazz programme doing it. I think that started me off . . . it really impressed me one helluva lot.

'It wasn't so much what you could play with your hands – you just got a lovely little tone out of the drums that you couldn't get with sticks. I thought it would be a good thing to do so I've been doing it ever since. You really get an absolutely true drum sound because there's no wood involved. It hurts your hands at first, but then the skin hardens. I think I can hit a drum harder with my hands than with sticks.'

Midlands musical contemporary Ed Pilling observed, 'John was a very aggressive drummer . . . and just like he drummed, he was.' Not infrequent bouts of fisticuffs also helped to toughen Bonham's hands.

'John was never afraid of a knock,' said Pilling. 'He didn't go out of his way looking for it but if it was there it was exercise and a chance to get a few things off his chest.'

Maturing as a drum stylist by the mid-1960s, Bonham couldn't help but be impressed by the astonishing percussion virtuoso, Ginger Baker. 'When I first started, Ginger was a big image in Britain. He was a star in his own right. In the old big band era, a drummer was a backing musician and nothing else. In the early American bands, the drummer played almost unnoticed with brushes, always in the background. Gene Krupa was the first big band drummer to be really noticed. He came right out into the front and he played drums much louder than they had ever been played before. And much better.

'People hadn't taken much notice of drums until Krupa came along. Ginger Baker was responsible for the same sort of thing in rock. Rock music had been around for a few years before Baker, but he was the first to come out with this "new" attitude – that a drummer could be a forward part of a rock band . . . not something that was stuck in the background and forgotten about.

'I don't think anyone can ever put Ginger Baker down. Of course, every drummer has his own idea of just when Baker was at his absolute peak . . . I thought he was just fantastic when he played with the Graham Bond Organization. It's really a pity that American and Japanese audiences didn't see that band because it really was a fantastic line-up consisting of Jack Bruce, Graham Bond and Ginger Baker.

'Personally I think Ginger Baker was more into jazz than rock . . . he definitely did play with a jazz influence. He was always doing things in 5/4 and 3/4 tempos which are associated with jazz. Unfortunately he's always been a very weird sort of bloke. You couldn't really get to know him – he just wouldn't allow it. Ginger's thing as a drummer was that he was always himself. It was pointless for anyone to try to do what he was doing. And Eric Clapton was the same in the guitar field.'

While Ginger Baker was astonishing audiences around the world with Eric Clapton and Jack Bruce as members of Cream (generally regarded as the epitome of 1960s British blues), Bonham again teamed up with Robert Plant, this time in the appropriately named Band of Joy. After serving their apprenticeship and getting their act together, American folksinger Tim Rose invited the band to open his 1968 UK tour.

'I think my first real break was backing up Tim Rose,' Bonham said. But the concerts appealed to a limited cult market, and Rose returned to the States. Band of Joy spluttered along for a time and then disbanded. Robert Plant elected to work with the veteran British blues stalwart Alexis Korner.

'Robert and I lost contact for two or three months,' Bonham explained. 'But Tim Rose was returning to Britain for another tour and he remembered me from the Band of Joy. He offered me a gig as the drummer in his band and I took it.'

Unbeknownst to the young drummer, bigger and better prospects were lurking in the shadows. Neither Plant nor Bonham could know that their lives – and their fortunes – were about to be changed immeasurably in the coming weeks.

John Paul Jones

When John Paul Jones took his first breaths of life as John Baldwin on 3 January 1946, in Sidcup, Kent, he inhaled the frothy fumes of full-on showbiz. 'My parents were both in the business,' he said. 'They were in variety – with a double act, a musical comedy thing. I've been on the road since I was two years old!'

His father, an accomplished jazz musician named Joe Baldwin, had played with Britain's renowned Ambrose Orchestra in the big band era. 'Dad was a pianist and we used to go out gigging together,' Jones said in 1990. 'He really wanted me to take up the saxophone because he believed the bass guitar would be just a passing sort of fad.

'He said I should play saxpohone because I'd never starve,' Jones laughed with the wisdom of hindsight. 'But I didn't want to play sax – I wanted to play bass. When he found out I could play the bass, he said, "All right, good bass players are hard to come by." And off we went doing weddings and masonics and the usual run of things.'

An only child, Jones had first taken up the bass as a fourteen-year-old student at Christ College boarding school. Once his choice of instrument was accepted, his father wisely urged Jones to learn to read and write music, a skill which would stand him in good stead in the diverse musical map which lay ahead.

Upon leaving school, John played an assortment of gigs at various Army bases in the area. 'Just after I turned seventeen I accepted an invitation to turn professional and to join Jet Harris and Tony Meehan's band.'

Tony Meehan vividly recalls that particular audition. 'It was held above the Roebuck Pub in Tottenham Court Road in London. We had a single called "Diamonds" at number one on the charts and we were putting together a band. John Paul heard about it and showed up. He was just out of school, very young and a bit nervous. Despite the nerves, he was a good musician and he knew his shit. He was cocky too in a certain way and I liked that. So we hired him.

'He toured with us for a year or so until the band broke up. I was doing some freelance production work for Decca Records at the time, and he played on a lot of my sessions. I liked to use the guys from the band; they knew their shit and it supplemented their incomes. They were making about £40 a week in the band, which was good bread in those days. Add to that the session income and TV fees – all told, it was a good gig for them.

'John Paul always displayed good taste and good ideas. He wasn't the usual run-of-the-mill player. I was playing drums and the relationship between bass and drums is very important. We worked closely and we worked well together. I always thought it was a great band, but far ahead of its time.'

Undoubtedly the Harris–Meehan line-up was ahead of its time. The widely acclaimed John McLaughlin was on lead guitar, while the late Glen Hughes, who achieved prominence with Georgie Fame's Blue Flames, was blowing sax.

'We were doing the sort of things which Chicago and Blood, Sweat and Tears came up with a few years later,' Meehan claimed. 'But we were booed off stage with some of it, the mainstream jazz things. People didn't want to listen, they just wanted to bop. It was dancing days – you didn't *listen* to music.

'All of us were depressed by the general pop scene, with the possible exception of the Beatles, who'd only just started. We were a progressive band and we loved what we were playing – that's what kept us together. We knew we were playing some good things but they were falling on deaf ears. Eventually Jet Harris had a nervous breakdown, and we decided to pack it in.

'John Paul's contribution to my band had been very significant – and he was only a kid then. He's well-read, a thinker, very intelligent. For John Paul, rock and roll was obviously neither the beginning nor the end of his musical potential. I think rock was really only a convenient vehicle for him; he would have been equally at home in either a jazz group or a classical orchestra. He is and was a musician's musician. He served his apprenticeship with us, and then he moved on to session work and arranging.'

The transition to professional session-playing has always been an arduous process. The London session scene was highly competitive and in many respects, a closed shop. Rampant nepotism and mates-based recommendations made it next to impossible to get a foot in the door. But John Paul's sheer ability made him hard to ignore and he was soon given the chance to make a record by himself – or almost. He played six-string bass with overdubbed orchestration on the traditional tune 'Baja'. It was 1964 and he was eighteen years old.

Partly through musical boredom – the bass remained a misunderstood and thoroughly underrated instrument in those dark ages of British rock – and partly through a desire for artistic adventure, John Paul started to investigate keyboard instruments. He'd played church organ as a lad, so he already possessed the rudiments of keyboard expertise.

'Organ was originally my favourite love,' he said, adding wryly, 'but for session playing, I found it much easier to carry a bass guitar to work than a Hammond organ. So there I was living with all I had – a guitar, a Hammond organ, and a table and bed in my room in London.

'As a bass player, I wasn't influenced by a lot of people because it was only in the mid- to late-1960s that you could even hear the bass properly on records. I had a number of obvious jazz influences – most of the good jazz bass players influenced me in one way or another . . . Charlie Mingus, Ray Brown, Scott LeFaro. I even got into jazz organ for a while until I couldn't stand the musicians any more and I had to get back to rock and roll.'

Like so many prominent rock bass players, John Paul was highly impressed by the arrival of Phil Upchurch, the Chicago bass guitar pioneer and seminal bass stylist. 'I've got to own up,' Jones said, 'the first record that really turned me on to rock bass guitar was "You Can't

Sit Down" by Phil Upchurch, which has an incredible bass solo and was a really good record as well. It was very simple musically but the record had an incredible amount of balls.'

The major music turn on in the mid-1960s for John Paul Jones was that thick, fat and jet-black Motown bass style, in many ways the definitive underlying rhythm of the decade, a fact often overlooked by rock historians. 'Bass was one of the Motown sound's biggest selling points for me,' said John Paul. 'Players such as James Jamerson, who was incredibly good. Motown was a bass player's paradise because they'd actually found a way to record the bass so that you could hear every note. The Motown bass players were just unbelievable – I think that some of the Motown records used to end up as sort of concertos for the bass guitar. I'll never forget when I first heard "I Was Made to Love Her" by Stevie Wonder. The bass on the record was incredible . . . and that's coming from the sort of person who really listens to the bass parts.'

Motown's musical motto, 'It's what's in the grooves that counts', meant what it implied. By revealing a broader bottom-line potential for the actual sound of a bass guitar, now widely regarded as one of the three crucial factors essential to any great record, the Motown sound out of Detroit led ultimately to a radical reappraisal of what British studio producers and engineers considered to be an acceptable sound for the instrument.

'So many bass players really got annoyed about what had been happening in Britain and they demanded better,' said Jones.

With much pushing, and such widespread player dissatisfaction, the position of the bass guitarist in a studio setting began to brighten. But there still remained for John Paul the broader issues of general session apathy and aspiring towards artistic satisfaction in his contributions. 'I discovered that musical arranging and general studio directing were much more interesting than just sitting there and being told what to play.'

By 1990, Jones had developed an interesting perspective on that period of evolution from playing to arranging. 'The only real impetus I had for arranging was panic. I put me hand up. You know how it is – somebody asks does anybody do any arrangements and you say, "Yeah, sure." Then as the session gets closer, you get a book and try and work out what goes where. After a couple of these situations, you find you're an arranger. It happens that way for a lot of people.'

John Paul's golden opportunity for a foray into successful arranging came through his association with the emerging British rock poet, Donovan Leitch. 'I'd been doing some sessions for Donovan. The first thing I really did with him was "Sunshine Superman". I happened to be booked on the session as a bass player and I ended up doing most of the arrangements. The original arranger they'd booked for the session really didn't know about anything . . . so I got the rhythm section together and we went from there.'

'Sunshine Superman' was a career revitalisation chart-crasher for Donovan (who'd lost his way after a string of earlier hits such as 'Catch the Wind', 'Colours' and 'Universal Soldier') and its massive global success in 1966 with sales of over 3 million naturally led to John Paul's intimate involvement in the follow-up single.

' "Mellow Yellow" I did entirely on my own as far as the arrangements were concerned,' said Jones. 'I was pleased with the results: the record was different to what was happening in the general session scene.'

This collaboration with Donovan led to Jones's first working session project with an up-and-coming young session guitarist named Jimmy Page. In fact John Paul booked Page to play lead guitar on another distinctive Donovan classic, the easy rocking 'Hurdy Gurdy Man'.

John Paul found himself heavily in demand as a skilled bass player with commercial arranging talents. 'There's no specialisation so you played for everybody,' he said in 1990. 'In England, everybody does everything – unlike America, you don't have country session players or rock or pop. In the mid-1960s, the London session scene was very large and active. You would do the Rolling Stones, the Everly Brothers, French rock and roll sessions, German ones, Engelbert, Tom Jones, Lulu – and all in the same day quite often.'

The good word about Jones echoed around London's music production enclaves. The noted American album producer, Jimmy Miller (Rolling Stones, Traffic, Spencer Davis Group) remembered arriving in London in September 1966 looking for new challenges. 'I started working with Island Records cutting solo artists like Jackie Edwards and Jimmy Cliff, who needed backing musicians for their sessions. Everybody told me I had to use John Paul – he was considered the best bass player around. And later on when I was working with the Stones and we wanted some really imaginative arranging, I naturally thought of John Paul.'

John Paul arranged the outstanding single 'She's a Rainbow' for the Rolling Stones and also worked on several tracks on the *Their Satanic*

Majesties Request album. All of these associations would stand him in good stead for what lay ahead. But the London life wasn't all joy and creative juices boiling – he also found himself toiling on boring Top-40 format fodder with producer Mickie Most and his bubblegum act, Herman's Hermits. His restlessness grew as an ivy of frustration took hold.

And so it was in that summer of 1968, at the age of 23 with eight years of diverse musical experience in his kitbag, John Paul Jones was ripe for a fresh outlet for his considerable skills. And more than ready to leap into a new creative course.

Robert Plant

According to the pundits of popular astrology, Leos are extremely sensual, dramatic, fun-loving people, born leaders in whatever they do. It is said to be *the* star sign of creativity, with the all-powerful sun as its symbol.

Robert Anthony Plant, born 20 August 1948 in the English/Welsh border county of Worcestershire, seems to fit all these generalisations. He pursued his own peculiar course, right from the beginning.

His father, a civil engineer, duly arranged for his only son to attend grammar school near Birmingham. 'It was decided by my teachers that I was intelligent but unwilling to concentrate,' said Robert. 'I do remember being a kid in short pants at Christmas time looking into the mirror and singing "Hound Dog".

'At thirteen, I liked girls all of a sudden and it all came down to attracting them the best way I could. So I grew my hair. It flopped down over my ears and was immediately chopped off by demand. I forgot about lesons for the next few years and kept joining pop groups.'

Robert's parents showed less enthusiasm for their son's rebellious interests in long hair and rock and roll. Nevertheless they didn't go out of their way to discourage him, and indeed his father used to drive him to the local club where Robert became intrigued with white men singing the blues, a new form of music to most Midlands rock freaks.

'There was this fellow called Terry Foster who lived near Kidderminster, my home village. Terry was an incredible eight-string guitarist, and instead of playing it in the normal way, he used to play like Big Joe Williams with the instrument half on his lap. He was a horrible bloke at times but he was a real white bluesman, and when

I was fifteen I fell immediately under his spell. I suppose he was the one who really introduced me to this music.

'My dad used to drop me off at the Seven Stars Blues Club in Stourbridge and we used to wail away on "Got My Mojo Working" and stuff like that. Chris Wood used to play with us, and Stan Webb and Andy Sylvester were in a competing band.' Wood later joined Steve Winwood's Traffic and Webb helped form Chicken Shack, a highly regarded late-1960s British blues band.

'We had a residency at the Seven Stars,' Plant added. 'All the other musicians who didn't have club residencies used to come along and sit right at the front with their arms folded. It was a good atmosphere – a real blues club like I'd love Smitty's Corner in Chicago to be. The sound was good and the people who saw me playing in 1963–1964 still remember it. People have said to me since, "You've come a long way, Robert, but the music's still the same."

'The Seven Stars Blues Club was really my initiation; our group was called the Delta Blues Band. When we weren't doing that number, a guitarist and myself would go around the local folk clubs playing "Corinna Corinna". The first music which really appealed to me – even when I was still at school – was stuff like Bob Dylan's "Corinna Corinna". When you look deeper into that kind of music, you find that it has a lot of the feelings that exist in blues. Then, of course, you realise that the blues field is a very wide one.'

Like most young rock musicians, Robert Plant ultimately stumbled into a crossroads in his blooming career path. 'It was really hard to combine school and the clubs and keep a compatible relationship with schoolmasters and parents, at the same time as getting into what I really wanted to do. At the time, I thought the combination was great. Apart from being able to have a drink under age, it gave me a break into a different society with different values.

'You can go to a grammar school and never see the light of day again for the rest of your life. The moment you pass your 11-plus exams, it could be all finished for you. I'm afraid it upset my parents a bit when I got in with this musician crew, and the cleft between mum and dad and me got gradually wider.'

At fifteen Plant had to make a major decision. 'I was supposed to start training as a chartered accountant. Although I was really young, I suddenly decided just where I was going. I packed up the accountancy training after only a couple of weeks and I went back to college to get some more O-levels. It was getting to the stage where I only dared to go home at night because my hair was so long. So at sixteen I left home and I started my real education musically – moving from group to group, furthering my knowledge of the blues and other music which had weight and was worth listening to.'

Ten years later, Plant looked back on that crucial period quite philosophically. 'That decision was the only thing I've ever looked at in my life from a long-term viewpoint. You've just got to have a go at what you really want to do first. I decided that if I didn't get anywhere by the time I was twenty, I would pack it in. Of course it didn't really matter what happened because I wouldn't have packed it in anyway.

'The whole scene was amazement, enlightenment, a total trip-out. You just couldn't reproduce those moments. You can't give up something you really believe in just for financial reasons. If you die by the roadside, then you die by the roadside – so be it. At least you know that you've tried. Ten minutes in the music scene was the equal to a hundred years outside of it.

'Fortunately my parents saw it too, but only *after* I'd proved it. Not before . . . I'm a little sorry about that, actually. They just couldn't relate to it at all, not even on a musical level. I just wasn't toeing any normal line.'

After leaving home, Plant joined the Crawling King Snakes. 'The group was into a bit more of a commercial sound than the other bands I'd played with. I'd be hopping around the stage with the mike stand in the air. A lot of incredible things happened to us and I met a lot of people who made sure that I'd carry on in the way I was going.'

Plant dedicated himself to finding out more about the blues and its origins, and attended any UK music festivals featuring American blues performers. 'I always got a shiver every time I saw Sonny Boy Williamson – the way he would strut out onto the stage. Finally I nicked one of his big bass mouth harps from backstage. I've still got it at home. Sonny Boy really did it for me. I couldn't believe the amazing control that he had.

'I used to seek out tales about him. For example, he always liked to eat some rabbit after a gig. One time in a Birmingham hotel, the only thing he could find in which to cook up his rabbit was a coffee percolator. So he put it in, turned it on and promptly fell asleep. The rabbit cooked and cooked and cooked. In the end, they had to evacuate the entire floor of the hotel and Sonny Boy was asleep, still snoring away. He had this strange charm about him though. He'd have a really good time yet he was really coarse – he was everything that I wanted to be at the age of 70.'

Another key influence on Plant's developing blues-tinged vocal style was Tommy McClellan, who recorded on the Bluebird label for RCA in the thirties. 'His rapport, the way he so completely expressed himself on record was great. It was as though he was saying "fuck . . . fuck you!" all the time. He was shouting out all these lyrics with such gusto that even now when hearing his records, you just have to go "Cor!" It was the same with Robert Johnson. I couldn't believe his empathy with his guitar playing.'

For Plant, B.B. King – the amiable genius generally regarded as a crucial inspiration on the evolution of British white blues – was a less vital influence. 'I do like to listen to B.B. and I like his stalking and leading up to things like "Don't Answer the Door" with that big rap style that Isaac Hayes got into later. But I think as far as taking things from him B.B. King is more of a guitarist sort of singer.

'My own influences were more blues people like Snoots Elgin, Robert Johnson, Tommy McClellan and even Bukka White. Bukka had a really nasal thing. His records from the 1930s, like "Fixing to Die" and "Bukka's Jitterbug" have a nasal vocal approach which I sometimes use. I'm not so sure about his newer stuff. Suddenly people like Bukka White are being grabbed hold of and shoved into a studio to make an ethnic blues recording.

'The artists think "Well, it's 200 bucks – that'll keep me in firewood for the next three months". So they get into their wheelchairs, do the thing and all the blues freaks say "Well man, this is the real blues", and it's really a load of bollocks. I've also always admired the real vocal bite of Tommy McClellan. And of course there was the Ray Charles influence. I'll never be able to sing like that.'

And then along came Steve Winwood, an emerging vocalist from Birmingham who made it obvious to Plant and his contemporaries through his gorgeous gravel-throated style, that white blues singers didn't invariably have to be plastic pretenders. 'Steve Winwood – I've always admired Steve. I just couldn't believe his incredible vocal range when the Spencer Davis Group first became popular in Britain – when they were doing songs like Slim Harpo's "Don't Start Crying Now" and "Watch Your Step" and "Ramblin' Rose".

'Steve Winwood was one of the finest white musicians in Britain and he didn't stick to the norm like the Hollies and all those groups which simply followed the arrangements and sang all the same things every night. Along came little Stevie Winwood screaming out all these blues songs, and I realised that he was only a bit older than me and I knew, "Gosh, that's what I've been trying to do." '

Other realisations took a longer time forming. 'I never really knew exactly where I wanted to end up. For a long time I thought that I just wanted to sing the country blues, maybe with only two people, or a very straight blues band. For example, the first time I heard Fleetwood Mac, I thought that they were the very straight blues band that I wanted to be in – they had that sort of Chicago-style tightness about them.

'Finally I found out that I was in a rut. I'd been singing with a lot of groups. And I'd written a few songs myself that really didn't have the right amount of balls behind them. It really just went around in circles until I formed the first Band of Joy.'

The Band of Joy, in its various incarnations, was to be a near-ideal vehicle for Robert's mid-1960s musical meanderings. It started out with a topical mixture of blues and soul music, gradually shifted back into pure blues, then ultimately added a veneer of Birmingham over the newly evolving US West Coast rock band consciousness. The Band of Joy eagerly assimilated diverse musical influences and – more than any other single factor – prepared Plant for his subsequent musical experimentations.

'Living near Birmingham, I naturally got in with a lot of Jamaicans and I started to like the old blue beat. Plus we'd been doing a Darrell Banks number, something by Otis Clay and even Little Milton favourites. Of course we were received everywhere with open arms. As a band, we were still learning . . . the drummer would slow down the beat every now and then, and the guitarist played a few odd chords. He never really ever played "Sunny" with the same chords on any two successive nights, God bless him. But it was a good time to be playing – I was starting to slip in a few blues things and they were going down as well as Darrell Banks, which was progress.'

Not everybody was impressed; the Band of Joy's manager wasn't a big fan of Robert. 'He just told me I couldn't sing and I was sacked from the group. He told me, "I'm sorry Robert but there's just something about you." I asked him to give me another chance but he wouldn't.'

Undeterred, Plant formed another Band of Joy. 'But somehow I was still tied in with this illustrious manager who'd given me the sack from the previous group. I'd gone back to him out of desperation. The new band decided to have painted faces on stage – before the arrival of the Crazy World of Arthur Brown. It went all right for a while but we were frightening our audiences to death. This big fat bass player would come running on and dive straight off the stage. I was howling with laughter at the sight of him in kaftan and bell bottoms billowing into the audience. The whole thing was absurd. I was driving the van as well and doing all sorts of jobs.'

Out of such untimely absurdities arose the third and final version of the Band of Joy, a combination which saw Plant teamed up with a powerful drummer, John Bonham. 'We got in a fantastic guitarist, a good bass player and Bonzo Bonham came in on drums,' said Plant. From its inception, this was a promising group, willing and able to tackle the odd bit of songwriting plus ambitious arrangements of other material.

Plant had recently become entranced by America's flowering West Coast rock scene. 'I got hold of a copy of a Buffalo Springfield album – it was great because it was the kind of music you could leap around to, or you could just sit down and dig it. Then I got the first Moby Grape album which was a knockout. It fitted together so well; I think I reacted to the spirit of it. I'd loved good blues for years but all of a sudden I couldn't listen to any old blues any more. It really was a big change – now I was sobbing to Arthur Lee and Love doing "Forever Changes".'

In the evenings after gigs, Plant and the Band of Joy hung out at the Cedar Club, a Birmingham musicians' after-hours spot. Ed Pilling, a friend from those days, recalled, 'We drank a lot together. Robert always came in smartly dressed, which sounds funny when you think of him now. I think he thought my long hair was a bit out of style. I looked a bit of a hippie type. Robert was more slick and into dressing mod.'

John Bonham, hammering away behind Plant on the drums, was also open to adapting the traditional Birmingham blend of blues and soul and he and Plant soon developed a close personal friendship. As long ago as 1970 Bonham remarked, 'He knows me off by heart and vice versa. I think that's why we get on so well. I believe that when you get to know someone – when two people get together and realise each other's faults and good points – you can then get on with them for a long time because nothing they do can piss you off when you're already accustomed to it.' To this Plant deftly countered, 'Bonzo Bonham is a good sparring partner.'

The singer and drummer worked together for a couple of mildly exciting years in the Band of Joy and three singles were released. 'Eventually,' said Plant, 'we were getting between sixty and seventy-five quid per night. But it didn't keep improving. In the end, I just had to give it up. I thought, "Bollocks, nobody at all wants to know about us!" And Bonzo went off to work with Tim Rose.'

In the meantime, Plant had met the serenely beautiful Anglo-Indian woman who would become his wife on 9 November 1968. 'I met Maureen at a Georgie Fame concert in 1966. I hadn't particularly liked what I'd heard of Fame's singing but I went along to see him perform. He didn't show up but I met my future wife instead.

'Seriously, I think marriage for me was the make-or-break of being a stable person, or just going on with this out-and-out looning. In the pop world, where everything gets blown up and unreal, you never know what is going to happen. You are going to have children here, there and everywhere if you lead that sort of life – and you've got to expect the consequences. I don't often admit it but being married is part of the peace of mind and stability thing I hope I've found.'

Tony Secunda, the astute former manager of Procol Harum and the Move and a long-time believer in Plant's potential, remembers his visits with Maureen and Robert in their early days together. 'Trevor Burton of the Move was a good friend of Robert's and they both had Anglo-Indian girlfriends,' both 'really beautiful ladies' in Secunda's estimation. 'Robert was living with Maureen in this house that was completely full of people. It really was a very busy place. We used to sit up all night together and then say good morning to other people just leaving for work. It was very nice and they were very good people. If ever there could have been a basis for soulful, urban blues in this country, it was right there in Birmingham with these first-generation immigrants from India. Robert had some good influences and I must admit I always felt he would be a star.'

But fierce dedication, grand aspirations and burning talent don't pay the rent. With no steady gig – and no savings to fall back on – Robert had little faith in his commercial prospects. He's admitted more than once that he thought he'd end up on the dole.

'I wasn't going to give up, though. For a while I was living off Maureen, God bless her. Then I did some road-making to earn some bread. I actually laid half the asphalt on the West Bromwich High Street. But all it did for me was to give me six shillings-and-tuppence an hour, an emergency tax code and big biceps. All the navvies called me the pop singer. Looking back I suppose it was really funny.'

The Band of Joy hadn't officially disbanded but gigs were few and far between. One of them took place at London's trendy Speakeasy Club and in the audience was Alexis Korner, the veteran British blues figure who had played with guitarist Jimmy Page at the Marquee. 'I rather liked Robert,' Alexis said before his death, 'and since the Band of Joy disintegrated a couple of gigs later, we worked out a loose arrangement and did some gigs around the Birmingham area.

'We started an album that was never finished. One of the tracks, "Operator", came out on an album called *Bootleg Him* on RAK in Britain and Warner in the States. It was just Robert, myself and the English piano player Steve Miller. We thought of forming a special trio at one point. We worked on and off for a year but it was all very loose – I just didn't want to reform a band at that point. It was a very, very satisfying relationship both musically and personally. We really enjoyed working together, even though it was only a temporary thing. Robert needed a regular sum of money – it wasn't a lot but it was more than I could afford. So he kept looking around.

'I always thought Robert had the makings of a very strong singer and harmonica player. I didn't think the rest of the Band of Joy were up to his talents. I always knew it would happen to Robert – I mean, it *had* to happen to him.'

A demo disc Plant had produced with the Band of Joy especially impressed Tony Secunda. 'It was worn out and covered with beer but it still sounded great through the scratches.' Secunda played it for a friend, producer Denny Cordell. 'We had the Regal Zonophone label happening at the time, so we got Robert to come down to London to make an audition test tape at the Marquee Studios . . . which later lost the bloody tape. When we made it, the people in the studio were quite stunned. It was just Robert and his harp, plus a bloody guitar player who couldn't keep up with him. People were coming into the control room saying, "Who's that?"

'Denny Cordell liked the tape but he had some reservations about Robert's timing. I said, "Just listen to the bloody voice – it's an insane lead instrument all by itself." So we arranged a meeting. Robert came bouncing in – thin and good looking and fit as a fiddle – and I think it overshadowed Denny a bit. Robert was bouncing off the walls: he was like an over-trained racehorse with all this excess energy. Denny was into a much slower relaxed pace and he had a few rolls hanging over his belt. And he just couldn't handle it and he blanked out. He told me later he had Joe Cocker and he couldn't handle anything else.

Plus I was up to my ears twelve hours a day just holding Procol Harum together, not to mention the Move, so we had to pass.

'I told Robert of the decision and he took it well. Since I was sort of his friend in London, I said I'd try and think of something else he might check out. I'd been telling him for years that he was gonna be a star and I really believed it. It was just a matter of finding a suitable outlet. With his energy and his talent, he *had* to make it. He was like so many people from the Midlands – down to earth, basic, extrovert. And that energy couldn't be stopped.'

Powerfully prophetic words, but Plant himself wasn't quite so positive. 'Looking back now,' he told me a few years later, 'I suppose I hadn't done much at all prior to joining up with Alexis Korner. I had been through a long period of trying to find out what I wanted to do musically. You go through the initial thing where you want to get up on stage and scream your balls off . . . then the next minute you want to play blues . . . and finally you find out that everything is a means to an end, to what you really want to do musically – once you've reached it. So I suppose that my first four or five years were spent finding out what I wanted to do. You could either end up going completely into the pop field on a commercial trip, or you could just stick to what you personally liked musically.'

Although Robert Plant hadn't the faintest premonition as he pondered his predicament through the long summer months of 1968, both the chance and the choice were literally right around the corner. His steadfast endurance and boundless enthusiasm were soon to pay off in spectacular fashion.

Jimmy Page

James Patrick Page's earliest memories revolve around idyllic days at his greatuncle's country home, an English manor house surrounded by 400 lush acres of bountiful farmland. 'We lived on this farm near Northampton. I can remember being fascinated by the animals.' An only child, he thrived in the lyrical serenity of the English countryside, riding his bike around the craggy hills, chasing butterflies, fishing and assembling a stamp collection on rainy days. Visits to local stately homes which displayed antiques and *objets d'art* gave him very early a taste for the aristocratic elegance of bygone eras.

That pleasant period lasted from his birth on 8 January 1944 until he was eight. Then his father, an industrial personnel officer, moved the family to Epsom, west of London. His mother remembered that as a child, 'Jimmy was fun, but quiet fun. He wasn't a screamer sort of boy. Like most other lads his age, I suppose, he liked to listen to records on the radio. He seemed mildly interested in music. He'd have a go on anybody's piano when we went visiting, but we didn't have one of our own.'

Until he was thirteen, Jimmy's only active involvement in music was singing in a choir. In 1957 his parents gave him a significant gift. 'We bought him a Spanish guitar,' his mother said. 'He just picked it up and started to play it. It all seemed so natural. He went along to a fellow in Kingston and had half-a-dozen lessons, but there weren't any guitar masters around in those days. After six lessons, the pupil was usually as good as his instructor.'

Jimmy's parents not only tolerated their son's growing infatuation with pop and rock and roll music, but actually encouraged it. Not everyone was so sympathetic. 'When I was at school,' Jimmy joked, 'I had my guitar confiscated every day. They would hand it back to me each afternoon at four o'clock. I always thought the good thing about guitar was that they *didn't* teach it at school. Teaching myself to play was the first and most important part of my education.'

Another essential part of his learning concerned curiosity about the opposite sex. In 1970, he looked back over his life and declared the most memorable occasion was the day in his fifteenth year when he first fell in love. 'It was one particular day in the summer and this girl and I wandered hand in hand through the countryside. It was the first time I felt I was truly in love.' It was also the occasion of Page's initial sexual adventure.

Jimmy's first electric guitar was a secondhand 1949 Les Paul, bought on hire purchase with his father as guarantor. After completing his exams, Jimmy applied for a job as a laboratory assistant. But before the position was filled, he accepted an offer as guitarist with a band called Neil Christian and the Crusaders. 'I took on Jimmy Page when he was still at school,' Christian enjoys telling people. 'I talked to his parents because they wanted him to stay on at school and not leave for some rock and roll band, but I talked them into it. He played with the Crusaders for several months before deciding he wanted to get into session playing.' Page said he quit the Crusaders because his health was playing up and he caught glandular fever.

Jimmy's reputation was beginning to spread. Prominent British drummer, B.J. Wilson, from Procol Harum, recalled, 'Many, many years ago when I was just starting to play drums, Jimmy Page was regarded as one of the best. One of the finest concerts I ever attended in my life was Neil Christian and the Crusaders the night Chris Farlowe got up and jammed with them. It was really incredible.'

John Gibb, a singer and guitar player who grew up in the same area as Page, regularly attended gigs by Neil Christian and the Crusaders. Looking back on those early days from his present Toronto base, Gibb reminisced, 'Jimmy was definitely the star of the band and he was a real raver. He had all the equipment that all the other young guitar players wanted but couldn't afford. He played a Gretsch guitar in those days, great finger-style stuff. He was also the first guy with a foot pedal. All of us young, aspiring players used to check out Jimmy regularly. He had more money to spend on equipment than most of us. He was getting twenty quid a week then, straight out of school, when bus drivers were only making about ten pounds a week. So it was natural that he quickly became a trendsetter, trying out all the new gadgets and sounds.'

An up-and-coming young bass player, John Paul Jones also picked up the good word on Jimmy Page in London rock circles. 'I've rated Jimmy for years and years,' Jones said. 'We both came from South London and even in 1962, I can remember people saying that you had to go and listen to Neil Christian's band because he had this unbelievable young guitarist. I'd heard of Pagey before I heard of Clapton or Beck.'

Jeff Beck did establish early connections with Jimmy Page. His own local group used to warm up the weekend crowd for Christian's Crusaders. 'I only had this one job a weekend,' Beck said. 'It was a big moment. Page was raving around with this big Gretsch Country Gentleman guitar, and it looked huge on him because he was such a shrimp. He was even smaller than he is now. So all you saw was this huge guitar being wielded around by a guy who was as thin as a pipe cleaner.

'But I must say I was most impressed by his ability. He used to play fiery sort of fast stuff. The trouble was that nobody was listening to it – they usually just wanted to hear Bobby Darin's song "Dream Lover". Jimmy wasn't playing funky at all – it was just sort of Hava Nagila stuff, terrible. But *he* was very impressive.'

Page himself was unmoved by the showbiz trappings of the Crusaders. 'They had me doing things like arcing over backwards until my head touched the stage – all those silly things that groups used to do.' Worse, his health began to suffer. 'We were driving around in the country, sleeping in the van and all that sort of stuff. We had breakdowns on the M1 motorway. That was great for a while but eventually it knocks you out. I didn't have good resistance and I came down with glandular fever. I just collapsed from exhaustion and fatigue. After only a few months with the band, I began to worry if I could carry on much longer.'

It was a major dilemma which confronts many musicians. All young rock groups had to battle through an indefinite, often interminable period of staggering from one gig to the next, never getting sufficient sleep or decent food. Jimmy didn't seem to have the constitution for this lifestyle, no matter how brilliant his talent. Reluctantly Page turned to his second love – the paintbrush – and enrolled at art college in Sutton, Surrey.

Although he attended the college for eighteen months, he maintained his intense interest in the guitar. Sunday jam sessions became regular events in the Page family household. 'It really was a lot of fun,' Mrs Page said. 'All of the boys that Jimmy knew, Jeff Beck and the other lads, would come to the house . . . the jam sessions forced Jim's father and myself to develop an opinion about so-called heavy rock music. I found that I have a thing for it myself. I adore it. You had to shut your mind to everything else and just get into it. So you either loved it or loathed it. I really took to it.'

John Gibb, who frequently rolled up for the Sunday sessions, vividly describes those days. 'The Page family had a typically small suburban London house, two rooms up and two down, on Miles Road in Epsom. You'll remember that Jimmy and Eric Clapton recorded a tune called "Miles Road" on that Immediate label album they did. The best part of the house was devoted to Jimmy and his music – there was no doubt about that. In most homes, the front room is usually a family room, but Pagey's parents had turned it over to Jimmy. There were records everywhere, a tape recorder, a couple of amps and guitars and other instruments. Plus a really good hi-fi system. Jimmy's mum usually stayed in the kitchen brewing tea for everybody.

'Pagey himself was about eighteen then and becoming a serious musician. He was bright too. He was really into music, not from the money angle but from wanting to learn more about it. Over a period of a couple of years, I'd go round to Jimmy's place sometimes twice a week . . . sometimes not for a couple of months because we were touring in separate bands. We'd just get into music – we'd play around with little riffs on guitars together, work on new songs, just mess around. They were great times.

'Although Jimmy wasn't much of a socialiser, we'd cruise quite a bit in my car around the Epsom area, usually shouting insults at people. Jimmy had a couple of funny sayings he used a lot – "Quim the Nun" and "Prick the Bish". We did strange things cruising around. For example, there were about half a dozen loony bins near where we lived and one of them was especially for girls who had sexual problems: they couldn't stop touching themselves and things like that. One afternoon we drove around and tried to pull a couple of them, but we couldn't get them out of the place. They were certainly ready for it, though.

'We were fairly wild in those days. One band I was in with Jeff Beck broke up because two of the members went to jail. They were real little hounds – breaking and entering, nicking musical equipment. It was all normal in those days.'

Jeff Beck remembered, 'I first met Jimmy through my sister. She went to art school and there was this guy Barry Matthews who was into guitars and he knew another guy, Jimmy Page, that he thought I should meet. Barry knew from my sister that I was wild about electric guitars and in those days not many people had even heard of an electric guitar. So I went straight over and met both Barry and Jimmy. Jimmy was a freak for the guitar but he didn't play one. He just used to draw strip cartoons of rock bands, starting from 1955. Then I discovered that I'd already met Jimmy through his gigs with the Crusaders . . . but I didn't know him then on a personal basis.

'I didn't live near Jimmy, but we were into the same musicians at the same time. We loved Cliff Gallett who was a fat guy of about forty playing lead guitar with Gene Vincent and the Blue Caps. He was the only guy we knew who was playing sharp, fast stuff. We both used to like him a lot.'

Page claims that through it all, he endeavoured not to neglect his art college training. 'I really wanted to be a fine art painter, I really was sincere about that. I didn't tell anyone at the college that I played guitar or else they would have had me playing in the lunch-hour. But gradually a conflict between music and art arose. When I first started art college, the music scene was pretty depressing. Nobody was interested in Chuck Berry or Bo Diddley. All the people wanted was Top-20 stuff and trad jazz. Then about a year later, everything started to happen. The Stones broke through and the Liverpool and R&B

scenes started coming together in England. I enjoyed playing and the R&B revival restored my faith in pop music. The Stones were playing a lot of old Muddy Waters numbers, while the Beatles were doing things by the Shirelles and the Marvelettes. Finally the point came when I had to make a decision.'

The significant developments which had been taking place in central London at the Marquee, a well-known Soho jazz club, influenced Page's decision in no small way. 'The whole thing started around 1960,' said John C. Gee, a former Marquee manager who later moved into music publishing. 'One of the club's directors was the jazz bandleader, Chris Barber. For a jazz musician, Chris was very broadminded and unlike many of his contemporaries, he was open to all types of influences. In 1960 Chris had a big hit internationally with "Petite Fleur" and as a result, he went on tour in the States.

'At that time all that we British jazz enthusiasts knew about American jazz came from listening to imported records. When Chris was over there, he wandered off into the black sections of big cities like Chicago, Detroit and New York, and he heard real rhythm and blues music live for the first time. He was really knocked out by it. When he got back to London, Chris started looking around for other people who might be into this type of music. There weren't too many of them about then, but Chris did find two musicians – Alexis Korner and Cyril Davies – who were in effect students of R&B music.

'Alexis and Cyril soon began to join Chris Barber and his jazz band on selected dates around the country and in a BBC Saturday night TV series, *Trad Tavern*. It was the middle of the trad jazz boom. But the reception the audiences were giving the blues numbers which featured Alexis and Cyril was so great that it led to the formation of a new band called Alexis Korner and Cyril Davies Blues Incorporated. They started out at a little club in Ealing and this was way before John Mayall surfaced. Their association with Chris Barber, still a Marquee director, brought them into contact with Harold Pendleton, the owner of the club. At this time, neither the Stones nor the Beatles had been heard of in London.'

Blues Incorporated began playing at the Marquee in May 1962 and provided an atmosphere which soon led to frequent jam sessions featuring the likes of Long John Baldry, Mick Jagger and others. 'But R&B still didn't mean anything,' said John Gee. 'It was still the trad jazz era of Barber, Bilk [Acker] and Ball [Kenny]. But we had one night a week, Thursdays, when there would be a blues jam session revolving around Alexis and Cyril's Blues Incorporated. For the first couple of months, they were lucky to draw a hundred people a night.'

Tuberculosis forced John Gee into hospital in June 1963. When he was discharged six months later, a musical revolution had taken place. 'The Beatles were the talk of the North, and the Thursday night blues sessions at the Marquee had become the rage of London. Alexis came up with the idea of getting a young supporting group for the Thursday blues gigs. He had heard the Rolling Stones at the Crawdaddy Club in Richmond and he decided to bring them into the West End for their first exposure in the heart of London.'

Even in the sophisticated West End, the Stones' rebellious image seemed bound to cause controversy. 'People all over London were talking about this strange group with long hair down to their shoulders and playing funny music,' Gee recalls. 'I was a jazz enthusiast basically and I came back to the Marquee at the start of 1963 to a whole new world of music. Jazz had just about died out and soon after the Marquee would discover and introduce to London audiences bands like the Who, the Spencer Davis Group featuring Stevie Winwood, and Manfred Mann.

'I'll never forget sitting one afternoon having a cup of tea with Alexis Korner in a little West End café. He leaned over to me and said, "This music is going to be the biggest thing to ever hit this country." And I replied, "Yes Alexis, sure man, go on and have another cup of tea." Now, of course, it's different. In retrospect you can see that the whole British music scene really was ripe for revolution.'

Korner and Davies had asked Jimmy Page to join them when they'd formed Blues Incorporated. But Page, then with the Crusaders, was on the brink of opting for art college. Later he attended their Marquee blues nights quite regularly. 'It was a fantastic band,' Page said. 'The best blues band of the day, better than Mayall or any of the others, no matter what Mayall may say. Cyril Davies was the real father of the City Blues in Britain, whether John Mayall knows it or not. A lot of groups owe a lot to Cyril, including the Stones.

'Cyril played electric harp. Alexis, who'd started off as a sort of one-man blues revival, stuck to playing acoustic guitar. They got in some rock musicians who were into blues and it just went from there.' The band specialised in the Chicago-based, Chess-label style of City Blues which went down extremely well with London audiences. 'Chicks used to dance on guys' shoulders. And it was a really good atmosphere – they used to do this really mad dance where everyone would be shaking,' said Page.

Predictably it wasn't long before Jimmy Page found himself up on stage joining in the jam sessions. 'Eric Clapton would be there too in the audience, only I never knew it at the time,' says Page. In those days Clapton played with a band called the Roosters. 'One day he came up to me, and said, "You play like Matthew Murphy, Memphis Slim's guitarist." I admit I *had* been following Murphy quite heavily.' Clapton's canny observation led to a long and serious (but publicly misunderstood) relationship between the two premier guitarists.

Cyril Davies died of a rare blood disorder and Alexis Korner soon quit the Marquee for what John Gee describes as 'political reasons', taking up a residency at the nearby Flamingo Club. But Page kept rolling up to the Marquee, and he soon began to 'play in the interval spot with three other guys including Andy Wren, the pianist, who was really good. We didn't know each other outside the Marquee; we just used to meet there and get up and play.'

Page also performed informally at the Crawdaddy Club in Richmond, and at nearby Eel Pie Island on occasion. 'It was a good scene then because most of us had the same upbringing. We'd been locked away with our blues records and then we came out with something really new to offer Britain. It just exploded from there.'

Then Jimmy received an invitation to join a different league of musicians – the world of studio session players. 'One night somebody came along and asked me if I'd like to play guitar on a record,' said Page. 'To tell you the truth, I can't even remember who it was. It was a nothing song, I remember that, and it became a minor hit. That led to other session offers and suddenly there were more than I could cope with – often as many as four or five a week.'

John Gibb, by then recording for EMI under the name of Brian Howard and the Silhouettes, approached Jimmy early on and asked him to play guitar on two singles, 'The Worrying Kind' and 'Bald-Headed Woman'. 'He played rhythm and lead guitar but nothing happened with the records. Nothing much was happening with any British records then, at least not the sort we were making. The Beatles were still a couple of years away.'

Another of the early producers to enlist Page's professional services was Tony Meehan, who'd recently met John Paul Jones. 'This tape operator at that time, Glyn Johns, kept telling me that Jimmy Page was a great kid,' said Meehan. 'He was young but he needed a break. Glyn said Page had the magic and that he should be given a chance. I decided to give him a try. He came down and I knew right away he was faking it – he couldn't read the music I'd written out. But he was doing well enough on his own. I switched him from lead to rhythm guitar and all went well. The session was at the IPC Studios in 1962 and I'm positive that the song we did, "Diamonds", was the first number one record that Jimmy had ever played on.' The first of many, as it would turn out.

At this time, there was basically one in-demand session guitarist in Britain, a guy called Big Jim Sullivan. When Jimmy Page underwent a crash course in reading and writing music, that situation quickly changed. 'If there were three sessions requiring guitarists going on at any given time,' Page estimated, 'Big Jim would play one and the other producers would end up with . . . well, we won't mention any names. Without Big Jim, the producers were desperate. When I came onto the scene, work quickly escalated. I became a new name. Big Jim had been carrying the whole weight on his shoulders and he was the only other young face on the scene.' Sullivan subsequently signed an exclusive deal with the Gordon Mills's management stable, providing back-up for such MOR heavyweights as Tom Jones, Gilbert O'Sullivan and Engelbert Humperdinck.

Jimmy Page had arrived at a creative crossroads; it was art versus music. 'I was missing lectures, taking days off and I finally had to make a choice. I suppose at that particular point I was really enjoying the session work. Many of the sessions were really good and I was allowed to do the solos, which I found to be really constructive work. So it was down to painting or playing. It wasn't too difficult a decision to make. Art college days were over.'

2 The Greening of Jimmy Page

ETWEEN 1963 AND 1965, Jimmy Page took part in literally hundreds and hundreds of recording sessions as a guitarist. Exactly how many sessions may never be known, although a gaggle of commentators have offered various estimates, largely because Page himself has been traditionally reticent about identifying which sessions he was involved in. One Alabama rock critic has claimed that Page played on 'anywhere from 50 per cent to 90 per cent of the records released in Britain in the 1963–1965 era'. This is an exaggeration, but there can be no doubt that Page's involvement percentage is relatively high. It *is* certain that Page performed in one way or another on records by the Who, the Stones, the Kinks, Donovan, Tom Jones, Joe Cocker, Burt Bacharach, Dave Berry, Screaming Lord Sutch, Cliff Richard, P.J. Proby and Brenda Lee. There were many more.

Page gained a substantial reputation as an accomplished studio guitarist in a very short amount of time. 'It really is astonishing when you realise that Jimmy was only twenty and he had become so well known in that field,' said his mother. 'In the music business, Jimmy didn't have anyone to introduce him around. Obviously there was a bit of luck involved. But Jimmy was never the pushy type – he just sort of glided into such a good position.'

Luck couldn't have been such a significant factor if Page hadn't been an extremely gifted guitarist. He was constantly in demand because he was a rock devotee at a time when most of Britain's session players were jazz enthusiasts. Many of them despised rock and roll for its simplicity and its popularity, and the way it had swept jazz into a mouldy corner of limited acceptance. Producers frequently wanted Jimmy on hand in case their big-name stars had trouble cutting it, especially early in their recording careers.

Page remembered one of his more easy-going experiences with a smile. 'I played rhythm guitar on the Who's first single "I Can't Explain". I really wasn't needed at the session but I was fortunate enough to find myself there. It was simply a case of strengthening the riffs, using two guitars instead of one.' The Who's Pete Townshend, unlike too many of his contemporaries in other British rock bands, freely acknowledges Jimmy's assistance.

Other session bookings proved to be less convivial to Page's presence, as with his collaboration with the Kinks, then produced by Shel Talmy. Page claimed that in 1969 he had been the first to use fuzztone guitar and that it was on an early Kinks record. 'What happened was that this guy who later went to work for Jimi Hendrix came up to me when I was playing at some club years ago, just after I'd started doing sessions. He told me he worked for British Admiralty in the Experimental department, and that he could probably build any sort of electronic gadget I might want. So I suggested that he try to make up this thing I'd heard years before on a Ventures record called "2,000 AD". It was a Gibson fuzzbox but it wasn't too good. In fact it was a disaster.

'So I said to this guy, "Why don't you try and improve on that with the Admiralty's facilities?" And he did, and that's how the fuzzbox got going. I used it on some sessions, and then the Pretty Things got one, and then Jeff Beck, and it swept through the scene and everybody got one. Jimi Hendrix was fortunate to ultimately get this guy to work solely for him. I believe that a lot of the sound Hendrix was able to get came through him. He really was a very clever chap.

'Concerning the Kinks' work though – and looking at it in retrospect – my presence at their sessions was to enable Ray Davies to wander around and to virtually maintain control of everything, without having to be down in the studio playing guitar all the time. Ray was producing those songs as much as Shel Talmy was – more so, actually, because Ray was directing them and everything. At one point, there were even three guitars playing the same riff.'

When news leaked out that Jimmy Page had been present at the Kinks' 'You Really Got Me' sessions – prompting spurious media inferences that the Kinks mightn't have been able to cut it musically – Ray Davies was understandably furious.

'I'll tell you about Jimmy Page,' he said acidly. 'Dave Davies [Ray's brother and the Kinks' lead guitarist] is a good guitar player and he played the solos on all our records. Jimmy Page played tambourine on "Long Tall Shorty" because he came into the studio as a friend of Shel Talmy. There was this particular thing happening when we were making our first LP that everybody was supposed to be friends. We'd all go into the studio together: just like Phil Spector played maraccas and Gene Pitney played piano on the early Stones records.

'Dave Davies did all those solos and Dave started that sound. The take of "You Really Got Me" that was actually released was the third take – there was a demo thing with Dave playing lead, a second cut which may have had Jimmy Page on it [and which Pye Records still has in its vaults] and a third which definitely had Dave on it. I know because I was standing right next to him when he played it. That's the one which was released. Jimmy Page did play tambourine on our first album. It's very good tambourine record.'

When such comments were brought to Page's attention, his diplomatic reply was, 'Fair enough – I didn't really do that much on the Kinks records. I know I managed to get a couple of riffs in on their album but I can't really remember. I know that Ray didn't really approve of my presence. The Kinks just didn't want me around when they were recording. My being there was Shel Talmy's idea. Too many writers were making a big fuss about the use of session men. Obviously I wasn't saying anything to the press about it, but things just leaked out . . . it often led to considerable bad feeling.'

It's possible now to trace Page's gradual disillusionment with session work – and his general mistrust of media people – to such uncomfortable session bookings where the producer wanted him around as insurance, while the artist didn't want him there at all. For many years, Page has been reluctant to discuss the specifics of his years of studio work. 'There is a code of faith between the session musician and his employer,' he said. 'Suffice it to say that during the period 1964–1967, I was in there grovelling around on a lot of sessions . . . but if I went into details, it would be a bit of a nause for the people concerned.'

While all of this artistic friction simmered throughout London studios Jimmy frequently got together with Eric Clapton, possibly to maintain his sanity. 'Eric and I became very close, I think. We got on very well and we used to go out and have dinner. We talked about a variety of subjects – education, art school [which Clapton had also attended], music, films, books. It wasn't just narrow conversation.

'One night Eric took me around to a friend's place. This guy was a music collector and he had incredible tapes of obscure musicians like Poppa Hop. It was the first time I'd even heard of Poppa Hop – he was from Houston and he played blues on a steel guitar. His was really amazing and his timing was impeccable. Eric was staying at this friend's house, really getting into those tapes and working off them, and learning this new technique. He was one of the first young guitarists to popularise the finger tremelo effect. Eric possibly picked it up originally from B.B. King. Soon other people were picking up on it, people like Jeff Beck.

'Eric was concentrating solely on blues artists in those days whereas I was and still am interested in other types of music. Even when he was playing in the Yardbirds and had to get involved in Chuck Berry stuff, he transitionalised more and more into the blues. He obviously preferred it to rock and roll or anything else. For him it was more emotional, more feelingful. During this period we were all getting into Elmore James and B.B. King. I'd like Elmore and B.B. and anyone else that I'd heard of, because obviously at that time − when you hadn't heard of too many blues people − it was a case of "who is going to turn me on to another guitarist I haven't heard before?" I suspect it was the same for Eric, as it would have been for any guitarist who was really into playing. It was really a whole year of just doing the groundwork, getting to know the different players and different styles.'

In 1965, Andrew Oldham, head of Immediate Records, approached Jimmy with a suggestion. Immediate, formed by Oldham with funds he'd accumulated as manager/producer of the Rolling Stones, planned a special British blues series. Would Page produce Clapton, Oldham asked? Although the four tracks they went on to record are among the finest examples of British blues from any period, the subsequent non-musical hassles left Jimmy with a very bitter taste. 'It was really a tragedy for me,' he claimed. Actually it was simply an early confrontation with the inherent music business malady − greed.

The tracks cut by Page at the Clapton sessions were 'Telephone Blues', 'I'm Your Witchdoctor', 'Sittin' on Top of the World' and 'Double Crossing Time'. 'I'll never forget how on one number Eric was using feedback,' said Page, 'and the engineer, a very straight conservative fellow, thought we were crazy. He'd never heard feedback before. At one point he screamed out and pulled down the faders on the console. "This is all unrecordable," he shouted. I told him to put the faders back up and let me worry about it. They were good tracks − I think "Telephone Blues" is one of Eric's best solos on record. It first turned up on an Immediate album called *Beginning British Blues*.

'I also have a theory that another of the tracks I did with Eric, "Double Crossing Time" turned up on that John Mayall album *Bluesbreakers with Eric Clapton*. I'm convinced that Mayall took the track away to Decca Records and did a separate deal with them for it. He was a real opportunist. They simply put a new guitar track in the background, that's the impression I got.'

Worse was yet to come. 'Eric used to come over to my parents' house in Epsom and we'd jam together. We did some "dirt" recordings between the two of us on a small two-track home recorder . . . mainly instrumentals with distortion and stuff. I happened to tell Immediate that I'd been doing some home tapes with Eric. Then Mayall and the rest of the Bluesbreakers were signed to Decca and Clapton left Immediate.'

When the Decca signing was announced, Immediate contacted Page and demanded that he deliver the Clapton home tapes to their offices. They'd been recorded, the company insisted, while Eric was still signed to Immediate and therefore belonged to them. Immediate's intention was to release the home tapes as an album, an idea which understandably annoyed Jimmy. But Immediate insisted and forced Page, who felt highly compromised anyway, to arrange the overdubbing of other instruments to give the tracks more depth and polish. Yet the songs, in Jimmy's opinion, were nothing more than eight takes of the same thing – variations on blues structures.

Despite Page's continuing protests, Immediate released the home tracks as part of a blues anthology. 'The liner notes were even attributed to me,' said Jimmy, 'but only on the first pressing. I didn't have anything to do with writing them. And I didn't get a penny out of any of it.'

Immediate also released tracks cut by the Cyril Davies All Stars, material put together for a laugh by a group of musicians including Bill Wyman, Charlie Watts, Mick Jagger, Jeff Beck, Nicky Hopkins and Page. 'They were just a few odd songs we'd done for fun when the real session had finished. Then Immediate hustled together those albums. I was really embarrassed. I think that everyone thought that I had been somehow responsible. Of course I wasn't!' said Page.

Clapton and Page received joint credit on the blues variations tracks done at Page's house, but Jimmy doubts if Clapton received any compensation either. 'I don't know if Eric got any royalties from it. He never knew what had really happened because it was released so long afterwards. Anyway he was in his heyday with John Mayall. I never heard anything from him about it.' Since that incident, the two once-close friends have barely exchanged more than a few terse sentences. Clapton refused to comment on this or any other part of his Page-related past. Presumably he genuinely, if incorrectly, believes that Page was just another opportunist in the great re-issue rip-off conspiracy which had haunted his early career.

Although Page was gaining a jaundiced outlook on record production, he tried again later in 1965. He cut his first and only solo single for Fontana Records, a song called 'She Just Satisfies'. 'I wasn't allowed to make a second single,' he said later. 'The first one was just a joke. It was very tongue-in-cheek. Should anyone happen to hear it now and have a good laugh, the only justification I can offer is that I played all the instruments myself except the drums. I even sang on it, too, which was somewhat unique. The other side is an instrumental featuring harmonica – I think the whole affair is better forgotten.'

Jimmy also dismissed any mention of other solo experiments, and much of his session work during the period, even Joe Cocker's brilliant début album which features Page wailing away on the classic title cut, 'With a Little Help from My Friends'. 'My playing was pretty bad then,' Page said. 'It's not that good now, but it was really bad then.'

As uncomfortable as he may have found the role, Jimmy Page had become recognised as a trendsetter in British rock circles. What Page did, others soon followed. Soon after he bought his first secondhand custom-made Les Paul guitar, diligently tracing its ancestry back to 1949, virtually every guitarist in Great Britain was pursuing a Les Paul.

'I chose mine purely because it had three pick-ups and such a good range of sounds,' Page explained. 'For me it seemed to be the best all-round guitar at that time. Now I would say that the Stratocaster is the best. But I think that Eric Clapton must take credit for establishing the "Les Paul sound" when he played with the Bluesbreakers.'

Later Page elaborated, 'Those old guitars made between 1952 and 1960 were made by the last of the post-War craftsmen. I find they're more responsive to the player's touch. Like the old Stratocaster. My favourite was the old Fender Telecaster.'

To his continuing credit, Page has consciously avoided imitating the tricks created by other enterprising rock guitarists or chasing after fashionable cult sounds, such as the sitar craze. 'I had a sitar sent over from India before any other people in pop, certainly before George Harrison, for instance. I'd been to see Ravi Shankar years before he became fashionable – the audience was almost totally adult. There were only about two young people there. I never used the sitar on a record, however, because I knew what was going to happen when someone eventually did do that. And I wasn't wrong. I just can't see using an instrument which has been developed over thousands of years as a quick gimmick. I will admit that I thought the Byrds' "Eight Miles High" was a great record, but I personally wasn't too happy with the way George Harrison used it on "Revolver", even though everyone else seemed to think it was incredible.

'As far as sitar playing went, it wasn't incredible . . . but later on when George did "Within You Without You" it was a different story. I think that record is unsurpassed to this day. So George really did do good things for Eastern music, and he was the one who woke people up to it on a mass media level. But we shouldn't forget that it was Davy Graham, the British acoustic player, who was into raga piece tunings and so on long before anyone else.'

Another British acoustic guitarist Page has always respected is Bert Jansch. 'Jansch is my all-time favourite. He's a real dream-weaver. He was so incredibly original when he first appeared and his début album had a great effect on me. Listen to "Alice's Wonderland" and "Finches" – they were so complex and full of weird things.'

In 1966 – the year of *Sgt Pepper*, *The Doors*, *Moby Grape*, *Surrealistic Pillow* and other psychedelic classics – Page felt that a replenishment of the musical soul was taking place, mainly in America. Rock and roll was ripping it up again and it found Page straining at his short but secure session leash. 'I was still getting the situation where say a violinist session-fixer, who really didn't know many other session musicians, would book me for what would turn out to be a ludicrous session – like muzak for supermarkets. Things in that vein were just a headache and I shouldn't have been doing them.

'The work was stifling. It was often like being a computer when you had no involvement with the artist. It should be stimulating to do sessions with other groups, but it wasn't working out that way.'

His dissatisfaction gnawed away at him and that summer Page found himself again confronting the crossroads of decision. He had taken up session work partly to preserve his health from the rigours of rock group activity. Now he discovered that he had to return to these rigours to preserve his creative wellbeing. He decided to take up an offer to join the Yardbirds – a group he'd already turned down once before.

The Yardbirds had formed in late 1963 in Richmond and Kingston, on the fringe of South London, the result of an alliance between the Metropolitan Blues Quartet and an unnamed band. 'It was kind of a local thing really,' said rhythm guitarist Chris Dreja. 'Eric Clapton, Anthony Topham and myself all went to the same art school. We used to take our guitars along and play in the cloakroom at lunchtime. We didn't have a group name or anything . . . it was all very informal. We knew two other guys, Keith Relf and Paul Samwell-Smith, who were members of the Metropolitan Blues Quartet. Paul brought along a friend, a fellow named Jim McCarty, and we all got together and jammed one evening at a club. It felt really good and we formed the Yardbirds that same night.'

Keith Relf generally gets credit for the group's name. Legend has it that he took it from an album by the renowned jazz musician, Charlie Parker, who was nicknamed Yardbird. (A yardbird was also American slang for a hobo who rode the rails in the Southern USA.) The original Yardbirds' line-up featured Chris Dreja on rhythm guitar, Jim McCarty on drums, Keith Relf handling vocals, Paul Samwell-Smith on bass and Anthony Topham on lead guitar. Eric Clapton meanwhile had joined another band known as the Roosters.

At their first gig, the band stood in for Cyril Davies. McCarty says the Yardbirds habitually depped for either Davies or another local group, the Rolling Stones. 'The Stones had this regular Sunday night gig at the Crawdaddy Club in Richmond. They had quickly built up a very big following at the club and their reputation around the country was growing too. It wasn't long before they'd gotten too big for the Crawdaddy, and we were asked by the club's manager Giorgio Gomelsky to replace them. Giorgio had originally managed the Stones and we signed a management contract with him when we started playing at the Crawdaddy,' explained McCarty.

Gomelsky, unquestionably one of the most perceptive visionaries involved in the early days of the British rock scene, moved to London from Switzerland in 1955 to make music films. 'I produced the first ever synchronised jazz film with Chris Barber in 1955 and a second in 1960. In the early 1960s, I spent all my time trying to convince people that something musical was going to happen in Britain. I could feel it. I knew that trad jazz was coming to a slow death – the bottom had fallen out of that business because of over-exposure. When Cyril Davies and Alexis Korner got their blues thing going in Chris Barber's band, I saw this as being a step ahead. I became more involved in what they called R&B. There was a certain feeling attached to this music and the bands weren't afraid of amplification. To me the scene was taking on some meaning.

'There was a jazz club operating at the Station Hotel in Richmond but audiences were falling off. I was given an opportunity to do something with the Sunday night segment. It took a total of eighteen months to really get going, but it worked. Eric Clapton, who went to art college nearby in Kingston, and other musicians used to drop by. The Stones worked their way up from there. I had no plans of getting into management or booking or anything like that. I simply liked the feel of this movement, and I wanted to prove something to journalists, to radio people, to the whole lot. By the time the Stones left, the Crawdaddy had built up into something very important. We had a loyal audience and we had to continue our policy.

'One night the Yardbirds came to see me at the club. After hearing them, I offered the band a gig. We did a few rehearsals before they started and I liked the doubling tempos and crescendos they were using. The lead guitar was more important than it had ever been before in a British group. What I wanted for the Crawdaddy – and what I saw in the Yardbirds – was the basis of an experimental blues band. Unfortunately Anthony Topham's parents thought he was too young to become a professional musician, so I asked Eric Clapton to join. We knew when we started the Yardbirds *had* to be different than the Stones – we didn't want people saying they were just another version of the Stones.'

The essential similarity between the two groups was that both blazed a pioneering path in British music circles with their fierce renditions of raw and earthy blues music. But soon the Yardbirds also outgrew the confines of the Crawdaddy and were forced to seek new venues. 'We started playing what they called the standard R&B circuit in those days,' said Jim McCarty. 'One night a week at the Marquee, the Ricky Tick in Windsor, Studio 51 in Great Newport Street and the Crawdaddy.'

From this London base they began to pick up other gigs further afield, including a visit to Liverpool's immortal Cavern Club. This led to the Yardbirds' first full-scale British tour, opening for Billy J. Kramer and the Dakotas. Gomelsky meanwhile had locked up a recording contract with EMI. 'The owner of the Marquee gave me an introduction to Norrie Paramor, head of pop A&R with EMI, and he put me on to a young guy named Tony Palmer. I'd had a sad fucking experience with Decca in getting a recording deal for the Stones, but EMI seemed a bit more civilised. I became the group's producer and Tony Palmer was the guy who pushed it all through at EMI.

'The first session yielded Billy Boy Arnold's "I Wish You Would" and the traditional blues tune, "Good Morning Little Schoolgirl". Rod Stewart came out with a totally different version of the latter tune at about the same time.' Neither single fared particularly well but a début album, *Five Live Yardbirds at the Marquee*, was released. Then came 'For Your Love', an innocuous but infectious little number which ultimately launched the Yardbirds not only at home but on many distant shores.

'As it happened, Brian Epstein owed me a favour,' Gomelsky said. 'Since I'd had some film experience, I worked out a film treatment for the Beatles and Brian gave it to Dick Lester who went ahead and produced *A Hard Day's Night*. Because of this, Brian agreed to put the Yardbirds on the Beatles' three-week Christmas tour of 1964.'

'We were playing the London date at Hammersmith,' remembered Jim McCarty, 'and this publisher, Ronnie Beck from Feldmans Music, was in the audience. He'd recently received a batch of new songs including "For Your Love" from a guy in Manchester called Graham Gouldman, and he thought it might suit us. It went straight to number one on the charts.' Gouldman subsequently wrote many hit songs for the Hollies and Herman's Hermits, and became a member of the highly regarded 10cc band.

'I'll admit that I just could not hear "For Your Love" as being right for the Yardies,' Gomelsky confessed. 'I told everyone it was just Manchester music. But I listened to other Gouldman demos and I detected a slightly Oriental influence – something to do with his synagogue experience and Hebrew music.

'It was very difficult in those days because we had the problem of trying to make a hit single that would work out for everybody. Eric Clapton didn't even play on "For Your Love" – there was simply no guitar part for him. We got Brian Auger in to play harpsichord. I can still remember Eric lying on his back at the IPC Studios while we were recording "For Your Love" – he just wasn't interested in it at all, and I can't blame him. It was terrible that we had to go through all that hit single bullshit. Personally I just wanted the band to make live albums – I thought that albums were going to be the important thing and they were, but not until three years later!'

Around this time, Jimmy Page was becoming a close friend of the Yardbirds. 'Jimmy had always been a friendly character,' said Chris Dreja. 'We'd known him for years . . . we're all from a similar background.'

Gomelsky said, 'I told Jimmy that I'd like to get him into the band. He had much more experience in music than any of the others, what with his session work. Jimmy was a bit more of a musician and less of a complete neophyte.'

Eric Clapton made no secret of his profound dislike of 'For Your Love's' blatant commerciality, as he didn't want to pander to the hit-single genre, and this was one key reason for his decision to quit the Yardies in January 1965. Another was Clapton's tenuous relationship with vocalist Keith Relf. 'Eric found it difficult to work with Keith musically,' said Gomelsky. 'Eric's favourite British singer was Stevie Winwood, but Relf didn't have any of the Ray Charles influence in his style. Eric felt he couldn't do what he wanted in that atmosphere, so he split, went off to Turkey and Greece and eventually wound up with John Mayall's Bluesbreakers.'

The group unanimously agreed to ask Jimmy Page to be Clapton's replacement. 'We really tried hard to induce him to join us,' said Chris Dreja, 'but it was only later that he felt that desire to be part of a band.'

Jimmy remembered the invitation a trifle differently. 'Yes, I was offered the chance to join the Yardbirds when Eric left. But I turned it down because I didn't like the way the invitation was put to me. Their manager came over and said, "Eric's having a holiday." "Holiday" was the manager's clever little euphemism for the fact that Eric had split the group. If I hadn't known Eric or if I hadn't liked him, I might have joined. As it was, I didn't want any part of it. I liked Eric quite a bit and I didn't want him to think I'd done something behind his back.'

Clapton himself never elaborated about the split and these days he maintains a stonewall silence. His only public comments, offered in 1968, were, 'I was with the Yardbirds for about eighteen months. They weren't too keen to have it known that I'd left. People leaving groups in those days were considered "dirty". It wasn't so bad at the start but after eighteen months I started to take music as a serious thing. I just realised I would be doing it for the rest of my life and I'd better be doing it right. Playing with a group like that puts you in a very strange frame of mind. You lose a lot of your original values. When I left, I was pretty brought down. I decided I wasn't playing well at all and I stayed in the country for a few weeks. Then John Mayall asked me to join which was great because I really was seriously going to do something else like painting.'

When Page declined the Yardbirds' original offer, he recommended Jeff Beck for the lead guitar gig.

'Jeff had a band called the Tridents,' said Jim McCarty, 'and although they weren't doing very well, Page used to help Jeff out financially by getting him session bookings that Jimmy couldn't handle himself because of prior commitments. Jimmy also recommended Jeff to us for the lead guitar spot in the band.'

Beck duly met with Gomelsky and accepted the offer on the spot. 'I was just doing nothing,' Beck recalled, 'and I had no money. I couldn't even afford guitar strings.' As Gomelsky saw it, 'Right away I knew that Jeff was very talented: he had a sound of his own. But he turned his back on the audience a lot because he was shy and timid. Coming into a successful group is difficult at the best of times – I think it was quite a fuck for Jeff. We took him to the hairdressers, had clothes made for him, the whole bit. Everything was still naive in those days – bands simply had to have stage clothes. Since we didn't have anyone in the Yardies who stood out like Jagger did in the Stones, we developed the strength of the lead guitarist. The group actually became a laboratory for lead guitar players.'

Jeff Beck, plunged headlong into the limelight, had to cut the mustard right away or risk critical crucifixion. 'I don't really know why the Yardbirds made such a feature of lead guitar, but they have always had to have a guitarist that was in Eric's sort of field, because he gave them their name. I hated the first few weeks playing in the band because Eric had a strong following and if you ever try to set yourself up in that position . . . well, you know how it is. But there were no problems.'

The Yardies had a second hit single with Graham Gouldman's 'Heartful of Soul', and on the strength of two international chartriders set out on their first American tour. 'It was quite funny really,' said Gomelsky. 'The Byrds had been number one with "Mr Tambourine Man" when "For Your Love" was number two, and a lot of people mixed up the two groups. We'd get lots of requests to do "Mr Tambourine Man". We had a lot of hassles with the Musicians' Union in the States but we were laying it down at the concerts. I think that people who saw any of those gigs will always remember them – the Yardies were possibly the most advanced group that was around then. The impact was being made in those live appearances. But the pressures of success can exhaust young and inexperienced people, which they all were. It was very exhausting – when you're twenty or twenty-one, you want to fuck a lot. There was no shortage of groupies. But no one had any experience of touring in America . . . it was a completely new trip.'

Two more hit singles followed – 'Still I'm Sad' and 'Shapes of Things'

– and by early 1966, the music press was seized by a flight of rumours that Jimmy Page might be joining the band as a second lead guitarist. 'Jeff Beck often used to say "I wish you would join us and we would play together" and I agreed that it would be good,' said Jimmy. 'But I never really took it seriously because there was this thing about the *five* Yardbirds and to bring in a sixth would have destroyed that.'

Giorgio Gomelsky was also growing a tad restless about the band's development. 'Eventually I became at loggerheads with them. It was tough working with Jeff Beck in particular. It was obvious he'd suffered some sort of trauma in his youth. I later found out that he'd fallen off a bike when he was around fifteen and had suffered concussion. This gave him terrible headaches and great pain, and it was often hard for him to work. I thought that the band needed a stabilising influence like Jimmy Page. Someone who could talk out problems and not forget the original aims and objectives. I do think that if Jimmy had joined the Yardbirds at this time, we could have saved them.

'We went off on a tour of Denmark and Jeff wouldn't come so we played without him. I thought we should find a keyboard player and forget about lead guitar for the moment. That would be a musical turning-point for the band, I figured . . . and Keith Emerson was reportedly floating around London looking for a gig. Keyboard players understand harmonics and they often have classical training: I saw a whole new direction for the Yardies. I was also getting into a Memphis thing, and I tried to turn on both the Stones and the Yardbirds to this sound coming out of Memphis with people like Otis Redding. But they couldn't see it. However I did persuade the Yardies to do a session at Sam Phillips's studio in Memphis one Sunday.

'About this time,' Gomelsky continued, his rotund face glowing with the memory, 'Paul Samwell-Smith had just met this girl Rosemary who was to become his wife. Rosemary was the assistant to Vicki Wickham, one of the producers of the TV series *Ready, Steady, Go!* Another of Rosemary's friends was a guy named Simon Napier-Bell. There was a bit of what we French called "Jesuitism" going down. I'd spent three years working my arse off for the Yardies – we'd formed a limited company and everything was organised in an impeccable manner. I don't know what really happened; when new people come into a band (both musicians and family) and they weren't there where it started, things begin to pull apart. The whole thing became just too much for me and I decided to pack it in. A settlement was arranged and I got to keep the rights to the records I'd produced with the band.'

Jim McCarty noted, 'One of the clauses in the settlement was that Giorgio would have all the rights if any of our old hits were re-issued. The next year out came *The Yardbirds' Greatest Hits* which sold more than 250,000 copies. Giorgio must have done incredibly well from that.' To which Gomelsky adamantly insisted, 'The early production royalties were all I ever got out of the Yardies.'

For the band, change was clearly in the air. That elusive shadow of history in the making was also making its presence felt. Simon Napier-Bell became the group's new manager, and the time seemed ripe for the long-anticipated involvement with old friend and sidelines booster, Jimmy Page.

'They were always a good band to go and see,' said Page. 'Then came this great night at an Oxford or Cambridge Union dance, I can't remember which, and the singer Keith Relf was incredibly pissed. Everyone was dressed up in dinner jackets and Keith was rolling around the stage, grappling with the mike, blowing harmonica in all the wrong places, and making up nonsense lyrics. He was shouting "fuck you" at the audience and eventually he just collapsed back into the drum kit. It was great, just fantastically suitable for the occasion, I thought. But instead of everybody seeing the humour of it — as three members of the group and myself did — the bass player Paul Samwell-Smith just blew up and said, "I can't stand this any more. I'm going to leave the group, and if I were you, Keith, I'd do the same thing".'

Page noted, 'Samwell-Smith was always after musical precision and adherence to strictly rehearsed neatness, and it was more than he could take . . . it was the last straw, he'd just had enough and decided to quit.' Samwell-Smith later drew widespread acclaim for his meticulous production work with Cat Stevens and others. Added Gomelsky, 'Paul was a very talented guy — he'd always wanted to experiment with sounds in the studio.'

With two upcoming gigs, the Yardbirds were really in a spot. They had no bass player but would be sued if they didn't fulfil the contracts.

'They were stuck,' Page said, 'so of course I said "Well I'll play". I offered to play bass for them even though I'd never played a bass guitar before in my life. But I knew their act and what they were doing and I learned enough to get through. The first gig was at the Marquee in London. Then they suggested that I stay on in the group and I did. Session work had become so predictable and boring. Herman's Hermits were into their own thing no doubt, but it wasn't my scene.'

Jeff Beck's recollection of how Jimmy Page joined the Yardbirds differs on several points. 'The Yardbirds were doing fine until Samwell-Smith started getting snobby. But I realised that if he did leave to become a producer, we'd lose an integral part of the Yardbirds' sound. So we had to think who was going to replace him. And I thought "well I don't know any bass players so we'll make up for that with another lead guitarist". I immediately got in touch with Jimmy but I didn't tell him why. We had to talk to him and bribe him with lots of money to come into the group . . . but he really wanted it anyway or he wouldn't have consented to have dinner and make an agreement.'

According to Beck, the original intention was for Page to join him on lead guitar with Chris Dreja switching to bass. For several months, Beck continued to play lead guitar with Dreja supporting him on rhythm and Page on bass. Whatever might have taken place later – and the potential for personal friction was always present, given Beck's temperament and Page's undoubted solo skills – things went smoothly on stage for a period. Backstage however it was a different matter as the Yardies were into their second management upheaval, and Simon Napier-Bell was on the way out.

'The whole trip with Simon has turned out to be absolutely ridiculous,' said Chris Dreja. 'Perhaps that's a bit unfair because Simon did do one good thing for us – he got us into the film *Blow Up*. We played a number called "Stroll On" and that was a good thing for our career. Although Jimmy was playing bass in the film, we actually recorded the track with both Jeff and Jimmy on lead guitars. Simon just wasn't a real managerial type. He couldn't handle the individual personalities and he just got out of his depth. We were all in too confused a state to know what was happening. Finally Simon just couldn't handle it any longer.'

As a first step in trying to reorganise the Yardbirds' management mess, Napier-Bell had brought in a man named Peter Grant. A British show business veteran who'd worked his way up through road-managing early tours of the UK by visiting American acts, Grant brought a new professionalism to the Yardbirds' activities. Napier-Bell initially wanted to arrange a split management deal, but when that didn't work out in practice, Grant assumed control. He would be their manager from the end of 1966 through to the band's demise in 1968. Everyone took to him, and as Dreja observed, 'If only we'd been involved with him earlier in life, things might have been a lot different.'

The Yardbirds' recording pinnacle had already been reached and their disc output, with a couple of exceptions, became meagre and mediocre. The only two studio tracks featuring both Beck and Page on guitar are 'Happenings Ten Years Time Ago' and 'Psycho Daisies', released in October 1966. 'I played bass on "Psycho Daisies" but there's a bit of a story attached to "Happenings",' said Jimmy. 'We were all in the studio waiting for Beck to turn up and Keith Relf had a little bit of music recorded on a tape recorder – it was sort of a riff pattern for a song. I worked on the riff and the structure of it, and we'd got it all ready by the time Beck eventually showed up. He just put some guitar on top of it and that was that. But I think it turned out well.'

That year the Yardbirds undertook a successful Australian tour and then took off once again to America. It wasn't long before the opportunity to play lead guitar live was suddenly thrust into Jimmy Page's hands – be they willing or not. 'The switch was necessitated earlier than planned because of one of Jeff's collapses,' said Page. 'We were playing a gig at the Carousel Club in San Francisco and because Jeff couldn't make it, I took over lead that night and Chris Dreja played bass. It was really nerve-wracking because this was at the height of the Yardies' concert reputation, and I wasn't exactly ready to roar off on lead guitar. But it went all right and after that, we stayed that way. When Jeff recovered it was two lead guitars from then on.'

The dynamic combination of Jeff Beck and Jimmy Page on dual lead guitars established a precedent in rock history. The Yardbirds had long since earned a reputation for top-drawer guitar playing but now with Beck and Page striving for a stereo effect on stage, they were on occasion absolutely devastating.

'I think we were the first to do it and it took the States by storm. The mystique grew because people liked Jeff and they knew Eric [Clapton] had been in the group. Plus there was the whole raver thing – English bands liked to loon and Hollywood went wild. It *was* an exciting group, but there is very little evidence of it on record,' Page confessed. 'There was "Happenings", which I feel went over a lot of heads in Britain although it perpetuated the Yardbirds' reputation in America; they were always into the more lyrical side of what we were doing. I would say that for the amount of time that it was working, the whole thing really was fabulous.'

Page swears that it was never a case of trying to blow each other off stage. 'I was trying to get it working so you had this stereo effect on guitars. There was no point in doing battle because that would've just led to a useless sound.' But the band did occasionally become immersed in one-stage guitar rivalry, according to other band members.

'When it did work,' reckoned Jim McCarty, 'it was really, really good. But now and then it became a bit of a jumble. Their different styles would get a bit confusing sometimes . . . and Jeff would get worked up into quite a state about it. Jimmy was quite a tight player – he usually played pretty much the same thing every night. Jeff on the other hand was great one night, and then for five nights he'd be awful.'

Chris Dreja, who had to try to drop in bass lines behind such erratic playing, said, 'I personally don't think Jimmy ever went out on stage with the intention of trying to blow Jeff off the stage. But with Jeff I think it got to be a "my-balls-are-bigger-than-yours" sort of thing. We went through some difficult times with Jeff – he was so much more temperamental than Jimmy. Jimmy was always a very business-like person. He's a bit like the business executive of the music world – but, of course, a really talented one. Jeff was the opposite – always larger than life. Which makes nice reading, I suppose, but I can tell you it got to be a bit hairy at the time.'

McCarty added, 'It was quite frightening at times: you were always wondering what was going to happen next. I remember one time we were playing in a little club somewhere in New Mexico. Right next to us was this huge open window, letting in fresh air. Something went wrong during the set so Jeff just kicked over the stack of amps and they smashed out through the window. If anybody had been walking underneath that window, they'd have been killed for sure.'

Despite omnipresent hassles and tantrums, the group undertook a major British tour with the Rolling Stones and Ike and Tina Turner, which opened 23 September 1966. Page recalled, 'I remember that one English music paper, reviewing the show we did at the Royal Albert Hall in London, said, "The Yardbirds appeared with their cacophony of sound." But in those days, groups had to use the Albert Hall's house PA system, which was terrible. So the guitars were really loud and bad.'

Singer Keith Relf could hardly ignore the heavy emphasis on guitar. 'Eric Clapton had always used a small amp when he was with the group,' said Page, 'and that was Keith's big complaint about Jeff and me. Keith got more and more reticent, but we weren't really trying to drown him out. There was a lot of tension.'

With insecurity rife in the band, they set out on another American tour at the end of 1966, only to have their severe internal difficulties compounded by appalling conditions on the road. 'It was a gigantic Dick Clark package tour,' explained Jim McCarty, 'and it really was a terrible scene. We'd be playing two gigs a night and then into the bus and on to the next gig between 200 and 300 miles distant, where we'd be playing the next night. You had to sleep in the luggage racks or the bus seats, depending on whether or not Gary Lewis and the Playboys would fly to the next gig or travel by bus. After three nights of this, Jeff Beck just blew up on stage, smashed his guitar and stalked off. And that was that.'

Added Page, 'We were sharing the bus with Gary Lewis and the Playboys, Sam the Sham and the Pharoahs, Brian Hyland and all sorts of people. We'd get to the gig and Brian Hyland, who opened the show, more or less went straight out on stage. There was no time to change or wash or anything like that. If it was a double gig – playing two different halls in the same city – the bus would do a sort of shuttle service. We'd come off the stage, get on the bus which had just returned from taking Brian Hyland and whiz off to the other gig. It's just ludicrous to remember how bad it was.'

Later Jeff Beck himself would comment, 'My problem has always been that during troubled times I have always been subjected to the moods of those times, and if I didn't feel right about the way things were going, then I didn't play right. It was a consistency which I now know I can only achieve in the right company.' Beck claims he left the Yardbirds over a clash of ideas, and because he wanted to work less because of ill health, exhaustion, and promoters' ignorant handling of acts.

Even to this day, Beck's departure – and the pointless press rumours of a raging Beck/Page feud – are extremely sensitive topics. 'This is all very touchy,' Page allows. 'There was a lot of cloak-and-dagger stuff going on and I didn't want to be part of it at all. Jeff Beck must wince every time he reads any of this, but I've never put him down. I've always said that he's a brilliant musician. When he's having a shining night, he is fantastic. He plays things of sheer genius – but he's got a funny temperament at times. I defy anyone to show me anything I've said against Beck in the press.'

Another well-publicised controversy centred around 'Beck's Bolero', a tune with origins dating back to shortly after Beck left the Yardies. Beck claims the instrumental was written in a 'little pokey room' in Page's house when the two of them were sitting on the arms of chairs and Page started strumming a Ravelian rhythm on a twelve-string guitar. Beck said he spontaneously added the melody line but he felt that some other element was still missing; when he got home he finished it off.

'Jeff claimed the song as his own,' said Page, 'but it's just not right. I worked out the chords in the studio and Jeff put on the steel part and other things afterwards.

'Nicky Hopkins, who was also involved in the sessions, is another who has some grievance against me about some Immediate tapes, which wasn't on at all. Things like that just get printed in the press and people seem to latch onto them and they don't know the full circumstances.'

Whatever the exact causes, Page's long friendship with Beck came to an abrupt and angry end, a situation which still saddens him. 'I'd known Jeff since I was eleven. He and I were very close. This strange sort of professional jealousy came between us and I really don't understand why.'

For his part, Beck refuses to discuss the matter.

Although personnel pressures eased off in the aftermath of Beck departing the Yardbirds, a new aggravation arose in their wake, one which profoundly influenced Page's opinion of the music industry and the often weird way it works. The problem revolved around the making of hit singles. Manager Peter Grant decided it might help the group if a commercially attuned ear could supervise the group's recording sessions. He nominated Mickie Most, the whiz-kid producer of Herman's Hermits, Donovan and others, as the man most likely to help the Yardbirds get back to the top of the hit singles charts.

'Our attitude was "we-want-a-hit-whatever-it-takes",' McCarty confessed. 'We did a couple of albums with Mickie that were hopeless – they were recorded just like a Herman's Hermits LP.'

The first Most-made album, *Little Games*, released in August 1967, was without question the worst Yardbirds' album ever, despite a highly inventive cello arrangement by one John Paul Jones on the title track.

'There is a reason why it's so bad,' Page insists. 'On half the tracks we didn't even hear the playbacks. Some of them were first takes. That's how it used to be done – we'd spend time on the singles but Mickie Most thought that albums were nothing . . . just something to stick out after a hit single.' This album wasn't released in Britain, nor were the two singles, 'Ha Ha Said the Clown' and 'Ten Little Indians'.

'Both of those tracks were a bit of a con job,' said Page. 'It happened like this: the producer would say, "Why don't we try to do 'Ha Ha Said the Clown', which had been a hit for Manfred Mann, but in the Yardbirds' style?" And we'd say "don't be silly". But he'd insist on trying it: "It'll be an interesting experiment and if it doesn't work we'll scrap it." Of course no sooner was it recorded than out it went, despite the fact that it was terrible. To cap it all, we fell for exactly the same line on Nilsson's "Ten Little Indians".'

Jim McCarty concurs completely. 'It really got into a very messy stage. We were doing any song that Mickie Most saw as a single. Even stuff that people had sent to him as unsolicited song demos. "Little Games" was one of them. The whole album was recorded as a collection of possible singles. Nobody wanted us to record any original material.'

Page himself has mellowed somewhat towards the Mickie Most machine with the passage of time. 'Mickie was far more into a commercial singles consciousness then, right up to the point where he started recording Jeff Beck and Rod Stewart, and his whole attitude obviously changed.' When one considers the far-reaching studio innovation of British bands like the Move, Cream and Free during that era, it's not difficult to sympathise with the Yardbirds' frustrating predicament.

Several tracks from the Most sessions have never been released. Page revealed, 'There was a song called "Tangerine" that was never actually finished – we'd only done the backing track. We recorded "My Baby" which Janis Joplin did, and it was a good version. There were also a few riffy rock things that sounded all right. Then there's another track, "Spanish Blood", which featured Jim McCarty doing his Roger Moore impersonation over a Spanish guitar backing – that track was really good, actually, and was like one of those old story singles [e.g. Lorne Green's "Ringo" and "Big Bad John" by Jimmy Dean], except that it was a romantic thing rather than the usual shoot-out Western theme. Most of these tracks were cut at the CBS Studios in New York, but they were never really completed.'

One more recording disaster occurred before the Yardbirds called it a day: an album entitled *The Yardbirds with Jimmy Page Live at the Anderson Theatre*, released briefly by US Epic records in the autumn of 1971. 'If you ever heard that album,' Page said acidly, 'you'll know why we had it stopped. What happened was that Epic said to us: "Can we do a live LP?" and they sent down the head of their light music department to supervise it. We had an agreement that if the results were good, they could release the album . . . but if not, they'd just file it away.

'Of course it was terrible. This character who'd been recording stuff like "Manuel's Music of the Mountains" was strictly into muzak, and the concert itself was bad. He had done things like hanging one mike over the drums so none of the bass drum came through. He'd miked up a monitor cabinet on my guitar instead of the proper amp through which I was playing all the fuzz and sustained notes . . . So all that was lost and we all knew it was a joke. But this fellow assured us it would be all right. "It's amazing what can be done electronically," he told us.

'When we listened to the completed master tapes, there were all of these bullfight cheers dubbed on it every time there was a solo, and it was just awful. You'd play a solo and then this huge "raaah" would come leaping out at you. There was one number where there was supposed to be utter silence and the guy dubbed in the clinking of cocktail glasses and a whole club atmosphere. But we had the right all along to say whether it would be released or not, and we made them shelve it.'

The tapes remained in the CBS vaults for four years and were then recycled by the company to cash in on Page's massive success with Led Zeppelin. But the album was withdrawn almost immediately after an injunction was slapped on it. Now that album, much to Page's chagrin, has become a collector's item fetching ridiculous prices. 'I just wish people would accept it for what it is, a pathetic load of crap! It was unfortunate that no live stuff of the Yardbirds was ever recorded properly.'

The same Epic executive was also responsible for the production of the Yardbirds' final single 'Goodnight Sweet Josephine'/'Think About It', released in January 1968. 'That was desperation,' said Page, 'because we were so anxious to get something done if only to prove to ourselves that we could do it.'

While the recording studio (and omnipresent plastic producers) had become an anathema to the Yardbirds, their live concerts – particularly in America – continued to arouse audiences to peaks of energetic enthusiasm. 'The reception to the Yardbirds in America had always been good,' summed up McCarty. 'We'd always done well there and it kept on getting better. Towards the end we were getting a much better reception in America than in Britain . . . of course it hadn't been like that when we started. The American audiences seemed to be much broader in their outlook – they were prepared to listen to a broader range of music. The heavy rock thing hadn't come to England much at that time. You were an outcast in England if you deviated from the basic blues thing. A hit single could instantly destroy your reputation with your audience. I suppose in England people had a preconceived idea of what you *should* sound like, while in America they were prepared to accept you for what you were.'

Even though riding the crest of widespread acclaim all the Yardbirds except Page were ready to pack it in. 'Towards the end, Keith and Jim just didn't have their hearts in the music. They were into very light things like Simon and Garfunkel, and the Turtles, probably to counteract the sort of stuff I was listening to. They were writing songs in that lighter vein which they wanted to record. I was all in favour of them recording their songs as the Yardbirds because I knew we had the potential to pull it off. But they just wouldn't have any of it. Keith was really the instigator, I think. He once said this very weird and interesting thing that I'll always remember: "The magic left for me when Eric left." I've always thought the Yardbirds' best stuff came from the Jeff Beck era when they did all that incredible experimental stuff. Since I didn't want the group to break up, I hoped there was a chance that Keith and Jim would change their minds and come back, if we could just keep it going. But they went off and made their own record with Paul Samwell-Smith.'

For a time, Chris Dreja shared Page's vision of a Yardbirds' renaissance. But ultimately he too departed from both the band and the rock scene at large. 'My attitude,' he recalled, 'was to try and see it through. But there were destructive influences at work within the band. Both Keith and Jim were under a strain. Eventually we all wanted to do different things so we just decided to can it. I left the rock business and became a photographer.' Dreja went to New York to study photography and ultimately became one of London's foremost advertising photographers. Relf and McCarty formed Renaissance, a band which recorded a couple of tasteful albums before submerging. McCarty then formed his own group, Shoot, with little success, while Relf pursued an unrewarding solo vocal career; he died on 14 May 1976, at the age of 33.

Looking back over the entire Yardbirds' career, Chris Dreja feels that of the group's three high-profile lead guitarists, he got on best with Jimmy Page. 'There's no doubt about it,' he declared. 'But as far as their playing was concerned, each of them had a different trip. Jeff got carried away at times and he sort of over-played. But at his best it was like magic – he could be unbelievable. He was always more emotional in his playing. Eric's playing was always very sweet, very calculated and entirely rehearsed. Sometimes he'd spend weeks getting a part just right. He was after perfection. It was sweet, fluid, well-oiled playing.

'Jimmy's style was at times very calculated, like Eric. But it was a lot more vicious, which added a new dimension to the group. But it was always so controlled. Jimmy could fall back on so many different ways of getting it across because of his years of session experience. They all played differently – they were all free-form players . . . especially Jeff and Jimmy, who ultimately pulled off some really original stuff. When Eric was with us, the whole scene was hung up on City blues and so Eric mainly stuck to that – just playing City blues in Britain then was innovation in itself.'

Page summarised the fateful Yardbirds years simply: 'There were a lot of incidents that led to the final break-up – something that had been there long before I joined the group. But while it worked it was good. Basically for me the Yardbirds are a mixture of good and bad memories. There certainly were some magic moments and it was a great time to be playing in a group, with so much new material reaching the public's ears.

'The whole group was a guitar precedent. Everybody was just into doing what's now known as jamming on stage. Eric began the precedent, and when he left Jeff felt that he had to be better than Eric, and when I was left, I felt I had to try hard too. It was excellent learning in that way.'

The Yardbirds played their final concert at the Luton School of Technology outside London in July 1968. Jimmy Page, for the third time, found himself down at the crossroads. He could return to session work. He could go back to art. Or he could lunge ahead and create a new band from the still-engrossing embers of the Yardbirds' fiery career.

3 The Launching of Led Zeppelin

I N THE EARLY SUMMER OF 1968, Jimmy Page – tired, temporarily depressed and a trifle disillusioned – retreated to his renovated Victorian boathouse at Pangbourne on the gentle twists of the Thames river, 30 miles upstream from inner London. He carefully mulled over his musical career to date, his achievements and his disappointments. Mainly he wondered how best his talents might fit into the rapidly evolving British rock scene.

Page had by now experienced a taste of both big-time success American-style, and of the numerous pressures which inevitably accompanied a British band on the road in a foreign country, and he felt confident that American audiences were impressed with his own style and sound. But could he find kindred spirits with which to create a brand new band?

The myriad musical questions gnawed away at him through the studied splendour of the English summer. He considered the spectrum of what was currently commercial, leaving aside the Beatles who were also in reclusion. Cream, featuring ex-Yardbirds guitarist Eric Clapton along with Jack Bruce and Ginger Baker, had become the top touring band in America; but after increasing indications that they had curdled, Cream officially disbanded that August. The Jimi Hendrix Experience was riding a crest, but their music had become too highbrow for the mainstream. The rock audience also was starting to buy albums by so-called 'underground' left-of-centre acts such as the Band, Spirit, Moby Grape, the Electric Flag, the Paul Butterfield Blues Band, Big Brother and the Holding Company, the Moody Blues, Deep Purple, Country Joe and the Fish, Steppenwolf and others.

Despite these artistically encouraging developments, the group which was selling the most albums in America in mid-1968 – at one point, they splattered an astonishing total of nine LPs on the *Billboard* US bestselling charts – was led by a monotonous trumpet player on the comeback trail, Herb Alpert and his Tijuana Brass. It was the final throes of the middle-of-the-road mania which major record labels had fostered so unflinchingly since the arrival of rock and roll. To the ears of an emerging late 1960s rock generation which wanted to boogie, the Tijuana Brass weren't blowing on the same planet.

The hit singles scene amply reflected the growing divisions in musical taste, the plunging chasm of creative division between conservative adult preference and rock free-form. The charts were a hodge-podge of mundane and masterful, grossout and glorious, – with little of substance in between. They swung from Bobby Goldsboro's sickly ditty 'Honey' to the hypnotic 'I Heard It through the Grapevine' by Marvin Gaye; from Jeannie C. Riley's drawling 'Harper Valley PTA' to the electric 'This Wheel's on Fire' by Julie Driscoll & Co.; from Don Fardon's insipid 'Indian Reservation' to the seminal 'I'm the Urban Spaceman' by the Bonzo Dog Doo Dah Band; from the yuck of 'Yummy Yummy Yummy' by the awful Ohio Express to the intrinsically brooding magnificence of Otis Redding's '(Sittin' On) The Dock of the Bay'.

During this confusing period, Jimmy Page's close friend and adviser was manager Peter Grant, the man who had 'inherited' the ownership of the Yardbirds' name. 'I always had the most respect and admiration for Jimmy,' Grant once told me. 'I felt that I was closer to Jimmy than any of the other members of the Yardbirds, and I had immense faith in his talent and ability. I just wanted him to do whatever he felt was best for him at that time. Of course it would have been a shame if he had decided to quit the business, but I don't believe the thought ever actually entered his head.'

What Page really wanted at that time was to reform the Yardbirds. To keep his hand in practice and to keep an ear to the studio floor in London rock circles, he returned to occasional session work. 'I only did a few sessions because I didn't want to fall into that trap of playing on every disc coming out of England.'

The word soon spread on the muso's grapevine that Jimmy Page was looking for some likely lads to create a new Yardbirds line-up. As fate would have it, the first player to link up with Page in this reconstituted Yardbirds line-up was bass guitarist John Paul Jones. A fan of Page's playing since the days of Neil Christian and the Crusaders, John Paul had worked with Page on many sessions in the mid-1960s and also on the Yardbirds' 'Little Games' production.

Page recalled, 'I was working at the session for Donovan's "Hurdy

Gurdy Man" and John Paul was looking after the musical arrangements. During a break he asked me if I could use a bass player in the new group I was forming. Now John Paul Jones is unquestionably an incredible arranger and musician – he didn't need me to get a job. It was just that he felt the need to express himself and he thought we might be able to get it together. Sessions are great but you can't get into your own thing. We talked about it and we agreed that in order to give what we had to offer, we had to have a group. John simply wanted to be part of a group of musicians which could lay down some good things. He had a proper music training and he had quite brilliant ideas. I jumped at the chance of getting him.'

'I worked at sessions for three or four years, on and off,' said John Paul Jones, 'I started running about and arranging about forty or fifty things a month. I ended up just putting a blank piece of score paper in front of me and just sitting there and staring at it. I joined a group, I suppose, after my missus said to me, "Will you stop moping around the house; why don't you join a band or something?" And I said, "There's no bands I want to join, what are you talking about?" And she said, "Well look, Jimmy Page is forming a group" – he'd just left the Yardbirds – "why don't you give him a ring?" So I rang him up and said, "Jim, how are you doing? Have you got a group yet?" He said, "I haven't got anybody yet." And I said, "Well, if you want a bass player, give me a ring." '

Next Jimmy began to think about a likely vocalist, and his mind flashed back to an impressive young singer he'd heard on the Yardbirds' British tour with the Rolling Stones. The opening act on the tour was a band called Peter Jay and the New Jay Walkers and their singer's name was Terry Reid. 'I'd seen what a good singer he was when we toured with them,' says Page. But it was too late as Terry Reid had recently formed a trio and signed a production contract. Page was disappointed: 'He was the only vocalist I knew but he'd just signed up with Mickie Most so he was out of the question.'

Another possibility was Small Faces singer/guitarist Steve Marriott, who died in a tragic fire at his home in April 1991, but he too was committed. While Page probed around exploring other vocal possibilities, the young Birmingham singer Robert Plant had just arrived in London seeking advice from an old friend, record producer Tony Secunda. Bogged down with production activities on his two hot bands, Procol Harum and the Move, Secunda couldn't fit Plant into his company's recording schedule. 'Then I remembered that the Yardies were rumoured to be coming unglued. I didn't think much of their previous vocalist [Keith Relf] anyway. To me he was weak, he had no stage presence, he had hunched shoulders and he was losing his voice. The Yardbirds had lacked vocal balls and I figured they could use Robert. So I pointed him in that direction.'

Coincidentally Terry Reid also suggested Plant as the voice that Page was seeking for his new band. 'I don't think he'd played much down in the south of England so consequently I hadn't heard of him,' said Page, who decided to informally audition Plant. 'I went up to see Robert sing, and his band Hobbstweedle were playing at a teachers' training college outside Birmingham to an audience of about twelve. It was a typical student set-up where drinking was the prime importance and the group was only of secondary importance. Robert was all right, though. He was singing really well although it was stuff that I didn't personally like very much. He was a Moby Grape fanatic and the group was doing all of those semi-obscure West Coast songs.

'I thought Robert was fantastic. Having heard him that night, and having listened to a demo he'd given me of songs he'd recorded in his Band of Joy days, I realised that without a doubt his voice had an exceptional and very distinctive quality. So I asked him if he wanted to come down to Pangbourne and spend a few days talking things over, listening to records, discussing sounds and whatnot, and to see what he thought.'

A penniless Plant spent several days in the plush confines of Page's Pangbourne boathouse getting acquainted. 'One day when Jimmy was out,' confessed Plant, 'I looked through his records and pulled out a pile to play and somehow or other they happened to be the same ones that Jimmy had put aside to play for me when he returned – just to see whether I liked them. When he saw that I'd picked them out too, we just giggled at each other for a bit. We found out that we had exactly the same tastes in music.'

Among the records they listened to were Muddy Waters' 'You Shook Me', 'She Said Yeah' by Larry Williams, Don and Dewey's 'Justine', albums by Buddy Guy, Elvis and the Incredible String Band, and a surprise choice – Joan Baez's dramatic rendition of the ballad 'Babe I'm Gonna Leave You'. ('We both liked her,' noted Plant.) As they listened, Page outlined his plan for a band that could play a song like that: 'I'd like to play it heavy but with a lot of light and shade.'

Page's plans made lots of sense to Plant. He remembers thinking to himself at the time: 'It's so fresh it's untrue . . . I don't know the person . . . but why not try it because it's something completely new. I mean, to begin with when someone comes along and says "come with us you're going to make a lot of money" you think he's got to be joking so you say okay.'

Plant sought advice also from an old associate, Alexis Korner. 'Of course,' said Korner, 'none of us had an idea what this new group of Jimmy's was all about. But there was strong management and Robert needed some money to pay bills.'

With Plant in place, the only ingredient still missing from the reformed Yardbirds line-up was a drummer. Plant suggested to Page his old friend from the Band of Joy, John Bonham. 'We needed a drummer who was a good timekeeper, and who really laid it down,' said Plant. 'And the only suitable drummer I knew was the one I'd been playing with for years and that was Bonzo Bonham.' Bonham was then on tour with Tim Rose. 'I got so enthusiastic,' added Plant, 'that I hitched back to Oxford and chased after John, got him to one side at a gig and said "mate you've got to join the new Yardbirds". But he wasn't easily convinced. He said, "Well, I'm all right here, aren't I?" He'd never earned before the sort of bread that he was getting from Tim Rose, so I had to try and persuade him. I had nothing to convince him with really except a name that got lost in American pop history – the Yardbirds.'

Unbeknown to Plant, Bonham also had other offers to contemplate. 'Joe Cocker was interested, and so was Chris Farlowe, along with Robert and Jimmy. It was baffling: I had so much to consider. It wasn't just a question of who had the best prospects, but also which music was going to be the right kind of stuff. Farlowe was fairly established and I knew that Cocker was going to make it.

'When I first got offered the gig, I thought the Yardbirds were finished. In Britain they had been forgotten. Still I thought, "well, I've got nothing anyway, so anything is really better than nothing." I knew that Jimmy was a good guitarist and Robert was a good vocalist, so even if we didn't have any success, at least it would be a pleasure to play in a good group. I already knew what music Robert liked, and Jimmy told me what he was into, and I decided that I liked their music ideas better than either Farlowe or Cocker.'

Page said, 'Although I had in mind the need for a very powerful drummer, I must say I wasn't ready for John Bonham. He was playing "Hey Joe" as an acoustic number – I could see the whole thing fitting together. He was beyond the realms of anything I could have possibly imagined. He was absolutely phenomenal and still sounds that way – his work's absolutely incredible.'

With the new line-up finalised, the four musicians met for their first rehearsal, the ultimate test of their chemistry. Would it fly? Would their combined creativity gel together? Would they find nirvana in this fresh transformation? Beforehand Page pondered what direction such a group might take: 'The trouble was I could play a lot of different styles but I didn't really know what to do. Sometimes I wanted to do a hard rock thing, at other times a Pentangle-type thing. But as soon as I heard Robert Plant, I realised it was likely to be the former.' John Bonham's booming drum chops cemented the decision completely.

By 1990 Page provided this perspective: 'I had it in my mind exactly what I wanted to try and get together. Then it was just a matter of searching around for the right personnel that could pull it off. By that I mean for the sort of work that I'd managed to expand around the Yardbirds' material . . . there were a lot of areas in there for improvisation and I'd come up with a lot of riffs of my own. And ideas and passages and movements and things. Along with the incorporation of the acoustic work – and the blues et cetera – that was the idea of it.'

Right from the start, the four hit it off more harmoniously than any of them had dreamed. To call it a marriage made in music heaven might be slightly over the top, but there was by all accounts a fiercesome fusion of hot musical skills. 'The four of us just got together in this four-by-four room and started playing,' said Page at the time. 'Then we knew . . . we starting laughing at each other. Maybe it was from relief, or maybe from the knowledge tht we now *knew* we could groove together. But that was it. That was just how well it was going.'

John Paul Jones recalled in 1990: 'We first played together in a small basement room in Gerrard Street in what is now Chinatown. There was just wall-to-wall amplifiers, Marshalls everywhere, and a space for the door and that was it. We were just literally looking at each other and we said "what shall we play?" Being a session musician, I didn't know anything at all. There was an old Yardbirds number called "Train Kept a Rolling" and Jimmy yelled out, "It's easy . . . just G to A and away you go . . ."

'The whole room just exploded. There were lots of silly grins and "oh yeah man, this is it man, yeah". It *was* pretty bloody obvious, actually, from the first number that it was going to work.'

Added Plant, also with the benefit of hindsight, 'I remember the little room. All I can remember is that it was hot and it sounded good. Very, very exciting and very challenging really. I could feel that something was happening within myself and to everyone else in the room. It felt like we'd found something that we had to really be careful of because we might lose it. The power of it was remarkable.'

Concluded Page: 'At the end of it, we knew that it was really happening, really electrifying. Exciting is the word. We went from there to start rehearsals for the album.'

Since the booking sheet contained several contracted Yardbirds appearances still to be fulfilled, the lads quickly dubbed themselves 'The New Yardbirds' and took off on a test tour of Scandinavia. On their return, they firmly agreed that a brand new band name was essential. 'We realised that it was working under false pretences,' commented Page. Plant added later, 'When we starting rehearsing the thing had gone beyond where the Yardbirds had left off. And when I introduced Bonzo to everyone, it was obvious that what we'd got was turning the corner again, and there was no point in calling it the Yardbirds.'

According to the ever-honest Plant: 'In Scandinavia, we were pretty green: it was very early days and we were tiptoeing with each other. We didn't have half the recklessness that became for me the whole joy of Led Zeppelin. It was a tentative start.'

Jimmy Page, Robert Plant, John Bonham and John Paul Jones were – individually and collectively – much more than just a new Yardbirds: they were a totally new creative entity and a change of name was entirely and urgently in order.

Not surprisingly, there are vastly contradicting tales on how the foursome settled on Led Zeppelin as the name for their new band. According to Page, 'We were sitting there kicking around group names and I suddenly remembered a name which Keith Moon had come up with some months earlier. This goes right back to the days when Simon Napier-Bell, who was managing the Yardies, was trying to get solo discs from each member. Jeff Beck and I were collaborating and in those days with these solo diversions it seemed we should use other musicians. So there was Keith Moon, John Paul Jones, Nicky Hopkins on piano, myself on twelve-string guitar and Jeff. We were doing "Beck's Bolero". After that session Keith Moon was really fired up – and I don't blame him – and he said, "We must get a band together – how about it?" He was fed up with the Who at the time, and he wanted to take the Ox – John Entwhistle – with him, with Jeff, myself and all the rest of us. It didn't happen because we couldn't find the right vocalist. But Keith's name for the band, Led Zeppelin, stuck in my mind.'

It popped up when the New Yardbirds sat down to paint themselves a new public image. 'We'd already considered Mad Dogs,' Page said, 'but eventually it came down to the fact that the name wasn't really as important as whether or not the music was going to be accepted. We could have called ourselves the Vegetables or the Potatoes. I was quite keen about Led Zeppelin. It seemed to fit the bill. It has something to do with the expression about a bad joke going over like a lead balloon. It's a variation on that – and there's a little of the Iron Butterfly light-and-heavy connotation.'

According to John Paul Jones, 'The name was coined by Keith Moon – and it was originally going to be for the band that recorded "Beck's Bolero". The thought of it all going on the road seemed horrific – they were quite a bunch of characters as you can probably imagine. That band never came about but we remembered the name and we asked Keith if we could use it.'

Robert Plant's interpretation is that the name 'refers to a joke which falls flat. It could only have been chosen by Keith Moon who was a complete lunatic. Since then it has gained something of a satirical flavour.'

That's the official version of events. However John Entwhistle, bass player with the Who and a budding solo star in his own right, swears that *he* thought up the name. 'There were several occasions during the Who's career when both Keith Moon and myself were going to leave the band,' Entwhistle claimed. 'Once when we were in New York, I sat down with Keith and our chauffeur, a guy called Richard Cole, and tried to come up with possible names for the new band we planned to form. That's when I flashed on Led Zeppelin. I also came up with the idea for a first album jacket with a Zeppelin going down in flames. The reasons behind it are quite simple. In those days it was a favourite line among British rock bands. "How did you go?" one group would ask another. "Cor, we went down like a lead zeppelin," they'd reply.

'Not long afterwards, the chauffeur Richard Cole went to work for Jimmy Page and Peter Grant and he must have told them the idea. But I was definitely the one who first thought of it. Later on Keith Moon claimed that he came up with it, which made me very angry. When I heard that Jimmy Page was going to use it, I was a bit pissed off about it. Later on, I didn't care that much: after all, they became an institution.'

Their new name, style and personal rapport confirmed, the group's next most urgent priority was the recording of a début album. Page had already selected a collection of likely songs, and rehearsals had started before the Scandinavian tour. Many of the tunes were further explored in front of the live audiences. 'In Scandinavia,' noted Page, 'the songs began to stretch out and I thought we were working into a comfortable groove.'

Bonham, Page, Plant and Jones adjourned to the funky atmosphere of London's Olympic Studios in suburban Barnes in November. 'The statement of our first few weeks together is our first album,' Page declared upon its release. 'We cut it in thirty hours at a cost of £1,700, and between us, we wrote six of the nine tracks. It was easy for us because we had a repertoire of numbers all worked out. We just went into the studio and did it. I suppose it was the fact that we were confident and prepared, which made things flow smoothly in the studio, and – as it happened – we recorded the songs almost exactly as we'd been doing them live. Only "Babe I'm Gonna Leave You" was altered . . . it was partly an attitude of "let's-get-the-job-done-and-not-mess-about-having-a-party-in-there". But it certainly wasn't just a first-take effort – we went on until we were happy with each number.'

Twenty years down the track, Page commented on his concept for *Led Zeppelin*: 'Well, certainly on the first album, I had a very good idea of what I wanted to try and get with the band. Because at that stage, I was extremely instrumental in the total direction of it. Obviously there was a definite concept of what one was trying to achieve there, and it was done. But we were definitely right out there on a limb, weren't we? Doing what we believed in. And it didn't really follow any sort of trend that was going on at all – or certainly nothing relative to any other band.'

Production management presented no problems. Page knew up front that he could direct it himself, although his only credited experience were the four tracks he'd cut with Eric Clapton years earlier. He had however spent several hundred hours as a player in various studios, and had observed all of Britain's best and worst producers in action. He'd always studied their techniques. With the Yardbirds he had also worked closely with Mickie Most, at that time the most successful chart singles maker in British recording history. The ultimate success of Page's studio efforts with Led Zeppelin perhaps belies the industry theory of the need for an outside producer, someone — as producers would have it — to provide an objective, detached, commercially oriented outlook.

Page himself credited engineer Glyn Johns with much of the studio success. 'He did a great job on the sound, which is the most important aspect of the production really. Glyn Johns is an ace engineer. Things like sound don't hang him up because he's both confident and competent.'

Only two of the tracks originated from the Yardbirds days — Page's own 'Dazed and Confused' [previously titled 'I'm Confused'], which many consider to be the *tour de force* of the album, and the closer 'How Many More Times'. 'When Led Zeppelin recorded those two songs,' said ex-Yardbirds drummer Jim McCarty, 'they'd been adapted for the new band. There certainly wasn't any bad feelings.' The second studio take of 'Dazed and Confused' is the one used on the album, and only the violin bow section was overdubbed.

'Babe I'm Gonna Leave You' is a traditional blues number which was also revived by Quicksilver Messenger Service around the same time. 'I got it from the Joan Baez version,' says Page. 'I used to do the song in the days of sitting in the darkness playing my six-string behind Marianne Faithfull.' Page and Plant worked together on the new arrangement although Plant received no credit on the album because he was waiting out the termination of an old songwriting contract.

Willie Dixon, the legendary Chicago blues composer and session bass player, wrote two of the stand-out tunes on the first Led Zeppelin album — 'You Shook Me' and 'I Can't Quit You Baby', which were considerably rearranged by the band. Asked in 1990 what studio techniques he'd originated as the producer of *Led Zeppelin*, Page replied, 'Backwards echo was a technique that I invented at the time. The engineer said it couldn't be done but I knew it could because I'd actually suggested it earlier on a Yardbirds track. You reverse the tape, record the echo, then put it around the right way again so that the echo precedes the signal. It created a fantastic sound but it was really only employed on the first album, on the end of "You Shook Me".'

Not surprisingly the first Zeppelin album predominantly consisted of Jimmy Page's ideas. The other three members had no objections — their individual influences and contributions would come through loud and clear in subsequent recording projects.

Page, always sensitive and sympathetic to the musical aspirations of fellow band members, was aware that Robert Plant in particular had somewhat different tastes and mightn't totally agree with the first album's direction. Yet at the time, Plant didn't appear daunted by the prospects. 'I don't think Jimmy was dominating anything as some might have suspected. I was able to suggest things and the two of us rearranged "Babe I'm Gonna Leave You". When we heard it back in the studio, we were shaking hands with our brains because it turned out to be so nice. It's been a good relationship all round. John Paul Jones has never worked with anybody like me before – me not knowing any of the rudiments of music or anything like that. It's been amazing how we hit it off.'

It was certainly an unlikely combination of acclaimed and established musicians and raw unproven potential, as Plant conceded in 1990. 'Everything is in the eyes of the beholder. Jimmy was a member of the Yardbirds and he was a session musician, so he was successful. Jonesy was much more the backroom boy – I didn't care really whether he'd produced "Mellow Yellow" or not, because it was a pop song and it just started and stopped. Pretty song, but somebody had to write the song, never mind organise it. So their sort of positions and previous roles weren't really that daunting.

'But how they handled themselves with us [Plant and Bonham] was important. Jonesy was a bit . . . not withdrawn, but he stands back a little and shoots the odd bit of dialogue into the air. It's good stuff but an acquired taste really. And Jimmy's personality initially was . . . I don't think I'd ever come across a personality like it before. He had a demeanour which you had to adjust to; certainly it wasn't very casual to start with. But then again, the music was so intense that everything was intense. The ambition was intense and the delivery was intense, and where we were going was intense. Nobody knew where the fuck it was, but we all knew that this power was ridiculous from the beginning. So it was very hard to relax, sit down and have a beer and be the guys from the Black Country. Bonzo and I were much more basic in every respect, in how to deal with everything – including Jimmy. Because he had to be dealt with.'

In late November 1968, manager Peter Grant, highly enthusiastic about the band's prospects, boarded a New York-bound jet with a suitcase full of audition cassettes, master tapes and jacket artwork. Grant's goal: a world distribution deal for the unknown entity, Led Zeppelin. Interestingly the only connection between the first Led Zeppelin album and the Yardbirds was the back cover photo by Chris Dreja; Page likes to boast that he never forgets his friends.

The Yardbirds had been signed to Epic Records in the US, a division of CBS, and to EMI in Europe. Grant declined to offer bidding rights to either company, which speaks for itself. Instead he steered his considerable bulk towards the New York offices of Atlantic Records near Columbus Circle. Company directors Ahmet Ertegun and Jerry Wexler immediately appreciated Peter Grant's personal style and the ferociously formidable sound of the group he represented. With landmark albums by the likes of Cream, Aretha Franklin and the Buffalo Springfield shooting up the charts, Atlantic clearly had an intimate understanding of the rapidly emerging 'underground' album-driven late 1960s music scene. A deal, reportedly involving an initial payment of $200,000 − a pittance by today's corporate rock standards − was rapidly concluded.

Then on a whim, Grant and his New York attorney Steve Weiss decided to drop in on Clive Davis, then president of CBS Records. Dick Asher, at that time a top CBS executive in New York, remembered that meeting extremely well. 'We at Columbia felt that Epic had done a really good job in promoting the Yardbirds . . . we thought we'd done very well on Jimmy Page. The Yardbirds had been signed directly to EMI in Britain and we in turn had an agreement with EMI for North American rights. Our contract specified that we had not only group but individual recording rights, in case the group broke up, and we assumed that EMI would have adopted the same policy. There's no point in merely signing a group by its name because groups break up every other day.

'When we heard that the Yardbirds had split up and Jimmy Page had formed Led Zeppelin, we naturally assumed that the rights to Page would go automatically to Columbia − the other three members being subject to mutual agreement.

'So Grant and Weiss duly arrived at Clive's office and we all sat down. It was Clive's first meeting with Peter Grant and we talked and talked about all sorts of things. It went on and on but there was no mention of Led Zeppelin. Finally Clive said, "Aren't we going to talk about Jimmy Page?" Grant replied, "Oh no, we've already signed Led Zeppelin to Atlantic." Grant then explained that Jimmy Page had never been signed to EMI as an individual artist, only as part of the Yardbirds group.

'Clive just went berserk . . . and I think with some justification.

The Yardbirds had been one of his pet projects. We were all stunned – especially after all we'd done for that group. It was a horrible, horrible meeting and I'll never forget it as long as I live.'

Clive Davis has never said anything publicly about this super-snub. Peter Grant had no comment to make about CBS, other than that he 'never' intends to do business with the company. Two other artists whom Grant managed at one time or another – Jeff Beck and singer Terry Reid – had also been signed to the CBS subsidiary, Epic Records.

As for Jimmy Page, he'd apparently soured on CBS when they greedily released the unauthorised Yardbirds live album, the one forced out of the marketplace by his injunction. 'I never signed any contracts with Epic – they didn't want me at the time,' said Page. 'Mind you, as soon as the deal with Atlantic was announced, they started saying things like "Hey you can't record him, he's signed to us". But when we asked them to prove it, all they could come up with was red faces and shuffling embarrassment.'

As 1968 wound to a close, Led Zeppelin had acquired a five-year worldwide distribution deal with Atlantic. Under its landmark terms, the band had acquired total creative control – their records would be independently produced without Atlantic input. The group would also control jacket artwork, press ads, publicity pictures, and anything else concerning their image. It wasn't that Peter Grant and the band were doubtful about Atlantic's abilities, but that they simply didn't want to trust anybody but themselves with these vital creative decisions. The basic outline of this remarkable contract later influenced the Rolling Stones in their subsequent label distribution agreement with Atlantic. Both bands completely controlled all creative processes, leaving only the physical record manufacturing and distribution, and to a limited degree, promotion, to Atlantic. Not that the Stones would come anywhere near Led Zeppelin's album sales figures in the decade that was to follow.

Led Zeppelin's inaugural North American tour was tightly co-ordinated to start late in December in Denver, the plan being to introduce the new band to US audiences and help stimulate sales of the initial album. A few days into the final year of the 1960s, Atlantic despatched a limited number of advance 'white label' copies of the début album to leading opinion-moulders: key press reviewers, radio programmers and sundry trend spotters. Enthusiastic reaction from the US West Coast in particular, long a stronghold of the Yardbirds, was encouraging and advance orders of 50,000 copies were generated, an impressive figure for a new band.

Then on 12 January, just three days after Page's 25th birthday, *Led Zeppelin* was officially released to the public. That same week the Beatles *White Album* was number one on the *Billboard* charts, topping such disparate artists as Glen Campbell, Diana Ross and the Supremes with the Temptations, the Association, Iron Butterfly and the Jefferson Airplane.

The week of the *Billboard* review, *Led Zeppelin* hit the LP chart at number 99. This probably happened through strong sales activity in the New York market where two weekends earlier, Led Zeppelin had played their first series of East Coast concerts at the Fillmore East. They had triumphantly blown headliners Iron Butterfly right off the stage and all but out of business. From 99, the album jumped to 40, then 28, and settled in for a long residence in the Top-20. Its highest chart position was number ten, reached on 17 May, but the LP remained on the charts for a phenomenal duration of 73 consecutive weeks, almost a year and a half. And it would return again on several occasions later in the 1970s.

Far from taking a dive as their name implied, Led Zeppelin took off like the proverbial show-biz rocket. And, remarkably, the group achieved their incredible success with no hit single (none was ever released from the first album), with little radio exposure and with next to no support from the rock press.

With a couple of notable exceptions, most rock critics either ignored the new band, or – as in the case of *Rolling Stone* magazine, which to its detriment became caustically critical of almost everything they did in the first half of the 1970s – proceeded to hammer them. John Mendelsohn, a peculiar reviewer who doubled as a mediocre drummer in a sour LA group called Christopher Milk, contributed to the 15 March issue one of the most ludicrous record reviews ever published. 'It would seem that, if they're to fill the void created by the demise of Cream, they will have to find a producer, editor and some material worthy of their collective talents.' These were obviously designed to be famous last words.

The handful of rock critics who were favourably impressed by Led Zeppelin's auspicious start included two Britons, Felix Dennis in *Oz* magazine ('a turning point in rock') and Chris Welch in *Punch* ('the definitive recorded rock performance of the year'), and yours truly in the *Toronto Globe and Mail*.

Having been literally swept off my feet on first playing of the advance test pressing shortly before release, I didn't hesitate to test whatever credibility I might have had by heading my 11 January piece: 'Led Zeppelin Climbs Before Its First LP.' My highly enthusiastic endorsement included such comments as, 'Led Zeppelin will be the next super-group in the US . . . they have emerged with a positive, driving, distinctive sound . . . Page's guitar work skims across the melody with a simple joy . . . Jones's bass and organ rhythms are forceful and invigorating . . . the whole is a rare pop experience . . . unlike many groups, Led Zeppelin has managed to maintain simplicity while striving for depth . . . the best début album by any group since *Are You Experienced?* by the Jimi Hendrix Experience.'

This review, according to Peter Grant – a man who never forgets the highs and lows of rock criticism – was the first press prediction anywhere of Led Zeppelin's looming international success. Twenty-odd years down the turnpike, I remain confounded by how any objective listener couldn't hear obvious commercial appeal within the grooves of *Led Zeppelin*. It reeks of broad acceptance, it cries out with mass market empathy. It was simply superstardom in the offing, waiting to explode. The public were quick to pick up on it, but apparently not the pop critics with tin ears or grudges to bear.

Jimmy Page offered this explanation for the group's immediate acceptance: 'We were a completely untried group of people who got together in the space of a few weeks to produce an album which really had only one ingredient that we were sure of – genuine enthusiasm. The secret of our success lies in the fact that we were unabashedly rock and roll and in our ability to interpret the excitement of those early rock sounds in the idiom of today.'

By the 1990s, Robert Plant had developed an interesting perspective on his contributions to the first album. 'If I'd been a little more relaxed and a little less intimidated, it would have been – for me – that much better. I would have sung the same songs with the same phrasing – but I just would have sung them . . . a bit less nervously. All the records are good – there ain't a bad record – but it's just when you look back you become very analytical. And when you analyse an entire piece, then it's usually something to do with the mood you were in, or the conditions that you worked under. I *was* very intimidated. Maybe I had a complex, maybe I was just neurotic or paranoid, but I thought, "This is all too much. Am I really here? Do I belong in this sketch?" So really, the record feels like that to me as regards my contributions.

But as a collection of tunes, and as a way to play and expand, it was great.'

The first Led Zeppelin North American tour was organised by the wily Frank Barsalona, head of Premier Talent, the most dynamic rock booking agency in America. Frank assembled a comprehensive schedule covering most of the US and Canada, with special emphasis on the West Coast where the Yardbirds had played to the most enthusiastic audiences. For Bonham, Jones and Plant, it would be their first exposure to the New World.

Before kicking off in the States, the band performed a number of minor warm-up gigs at home in Britain. The first London gig had taken place at the now defunct Middle Earth club on 9 November. Although they'd only had six hours of rehearsal time on the board, they managed to impress the audience sufficiently to score two standing ovations and a couple of encores. They were paid £150. A week later they played the College of Science and Technology in Manchester for £225, then Sheffield University on 23 November.

On 10 December they performed for the first time at London's blues/rock showcase, the Marquee Club on Wardour Street. John C. Gee, then manager of the club, didn't regard it as a particularly auspicious start. 'Peter Grant was all geared up before the gig. He told me this was going to be a fantastic new group. He really had a lot of faith in them. But the group was very loud – I thought they were overpoweringly loud for the size of the Marquee. Anyway the lads received an enthusiastic but not overwhelming reaction from the audience.

'After the gig Peter Grant came over and asked me what I thought. I told him I wasn't very impressed. Peter insisted that I tell Jimmy the comment personally. So I told Jimmy that they had been OK but that they didn't kill me. I'll willingly admit now that I just couldn't see them making it. Basically I was a jazz enthusiast. The only reason I listened to this hard rock stuff was because it was my job. I don't know – maybe their sound just wasn't quite right that evening. It was just too damn loud for me.'

Two more British dates followed – Bath Pavilion on 16 December (for £75) and Exeter City Hall three days later (£125). At most of these early gigs, promoters insisted on billing the band as the New Yardbirds, despite their name change. They presumed the band's drawing power would only come from the old association. Quite a few other UK promoters simply weren't interested in booking the band until they'd proven themselves.

Led Zeppelin had fared fairly well in impressing the early English audiences, but it could hardly be termed a rip-roaring start. With expenses balanced against the meagre returns, Page personally had to subsidise the band to keep it afloat. The British market clearly wasn't quite ready for Led Zeppelin. So it made good business sense – let alone as a creative stimulus – for the band to take off on its first North American tour a few days later. The British rock press acted as if it couldn't care less, an outlook it would come to regret.

'In England,' John Bonham pointed out, 'with just the reputation of Jimmy Page and the old Yardbirds – even though we'd changed our name – everyone's attitude was that the Yardbirds hadn't done anything in England for so long and they didn't want to book us. When we came over to America with the album coming out, we were able to get some bookings. The Yardies weren't the biggest thing in America, but they were the innovators of something that smelled refreshing to the American public. There's no question that America gave us our chance. In the very early days, I suppose we did lose faith in Britain.'

'It was just a joke in England,' said Page, passionately. 'We really had a bad time. They just wouldn't accept anything new. It had to be the New Yardbirds, not Led Zeppelin. We were given a chance in America. We started off at less than $1,500 a night. We played for only $200 at one gig, but it was worth it – we didn't care – we just wanted to come over to America and play our music. I'd assumed that even though the Yardbirds had been getting $2,500 a night, Led Zeppelin could only hope to start off at about $1,500 mark, and work our way up from there. That was all I expected.

'Bill Graham booked us in both the Fillmores and other underground club promoters gave us a chance. Then it was on our own shoulders. The attitude was "come over here work as hard as we can give them all we can and if it doesn't work we would go back to England and start again". Mind you, no one would have had us back if we had died. It was really up to us.'

The vital North American live début kicked off in Denver, Colorado, on 26 December, one of a series that Peter Grant was able to set up after another of his clients, Jeff Beck, had blown out a tour at short notice. 'Jeff wasn't consistent about his playing,' Robert Plant noted, with a measure of understatement. 'That's a nice way of putting it. Jeff had run away a lot and quite rightly so. Playing on the road can be strange – some people like it and some people don't. Anyway whatever happened, happened, and we ended up in Denver on 26 December with a silly look on our faces and well, it just happened from there.'

Playing wherever and whenever they could – and performing with the sort of total unswerving commitment that literally shook rock clubs from coast to coast – Zep made a volatile impression, to put it mildly. When they came out on stage, they played as though their lives depended on it. Their sound was raw and loud and hammer-like; they seemed to tear it out of themselves. It was white man's blues – 'contemporary blues' is how Page liked to describe it – but it wasn't that far removed from the gutsy authentic blues then in vogue and being performed almost every weekend at these same rock clubs by Muddy Waters, Howlin' Wolf, Albert King, Freddie King and even the Butterfield Blues Band. America was in the grip of another blues renaissance – first-, second- and now third-generation.

As Page had said, the raw basic quality of Led Zeppelin 'was also the whole thing that made the Yardbirds happen. Getting into your own thing is fine, but it has to be a form of experimentation that evolves from a basic sound that everyone else knows and can relate to. Perhaps that's why blues is so big – you can recognise the roots.

'Led Zeppelin is basically a hard rock group. Rock is refreshing and exciting. I've always been a rock musician – I can't play anything else. When rock is on, you just can't pull away from it. At the start, we had a hard rock core. There were a couple of blues tunes too – the whole idea was hard rock and blues.

'I can't really comment on why we broke so big in the States. I can only think that we were aware of the dynamics at a time when everyone was into a drawn-out West Coast style of playing. We knew we were making an impression after the incredible response at the Boston Tea Party and the Kinetic Circus in Chicago, but it was the Fillmore West in San Francisco when we knew we'd really broken through. It was just bang!' said Page.

The West Coast was of crucial importance. Robert Plant recalled the band's first arrival in the surreal environment of an LA Christmas season, 'Bonzo and I were amazed. We'd barely even been abroad and here we were. It was the first time I saw a cop with a gun, the first time I saw a twenty-foot-long car. The whole thing was a complete bowl-over. It was Christmas, and Christmas away from home for the English is the end of the world. I went wandering down the Sunset

Strip with no shirt on. Frank Zappa's girl group, the GTOs, were upstairs. We threw eggs, had silly water battles and had all the good fun that a nineteen-year-old boy should have. We met a lot of people who we still know, a lot of people who've faded away. Some of them literally just grew up. I don't see the point in growing up.'

A master musical strategist, Peter Grant considered the Fillmore West gig with Taj Mahal and Country Joe and the Fish to be especially vital. 'Peter told us if we didn't crack San Francisco, we'd have to go back home,' Plant stated later. 'That was the place that was considered to be essential, the hotbed of the whole movement. It was the acid test, forget the Kool-Aid, and if we weren't convincing, they would have known right away. I said, "I've been singing for years. I'd be happy to sing anywhere". But Peter had his eyes set on something I couldn't even imagine.'

Billed only as 'Supporting Act', Led Zeppelin obviously faced an uphill battle but they pulled it off with formidable style. 'It felt like a vacuum and we'd arrived to fill it,' Page recalled. 'You could feel something happening . . . first this row, then that row. It was like a tornado, and it went rolling across the country.'

Shrewdly the band had anticipated the one double-edged problem they encountered regularly from reviewers – Jimmy's connection with the Yardbirds. 'With Jimmy's reputation,' Plant observed, 'we could get into the right clubs. But had Jimmy been the only member of Led Zeppelin who was any good, it would have been pointless. Obviously on that first tour it was all "Jimmy Jimmy Jimmy" – which is fair enough because he deserved it. But fortunately each of us shone in our own little way.'

John Paul Jones reckoned 'If Jimmy had been incredibly insecure and really wanted to do a star number, he would have picked lesser musicians and just gone on the road and done the whole star trip. Once we'd realised that Jimmy's name was a boost to Led Zeppelin and became aware that we had a job to do, it worked out all right. I don't care if people don't recognise me or say "Oh, you're not Jimmy Page". I'm quite happy – I'd rather be in the background, anyway. It's just my way. I've been into this for too long to have ego trips.'

Page expected that after the initial impact, audiences would willingly accept Led Zeppelin as four talented musicians – not just one guitar star, a singer and a couple of backing musicians. 'The other three,' noted Page, 'knew that it was on their shoulders. I felt that as soon as people saw us on stage, they would be able to see merit in everyone there. Led Zeppelin didn't have any passengers – everyone had as much to show as I did.'

Nonetheless it was an awesome responsibility for Bonham, Jones and Plant, seen under the cold light of retrospect. Particularly so, as many other aspiring British groups of the period appeared to be labouring under countless difficulties in establishing American acceptance. 'Obviously we owed a lot to Jimmy in the first place,' said Plant, 'because he gave us the chance. People like Spooky Tooth had such a hard time trying to get any sort of reputation in the States. Eventually this leads to a rapid decline in inspiration. Spooky Tooth came over here and did about seven gigs all summer. It was very bad for the band. I thought they were really good. But I suppose coming to America and being faced with all the hang-ups they had – and no money – must have been a real drag. Why we did it I'll never know. I haven't a clue. Maybe you could say that we were good or that we were exciting.

'American audiences just seemed to appreciate our music. When we started the tour on the West Coast, we weren't even listed on the bill. By the time we got across to the East Coast, we were up to second on the bill – it was quite a feeling.'

John Paul Jones felt that many American bands had simply become lazy, thus allowing their British counterparts to overpower them on stage. 'The Americans had it their own way for so long. But as soon as some competition comes along and succeeds, the not-so-good American groups get uptight because they think they're missing out on all the work. The better bands just pull their fingers out and come up with something really great – then they do as well as the best English bands. Of course I think it can be taken as a criticism of American bands that so many English groups are getting into the US charts. They should take another look at themselves and their music.'

Later on Jones would cite the Boston Tea Party gig on that first tour as one of the best moments of the entire Zeppelin career. 'That was the biggie really for us, and we really knew that it was working. Plus it was the longest concert we ever did. We played four and a quarter hours I believe, which – with a ninety-minute set – is some going, I can tell you. We played four nights at the Tea Party and on the last night, we did our act twice and then we did everybody else's act – we did Beatles songs, Stones songs, Who songs and everything. It was really good and it was really steaming.'

Summing up that historic first American breakthrough tour, Page observed a few years later, 'I think that what did it for us was the stage thing. We came here unknown on that first tour, we did our number and the word got out that we were worth seeing. We tried as hard as we could on stage and it worked.

'Before they saw us in America there was a blast of publicity and the public heard all about the money being advanced to us by the record company. So the reaction was "Ah, a capitalist group" . . . but they realised we weren't when they saw us playing a three-hour non-stop show every night.'

The band returned to Britain at the end of February 1969, dazed, perhaps, but certainly not confused. They were buzzed by their early success — it had been a tough tour but the usual rigours of the road had not deterred the band's sense of purpose. In their first battle with the usually elusive American market, Led Zeppelin had won hands down.

Back home, not surprisingly, life seemed somewhat anti-climactic. Peter Grant organised an extensive series of club gigs in an attempt to expose the band to as many British punters as possible in order to let the public decide for themselves. Between 1 March and 17 April, the lads played eighteen dates over a broad geographic spread — from Plymouth to Leicester, Cardiff to London, Sunderland to Stoke-on-Trent. Audience reaction was good but the money was pitiful. Examination of the band's private files revealed a low of £60 against 60 per cent of the gate, to a high of £140 flat.

But the group wasn't disheartened. At the end of the tour, Page told the British music press, 'We've been very lucky. It's been a very rapid success. It is amazing. I think Atlantic Records had a lot to do with it — they made sure that people knew each member of the group as an individual.'

Instead of sitting back and resting on their newly earned laurels, Grant and the band decided to push on. A start was made on some tracks for the second album, and then they headed back to America. The first leg of the second Led Zeppelin US tour in only a few short months opened in May 1969 with four extremely well-received performances at San Francisco's Fillmore West. Then on to LA where the gigs had sold out the day prior. The group's sizzling reputation on the rock grapevine seemed to be hotting up by the hour — and if we are to believe some reports, so too were the group's diverse activities as rock and roll ravers extraordinary. Writer Ellen Sander, no hearty enthusiast of Led Zeppelin's morals (or alleged lack thereof) claims their assorted antics at the Continental Hyatt House hotel on Hollywood's Sunset Strip 'set the popvine aghast'. She reported that John Bonham had dressed himself up as a waiter and served Jimmy Page on a room service cart to a flock of eager young nubiles.

Such frivolous frolics notwithstanding, the second tour wasn't all donuts, mud sharks and plaster casters. The band arrived at a Detroit motel only seconds after a murder had taken place. Fresh blood stained the reception carpet. It was early morning and the band had been flying all night. Even in their dazed condition, such ugly episodes weren't that easy to shrug off as just the normal rigmarole of the road.

The beat went marching on. 'I think that on the second tour,' Plant said, 'people really started taking an interest in the other members of the group and not just Jimmy alone. Each of us has a different personality which is now coming to the fore. People can identify with John Bonham for example when he jumps into the air above his drums. I think that audiences now know each member of the group for his musical ability and for himself.'

The first leg of the long 1969 summer tour came to a spectacular conclusion at the Fillmore East in New York on 30 to 31 May to sold-out crowds and ecstatic encores. But still some members of the press couldn't come to terms with the burgeoning phenomenon. Witness a period review from *Variety* magazine, 'Led Zeppelin have carried the British bass-drums-lead-guitar format to an extreme. Following the footsteps of Cream, the Who, Jeff Beck, Jimi Hendrix et al, this quartet's obsession with power, volume and melodramatic theatrics, leaves little room for subtlety the other Britishers employ. There is plenty of room for dynamics and understatement in the Zeppelin brand of ultra-hard rock. But the combo has forsaken their musical sense for the sheer power that entices their predominantly juvenile audience.'

The band went back to Britain in June, thrilled with the extent of their North American success, and certain that the time had come to take on the UK rock scene on their own terms. The promoters of the Pop Proms series at London's prestigious Albert Hall gave the band a chance to show the locals what the fuss was all about across the Atlantic. The gig sold out and although the Hall's capacity is only 3,000, Zep performed before their largest British audience to date.

Tapping his foot in the wings was Phil Carson, a former bass player and group manager who'd just been appointed Atlantic Records' new British director. 'It was the very first time I'd seen the lads play,' Carson recalled, positively glowing with the memory. 'It was just an absolutely am-aaaaaz-ing concert. No band has ever played rock and roll like they played it that night. It was just an incredible experience to see that band in the Albert Hall environment. They were just so good. They closed the show with a rock and roll set which was probably the best that I've ever heard them play. Even better than the rock and roll set they later played in Osaka, Japan, with me on the bloody bass! Certainly they were better than I've ever heard anyone else ever play a rock and roll set.'

It was the landmark gig to take them over the top in Britain.

Wrote Peter Cole, respected reviewer with the *London Evening Standard*, 'Led Zeppelin are electrifying. They are one of the new wall-of-sound bands who aim to reorganise the central nervous system first, and entertain afterwards. They did both to great effect.' *Disc* noted the audience 'stormed the stage, danced in the aisles and the boxes, and were screaming so hard that the band did three encores'.

So it was that eight months after their formation, Zeppelin had finally cracked their homeland, after literally forcing focus on themselves based on their impressive American achievements. They could not be denied.

Anxious to maintain their momentum, Led Zeppelin hopped on a plane to the States on 5 July to kick off the second part of their 1969 summer tour. They swung into it at the Atlanta pop festival and followed with appearances at jazz festivals in Newport, Baltimore and Philadelphia. While their sound is a long way removed from jazz, festival organisers desperately needed broader audiences. For Led Zeppelin, it was wider exposure and more money.

Elsewhere, too, they were rapidly outgrowing small rock clubs which had spawned them, such as the Boston Tea Party, Toronto's Rock Pile and Chicago's Kinetic Circus. The time had clearly arrived for the band to move up to larger venues. In New York they played in Central Park, and *Cashbox*, the music trade weekly, described their appearance as the highlight of the 1969 Schaefer Music Festival, 'Outstanding candidate for super-stardom is the group's luminary vocalist, Robert Plant. His soaring, spell-binding voice revealed an extraordinary physical and emotional range, as he wove Zeppelin's demanding musical atmosphere with apparent ease. This, combined with his wantonly awesome stage presence, drama of movement and searing improvisation, all testify that Robert Plant may very well be the artist who can employ all nine muses at once.'

While few other critics were as wildly complimentary, the fans were exultant. The summer tour turned into one stormy triumph after another, peaking at the Dallas Festival on 31 August. There the band received its largest single concert fee to date – a flat $13,000. Although severely exhausted, the band members knew they'd totally broken through in the American market – the battle had been won. Even so, Page's parting comment as he left New York for home was – as ever – cautious and modest. 'This tour has been fantastic. But you can never be too sure. We've got to work even harder now. You can't rest on your laurels. It's easy to go down just as fast as you go up.'

Not only the media maintained a sceptical outlook on Led Zeppelin, as some of their high-profiled contemporaries also demonstrated various degrees of reticence about the spiralling success of the unexpected little quartet which Page had put together. Early in 1970 I sought personal impressions of Led Zeppelin from four of the world's most prominent rock musicians: John Lennon, Keith Richard, Pete Townshend and Eric Clapton.

John Lennon: 'From what little I've heard, they sound all right. Jimmy Page has always been a bloody good guitar player.'

Keith Richard: 'I played their first album quite a lot when I first got it, but then the guy's voice started to get on my nerves for some reason. I dunno why – I imagine it was just a bit too acrobatic for me. Jimmy Page is a great guitar player and I've known him for years . . . even before he was with the Yardbirds. He's always been a very respected player.'

Pete Townshend: 'I'm not one of their biggest fans which doesn't mean that I don't like them, but means that I don't really get into their music a lot. I don't know their music very well – and I haven't seen them work very often. We played together only once. I think it must have been the last gig they did playing before another group on the bill . . . and we [the Who] just about got it together, we just about topped what they'd done.

'When we did the Murray the K show in New York some years back and Cream was working with us, it just seemed logical to me that there was no reason why Americans would absorb a group like Cream – which was only throwing their own music back at them. At that time Cream was doing very badly and it was only later on that suddenly – after playing the Village Gate in New York – they picked up the pieces and smashed home to a huge proportion thing. The fact that Zeppelin did the same thing was no surprise, because by then I was aware of that market.

'Now I'm beginning to understand why Jeff Beck was such a huge success in America but nothing here in England. And why people like the Yardbirds were appreciated there but not here. They were all solo-guitar-based groups. They had guitar idols in them – which is something I've never been. I've always been very much a part of the Who. Let's face it – you can't worship a guy for destroying an instrument in the name of rock.

'The following for groups like Led Zeppelin consists of music lovers, people that haven't got the whole thing about rock and roll that you and I probably have in an abstract way . . . and let me hasten to add that the Zep members themselves fall into our category.

'But when you get this ideology thing happening for the ideal rock guitarist – like the B.B. King syndrome, the Eric Clapton thing, the Jimmy Page trip – and I think Jimmy Page has been right in it and probably invented it. Jimmy played fuzz guitar on the B side of the Who's "I Can't Explain", a song called "Bald-Headed Woman". I just sat there and thought, what is this? Fuzzbox? I'd never even heard of it. I wondered what the hell he was doing. But I knew that this was going to be *the* sound. Jimmy just ran his fingers over the guitar a couple of times. Me, I just used to play chords!'

Eric Clapton: 'I don't know about them. I've heard their records and I saw them play in Milwaukee – we were on the same bill. They were very loud – I thought it was unnecessarily loud. I liked some of it, I really did like some of it. But a lot of it was just too much. They over-emphasised whatever point they were making, I thought.'

But no matter what musicians and music critics might think, Led Zeppelin's future was assured. The public had made up its mind. The question now remaining was what Led Zeppelin might do with the brewing fame and acclaim, and where it might lead them.

4 Whole Lotta Follow Through –
The Band in Dynamic Motion

WITH THEIR NEWLY FOUND MOMENTUM HUMMING, Led Zeppelin members at last stopped to catch a private rest in the early autumn of 1969. Bonham, Jones and Plant retired to the solitude of their country retreats, such as they were. Page and his partner, Charlotte, took a month off and travelled through Morocco and Spain for a change of pace and place. They obviously deserved a rest, not just from touring but from the intense pressure of trying to create the framework for a new and vital album in between concerts. Since the band had formed eight months earlier, they'd been on the road almost incessantly. Any free days between gigs had usually been devoted to brief but prolific recording sessions, ad hoc and at random, but inevitably under pressure.

Led Zeppelin was soaring serenely at number sixteen on the *Billboard* album charts and selling sweetly. An excited Atlantic was pushing strongly for the completed master tapes of the eagerly anticipated follow-up. Initially the company had hoped to rush the second album on to an eager market by the end of July, to capitalise on the second North American tour – but the band seemed annoyed at the record company's apparent indifference to the logistic problems of trying to cut an album on the run while zipping around the continent on tour. They expected compassion from Atlantic, but the company – not unexpectedly – was too inflamed by the presence of a super-hot new act and thought only of the awesome prospects of new product and heavy chart action, not to mention fabulous profits.

Somehow the band had made sure it kept delivering, both on stage and in various studios, no matter how impossible the schedule. Unlike virtually anybody involved with the band or the record company, I could see the situation from both sides and it was none too comfortable. Before one of these amazing on-the-fly studio sessions, manager Peter Grant and a very privileged journalist in the person of yours truly, cruised the freeway out to Kennedy Airport from downtown Manhattan to meet Jimmy Page who was jetting in from Salt Lake City the morning after a concert.

Later that same afternoon, he would wing back across to LA to rejoin the group and then proceed on to Phoenix for a performance the next day; such was the luring late-1960s reputation of a mix-down facility like A&R Studios in New York for a committed production perfectionist such as Page.

My presence on this particular journey shouldn't be interpreted as an indicator of the Led Zeppelin camp's mellowing attitude towards the media – far from it. As John Paul Jones noted in recent years, reflecting on early media resistance to the band, especially from *Rolling Stone*, 'The first review we got from *Rolling Stone* was all about the *hype* of Led Zeppelin. You know – "It's just another band of do-nothings, and here they are hyped up by everybody, and it's a bunch of shit anyway." And that was really hurtful at the time, because we knew we'd done a good record. It helped foster my general hatred of the press.'

Later on I would realise that the only reason I had attained unrestrained access to the band in the early 1970s wasn't because they needed the publicity – though God knows I churned out heaps of Led Zeppelin articles from these on-going 'progress reports' from within the mystical walls of the Zep inner sanctum. Eventually I came to understand that this freely-given access originated out of an unusual feeling of loyalty – I'd been one of the first to acclaim Led Zeppelin's first album and they appreciated any support which arrived in the early days of wholesale press slag-offs. They wouldn't forget the handful of people who'd acknowledged them. And encouraged them.

'We had appalling press at the time,' Plant said. 'Nobody seemed to want to know us for one reason or another. We got to America and read the *Rolling Stone* review of the very first album, which was going on about us as another hyped British band. We couldn't believe it. In our naivety we thought we'd done a good album and were doing all right, and then all this venom comes flying out. We couldn't understand why or what we'd done to them. After that we were very wary of the press, which became a chicken-and-egg situation. We avoided them and so they started to avoid us. It was only because we did a lot of shows that our reputation got around as a good live band.'

So I wasn't exactly engrossed in the attitudes of other members of the media as the limo tooled down the highway to JFK that very warm

Tuesday afternoon. I was in New York doing some liner note projects for Atlantic Records and Jimmy was flying in for a few hours – naturally I'd whip out to the airport to meet and greet him. And Peter had hinted that – scoop of scoops – I might, just might get a chance to hear at least a couple of tracks from the forthcoming album, the second LP that even rival record companies were anticipating in their private corridors.

Like the rest of the world, I couldn't wait to hear what that soul-stirring stimulant of broad acceptance – artistically and commercially – would incite in their creative spirits. After all the first album had probably shown as much promise as any rock début album – certainly they'd kicked off from a musical proficiency level that very few bands could even dream of. Massive expectations had been imposed upon the band – from their record company executives through to the intrigued punter on the street. The groundswell around the band had reached such proportions that much was anticipated from the lads, despite the well-known fact that they'd constantly been on the road since the release of the first album.

A relatively relaxed Peter Grant pulled out a large white hanky and mopped his brow as we finally glided into the Arrivals level at JFK. But he was mortified – and I choose the word carefully – to discover that a mistake had been made. Jimmy's flight from Salt Lake City had landed a couple of hours earlier, and the presumably jet-lagged guitarist had been forced – none too willingly – to jump a cab downtown. Grant's abundantly clear crease of concern resulted from Page's well-known paranoia about riding in taxis. It wasn't all that difficult to see that Peter figured he'd been fucked up in a big way. Those less suspicious than your observer might well have concluded that Grant himself had a major paranoia about screwing up Jimmy's sweltering schedule – after all, he'd humped his way in all the way from Salt Lake City and all we had to do was sweat out the expressway from Columbus Circle to JFK. This could be construed as a major fuck-up, no doubt about it. I merely assumed that Grant was particularly diligent in taking care of his increasingly valuable clients, especially his long-time associate and confidant, the one and only (but occasionally fragile) Jimmy Page. Especially on this particular mercy mission from halfway across the bloody continent.

In what was to be easily the fastest airport–downtown dash I've ever witnessed, we tore back into the city with a volatile Grant urging on the silent chauffeur like a mule driver. Even to a fringe insider like myself, Grant readily indicated that he expected severe words from Page, who had been under 'heavy strain'. 'Cor,' Grant croaked breathlessly, the sweat tumbling from his broad forehead, 'Jimmy's not gonna like this . . . he's not gonna like this at all. Jeeeeesus – hurry up driver! Are we *ever* gonna get there?'

By the time we squeezed into the mini-elevator heading up to the A&R Studios, I'll admit to feeling a tinge of nerves myself. If Peter Grant was this worried about how pissed off Jimmy might be, then it seemed logical that he was unlikely to be thrilled to see a possibly intruding journalist. With all of his constant travelling and the odd bit of partying, we were expecting to find Jimmy looking like an emaciated rake, albeit a rake with a few odd quid left in his pocket. As it turned out when we finally stumbled into the studio, he was fine. Not only that, he was most agreeable and convivial – Peter Grant beamed like a warrior finding himself miraculously recovered to fight another day . . . the ups and downs of looking after a rapidly rising red-hot rock group. Grant, more so than any other manager I've ever scrutinised in action, knew how to roll with the punches, and rock with the rollers.

Dressed in Chelsea King's Road-style Regency splendour – the buckled burgundy patent leather boots, the flaming red velvet bell-bottoms, the dusty pink brushed-velvet jacket (no wonder he'd been nervous about riding with strange taxi drivers) – Page was calmly slouched behind an extensive mixing console with engineer Eddie Kramer. He looked up from munching on a prune Danish pastry which he was coaxing down with a plastic cupful of teabag swill. He greeted us warmly which relieved Grant no end, and bid us relax on the studio sofa while he and Kramer put the finishing flourishes to a blues blaster called 'Bring It On Home', considered by the band to be the quintessential closing track of *Led Zeppelin II*.

We sat enthralled as Page issued simple, clear-cut instructions, quietly but forcefully. No ifs, buts or maybes. He knew what he was after and he would endure and inquire until he found it. Eddie Kramer, one of the finest in his field, manoeuvred the myriad of dials and faders, translating Page's notions into sounds. Occasionally Kramer tossed up a suggestion and Page listened. More often than not, he had an intuitive projection of what the outcome would be. The sound splintered into muddier and dirtier incarnations as Page pushed for the raw and heavy echo sound he wanted, a style of recording closer to the classic early Chess milieu. Three more playback runthroughs, some minor adjustments on the left channel and finally Page grinned with apparent satisfaction. 'Phew!' he sighed, turning a delighted smile upon Grant and myself. 'It's nice to get that one finished. I think we might close the album with that one.' Suffering from sonic shock, we nodded in overwhelming agreement. It was overpowering and it was absolutely brilliant. But as always on rare occasions like this, it's absurdly difficult to find any appropriate critical comments.

Peter Grant plunged into a humorous explanation of how some travel agent twit had confused Jimmy's flight details earlier in this memorable day, while Eddie Kramer lined up the playback machine to provide us with a taste of the final mixes on three of the finished tracks from the upcoming album. Like myself, Grant had yet to hear these completed mixes. We sat in stunned silence as the speakers burst forth with 'Living Loving Maid', 'Heartbreaker' and 'What Is and What Should Never Be' – all stunning introductions to the album to come. Rising above the occasion, I begged for acetate copies of the three tracks to take back to Toronto with me later in the week – I couldn't live without them, I said, and I meant it. Jimmy obliged me.

Page seemed genuinely pleased by our natural enthusiasm for what we were hearing – it was the first reaction he'd observed outside of the four band members and engineer Eddie Kramer. But being the permanent perfectionist, Pagey had a hatful of lingering reservations. Even an overwhelming endorsement which followed a few weeks later from the spiritual Godfather of rock and roll, Atlantic Records' Jerry Wexler [to quote, 'On the strength of these three tracks from the next Led Zeppelin album, I would have to say that this is the best white blues I have ever heard' – rating them superior to Cream], didn't put Jimmy's stubborn Capricorn heart at rest. Not that he could have hoped for a more sincere or profound endorsement than that accorded them by Wexler, a princely purist to the *n*th degree. If Led Zep were making it sound great to Wexler's ears, then they were taking it over the top, full stop.

As it had turned out, a combination of record company pressure, the need for simple expediency, the constant travel and touring diversions had given Jimmy no time to sit back, relax and evaluate at leisure, thereby placing the album as a whole in some sort of realistic focus. Stuck midstream in a neverending battle to get on top of it all Jimmy could only feel the dampener of confusion. His misgivings and minor concerns were in fact a reflection of that conclusion.

As he put it himself at the time, 'We've been so busy that we just weren't able to go into one studio and polish the whole album off. It's become ridiculous – we put a rhythm track down in London, add the vocals in New York, overdub harmonica in Vancouver and then come back to New York to do the mixing here at A&R. We never really expected to be as big as this,' he said quietly, and I'm sure he meant it. 'We just wanted to be able to come over to America to play some gigs a couple of times a year. It's almost gotten out of hand now.'

A tinge of paranoia perhaps? 'I do worry that the second album is turning out to be so different from the first – we may have overstepped the mark,' Page surmised as Kramer ran off safety copies of the new completed two-track mixes. 'But then again, I suppose there are enough Led Zeppelin trademarks in there. It's very hard rock, there's no doubt about that. There aren't many bands into hard rock these days and I think that might account for some of our success. All sorts of people are into folk and country and softer stuff. We just like to play it hard and bluesy. There aren't many exponents of real contemporary blues either. John Mayall doesn't do it any more. But there's always a market for it, I think. Taj Mahal is my idea of contemporary blues. Our stuff I think is a combination of everything.'

How, I enquired, had he hung onto his trademark modesty and honesty throughout the recent hectic period capped off by their overwhelming North American success? 'There are so many guitarists around who I think are better than me,' he replied. 'Everywhere I go I hear some cat who sounds better than I do. That's the trouble: everyone's good these days. I'm a trifle disappointed with some of the guitar playing on the second album. When I'm in the studio, I really do miss the rapport you get with a live audience,' he continued in the true spirit of a veteran tour campaigner. 'There's only a few people there looking at you through a window: it's all very depressing really. The hardest thing in the world is to get excitement on to a piece of plastic. I really do think that we all play better on stage than we do on record.'

At the time Page offered these comments, the second album was less than half-finished and he was in a bit of a frazzle. Later when it was wrapped up we spoke again, but Pagey was still clinging to some lingering doubts which I for one tried unsuccessfully to dispel. 'The album took such a long time to make . . . it was all on and off. It was quite insane really. We had no time and we had to write songs in hotel rooms. By the time the album came out, I was really fed up with it. I'd just heard it so many times in so many different places.

I really think I lost confidence in it. Even though people were saying it was great, I wasn't convinced myself.'

If Page was too concerned about technical flaws, then at least he knew that the second album didn't lack balls. 'There was probably more attack on the second album because it was written while we were on the road and only getting into the studio when we could find an opening. I suppose that feeling of playing all the time is evident in the new album. There wasn't much time to sit back and think about it.'

It's worth noting that Page's prime ambition at this time was 'to keep a consistent flow of record product coming out'. 'Too many groups,' he said, 'sit back after the first album, and the second one is a down trip. I want every album to reach out further − that's the whole point of it.'

Rather late one evening after the stunning Carnegie Hall concerts in New York, just prior to the release of *Led Zeppelin II*, Page sat back and gave me an insightful track-by-track account of how he felt about the songs which would sent the second album soaring.

'Whole Lotta Love', the fiery riff song which would become a Led Zeppelin anthem, opened the album in spectacular style. No one is sure when that unforgettable riff first appeared: John Paul Jones reckoned it probably first surfaced during an on-stage jam as part of 'Dazed and Confused'. Plant added recently, 'Wherever it came from, it was all about that riff. Any tribute which flows in must go to Jimmy and his riffs. They were mostly in the key of E and you could really play around with them. Since I've been playing guitar myself, I've realised more than ever that the whole thing, the whole band really, came straight from the blues. Everything.' To Jimmy Page, the song 'was just a basic rock tune, using some electronic sounds in the middle section. It does sound great on headphones, I think. It reminds me of a sort of Rolling Stones feel.' Other observers claimed to hear traces of Willie Dixon's 'You Need Love' in the track. Blues cross-currents aside, this tune set the scene not just for this album but, more broadly, for the entire hard rock genre. Two decades down the track, it remains one of the greatest songs that hard rock has tossed up in its stormy evolution, epitomising what talented musicians can derive from one basic riff. It is without doubt the definitive heavy metal mould-maker.

Later Page explained how he'd got the riff together. 'I had it worked out already before entering the studio. I had rehearsed it. And then all that other stuff − sonic wave sound and all that − I built it up in the studio and put effects and treatments on it. The descending riff was done with a metal slide and backwards echo. I think I came up with that first before anybody. I know it's been used a lot now, but not at the time we did the second album. Some of the things that might sound a bit odd have, in fact, backwards echo involved in them as well.'

The next cut 'What Is and What Should Never Be' Page saw as 'a change for the band. We wanted to try some new ideas on the second album and this is one of the first things that we came up with. We put a lot of thought into it and I like it a lot. In the chorus you can hear in Robert's lyrics a serious lyric writer starting to emerge.' John Paul Jones also found particular significance in the song. 'I always did like a good tune on the bass, and as an example you can listen to "What Is and What Should Never Be". The role of a bassist is hard to define. You can't play chords, so you have a harmonic role: picking and timing notes. You'll suggest a melodic or a harmonic pattern, but I seem to be changing anyway towards more of a lead style. The Alembic bass guitar [built by the Californian Alembic guitar maker, Rick Turner] is doing it: I play differently on it. But I try to never forget my role as a bass player: to play the bass and not mess around too much up at the top all the time, and that's the most important thing.'

'The most basic blues thing on the album,' Page asserted, 'is "The Lemon Song". We cut it live in the studio with just a guitar overdub on the bridge – I think it was a Fender or Rickenbacker electric twelve-string.'

As for 'Thank You', in Page's opinion it signifies Robert Plant's true emergence as Led Zeppelin's lyric master. 'I never felt at all confident with my own lyrics,' Page admitted, 'and I was hoping that Robert could do all that side, which I think developed from this track. We did very little overdubbing on this number.'

Moving on to side two and 'Heartbreaker', Jimmy noted, 'This tune "Heartbreaker" has become a real workout number at concerts. It's really just a riff number, a collection of riffs with Robert's words. "Living Loving Maid" was again a basic sort of rock number built around a riff. It's all about a degenerate old woman desperately trying to be young again.'

Of 'Ramble On', one of the tunes requiring several guitar overdubs, Page said, 'It's a very nice track but it's very hard to do on stage – the acoustic guitar over the electric guitar. I know it's Robert's favourite song on the entire album.' Plant readily confirmed this, 'Yeah, that song was my baby and I hoped everybody would suss it out and realise that this is where I want to go.' About the two closing tracks, Plant added that 'Moby Dick' was especially written to feature John Bonham's drumming, while part of the closing cut 'Bring It On Home' was dedicated to Sonny Boy Williamson.

Page said, 'My particular favourites are "Thank You", "What Is", "Ramble On" and "Whole Lotta Love". But I like to feel that each of the tracks has something to say for itself. Some of the things definitely are a departure from what we've done before. And there was no violin bow playing used on this album.'

For Robert Plant, *Led Zeppelin II* offered the chance to express himself outside the usual limitations imposed on a 1970s rock band frontman. He felt the album demonstrated 'more of a musical empathy with Jimmy, and our styles and variations have widened considerably. With things like "Ramble On" and "Thank You", we are definitely deviating from the original Zeppelin intensity, but without losing any quality. I think we've probably gained quality because my voice is being used in different ways instead of confining it to a good safe formula. I think the open chord sort of thing, like Neil Young also uses, is beautiful. I'm obsessed with tht kind of music, particularly when it has really good lyrics – intense lyrics. What I want to do is sit down and write songs and say to the rest of the band: "Listen to this!" '

Led Zeppelin II was released on 22 October 1969, a few days after the band had arrived back in North America for its third tour in less than twelve months – and with their first album still holding strong on the *Billboard* charts at number eighteen after 38 weeks. Ironically Leonard Chess, one of the founders of Chess Records in Chicago – a key influence and inspiration for the band – had just died. The first album had already sold 780,000 copies, a phenomenal figure by any standards, and *Led Zeppelin II* was certified gold the day it was released, with advance orders in excess of half a million copies. Both the Beatles [with *Abbey Road*] and the Stones [*Let it Bleed*] had also just released new albums, and it was abundantly obvious that a fierce battle was about to take place for the number one position on the charts.

Although *Led Zeppelin II* entered the US charts the week of release at a lowly number 199, the following week it made one of the largest leaps in chart history – an astonishing total of 184 positions to thunder in at number fifteen. By 22 November it hit number two, where it sat stalled for a month. The Beatles' *Abbey Road* – containing some of that group's finest recorded moments – appeared to be irretrievably entrenched at number one. It looked impossible to dislodge.

But a couple of days before the last Christmas of the 1960s, Atlantic New York ecstatically wired Peter Grant and the group in London to proclaim the unexpected – by the 27 December chart listing, *Led Zeppelin II* had knocked *Abbey Road* off the pinnacle and into the number two slot. *Led Zeppelin II* spent seven weeks on the top spot before being dislodged by Simon and Garfunkel's classic folk-rock bestseller, *Bridge Over Troubled Water*. All in all, *Led Zeppelin II* would remain on the *Billboard* charts for eighteen months. It then returned early in 1975 on the strength of an enormously successful US tour.

So Led Zeppelin had actually knocked off the supreme musical gods of the 1960s and entered the new decade as the world's number one rock band, a position they would maintain until the end of the 1970s. On hearing the chart news, the band was naturally over the moon. 'None of us expected to be this big,' Page later admitted. 'Frankly I was surprised when the first album became a gold disc, but I just didn't believe all the people who said our second would do just as well. It was a total shock when I heard that *Led Zeppelin II* was actually selling faster than the first one. I just can't believe that they're both now platinum discs. It's really frightening the way it has snowballed – especially because it wasn't a contrived thing. It was just good luck and good timing.'

Page was being unduly modest. One has only to compare Led Zeppelin's album track record at this point in time with that of the top American hard rock band of the period, the Doors. It wasn't until late 1981 that the Doors would receive their *first* platinum album, that being for a repackaged *Greatest Hits* collection. Obviously Led Zeppelin's popularity in North America was infinitely larger than that of the Doors.

For rock observers, the biggest mystery was that such a successful group still hadn't received due critical attention and acclaim by rock media. And perhaps worse, American AM radio seemed disinterested. Since the group wouldn't release trimmed-down and edited three-minute singles, Top-40 radio ignored them, figuring theirs was a temporary success, a storm in a heavy metal teacup. Gradually, though, listener enthusiasm and incredible chart gains by the second Led Zeppelin album forced some AM programmers to reevaluate attitudes. A few suggested that 'Whole Lotta Love' might be a potential singles hit, if it could be chopped down from its original five minutes and 35 seconds to something more manageable for tight format playlists. This request of course had nothing to do with musical content – any song had to fit the three-minute framework or it didn't get on.

When the band refused to comply with any editing request, a few of the more adventurous stations chopped a couple of minutes out of the solo section in a classic example of sleazy rock censorship. Audience reaction was instantly favourable at these stations where listeners were anxious to hear *any* Led Zeppelin on AM airwaves. Within days Atlantic felt itself forced by broadcaster demand – and its bottom line – to release this edited and adulterated version of 'Whole Lotta Love' as Zep's first-ever single. The band still swears that it completely disagreed both in principle and in practice with the decision from a creative standpoint.

Billboard magazine of 22 November reviewed the single and gave it a Top-60 Spotlight prediction, under reviews of two Top-20 Spotlights, new singles by Jimmy Cliff and the Isley Brothers. 'Whole Lotta Love' was listed under the 1910 Fruitgum Company's 'When We Get Married', Electric Indian's version of 'Land of a 1000 Dances' and O.C. Smith's 'Me and You'. The review simply noted, 'The hot LP sellers make a strong bid for the singles market with this powerful, commercial swinger that should have no trouble putting them up the Top 100'.

'Whole Lotta Love' would in fact be the biggest hit single by far in the group's entire career. It leapt up the chart from number 91 to 45, 28, 21, twelve, nine, six, five, peaking at number four. That week of 31 January 1970 it was topped by the Jackson 5's 'I Want You Back' at number one, the Swinging Blue Jeans' 'Venus' at two, and 'Raindrops' by B.J. Thomas at three. Total sales of 'Whole Lotta Love' in the US were over 900,000 copies, just short of the gold disc mark. The flip side ['Living Lovin Maid'] also saw some chart action after 'Whole Lotta Love' had run its course. It spent five weeks in early spring reaching number 65 before dropping off the charts.

However the band itself felt extreme dismay over what they viewed as compromised success with 'Whole Lotta Love'. A few US stations had programmed the original uncut album version, but most of the Top-40 sector stubbornly and stupidly stuck with the scissored version.

'I just don't like releasing tracks from albums as singles,' Page explained. 'The two fields aren't related scenes to my mind.' Added John Bonham, 'The record was only put out in the US so AM stations had something to promote the LP with. We only wanted the full-length version out, but there were some misunderstandings.'

One of these was a widely publicised announcement from Atlantic UK that they would be rush-releasing the edited version of 'Whole Lotta Love' in Britain. Peter Grant immediately issued a disclaimer to the effect that 'Led Zeppelin had no intention of issuing this track as a single, as they felt it was written as part of their concept of the album. They've written a special number which they intend as their first British single which they will be recording next week.'

That projected single was in fact never released, but in the meantime the newly installed Atlantic boss in Britain, Phil Carson, suddenly found himself plunged into the controversy at the deep end. 'I'd only been in my office a day or so,' Carson said, 'and I received this phone call from Peter Grant's office telling me that in no way did they want "Whole Lotta Love" out as a single. Peter said it wasn't their policy to put out singles in Britain. I put the phone down and said to myself, "They're crazy. You know, what the hell do they know about it? I'm running the record company." So I went around to see Peter Grant and I tried to say, "Well, I'm the marketing genius around here, you know, and I'm telling you that if you want to sell albums, you've got to have a single." He replied that he just didn't want a single, because the band didn't feel that singles were the thing to do in England. In the end, he convinced me that it shouldn't come out – in his own subtle way. He was really insistent. He said that we should call Ahmet Ertegun at Atlantic in New York and Ahmet could refer to the group's contract which states that Grant has the right to say whether he wants singles out. And of course history has shown that Peter was absolutely right because at one point, *Led Zeppelin II* was selling as fast as a single could sell in those days. The sales really were phenomenal – after a heavy advance sale, it was repeating orders of three, four and five thousand units a day, and it went on for weeks selling like that. So I could never again say to Peter Grant that he was wrong about not having Zeppelin singles.'

In those dismal days before commercial radio was finally launched in Britain, Phil Carson felt that the American market had to be viewed entirely differently. 'Stations in the US will play a Zeppelin single but those schmucks at the BBC here just won't play singles by heavy groups. Tony Blackburn seems to hate the word "progressive" – he may be a very good DJ but he won't play this kind of music. In addition to the lack of BBC radio exposure, an artist has to do things like the TV show *Top of the Pops*. There's just no way that Led Zeppelin could be presented properly on *Top of the Pops*. It may be all right for Gary

Glitter and Alvin Stardust but it's just not right for the Zeppelin. They just wouldn't and couldn't do it.'

The band remained unanimously adamant about no singles in Britain. John Bonham told a reporter from a local Birmingham paper, 'We refused [to release "Whole Lotta Love" as a single] because they wanted to take the middle section out and we didn't like it. We don't want kids to think we are releasing an LP track just to get into the chart. I'm dead against tht sort of thing – we feel it's conning the public.' Jimmy Page added, 'We just didn't want any of that to happen, and we weren't going to be pressurised into things like that any more. We want to give the best value we can. We have no intention of resting on our laurels. We're going to keep on striving to get better. All we can hope to do is continue to put out product that people will like. It's pointless getting obscure and recording material that people aren't likely to appreciate or enjoy. We just want to carry on getting together and putting in ideas. And I hope that what comes out on the records will keep people happy.'

Although the lads only had six weeks off after their US summer tour – and could easily have used several more months of rest and relaxation – it was soon time for another dose of R&R of the musical variety. A few days before the release of their second album, Led Zeppelin set forth on their third North American tour in less than a year. They kicked off in spectacular style with two upmarket New York concerts on 17 October 1969, not as before at the Fillmore East in the Village, but this time uptown at the prestigious Carnegie Hall. The gigs had sold out weeks earlier and it turned out to be a memorable evening. For the first time on a regular basis, the act exceeded two hours in length. The reason? An additional three concert songs as they dropped 'You Shook Me' but added four cuts from the second album: 'Heartbreaker', 'What Is and What Should Never Be', 'Moby Dick' and 'Bring It on Home'.

The show flowed like molten fury – I was beginning to think that nothing could stop these lads from taking their success to unprecedented and unrestrained heights. Fighting my way backstage through a herd of beautiful New York young women – for whom Led Zeppelin had become the touring circuit's main attraction – I found Jimmy Page still towelling the sweat from his curly black locks. I praised the new additions to the concert set, the fresh emotional patterns imposed by the flow of the four new tunes. 'It was really hard to know what to drop,' Page said, a grin from ear to ear, at the reception to the new show. 'We couldn't take out "Dazed and Confused" or anything like that. So our show just grew to two hours and upwards. I'm really pleased that people have responded so well to the set tonight in this venue.'

Earlier that day – which stretched into a monumentally long evening – Peter Grant had learned from Atlantic executives that the first album was edging platinum. Advance orders for the second album had long since passed the gold disc figure. At that point, they hadn't released a single and the band was still less than a year old. Serious celebrations were in order (and certainly took place), and then it was back to the air again. Next stop Detroit, then Chicago, Cleveland and Boston. There the band drew 17,000 addicts to the Gardens and earned the largest concert fee of their career to date – a respectable $45,000. 'It was just incredible,' Page said. 'We take the artistic side so far, and then the managers take over the business and start working on percentages above guarantees. In the end it obviously depends on how big the venue is, and the Boston Gardens had been the biggest place we'd played up to that point.'

The tour rolled on through Buffalo, Providence, Syracuse, Toronto, Kitchener and Kansas City, culminating in three sold-out nights at the Winterland Ballroom in San Francisco. During this same period, highly touted British supergroup Blind Faith had been formed – from remnants of Cream, Traffic and Family – played one tour and then packed it in. There seemed nothing that could stop Led Zeppelin's spiralling ascension of the North American concert scene.

Nothing, that is, except the pervasive effects of the group's grim touring experiences on American soil. Off stage the lads were regarded as just street hippies in fancy clothes to the casual observer. And in the late 1960s and early 1970s the casual observer in America rarely liked long hair; it somehow threatened a tenuous security and invited an ugly response.

Robert Plant vividly recalls his casual search for a drugstore in downtown Detroit. As he crossed the road – golden locks bobbing behind him – a motorist screeched up next to him and spat in his face. John Bonham, ever vigilant for any hints of violence, remembered the hiring of armed bodyguards as insurance so that the band would emerge unscathed from a tour of Southern cities where lamebrain rednecks were prevalent. 'The restaurant scene in the South can be unbelievable,' said Bonham. 'We've stopped for a coffee and watched everybody else in the place get service, people who came in after we did. Everybody sits and glares at you, waiting and hoping that you'll explode and a scene will start.

'We even had a gun pulled on us in Texas. Some guy was shouting out and giving us general crap about our hair and all, so we simply gave it back to him. We were leaving after the show and this guy turns up at the door. He pulls out a pistol and says to us: "You guys gonna do any shoutin' now?" We cleared out of there *tout de suite*. The adults, the older people are the trouble – some of them are crazy.'

While Led Zeppelin was never an overtly politically motivated group, they found it extremely difficult to remain apolitical during their tours of America as the 1970s began. Everyday violence and all-too-frequent police brutality at concerts alarmed even the easy-going undemanding introvert, John Paul Jones. 'Yes, it does frighten me,' Jones admitted, 'mainly because the US is the biggest power in the world – it has the most to say in things. It just seems to me to be in a terrible mess at the moment . . . the glaring fact which you just can't escape is that there's just so much money involved. No other country in the world could possibly get into this state, except perhaps Germany, because no other country has ever had this amount of money. The government here seems to be so corrupt. I'm sure it can't be that corrupt in England because over there, we're working in thousands of pounds, and here they're dealing in billions of dollars, and that's what seems to be the point of it all.'

Jones said he always felt relieved to return to Britain. 'The policemen don't carry guns and they don't start trouble. In the States it seems that the police are always starting trouble. In England there hasn't been a war for twenty-five years and people are starting to get a bit restless. They can't really scream at the government because it's only a sideshow. British kids can't really get their teeth into anything. The students are just revolting against their teachers – that's about it.' He paused for a moment to collect his thoughts. 'Touring makes you a different person I think. You always realise it when you come home after a tour. It usually takes weeks to recover after living like an animal for so long.'

For Jimmy Page, America was difficult because of 'all that narrowmindedness that you have to cop. I think it's the same for anyone with either long hair or general feeling. I'm fed up with people making nasty comments. We were discriminated against all the time. If we were coloured, we'd really be able to kick up a stink about it. I'm not, so I have to put up with it. Everyone with long hair does. It's a bit of a drag. I can't stand restaurants where they give you a bad time. Or trying to check into hotels where they don't like the look of you and don't want you messing up the swimming pool. It's just unfortunate that this is the age we live in – a very hostile age.

'But,' he went on, 'there are many things about America that I like. Things that Americans take for granted like a good telephone system. And they don't force you to go to bed at 10.30 p.m. by switching off all the TV programmes and stopping the trains.' Not to mention the incredible joy of real authentic American blues music, performed by the original masters at local clubs in almost every major city.

At the end of that third tour, the band celebrated its first anniversary in appropriate style. Since they hadn't faded away as the cynics had predicted, it was an appropriate occasion for the media to dumbly dissect the Led Zeppelin phenomenon. What, idiot critics asked, was the rationale behind the band's steamrolling popularity with the punters? While only a wise handful put it down to extraordinary musicianship and incomparable performance values, the majority of media observers in those early days couldn't come to terms with Led Zeppelin's full-blown success. To the regiments of tin ears, Led Zeppelin was an anomaly, an accident, a quirk of fate. It was even suggested that Led Zeppelin was a cunningly contrived money machine, that only super-hype had taken them over the top, that Robert Plant merely imitated Jim Morrison of the Doors, and that the Zep audience primarily consisted of heavy dopers. Missing out on foreseeing Led Zeppelin's success, the media seemed keen to make amends by trying to justify its lack of perception with outrageous accusations.

Ellen Sander, the critic, offered a typical barb in her book *Trips* (Scribners, 1970): 'Their success was built on a well-engineered promotional strategy. Recordings, airplay, personal appearances and publicity have to be co-ordinated for the greatest impact. A constant flow of albums, the release of a new one timed with the denouement of the current one is desirable. Their names must appear somewhere at all times in some sort of press, columns, fan magazines, critical journals, underground papers – no possible exposure is left untried. Their English manager, American lawyer, road manager and publicity agency, one of Hollywood's heaviest, conspired to pack the heaviest possible punch.'

Much of this was patently untrue. For example, I doubt if any major rock act in either Britain or America was *less* motivated by promotional strategy or publicity manipulation than Led Zeppelin – their press relations had been all but non-existent and with the exception of early get-to-meet-you months, the band has seldom been freely available for media inspection or indulgence. The fact that they tried hard was misinterpreted – in our free enterprise society, there is nothing wrong with doing one's best to achieve success. Even a disinterested observer of pop culture over the past three decades must have reached the conclusion that almost everybody is in it for the money, from the Beatles on down. Is that a crime? Do we expect only noble altruistic aspirations from those who have the talent to entertain us? Rock and roll, like virtually all areas of artistic endeavour, is profit-driven.

What were all of the Beatles' British legal battles concerned with? Prestige? Power? A masochistic need to keep their mugs in the papers? No, they were directly related to money – royalties and ownership and control of publishing copyrights and tape masters, and the marketing thereof. Very few artists or writers are involved in rock music for mere artistic satisfaction, thrills or egomania. They work for money just like everybody else who toils in Western society.

Entertainers, it could hardly be denied, make an enormous amount for what they do, and whether that is right or wrong is a valid but separate argument. So far Western society has deemed that large amounts of money are the right reward for top-of-the-line success in popular culture, particularly the electronic arts. To my mind, Led Zeppelin has certainly earned its just reward by working extremely hard and providing their audiences with outstanding musical performances which ultimately evolved to over three hours in length.

The fabricated rip-off allegation disregards completely the musical sensitivity and integrity of the four members of Led Zeppelin. In the early days certainly this caused them considerably more mental anguish than the public ever became aware of. 'For anyone to imply that Led Zeppelin were prefabricated or hyped up on a gullible public is grossly unfair,' Page exploded when the accusation first surfaced in print. 'You can't compute or calculate for a situation like that, or the chemistry which arises when you put together a band. The only people with a similar approach at the time was Cream, but I always felt that their improvised passages used to go on and on. We tried to reflect more light and shade into the spontaneous pieces, and also a sense of the dramatic. If there was a key to why we made it, I think it was in that.'

Robert Plant was equally outraged. 'Had the fusion of people and their individual ideas not been the way it was, we might have been like anybody, Edmondo Ros if you like. It didn't *have* to be the way it turned out. You just can't tell someone how to write a song. Had I been a different person, or had anybody else in the group been even fractionally different, it would have been a different kettle of fish. Had it simply been a gap to be filled, it would have been easy to take every cliché from the Yardbirds, everything from everybody else who was phasing things or messing around, and build something on that. I've seen a lot of groups do that – a lot of groups who are now supposed to be Led Zeppelin clones – and no matter how much you take, that doesn't make you original. I think that Led Zeppelin *was* original, despite the orientations that were there and always will be there because we all have to listen to other sounds. You can't avoid them. But we weren't created to fill any gap. It would have been pointless for me just to do anything, to accept being told to do something just to fill some gap.'

As for the comparison with Jim Morrison, Plant told me quite emphatically, 'We only played with the Doors once – in Seattle – and it seemed to me that Morrison was really fucked up. Some of the things he was doing were great – for example "Cancel My Subscription to the Resurrection". Then he stopped getting into any of the things from the past, the sexual thing was gone and he was just miles above everyone's heads. I think he realised that the Doors were on the way down. I think he went out on stage with that opinion, and immediately went into those strange things that nobody else could get into. Almost nobody anyway – there were one or two people yelling out "Jim, you're god, you're king" and I was thinking to myself "why?". Then the Youngbloods went on stage and wiped the audience out because they were so warm. They'd laugh, and the audience would laugh. That's how music should be. It isn't a real fucking serious thing. We don't come over to the States to have a bad time. We're over here to have a good time and people pay money to have a good time as well.'

Plant insisted that he had always tried to wear his so-called 'sex symbol' role as lightly and as frivolously as possible. 'Once you take that sort of thing seriously, I think it's the end of your life. You can't go out on stage thinking things like that. You can take in all that applause at face value, and it can turn you into a bad person, it really can. All this sort of popularity can do you terrible harm and I'll admit that I really thought that it would do once we started getting off. "Christ if this keeps going, what will happen to me?" I thought. You could go right off your rocker and get into a trip of "Here I am, the greatest singer in the world". But it's not worth it because there's always someone who will come along and will sing better than me, and I fully realise that. So all you can be is honest and be yourself.

'It seems a trifle funny that a few short months ago I was an ungratified singer, and now they're calling me the next sex symbol. It can't be bad. I must admit that I don't really know what or how people think about sex symbols. Maybe if the audience can see a cock through a pair of trousers, then that must make you a sex symbol. Since I'm the only one of us who doesn't have a guitar or drums in front of mine, I suppose I started out with a bit more chance than anybody else in the band. Really you can't take it seriously. You just get into your music and the sexual thing isn't really apparent to you. It's simply not what we're there for.'

At the same time, Plant didn't feel that musical virtuosity was his ultimate aspiration either. 'You can't get hung up on a musical ability trip, I don't think. I mean, I know that my timing is ridiculous and I don't make any bones about it. I would rather leave a band than be forced to get it together, timing-wise. I'd much rather express myself just the way it comes out.'

Plant's personal vocal style came very much from spontaneity and bounced off audience reaction. 'Without the audience throwing back vibrations, I just couldn't do it,' he said. 'I couldn't extend myself. When you're looking into those thousands of faces, it just seems to pour out of me. By allowing your mind to be free and open, you get a new dimension going and the audience comes back at us. I suspect that you could put a lot of the group's success down to that. We've never had the attitude of just going out on stage, playing like clockwork for the allotted time and then pissing off. That's not our trip at all.'

Over a year later, Plant continued to be astounded by the band's success, the extent of it. 'I just don't think anyone could have expected it. Not even Jimmy, and he already knew that American audiences were much more responsive to hard work. It was just BANG! We really have never known just how big we were. You can't fully realise it until you arrive at each individual town that you have never been in before, and people are running down the street banging on your car windows. And when you get a fantastic reception the moment you walk out on stage, then you begin to realise just what's happening. I never could have dreamed of anything like this. Certainly we've had some criticism of our stage act and what we do up there. But it's the *people* we want to impress – not the bloody press! After a while, I find that you go out on stage and you can feel what's going to happen. The moment you set foot on stage you can let go, and the audience is like a piece of blotting paper. What makes it is what you give it, and you've simply got to give it good.'

Another classic media barb originated in the august pages of *Rolling Stone*, which continued to crap on all the band's endeavours until the mid-1970s when they changed their tune and desperately wanted a cover story/interview. *Rolling Stone* suggested that the audiences for Led Zeppelin's music consisted mainly of 'heavy dope fiends', a story that was widely circulated on the industry rumour mill. The *LA Times*, for instance, noted on 7 September 1970 that 'their [Led Zeppelin's] success may be attributable at least in part to the accelerating popularity among the teenage rock and roll audience of barbiturates and amphetamines, drugs that render their users most responsive to crushing volume and ferocious histrionics of the sort Zeppelin has heretofore dealt in exclusively.'

Page responded to this fruitcake accusation with a nice little slice of wry irony. 'It's really nice of people to say that,' he grinned. 'Actually I'd been a bit frightened that the band would be too loud and would annoy people that were stoned. So it's really good that it's not like that.'

'Percy' Plant naturally offered some down-to-earth observations of his own. 'I think that any group, except straight groups, can hit you differently when you're stoned. You can listen to a group when you're straight and it feels one way, and you can listen to it stoned and it just becomes more intense. You're just able to pick out more of what the group is trying to show you.' Added John Paul Jones, 'I hope we can be appreciated by people stoned out of their minds. But I think we can be appreciated by anybody. We don't make our stuff with any intention of it being either drug music or acid rock. We're just playing for people who go to the concerts, whether they're stoned or not. I really believe that anybody can appreciate what we're into – no matter what condition they're in.'

And what did the group feel were the often-debated reasons for their immense popularity by this time? Page thought that 'the initial success was due to the fact that so many of the good American groups were moving to a softer sound which made Led Zeppelin's heavy rock appear more dramatic. Blind Faith were a disappointment to many people who expected the band to lean more towards the Spencer Davis/Steve Winwood end, rather than turn out to be an extension of Traffic, which I think they were. It meant that no one was filling the gap left by Cream, and in many ways I think it is their audience that we have captured.'

Page expressed amazement at the broad age spread in typical Led Zeppelin audiences, especially the pre-teens. 'I'm sure they can't really be into the music – they can't understand it. It's incredible that this happened to groups like Cream and ourselves.' Plant felt, 'There are many different kinds of people who come for different reasons. I really don't think our popularity is down to one simple reason. I just don't think there's any real reason why we're as big as we are. Except,' he added with a twinkle, 'that we were lucky.'

Plant was as amazed as Page about the tender age of some of the concert-goers. 'It beats me why they come. I really don't think our first album was commercial at all. To me, Crosby, Stills and Nash were far more commercial than Led Zeppelin – inasmuch as the vocal thing was there to hang on to. With us there were all sorts of different things going on. Every member of the group was into something different. I suppose the audience is just fanning out more and more in a musical sense.'

John Paul Jones had a theory too. 'If you look at it from a purely popologist's point of view you could say, well, it was foreseen, inevitable, predictable. There was a gap there and we filled that gap. But I suspect that there's a lot of other things which may be involved. I do think the music business did need something different because Cream had been going around in circles. It seemed as if the members never talked to one another. The groups that did have a good sound were successful, but they always seemed to have internal troubles. While the groups who did get on with each other never got heard. Somehow you had to get the two elements together – an amicable group, a good sound, plus exposure.'

Robert Plant was able to provide a more profound perspective ten years after the band called it a day. Discussing whether Led Zeppelin regarded other bands as competition, he pointed out, 'We were more concerned with diversity, self-satisfaction, creativity. So really there was nobody to compete with, because we were trying to entertain ourselves first and foremost, with no intentional stab at a pretty song for a pretty song's sake.

'From the beginning, really, it was a group policy that singles were not to be considered, that the whole game would be that if you wanted to find out about Led Zeppelin, you had to get into the whole thing. We would not put out singles as calling cards. It would be nice to think that we could walk alongside Kaleidoscope or Buffalo Springfield for diversity. I don't think Jimmy would agree with that, because I don't think he thought much of Buffalo Springfield.

'I think the way the music moved around – in its Englishness and its blues roots – the inspiration didn't allow it to compete with anybody, really. Because it wasn't a pop band. I mean, it's popular, but it certainly wasn't pop.'

In the end, the most accurate reason put forward for Led Zeppelin's success – an explanation that flies above all rational reasoning and critical theorising – was suggested, perhaps tongue-in-cheek, by Pagey himself. 'We must,' he said with timely understatement, 'have presented the right thing at the right time to the right people.'

5 A New Decade and Stunning New Directions

THE SWINGING 1960s had shuddered to an end. John Lennon was encamped in Canada talking peace with communications prophet Marshall McLuhan and Prime Minister Pierre Trudeau. Back in London, Paul McCartney was preparing his proclamation of the death of the Beatles. Richard Nixon ranted and raved about his peculiar brand of law and order, while napalm rained down on Vietnamese peasants. Led Zeppelin, barely a year old, returned to Europe for concert dates.

A few days into the new decade and Denmark suddenly became the focus of global rock attention. John and Yoko Lennon took the plunge in the freezing heart of a Jutland winter and had their hair cut off. John's locks had barely been swept up and sent off to Michael X (and subsequently auctioned at Sothebys to raise money for the Black Power movement) when Led Zeppelin arrived to play a Copenhagen concert.

It was the band's first Danish visit since the New Yardbirds days and this time around, they found their name getting them into a spot of hot water. It turned out that a certain Ms Eva von Zeppelin, a local relative of the German designer of the airship, had worked herself into a full-on frenzy and was threatening to sue the band if they appeared in Denmark using *her* name. 'They may be world famous,' she hissed to the bemused local press, 'but a couple of shrieking monkeys aren't going to use a privileged family name without permission.'

'She actually dashed into a studio where we were recording and wanted us thrown out,' reported Plant. 'She wasn't going to have any "babbling apes" making so much money from the family name, she said. I can't see that it's anything to do with her.'

For Eva, of course, it was a big publicity break. For Led Zeppelin, it necessitated a temporary, overnight change of name before the concert, to avoid any legal hassles. They billed themselves as the Nobs, Cockney slang for genitalia. Strange as that might have been, more of the unique brand of Led Zeppelin humour would come to the forefront the next day.

Phil Carson, now promoted to European director of Atlantic Records, had been asked by Grant and the group to accompany them to Denmark for a bit of fun, which the label executive wasn't averse to. Although Carson had only joined Atlantic the previous October, he'd struck up a firm friendship with the Led Zeppelin camp – not only because he possessed empathy, having plucked some bass in his own past, but also because he had an affinity with the band's boisterous behaviour. Sensing this, the band tended to push things to the very limit when Carson was on hand, which dear old Phil obviously appreciated.

'They asked me along on that tour,' Carson said, 'to sort of take care of the promotional aspects of the group vis-à-vis the local record distributors. Making sure that the group wasn't being over-hassled because distributors of Led Zeppelin product can become over-enthusiastic. It's very important to draw the line between what *is* advantageous for the band to do, and what is just time-filling. The group is only going to do so many interviews before they get bored with it, so the important thing is to make sure that the important ones get done first. Then if they do get bored halfway through, it's only the media of lesser importance that you have to elbow. Having me there helps too because instead of Peter Grant having to say "Well they're not going to do your interview, fucking bad luck sunshine" which isn't necessarily what he would say – but to prevent that sort of attitude coming across to the local company, I can explain things in terms they'll understand.

'I suppose you could say that my most embarrassing moment with them came on that visit to Denmark. Peter Grant had flown the European licensees into London a few weeks earlier to introduce the second album and to discuss the promotion of the Continental tour. At the meeting, the guy from Denmark stood up and asked if it were true that Led Zeppelin members were very interested in art. So Peter says, "Well yes, Jimmy and I *are* collectors and so is John Paul Jones." So the Danish exec suggested that a press reception might be organised in a new Copenhagen art gallery. Only one thing worried him, he said. He'd heard somewhere that the group tended to be a trifle violent at times. "Well yes," we said, "that can be true occasionally, but of course they do respect fine art.' I told him not to worry about a thing. The lads have fine art in their homes – they're not going to be silly. We actually acted a bit insulted at the suggestion.

'So off we go to Copenhagen and to the press reception in this modern art gallery. Pagey is a connoisseur of art, and I was horrified when I overheard Jimmy saying that the gallery was full of bullshit art. So I raced over and I said to Jimmy that we had to be cool. And he replied, "But look, Phil, it's only bullshit art. It really is; it's just bullshit bad art. It's a take-on for the public." I agreed with him in the end but I made him promise not to do anything about it. It wouldn't have been fair. And I did believe that they *would* remain cool.

'But the drink kept flowing and our attention was drawn to a series of paintings – which I was assured was fine art – by a well-known impressionist from Sweden. I must admit that to me they looked like a mess of oil on canvas in relief. The oil actually looked like it had been thrown on to the canvas or sculpted on it. It was just a weird mess of colour and I couldn't see anything in it at all. Anyway I went upstairs for something and while I was gone, some of the lads decided that since the oil was still not yet dry, they'd change things around a bit. I came back and they'd moved the oil on three paintings from one side to the other!

'You can imagine that I was really horrified. The guy from the record company who'd been in London nearly fainted, and it was pretty clear that I'd have to work something out with the gallery owner. He went down to survey the damage but found only *one* painting in disarray. So Jimmy had been right – it *was* bullshit art. The owner of the gallery didn't even know what had been changed on the other two pictures. So we paid up for the one picture.

'The whole thing could have been a disaster scene but in retrospect it's quite funny. We also had a couple of idiot journalists at the reception – you know how stupid some journalists can be with ridiculous questions – and they had to be thrown out bodily by Bonzo and Richard Cole. The next day Led Zeppelin didn't figure too well in a couple of the papers. But I think the Copenhagen audiences thought it was really funny because these were two journos the kids were rumoured to really hate.'

For Grant and the lads, it was some much-needed light relief of a variety for which the band would ultimately become infamous around the globe. When the Led Zeppelin members returned to England, they were absorbed in the realisation that their music was in a subtle process of change, part of it in subconscious response to short-sighted media accusations that they were all noise and amplification.

The essence of the Led Zeppelin sound at the close of the 1960s could be summed up in one word – motion. Their two first albums had offered glimmering crucibles of energy and movement, and reflected musically the dischord and underlying tension of technological society. The machine age had arrived and Led Zeppelin were there to document its dazed and confused denizens. Live and on record, the band mirrored the panic and paranoia of their time more so than any other rock group, including the Rolling Stones who have never exhibited the sort of power, energy and mystique which naturally flowed from a Led Zeppelin concert event.

Among all their other supreme vinyl achievements from a mere two albums, the band had created one classic monument – a literal era anthem – synthesising world chaos and corruption in five furious minutes. 'Whole Lotta Love' had perfectly portrayed the pathos of the dying decade: a driving machine-like beat underlying one of the most insidious riffs ever to arise from the intellectual rubble of rock. It was the soundtrack for a scenario of mass confusion – lyrically it reduced the dilemma of contemporary youth to its most basic jungle frustration, the need for love, for caring and sharing.

Although 'Whole Lotta Love' had been a massive landmark achievement, the band had no desire to pursue its commercial acceptance by pop radio ad infinitum. Having been dragged into the hit singles arena, the band's musical direction was now turning away from the raw and savage power that had made this and so many other Led Zeppelin tunes so dynamic. Ever cognizant of the artistic ruts which had marred the careers of so many of their British contemporaries, the group instinctively understood that they had no over-riding desire to become imprisoned by the form which had made them famous, hard rock. They had no immediate plans to forsake that particular medium, but they did feel the time had come to expand their musical horizons. The signs had already been evident in the previous tour, when Led Zeppelin fans had been treated to a taste of the band's acoustic virtuosity in the person of Jimmy Page.

Late in 1969, Page had hinted to me how he felt the overall sound might change. 'We've always had this desire to do acoustic things. The audiences, especially in the States, have shown us that they are ready to accept us doing things other than hard rock. The really good thing is that people don't expect us to follow one straight line. They know this band isn't confined to any one particular bag. A lot of bands split up because members want to go in different directions. Zeppelin wants to expand too – but as a group. A lot of bands like to sit back and rest on their laurels once they reach the top, but not us – we want to keep working at it as a band. We want to stay together and explore new dimensions together.'

Albums produced by successful acts who don't need to stretch themselves or wish merely to keep on doing what they have already made money from more often than not reflect the stagnant surroundings in which they are produced. *Led Zeppelin* and *Led Zeppelin II* mirrored a band always on the loose, venturing forth, on the move. 'In the normal course of events,' said Plant, 'we are always going somewhere working. In general, we are always going. The effect of that on our music is motion.' To vary the influences, to re-adjust the focus, and to simply get some much-needed rest, the band decided to seek out a fresh creative environment.

'We'd been working solidly and thought that it was time to have a holiday,' Page said, 'or at least to get some time away from the road. Robert suggested going to this cottage in South Wales that he'd been to once with his parents when he was much younger. He was going on about what a beautiful place it was, and I became pretty keen to go there. I'd never spent any time in Wales but I'd always wanted to. So off we went, taking along our guitars of course. It wasn't a question of "let's go out and knock off a few songs in the country". It was just a case of wanting to get away for a bit and to have a good time. We took along a couple of our roadies and spent the evenings sitting around log fires, with pokers being plunged into the cider and that sort of thing. As the nights wore on, the guitars came out and numbers were being written. It wasn't really planned as a working holiday but some songs did come out of it.'

Jimmy brought along his girlfriend, Charlotte (a French model first promenaded on the London rock scene by Eric Clapton, and introduced to Page on his birthday, the night of the magnificent Royal Albert Hall gig), while Robert squired wife Maureen and baby. Three roadies were responsible for security and generally taking care of things.

The cottage, named Bron-Y-Aur (reportedly for the bolt of sunlight that daily crossed the valley) lay off the beaten path near the River Dovey in the South Snowdonia region of Wales – stunningly beautiful especially in the rebirth of spring, a suitably remote black mountainside scenario. 'The great thing about our stay there,' noted Plant, 'was that there was no motion, just privacy and Nature and the beauty of the people who were there. It was a good experience in every way. The cottage has no electricity and is right away from everything. There's no road – you have to drive across the fields and mountains to get to it. We drove around the hills in a jeep in the daytime and sat by the fire at night. We just wanted to see what we could come up with when there's nobody around.'

There were a predictable number of lighter moments during the Bron-Y-Aur adventure, including the arrival of the first outside invaders. One splendid morning three motorbikes roared out of the green haze and across the field, shattering the serenity of the cottage surroundings. Plant tore out the door, armed with a log, prepared to do battle if necessary for the maintenance of their privacy. The riders turned out to be local kids, sons of nearby farmers with hunting and fishing rights in the vicinity. Staring incredulously, one of them finally managed to mutter, 'Are you *really* Robert Plant?'

On another occasion, the party decided to venture forth into the outside world with a visit to a nearby stately home that was being restored by a group of young volunteers. Page, Plant and families arrived in their jeep and quietly looked around the mansion. One of the restorers had a guitar and was fooling around with a song he'd written. Plant shuffled over and asked the kid the name of the tune. The kid mumbled, 'Oh, it's nothing.' 'I wish I could play like that,' exclaimed Plant, demonstrating his scant skills on the instrument. One of the other kids offered Page a quick strum too, but Jimmy declined, saying he had absolutely no idea how to play the guitar. Plant swears that those kids didn't recognise their visitors.

Bron-Y-Aur was a bountiful period in Zep's evolution, creative and otherwise. 'It was the first time I really came to know Robert,' Pagey admitted later. 'Living together at Bron-Y-Aur, as opposed to occupying nearby hotel rooms. The songs took us into areas that changed the band, and it established a standard of travelling for inspiration . . . which is the best thing a musician can do.'

Certainly the circumstances surrounding Led Zeppelin's stay in rural Wales were a lifestyle removed from the pandemonium of the Beatles' first visit to Wales a couple of years earlier. The Fab Four had decided to accompany their guru, the Maharishi, to his summer conference in Bangor, Wales, on the August bank holiday weekend. They'd not kept their destination secret and had been mobbed in scenes of near chaos, fuelled by a lull in hard news in the editorial offices along Fleet Street. Thousands had turned out to see the lads off from London's Euston Station (John's wife Cynthia missed the train in the mêlée) and almost as many were awaiting their heroes on the platform in Wales.

The daily papers were full of it. The Beatles' biographer Hunter Davies, who accompanied the group on that trip, later wrote, 'What they thought was going to be a private, spiritual experience developed into a carnival. Thirty-six hours later, the news of manager Brian Epstein's death reached them, cutting short the most circus-like sabbatical in recent history.'

Led Zeppelin, on the other hand, had managed to effect a discreet presence in the West Country and the 'private spiritual experience' the Beatles had failed to find. Although some observers had already begun to refer to them as the 'new Beatles', their lifestyle and outlook were a generation removed. They represented separate eras, different equations.

Robert Plant was clearly happy about such differences. 'Being recognised isn't nearly so bad today. But I can understand now that the Beatles must have been the most pestered people on earth. If I decide to go and see some old musician friends of mine, it's a different trip. There's a lot of whispering going on, but you're in a village hall in the middle of nowhere and it's cool. People can come up to you and say "nice one" if they wish and simply leave it at that.'

By the time the band headed out of England for their fourth North American tour which opened in Vancouver on 2 March, the third album had begun to take shape. Before departure Peter Grant announced that Led Zeppelin would earn roughly $800,000 for the coming month's work. And a few bellylaughs could be heard echoing around the camp when the *Financial Times* writer, Anthony Thorncroft, described Robert Plant as 'A painfully thin, pre-Raphaelite heroine, with delicate features and wild curls which cover his face completely when he tosses his head. Plant screams into the hand mike, which he holds close and low, pessimistic snatches from American blues singers of the 1930s, and culminates with a belligerent cry from the silent depths of the hall: Squeeze my lemon until the juice runs down my leg.'

The juice certainly was running at the first gig on the fourth tour. In the Vancouver audience, tour manager Richard Cole spotted a man holding an extended microphone in the audience. Mistaking him for a dreaded pirate product taper, Cole had a couple of roadies drag the man backstage where his mike and tape machine were smashed up in Grant's presence. But the man turned out to be an official agent of the Canadian Government, testing concert decibel levels. Peter Grant was charged over this incident, and was unable to travel with the band to Canada until it was resolved years later. Backstage in Vancouver, an angry Bonham kicked in the dressing room door causing $1,500 damage for which Grant, as always, provided monetary compensation. It was, one assumed, the price of doing business with such a volatile group.

But piracy was a mounting problem and Led Zeppelin suffered more than most from its network of sales outlets – losing millions of dollars over the years, mainly on pirated live recordings of their gigs. Grant had every reason to be eternally vigilant, but his methods of dealing with it were somewhat questionable.

Media matters and Grant's never-ending battle with bootleg pirates were of less concern to the group than the new music they were now laying down. As the tour kicked off, Page speculated on how the third album might turn out. 'I feel that the new album is perhaps our most significant of all. We're not changing our policy. It wouldn't be fair if we just *completely* changed our sound and announced that we were going to do all new things. On the new album, we'll be including some quieter acoustic numbers. But we're still a heavy band. We can always infiltrate new material in with our older songs, without making everything from the past seem obsolete. I think that some so-called progressive groups have gone too far with their personalised intellectualisation of beat music. I just don't want our music to be complicated by those kinds of ego trips. Our music is essentially emotional, I think, like the old rock stars of the past. It's very difficult to listen to those early Presley records and not feel something.'

'You can just see the headlines, can't you?' laughed Plant. ' "Led Zeppelin go soft on their fans" or some crap like that. The point is that when you begin a new album, you don't know what you'll come up with that might be different. When we conceived the original songs at Bron-Y-Aur, we started to see what we wanted this album to do. From the start, it was obvious that it was going to work, and it just grew from there. Some of the things we're doing on the album – like the mandolin – will really come as a surprise. I must admit that I never thought we'd get to this. Of course we always wanted to do acoustic things, but now we've managed to do it in such a way that although the guitars on some of the tracks may be acoustic, we are still laying it down. It's really just an extension of some of our heavy electronic things.

'I don't think we'll go into a decline just because we've got into some different things. We've already made people aware of us and what we've got to do now is to consider the position we've arrived at . . . so that eventually we'll be able to say what we really want to say, and people will listen to it because it's us.'

More recently, Plant offered some astute perspectives on the Welsh inspiration connection. 'All we wanted to do was keep stretching. That's the whole thing about Led Zeppelin or about Jimmy and myself. We wanted to try and stretch it out and open it up and change – just shock ourselves to see exactly what we could do. So we started going back into more of an acoustic vein. It wasn't an area that we hadn't touched before – because of "Your Time Is Gonna Come" and "Baby I'm Gonna Leave You" and being exposed to the Incredible String Band and Roy Harper which was music for the head coming from a more acoustic base.

'I think it was a great success. But it was the least successful Led Zeppelin album, and we had the critics screaming for our lives, saying, "what's this crap?" Yet it was probably one of our finest moments. And the fact that we'd deemed that we had to do it at all was a fine moment.'

By late April 1970, Led Zeppelin had played a total of 26 concerts on the fourth North American tour, all large gigs in stadiums, coliseums, arenas, forums and the occasional auditorium. The group received ecstatic audience response at every concert. While in Memphis on 17 April the band were made honorary citizens, the first time that such a civic recognition of rock music had taken place there since the early days of Elvis Presley and Carl Perkins. For Page, long addicted to the brilliance of the Memphis-made early Sun label singles, it was a moving and memorable honour.

Backstage in Memphis, a different vibe prevailed. Seeing 10,000 young Southern kids in a frenzy over a performance by their favourite band, the promoter flipped out and demanded that Peter Grant pull the lads off stage. When Grant refused, the promoter whipped out a pistol and shoved it into Grant's considerable midriff, telling him, 'If you don't cut the show, I'm gonna shoot you.' To which Grant replied, 'You can't shoot me, ya cunt. They've just given us the fucking keys to the city.'

Further into the deep South, the group hired eight additional bodyguards to protect them from hostile locals enraged by the group's long hair and allegedly effeminate style of clothing. Constant hassles, constant travel, weariness and ill health possibly accentuated by over-indulgence and the state of the torn American nation continued to frustrate them. Back in Blighty, Page commented, 'People [over there] have no faith in anything. Everyone seems to carry a gun for protection – it's just like being back in the Jesse James era. We had to have armed guards in every car in Georgia. The constant pressure does get to you. But we will go back to the States because people, our audience, want to see us again. I just hope it's cooler next time.'

Despite the rigours of touring in the prevailing uptight atmosphere, Robert Plant felt he was making rapid gains in his musical development. 'I think I'm now finding my musical niche,' he explained at the time. 'Led Zeppelin has given me a chance to express that in lyrics on the second album, and I hope the third album will bring that exercise even more to the point of what I'm trying to get into. Gradually, bit by bit, I'm finding myself now. It's taken a long time, a lot of insecurity and nerves and the "I'm-a-failure" stuff. Everybody has to go through it. Even Jimmy did when he was with the Yardbirds, but now everything's shaping up nicely.'

Work on the third album continued through the English summer, this time using mobile recording facilities set up in an old Hampshire stately home called Headley Grange which proved more suitable to the laid-back flow that the album would proclaim. Asked in 1992 why Led Zeppelin started using mobile recording facilities, John Paul Jones noted, 'It was just like the idea of going somewhere to write – it was a focus, somewhere you could go to write songs and then when you're ready, roll in the mobile truck. It was better to do it that way, rather than be in a place where you write and then moving to a place where you can record. Or being in a place where you can record while you write – which is the worst and most expensive thing. Studios really aren't that conducive to making music.'

The band took a few days off from third album sessions to play some European dates, the highlight of which was a spectacular show at Frankfurt's Festhalle where they broke all existing attendance records by drawing 11,000 fans. Somehow through it all, they succeeded in getting the tracks down on tape, and Page mixed the album in the US during August when the band returned, yet again, for a late summer series of appearances (their fifth tour).

Apart from the completion of *Led Zeppelin III*, this trip brought two other noteworthy occurrences. The group moved up to a basic minimum fee of $25,000 per performance, and they decided to cease working with any opening acts. This allowed them to extend their appearances to well over two hours on a normal night without worrying about curfew limitations should the support band run overtime. At the sensational wind-up concert at New York's Madison Square Garden on 19 September, Led Zeppelin for the first time grossed in excess of $100,000 for a single performance.

Back home Jimmy Page surfaced briefly to describe to the local press the extent of their North American success. 'They are talking about Robert Plant as the next Mick Jagger, but we never set out to contrive a big, sexy image . . . it's stupid to base your image on a big sex angle. MUSIC is what it's all about today.' Obviously Pagey felt confident about the new music to be unveiled on *Led Zeppelin III* which had the distinction of following up one of the most successful albums in Atlantic's star-studded history (*Led Zeppelin II* had remained at number one on *Billboard* LP charts for seven weeks longer than any other album the label had ever released).

With *Led Zeppelin III* the group instinctively knew they were about to spring a drastic shock on their hundreds of thousands of hard rock fans. It was absolutely inevitable – yet group members maintained a stony silence about the album's content right up until the time it reached the record stores.

The new album opened with typical Zeppelin high-flying velocity in the 'Immigrant Song' and a fierce and lusty Viking-like Plant war cry, before proceeding into an equally stunning soft track featuring layers of acoustic guitar. The stage for a new era had been set. 'I considered "Friends" in particular was really quite special,' Page said. 'Overall I was pleased with the album.'

' "Since I've Been Loving You",' Plant explained, 'is virtually a live track recorded in the studio. I think the sound is great. If bootleg record-makers got it together properly instead of waving those evil mikes on the end of broomsticks, this is the kind of sound they would get at a Led Zeppelin live concert.'

For many Led Zeppelin fans 'Gallows Pole', a traditional British folk standard, was the biggest surprise of all. 'I heard it first,' Page recalled, 'on an old Folkways LP by Fred Gerlach, a twelve-string player who I believe was the first white man to play the instrument. He'd been influenced originally by Leadbelly, and there certainly are heavy Leadbelly overtones on the Gerlach album. As far as I know, the album wasn't well received which made Gerlach despondent, and he retired to Venice near LA and remained out of the public eye. He recently made a new LP for Tacoma Records which I think is very good. I used his version as a basis and completely changed the arrangement.' Page also debuted his banjo-playing skills.

'Tangerine' had been written by Page years earlier and the Yardbirds had attempted to record it on at least one occasion. 'I'd written it after an old emotional upheaval, and I just changed a few of the lyrics for the new version,' said Page.

The track also features him playing pedal steel, which he'd first demonstrated on 'Your Time is Gonna Come' from the first album. 'I'd never played steel before but I just picked it up. There's a lot of things that I do first time around that I haven't done before. In fact, I hadn't touched a pedal steel from the first album to the third. It's a bit of a pinch really from the things that Chuck Berry did – but nevertheless it fits. It was more out of tune on the first album because I hadn't got a kit to put it together.'

'That's the Way' represented another significant change, this time lyrical in nature. Plant explained, 'I'm a reflection of what I sing. Sometimes I have to get serious because the things I've been through are serious. We've been to America so much and seen so many things which we don't agree with, that our feelings of protest do reflect in the music. When you have the justification, it must be done. I believe that America makes you aware of the proximity of Man's fate. You see so much that is great but so much that is terrible. The rush, the hassles, the police . . . you know, people may think that we make a lot of bread but in some cities it's so rough that people are scared to come to our concerts. Our manager once had a gun pulled on him, and we've been threatened with arrest if we returned to the stage for an encore. The police have even accused us of being drug addicts. That's all part of where "That's the Way" came from. It was one of the five or so songs that we wrote at Bron-Y-Aur. We also started work on the arrangements and got the idea for the violins.'

'Bron-Y-Aur Stomp' reflected yet another colour of the Zeppelin spectrum. Commented Plant, 'I like it as a track because it is so simple yet effective. It's just a song about my dog, Strider.'

'Hats Off to (Roy) Harper' had started out as a Robert Johnson-like improvisation on Bukka White's 'Shake 'Em On Down' and evolved into a sincere salute to the eccentric British folkie, Roy Harper. 'Me and Pagey,' Plant recalled, 'just sat in the studio at Headley Grange and played through some distortion machines and said "Hats Off to Harper" along with all the roadies up the back singing "Yeah" and banging tambourines. When we played it for old Harper, he didn't know what to say. But his time will come – I personally think Roy Harper is one of the best spokesmen this generation has. Despite the subsequent confusion of critics who somehow misconstrued the meaning and thought that it was some kind of putdown, "Hats Off to (Roy) Harper" is just an acknowledgement of a friendship.'

The variations in the group's trademark style could instantly be heard on first playing of the third album – acoustic and semi-acoustic material; a mix of Celtic mysticism; intricate lacey songs to parallel the straightforward pounding riff numbers; and an amazing and tenacious intensity which pervaded all of the tunes, soft or heavy. The main influences at work were Plant's youthful musical leanings and Page's hitherto suppressed admiration for traditional folk music. When Plant joined Led Zeppelin, he'd insisted that he could combine his preference for the Moby Grape/Buffalo Springfield genre with the gutsier, grittier Led Zeppelin approach. Obviously he was right.

'You see,' he noted, gently but firmly, 'here I am the lead singer with Led Zeppelin and underneath I still enjoy people like Fairport Convention and the Buffalo Springfield. Some people may find that surprising. To tell the truth, I've always wanted to go into the realms of that sort of music to a certain degree, without losing the original Zeppelin thing. Some people may have gotten the impression that I had some unfulfilled ambitions while the last two albums were getting done, but all I can say is that this album is really getting there.'

In the group's eyes, the only real problem with *Led Zeppelin III* was the jacket, which the band regarded as a big downer. Planned to be a spectacular and innovative cover design (to augment the freshness of the music contained therein), Page felt that it didn't meet his expectations when it was completed, not by a long shot. It *was* without doubt a distinctive design but it didn't feel quite right, even to an untrained eye. Page said, 'It was intended to be something like one of those gardening calendars or the zoo-wheel things that tell you when to plant cauliflowers or how long whales are pregnant. But there was a misunderstanding with the artist – who is very good in fact but hadn't been correctly briefed – and we ended up on top of a deadline with a teeny-boppish cover which I think was a compromise.'

Led Zeppelin III was released by Atlantic on 5 October 1970 with advance orders in excess of 700,000 copies in America and more than 60,000 in the UK. *Led Zeppelin II* was still holding down number 89 after exactly 52 weeks on the chart. A new Stones album, *Get Yer Ya-Ya's Out!*, had been issued a week earlier. *Led Zeppelin III* rocketed into the bestselling charts at number 3 on 24 October, blanketing the

Stones, an accomplishment which had become a regular feature of the Led Zeppelin career. The Stones simply weren't in the same sales league. That same week saw the first chart placing (at 77) of the second Allman Brothers Band album *Idlewild South*.

In its second week, *Led Zeppelin III* shot to number one and stayed there for a month. Predictably AM stations cried out for a single – after all, they weren't about to grow up, face the facts and simply playlist a variety of cuts from the world's bestselling album. They only played seven-inch records and acted as though the twelve-inch variety was programming poison. Atlantic pushed for the release of 'Immigrant Song' from the album and while the group wasn't too excited at the prospect of *any* single release, the record company finally got its way. *Billboard* reviewed the single on 14 November, under an assortment of pop-oriented Top-40 ditties by Michael Nesmith, Tommy Roe, Tom Jones, Dawn, and Gladys Knight and the Pips, and awarded Led Zeppelin a Top-60 Spotlight prediction. 'Immigrant Song' hit the Hot 100 chart the following week at number 85 and remained for a total of thirteen weeks, peaking at number 16. The track had been a bit too full on for daytime play on conservative Top-40 outlets. It was not released in Britain . . . Phil Carson hadn't even bothered to discuss the possibilities with Peter Grant. Meanwhile in its year-end survey for 1970, *Billboard* accorded *Led Zeppelin II* the number two album of the year award, based on chart standings over the past twelve months.

The critics, true to form, were mostly unimpressed – they were especially cold towards the acoustic changes the band had introduced. The widespread critical response may have been a minor factor in influencing the album's ultimate fate. Although it had torn up to number one, *Led Zeppelin III* had a relatively brief chart life of only 31 weeks, the shortest stay of any of their first five albums.

The media panning accorded Led Zeppelin – after they'd bravely endeavoured to bring more substance and contrast to their style – had a profound effect upon the band, Page in particular. 'The third LP did get a real hammering from the press,' he admitted later, 'and I got really brought down by it. I thought the album in total was good – but the press didn't like it, and they also went on about this alleged enigma that has blown up around us. I admit we may have made it relatively quickly, but I don't think we ever over-played our hand in the press or anything. Yet we were getting all these knocks and we became very dispirited. The result was that we left off for almost a year.'

Ironically many of the pundits who had derided their original knockout-rock approach turned around and ridiculed the band for evidently abandoning that style. Some moaned for a return to 'Whole Lotta Love' which ultimately led to the band's dislike of being associated with a hit single, a tiny taste of what the band actually represented in the musical sense. 'There's just no yardstick for what we turn out,' Plant commented. 'We're all learning all the time, so that we can look back on stuff we'd done a couple of years earlier and see the progression. Somebody came up to me and said, "The second album was so good, but whatever happened on the third?" What can you say to that? They just don't seem to understand that you can't do "Whole Lotta Love" eight times on an album.

'To a certain extent, I suppose, there's something of "Whole Lotta Love" in everything we do. Even if we're not singing the same lyric, the feeling is still there – even when it's mainly acoustic guitar instead of electric. Music doesn't just stop at any one point – you can't restrict it into categories. What we want to do is combine the whole bloody lot. There are different moods to our music, just the same as people have different moods. Sometimes they laugh, sometimes they cry. There's both a physical approach and a more pensive approach to singing and to me, both are natural. The lighter songs are not really light, if you can grasp the atmosphere and the intention.'

Plant elaborated at some considerable length on how the band didn't want to disown 'Whole Lotta Love', but at the same time didn't want to be confined to it or by it, as some rock writers had tried to do. ' "Whole Lotta Love" is something that I personally need, something that I just have to have. We bottle it all up and when we go on stage, we can let it all pour out. The song is very good for us. I suppose in a way it's become a Zeppelin cliché. But it's also a vehicle to other things . . . to give people the chance of hearing things that we reckon are worth hearing.'

Nick Logan, a journalist who went on to become editor of Britain's *New Musical Express*, was among the first to notice the group's urgent creative need to evolve. The third album, he observed 'may prove to be an important turning point in the group's career'. *Melody Maker's* Chris Welch also saw the light: 'In many ways, this is a much better album than *Led Zeppelin II* with many varied approaches and they maintain a steady standard of taste and execution.'

With more concentrated success came inevitable but ignorant rumours that the band might be breaking up. Plant dismissed them with a single word – 'crap' – adding, 'You can never say what's going to last for how long – but it's refreshing to all of us to be able to sit down and come up with these things. With all of us having ideas that we've never had before, and with everybody being part of the finished article. It's really good and it'll last as long as it'll last. We've been producing something different all the time.'

Jimmy Page chimed in more recently, 'The element of change has been the thing really. We put out the first one, then the second . . . then a third LP totally different from them. It's the reason we were able to keep it together.'

Despite the nagging media negativity about their artistic growth – and even before the release of the third album – something more profound was brewing in the cauldron of their creative union. Page and Plant were engrossed in a forthcoming project, a mysterious new song with roots in the glow of the log fires at Bron-Y-Aur, the derelict little Welsh cottage from whence so much inspiration had sprung. Like a climber with his first view of the pinnacle, the lads had felt a taste of a coming crossroads, something they both knew was supremely special.

Jimmy Page hinted at the future as we tooled down the highway to the airport after a sensational appearance in Toronto, long a stronghold of the band. 'It's an idea we've got for a really long track,' Jimmy confided. 'You know how "Dazed and Confused" was broken into different sections. We want to try something new with the organ and acoustic guitar building up and building up, and then the electric part will start. It may turn out to be a fifteen-minute track and we're really looking forward to it. I can't really tell you any more in case it doesn't work out . . . but I think it will.'

Plant anticipated that this mysterious new potential *tour de force* would involve the band as much as the entire third album. 'You might say we keep setting ourselves new limits,' he joked, but I could detect an underlying hint of resolution.

With the commercial and critical disappointments of the third album, one might have expected the members of Led Zeppelin to be laying low, licking their wounded egos. Far from it, they had stumbled into the initial structure – the first fleeting visions of magic looming – of a song which would become the most popular statement in the history of rock. They were poised to ascend the first steps on their 'Stairway to Heaven'.

6 There's a Feeling I Get When I Look to the West

THE BONE-CHILLING WINDS OF MID-WINTER 1971 and George Harrison's splendidly peaceful Christmas coupling of 'My Sweet Lord' and 'Isn't It a Pity' had a warming hold on number one – the first Beatles solo single to reach the top. Before long – sliding down from the sublime to the frozen depths of ridicule – George will be elbowed after four weeks by 'Knock Three Times', an insidious studio concoction featuring a lead vocalist resurrected from 1961 and two background singers. In time Dawn would be eclipsed by a fortuitous family of Mormons from Utah called the Osmonds with their 'One Bad Apple', and then that too would make way for an intense blues shuffle entitled 'Me and Bobby McGee' written by a Rhodes scholar and raunched out by his sometime girlfriend, a barnstorming Texas wailer who'd overdosed a few months earlier – Janis Joplin. I'm talking of very strange times, an era ripe for revolutionary change.

On American AM hit radio, the audio spectrum was murky and all too often mundane, as the music zigzagged and staggered on – from brilliant to abysmal, from sensational to banal, from absolute gems to total horseshit. The seesawing merit of chart hits reflected a frantic fluctuation in values in the mainstream. But beneath the outward confusion, a powerfully fresh current of hot album-driven rock was surging to the surface, bent on submerging the status quo. Ultimately the fast-rising underground breed of new music would celebrate its ascendence when a non-hit album track would surpass all of the hits in rock history. It would set new yardsticks by which the popularity of rock songs would be measured. One era was evolving into another, but it was happening much more dramatically than the rock Establishment was ready for.

In the rural English county of Hampshire, the members of Led Zeppelin could be found privately laying down a very impressive beat at their Headley Grange mobile studio headquarters. They'd started out just before Christmas with a week at the Island Studios in West London, and then moved on to Headley Grange after the holidays. Living together, playing together, getting a buzz on being together alone, except for essential entourage, renewing that natural spiritual union which was their greatest strength.

After a week it was obvious they were ready to switch on the tape machines, and the Rolling Stones' mobile recording truck was carted in for the fireworks to begin. The sales and critical disappointments of the third album were left far behind as the band soared into what promised to be their finest studio work.

The third album was by no means a failure, but its chart duration had left something to be desired, although the band wouldn't publicly admit it. Undeterred – at least on the surface – Led Zeppelin took off on an extensive British and European tour, their largest to date. On the Continent the high-flying Led Zeppelin rock ship collided with its toughest obstacle to date, an ugly event which would affect the group's outlook on dubious police crowd control methods for years to come.

Although the group had become acknowledged experts on authoritarian audience brutality during their five American tours, nothing approached the free-for-all mêlée which devastated their performance in the Italian industrial city of Milan. They'd been booked to headline in the 12,000-capacity Vigorelli bicycle stadium, but upon arrival, they discovered that 28 other acts were on the bill and the venue was 'guarded' by hundreds of fully armed riot control centurions.

Months later, Jimmy Page was still seething about the event as he recounted the horror story to me during a limo airport ride in Canada. 'It was a festival organised and sponsored by the government and we were playing on the grass in a huge football ground. Five or six other acts went on before us, and then we finally went out and started playing. All went well for several numbers and then we suddenly noticed loads of smoke coming from the back of the oval. The promoter came out on stage and told us to tell the kids to stop lighting fires.

'Like twits, we did what the promoter said. We warned kids the authorities might make us stop playing if there were any more fires. We went on for another twenty or thirty minutes, but every time the audience stood up for an encore, there'd be loads of smoke. We kept on asking people not to light fires then we suddenly twigged – it wasn't fire smoke but bloody tear gas that the police were firing into the crowd. It wasn't until one canister lobbed about thirty feet from the stage that we realised just what was happening.'

'The eyes were stinging a bit by then, I can tell you,' interjected John Paul Jones from the other corner of the limo, 'but we kept on playing.'

'Oh yes,' muttered Page, 'true to the end, the show must go on. But it was getting ridiculous. We'd noticed when we'd arrived that the whole militia was out and I told the promoter, "Look, this is absurd . . . either get them out or get them in trim, or there's gonna be a nasty scene." Plus the backstage area was swamped with people, you could hardly move through it. I told the promoter that if we were going to have the militia squad, he should at least get them to keep the backstage area free of people.

'We were still playing in the middle of this cloud of tear gas but it was hopeless. So we said, "Blow this – it's got into tear gas – let's cut it really short." We did one more number then went into "Whole Lotta Love" and the whole crowd jumped up. By this time there'd been forty or fifty minutes of tear gas attacks, and finally somebody heaved a bottle at the police. It wasn't entirely unexpected since the crowd had been getting bombarded for no reason. But of course the moment the bottle went up, that's what the police had been waiting for. They fired thirty or forty canisters at once.

'Our only way out was through a tunnel filled with tear gas. We had no idea of what would be on the other side of the tunnel, but we got through and locked ourselves in a dressing room. All sorts of people were trying to break into the room, probably thinking it was immune from the rest of it. Plus we'd left the roadies running around trying to save our instruments.'

'Actually,' added John Paul Jones, 'some of our roadies had to be carried off in stretchers. Mick Hinton, Bonzo's drum roadie, was badly cut on the head by a broken bottle and had to be carried to hospital. These guys were just trying to save our gear – the police had cordoned all the audience around the back. The only way they could move was forward on to the stage. So about 10,000 kids were forced up through the stage area. It was a war.'

'And to top the evening off,' Page noted wryly, 'we finally got back to our hotel and collapsed into the bar to try and calm down. Along comes this reporter, a guy who'd been there and seen the whole thing and *knew* what happened. There we are, completely shattered emotionally, and he comes up to ask for our comments. We just tore him apart, saying, "C'mon man, you saw it, now *you* write it up. Don't ask our opinion. You've got your own." But he kept on bugging us for a comment and in the end, Bonzo told him to piss off or get a bottle smashed over his head.'

It would be the worst riot of the entire Led Zeppelin career and the band was absolutely stunned by it. On the plane back to London, Robert Plant was moved to tears trying to describe the irony of a band aiming to make uplifting music in the face of fascist crowd control measures. None of it added up, and memories of Milan would remain with them for many a concert tour.

After the pandemonium of Milan, the seventeen-date North American tour in May and June seemed relatively calm. Ahead of them later in the summer would follow a more extensive US and Canadian itinerary, and a series of performances in Japan, the group's first visit to the world's fastest-growing rock market. But in between the two American tours, they spent a few weeks back in Britain finishing off the fourth album.

Despite Milan memories, the band was riding high. They had had three consecutive platinum discs. They were receiving exceptionally large concert fees. And their overall presence in the marketplace, already exceeding that of any other rock act, continued to spiral. Even the winter of paranoia over their carping critics – the result of inexplicable constant bad reviews and the spreading of malicious breakup rumours – seemed to be on the wane. Remaining on top however was a problem in itself. They had to learn to cope with the pressures of staying number one, when they were still as amazed as anybody else in the industry about the actual extent of their enormous success.

Other second-generation British album bands – more than a few of them possessing the odd Led Zeppelin leaning – were also expanding their audiences at a fairly rapid rate. Black Sabbath, Emerson, Lake and Palmer, Jethro Tull, and Uriah Heep were all climbing steadily. In America, Led Zeppelin-styled groups like Grand Funk Railroad, Bloodrock, the Buddy Miles Express, the MC5, Lee Michaels, Rare Earth, and to a lesser extent, Mountain, the James Gang and Steppenwolf, tumbled into the new hard rock chart territory that Led Zeppelin had blasted open. It was becoming highly lucrative to be a part of the new hard rock hierarchy.

Despite the inherent pressures, the band had set about putting together the vital fourth album with a marked degree of fresh enthusiasm, and had several outstanding new numbers in the pipeline and a handle on the 'mystery song' they'd been playing with for months.

They were so in tune with each other that unanimous intuitive confidence and their unique faith kept them hard at work – they really knew in their hearts that the 'mystery song' was evolving into an absolute rock blockbuster. All the while, they maintained a low profile, avoiding the media except for closest confidants. 'We felt,' noted Page, 'not only that the new album would make or break us, but that we had to prove something to ourselves.' It was this dogged determination which in the end saw them survive horrors they hadn't begun to imagine as they got down to the serious recording of *Led Zeppelin IV*.

The first upset in the schedule turned out to be the taping location. Almost all of their previous recording work had taken place within the multiple confines of conventional recording studios, an awkward creative environment which the group had to battle to overcome. It wasn't until someone suggested a complete change of venue (and indeed creative *modus operandi*) that the band realised they needn't be dominated by the hardware technology when it intruded on the art of making music. Furthermore they would soon find they could not only survive but prosper without its four foreign walls of restraint.

'We started off doing some of the tracks at the new Island studios in London in December,' said Page, 'but after that we moved to our house, Headley Grange in Hampshire, a place where we often rehearse. For some reason, we decided to take the Stones' mobile truck there – because we were used to the place. It was familiar territory: we'd even lived there during long rehearsal sessions. It seemed ideal – as soon as we thought of an idea we were able to put it down on tape right away.

'In a way, that was a good method. The only thing wrong was that we'd get so excited about an idea that we'd really rush to finish its format to get it on to tape. It was like a quick productivity thing. It was just so exciting to have all the facilities there.

'Looking back, I suppose what we really needed was at least two weeks solid with the truck. But as it turned out, we actually only had about six days. Usually we need a full week to get everything out of our system and to get used to the facilities. Then we could be really getting it together in the second week. You really do need the sort of facilities where you can take a break for a cup of tea and a wander around the garden, and then go back in and do whatever you have to do. Instead of that feeling of walking into a studio, down a flight of steps and into fluorescent lights . . . and opening up the big soundproof door and being surrounded by acoustic tiles. To work like that, you've got to programme yourself. You're walking down those stairs telling yourself that you're going to play the solo of your life. But you so rarely do in those conditions. It's that hospital atmosphere that all studios have.

'Personally,' Page continued, 'I get terrible studio nerves. Even when I've worked the whole thing out beforehand at home, I get terribly nervous playing anyway – particularly when I've worked on something that turned out to be a little above my normal capabilities. When it comes to playing it again in the studio, my bottle goes. It's the studio nerves – you never lose them. I might as well be back there three years ago making all those dreadful studio records.

'Those nerves are one reason why I'm getting into my own studio at home. It's not going to be as expensive as I thought it might be, and obviously the whole band is going to benefit from it. You can work in your own home and in your own time without the red-light pressures.'

The rest of the band solidly agreed. Said Robert Plant, 'A recording studio is an immediate imposition on you. It's rather a limiting factor as compared to sitting around a fire playing away. You can also do quite a lot of experimenting when you've got a mobile truck. Most of the mood for this album was brought about in settings that we hadn't come across before. We were living and recording in this old falling-apart mansion way out in the country . . . the mood was incredible. We could put something down on the spot and hear the results immediately.'

In the can, Led Zeppelin already had at least a dozen studio tracks in various stages of completion from assorted earlier sessions. Adding to this the fruits of their labours at Headley Grange (some eight tracks in all), they finally pruned the choice of repertoire for the fourth album down to fourteen songs. 'We have enough here for two albums,' said Page, 'but we won't put out a double album. I think people can appreciate a single album better.' According to him, 'almost everything' on the fourth album turned out to be from the mobile truck sessions. The feeling was clearly right.

With the next stage however, the real traumas began. By mid-summer, the eight chosen tracks were ready for the formidable task of mixing down to two-track stereo. Page described the fiasco which followed. 'There were so many foul-ups, basically by engineers. Andy Johns said he knew a place where we could mix the album, Sunset Sound in LA. He convinced us it was the best place to do it, the best mixing room. In the right room, you can hear the tapes true to form and the record will sound exactly the same as it did in that room. But of course it didn't – and we wasted a week wanking around.

'From that point on, Andy crapped himself and he disappeared. We then had to find a new engineer to tie it all together. That's when the fiasco really started. It had sounded all right to me but the speakers were lying. It wasn't the balance – it was the actual sound that was on the tape. When we played it back in England weeks later, the tapes sounded like they'd gone through some odd processes. All I can put it down to was the fact the speakers in LA and the monitoring system in that room were just very bright – and they lied. It wasn't the true sound.'

The suspense dragged on. Plant said, 'We were just disgusted at the amount of time it had taken to get the album finished. The sound of the mixing room that Andy Johns took Jimmy to was really duff. Then there was a hold-up about pressings, and whether the masters would stand up to how many pressings.'

The final struggle – and the one which appeared to close insiders to cause the most consternation within the group – boiled down to the album title and what should (and what should not) be displayed on the jacket. Such artistic battles between creators and merchandisers are nothing new, of course. Not until the creative revolution of the Beatles did recording artists begin to have any input into album packaging – which may account for many of the cover art abominations that have been fobbed off on the public over the years. Nowadays most major artists insist on controlling as many of the creative procedures as possible in the marketing of their music – jacket design being an integral part of this. Led Zeppelin was no exception, especially with Page's art college training and love of fine art. But record companies insist on a right of refusal clause in case an act's concepts are totally off the planet. After all, record executives insist, the label is responsible for merchandising and marketing the product and they therefore know best what's required in the retail marketplace. From the group's point of view, the problem was different and this difference, on the fourth album, led to a major controversy.

Because of the intense media slagging of Led Zeppelin III, the group was carrying a certain insecurity. The band's image had come under the gun too, with more than a few catty comments about their sexuality and appeal to young females. Because they resented these accusations, the band decided to ensure that nothing would come between the listener and the music. This album, the group specified, was to be presented purely and simply as a collection of new music. The band had been unhappy with the printing of the jackets on their first three albums, and both Page and Plant had said so, loudly. Still nobody at Atlantic was prepared for Peter Grant's announcement that the band had decided the fourth album would have *no* title, *no* mention of the group on the outside jacket, and *no* record company logos or catalogue numbers and credits. Zep wanted raw, untarnished, unmutilated jacket art.

'We decided,' Page explained, 'that on the fourth album, we would deliberately downplay the group name and there wouldn't be any information whatever on the outside jacket. Names, titles and things like that don't mean a thing. What does Led Zeppelin mean? It doesn't mean a thing. What matters is our music. If we weren't playing good music, nobody would care what we call ourselves. If the music was good, we could call ourselves cabbages and still get across to our audience. The words Led Zeppelin don't appear anywhere on the cover of the fourth album. And all the other usual credits are missing too. I had to talk like hell to get that done – the record company told us we were committing professional suicide. We said we just wanted to rely *purely* on our music.'

Plant was equally emphatic. 'We wanted a cover with no writing on it. No company symbols or anything. The hierarchy of the record business aren't into the fact that covers are important to a band's image. We just said they couldn't have the master tapes until they got the cover right.'

A stalemate extended over several uncomfortable days: neither side wanted to budge an inch. Atlantic were obviously freaked at the prospect of setting a precedent – what might happen in the future if Led Zeppelin and other acts rammed through such a break with tried-and-tested tradition. Page said, 'They were all dead frightened of giving away too much. The LP was a whole experiment really because everything was underplayed, rightly or wrongly. When you haven't put out an album for a year and there's this huge enigma that's blown up, and then you put out an album with no title whatsoever . . . and with no reference to the group whatsoever apart from the piece of plastic inside, then some people would consider that to be suicide. But the whole thing had to be done to satisfy our own minds after all the crap that had gone down in the newspaper – and still does.'

Eventually the landmark jacket design was reluctantly approved by Atlantic, and it emerged as a stunning piece of visionary art. The front featured a picture hanging on the derelict wall of a slum house, a portrait of a weary old man carrying a load of twigs strapped to his back. The rear showed a typical slice of urban society, in London or anywhere – soaringly ugly concrete high-rises casting shadows over Victorian-era housing projects crumbling from neglect and the wrecker's ball.

The inner sleeve highlighted an old man in a long white cloak (representing the hermit of the tarot) peering down from the top of a mountain, observing a walled village situated in a valley. A young man is seen climbing the mountain. There is no mention of titles or group names. The actual credits for the album, its track listings, and the lyrics to 'Stairway to Heaven' are contained on the inner paper sleeve – marking the first time that Led Zeppelin (or any other Atlantic artist) had refrained from the conventional Atlantic catalogue promo sleeve. And it was the first time Zep had utilised a lyric sheet.

'Unfortunately,' noted Page, 'the negatives were a bit of a bluff so you can't quite read an Oxfam poster on the side of a building on the back of the jacket. It's the poster where someone is lying dead on a stretcher, and it says that every day somebody receives relief from hunger. You can just make it out on the jacket if you're familiar with the Oxfam poster. But other than that, there's no writing on the jacket at all.'

Pagey also explained his interpretation of the jacket's omnipresent symbolism. 'The old man carrying the wood is in harmony with nature. He takes from nature but he gives back to the land. It's a natural cycle and it's right. His old cottage gets pulled down and they move him to these horrible urban slums, which are terrible places. The hermit on the inside was painted by a friend of mine, Barrington Colby. The hermit is holding out the light of truth and enlightenment to a young man at the foot of the hill. If you know the tarot cards, you'll know what the hermit means.' [It is generally regarded as a special warning against proceeding on one's present course without retirement and contemplation.]

Page himself is at home with the tarot cards, but more particularly with the philosophy of Aleister Crowley. Page is likely the world's foremost collector of Crowley memorabilia, and cynics have often suggested a sinister link between Crowley and his modern-day mentor. A controversial character who liked to call himself 'The Great Beast 666', Crowley was a notoriously flamboyant British musician, poet, writer and mountain climber who caused an uproar among occultists in the 1920s and 1930s becuase of his allegedly reckless psychic experiments involving elements of so-called 'black' magic.

It could be fairly stated that Aleister Crowley has had a profound impact on Jimmy Page's life, and in that light, his background should be considered. Born to a comfortable middle-class British family in 1875, Crowley matured into a somewhat charismatic young writer who published his poems while at Oxford and also gained recognition as one of the foremost rock climbers and mountaineers of his era. Eager for esoteric, informed knowledge, Crowley teamed up with the celebrated Order of the Golden Dawn, but was prevented from gaining higher achievement by William Butler Yeats who wrote to Lady Gregory that 'we did not think that a mystical society was intended to be a reformatory'.

Crowley spent a year in Mexico attempting to make his image vanish through a mirror. He rejected totally conventional morality, and his credo was contained in the motto he used to introduce his letters: 'Do what thou wilt shall be the whole of the law.' In between Himalayan mountaineering expeditions and maintaining a satanic temple on the Fulham Road in London, Crowley achieved legendary status with his unabashed abuse of then misunderstood drugs such as hashish, opium, cocaine and heroin, and with his 'sex magick', in which long sessions of sexual intercourse *sans* orgasm were the gateway to apparently incredible periods of ecstasy and intense intoxication.

There can be no doubt that Crowley had some interesting and revolutionary concepts on enjoying one's brief stay on Earth. He wound up dodging from one country to the next, a heroin addict suffering from asthma and a bronchial infection, and he died in Brighton in 1947, when Jimmy Page was just three years old. But Page obviously found a soulful sustenance in Crowley's unorthodox beliefs and has propagated his theories and concepts.

In 1970, Page acquired probably the ultimate Crowley artifact – his country manor seat, Boleskine House on the mysterious shore of Loch Ness in Scotland. An eighteenth-century U-shaped pile, Boleskine boasts a grim history by any definition. The house had supposedly been built on the site of a church that had been burned with its flock in attendance. Local legend claims that a man was beheaded there, and his skull rolls around the halls on certain nights.

Crowley moved in shortly after the turn of the century and called himself the Laird of Boleskine. He used magic spells to summon up demons such as Thoth and the Egyptian deity, Horus. Ultimately, it is said, Crowley's magic induced the house and terraces to be surrounded by 'shadowy shapes'. The lodgekeeper apparently went nuts and attempted to murder his family. Even Crowley himself reported that the Boleskine rooms sometimes became so dark in the middle of a sunny day that he had to introduce artificial light while copying magical symbols. Clearly Boleskine House has a special vibe, and one not especially suited to the uninitiated. Yet Jimmy Page has flourished in its precipitous precincts.

Jimmy's growing infatuation with the occult *à la* Aleister Crowley had already led him to inscribe the Beast's credo 'Do What Thou Wilt' on the masters of *Led Zeppelin III* (look on the inner spirals of the album). Now it (and Robert's fascination with Celtic mysticism) led to the most striking and obvious feature on the fourth album, four very mysterious symbols above the track listings. The entire international rock media was baffled by this latest mystery episode. Were these symbols supposed to be the title of the new album? Or were they some private personal joke as the inscriptions of 'Porky' and 'Pecko Duck' on the pressing appeared to be? At first, the band did absolutely nothing to enlighten the media or the public.

Then an unsubstantiated rumour was circulated widely in the press that the four symbols were Icelandic runes, ancient alphabet-like letters of mysterious origin. In discussing the symbols, John Bonham would only say, 'The runes are symbols which apply to each one of us. I wouldn't like to state what they mean. Each one of us picked one.'

A year later, Jimmy Page confessed that the symbols were 'not Icelandic. That was just a red herring-type rumour. Only the middle two are actually runes. What happened was that we all chose a symbol and the four together became the title of the album.'

Robert Plant also added grist to the mill, contributing further information on the surreal symbolism. 'We'd decided that the album shouldn't be called *Led Zeppelin IV* and we were wondering what it should be. Then each of us decided to go away and choose a metaphorical-type symbol which somehow would represent each one of us individually – be it a state of mind, an opinion or something we felt strongly about or whatever.'

Ultimately, Page informed the bewildered British press, 'Robert's symbol is his own design – the feather, a symbol on which all sorts of philosophies have been based, and which has a very interesting heritage. For instance, it represents courage to many red Indian tribes.' Plant himself finally elaborated, 'My symbol was drawn from sacred symbols of the ancient Mu civilisation which existed about 15,000 years ago as part of a lost continent somewhere in the Pacific Ocean between China and Mexico. All sorts of things can be tied in with the Mu civilisation, even the Easter Island effigies. These Mu people left stone tablets with their symbols inscribed on them all over the place – in Mexico, Egypt, Ethiopia, India, China and other places. And they all date from the same period. The Chinese say that these people came from the East, and the Mexicans say they came from the West – obviously it was somewhere in between. My particular symbol does have a further meaning, and all I can do is suggest that people look it up in a suitable reference work.'

John Bonham's symbol was the three circles. Observed Plant, 'I suppose it's the Trilogy – man, woman and child. I suspect it had something to do with the mainstay of all peoples' belief. At one point though – in Pittsburgh, I think – we observed that it was also the emblem for Ballantine beer.'

Page continued the explanation, 'John Paul Jones's symbol, the second from the left, was found in a book about runes and was said to represent a person who is both confident and competent, because it was difficult to draw it accurately. Bonzo's came from the same book – he just picked it out because he liked it.'

Which leaves only Jimmy Page's symbol. The guitarist had only let the claws of the cat out of the bag, which was typical of him. 'Mine was something which I designed myself,' he revealed rather slyly. 'A lot of people mistook it for a word – "Zoso" – and many people in the States still refer to the album as "Zoso" . . . which is a pity because it wasn't supposed to be a word at all but something entirely different. Basically the title thing was just another ruse to throw the media into chaos. We all had a good laugh when the record went into the charts and they had to reproduce the symbols instead of a conventional title. Atlantic did supply all the trade paper charts with the appropriate artwork for the symbols, but they didn't like it at all because it set a precedent. The album actually set two precedents – first the title, and secondly the sleeve bearing no wording at all.'

With master tapes and artwork finished, the band left Atlantic in a state of some confusion over the forthcoming fourth album jacket and proceeded on to their late summer North American tour. They then headed across the Pacific – stopping in Hawaii for a week of well-earned rest with wives temporarily in tow – before continuing on to Japan for their début tour in that territory where 'Immigrant

Song' was entrenched at number one on local charts. From start to finish, this tour would be one of the most enjoyable in their entire career.

'It was just a fantastic place to play,' John Bonham later enthused. 'Rock music only started to happen there a few years ago, but now it's the second biggest market in the world. The people were so friendly and we had the best promoter in the world there looking after us. It turned out that "Immigrant Song" is one of our biggest favourites in Japan, and it's the number we always open with. So the audiences were going potty right from the start.'

Atlantic's Phil Carson accompanied the band to Japan for the usual reasons and found himself in an assortment of hilarious and sometimes compromising situations and predicaments – among them being banned for ever from staying at the Tokyo Hilton because of their over-the-top escapades. 'The only way of relieving the boredom of this constant grind of Hilton hotel rooms is just to have a bit of fun from time to time,' Carson explained with the accent on justification. 'The lads had been playing in America for four weeks and then straight to Japan for another ten days. They'd been away from their homes for six or seven weeks, so things kind of build up and there's a need to let off a bit of steam.

'We all play jokes on one another. Everybody gangs up on one particular person for a spell, and then it's someone else's turn. These things can become very funny. On one occasion, Robert Plant accidentally knocked one of my pillows out of the window of my room at the Tokyo Hilton. So I thought I'd climb out the window and retrieve the pillow from a ledge. All I was wearing was a bath towel. There was no danger of falling off, but it did take quite a bit of explaining when they phoned the house detective and complained there was a peeping tom on the ledge outside their room.'

On another occasion, a drunk and comatose John Paul Jones had his door chopped down with newly acquired samurai swords. Jones was then dragged out into the corridor while John Bonham and Richard Cole butchered his room with their blades. Hotel staff found Jones asleep in the corridor the next morning, and were roundly abused for disturbing him until he found he wasn't waking up in his bed.

A subsequent messy corridor episode of fruit throwing led to Hilton management banning the entire entourage.

Even a sobering one-nighter at the Hiroshima Municipal Auditorium (a benefit for victims of the 1945 atom bomb attack, which saw the mayor present the group with a Hiroshima peace medal) wasn't able to totally stifle their desire for sundry light entertainments. The next day the party boarded the Bullet express train for Osaka and Kyoto, a journey which has become something of a legend in Japanese rock circles. They boarded the gleaming blue and white jet-like train with a case of local Suntori whiskey and a dozen flasks of hot sake, the Japanese rice wine. Reported Carson, 'Well, by chance it was Jimmy's turn to be gotten by the rest of us. It was one of those sleeper trains with canvas sides on the bunks, like in America. John Paul, Robert and Bonzo had this idea of pulling aside the curtain to Jimmy's bunk and tossing in a load of cold tea, stale sake and rice at about three in the morning.

'So they pulled the curtain aside and John Paul heaved in the stuff. The trouble was that it was Peter Grant's bunk by mistake and not Pagey's. I've never seen Peter move so fast – he dived out of his bunk and went chasing down the corridor after Jonesy and caught him and threw him into his bunk. Along came Richard Cole to see what the fuss was about, and Peter took a swing at him. He ducked and the punch hit Bonzo. Peter had a few very sharp words with Richard, who'd had nothing to do with the incident. One of the local record company promo men was with us on the train and he was about ready to commit hari-kari. He thought the group was splitting up right before his eyes, and he might get the blame. I had to explain to him that this sort of thing does go on quite often. The next morning we got off the train as if nothing happened, but it was all over the front pages of the Japanese newspapers.'

Carson flew back to London with Grant, Jonesy and Bonzo while Plant, Page and Richard Cole decided to take a quick whizz through the Orient. 'We all bought cameras in Japan,' Plant said on his return, 'and became sweaty photographers. Page must have lost a couple of pounds rushing about taking pictures in the red-light district of Bangkok. In Thailand all the kids followed us around calling out "Billy Boy, Billy Boy" which means queer – all because of our long hair. But it was friendly stuff. When we landed in Bangkok, we saw a sign saying that the band Marmalade were coming to play here soon. Led Zeppelin had never even been heard of in Thailand, but here was Marmalade playing there, and then heading off somewhere else exotic. It made us think.' [Marmalade only had one hit, 'Reflections of My Life'.]

The group reassembled in Europe shortly before the long-delayed release of the fourth album. Once again members of the band ran down the album for me on a track-by-track basis, always a fascinating insight into their creative processes.

The opening cut, 'Black Dog', was a sizzler in the powerhouse Led Zeppelin tradition of 'Immigrant Song', 'Whole Lotta Love' and 'Communication Breakdown'. The tune had been first introduced to audiences on the 1971 summer tour, and had become an instant favourite. 'It's a bit of a hairy one,' Pagey laughed, 'on which John Paul Jones worked out the impossible part of the riff.'

Jones said he had been inspired by the Muddy Water's 1968 comeback album *Electric Mud*. 'I wanted to try an electric blues with a rolling bass part. But it couldn't be too simple. I wanted to turn it back on itself. I showed it to the guys and we fell into it. We struggled with the turnaround until Bonzo figured out that you could just count four-time as if there's no turnaround. That was the secret. We titled it after a dog that was wandering in and out of the studio – the dog had no name so we just called the song "Black Dog",' he said in recent years

Plant observed, 'The band is really getting attuned to time skips. They're not really intentional, just little whims which we'll no doubt expand upon in the next album. We were messing around doing those kind of time skip riffs when the other lads suddenly came up with that passage in "Black Dog". They just played it, fell about all over the place for about ten minutes in fits of laughter, played it again, burst into more laughter, then put it down on tape – as simple as that.'

' "Rock and Roll" is just what it says,' Page explained, 'just a rock and roll thing. We were messing around working on another song and suddenly Bonzo played that drum thing. I joined him on guitar in the riff and although it only lasted for about fifteen seconds, we listened to a playback and heard the basis of a whole song which we then got together in the space of about fifteen minutes. Things like that often happen now, spontaneous things. Usually they're only riff numbers but I think they're still loaded up with an immediate excitement and communication.'

'The Battle of Evermore' has an altogether different style and feel – quiet and wistful and unimposing – and features the outstanding voice of Fairport Convention singer, Sandy Denny. It came to life spontaneously. Page said, 'I picked up Jonesy's mandolin and those chords just came out. It was my very first experiment with the instrument, and I suppose all mandolin players will have a bit of a laugh because it must be standard to play those chords. Afterwards it sounded like a dance-around-the-maypole number I'll admit. But it wasn't purposely a "let's do a folksy number now".'

The lyrics also fell into place quickly. 'I'd been reading a book on the Scottish wars just before going to Headley Grance,' said Plant. 'The number is really more of a playette than a song. After I wrote the lyrics, I realised that it needed another completely different voice — as well as my own — to give the song its full impact. So I asked Sandy Denny to come along and sing — I must say I found it very satisfying to sing with someone who has an entirely different style than my own. So while I sang about the events in the song, Sandy answered back as if she was the pulse of the people on the battlements. Sandy was playing the role of the town crier, urging the people to throw down their weapons.'

Then out of the clear blue pool of creativity arose the eight-minute extravaganza which would become Zeppelin's ultimate trademark, a song of shimmering and flourishing beauty, a supreme accomplishment which Robert Plant would later describe as 'our single most important achievement'. To Plant — and indeed to Led Zeppelin fans everywhere — it proved once and forever that Led Zeppelin wasn't just another noisy hard rock band. Said Plant, 'That song gave us the musical respectability we've deserved all along.' An authentic, incomparable rock classic, 'Stairway to Heaven' combines the diffuse elements of both Led Zeppelin's ever-broadening style, and of the entire white rock genre. Even staunch R & B addicts admitted it was a mean mother of a track.

'I was just sitting there with Pagey in front of a fire at Headley Grange,' Plant recalled. 'Pagey had written these chords and he played them for me. I was holding a pencil and paper and for some reason, I was in a very bad mood. Then all of a sudden my hand was writing out the words: "There's a lady who's sure, all that glitters is gold, and she's buying a Stairway to Heaven." I just sat there and I looked at the words and I almost leapt out of my seat. Looking back I suppose I just sat down at the right moment. Obviously it *was* the right time.'

Jimmy Page picks up the tale of 'Stairway's' creating. 'I'd written the music over a long period, the first part coming at Bron-Y-Aur one night. The other parts came together piece by piece. When we went to record it at Headley Grange, we were all so inspired by how the song could come out — with the building passages and all of those possibilities — that Robert suddenly burst out with the lyrics. He had forty per cent of the lyrics together almost immediately. Then we all threw in ideas — things such as Bonzo not coming in until the song was well underway to create a change of gear – and the song and the arrangement just came together.'

'It took a little working out,' Plant reflected recently, 'but it was a very fluid, unnaturally easy track. It was almost as if it just had to be gotten out at that time. there was something pushing it, saying "You guys are OK, but if you want to do something *timeless*, here's a wedding present for you".'

'I remember playing it for the first time at the LA Forum,' Page said in 1991, 'and – I'm not saying the whole audience gave us a standing ovation – but there was this sizeable standing ovation there. And I thought, "This is incredible, because no one's heard this number yet. This is the first time they're hearing it!" It obviously touched them . . . so I knew we were on to something with that one. Because it's always difficult to hear a number – especially something that long – which you've never heard before.'

The appeal of 'Stairway to Heaven' as a musical piece is self-evident: its lyrics seemed to embody the individual's prevailing quest for a spiritual rebirth. Plant has since cited the book *Magic Arts in Celtic Britain* by Lewis Spence as one of his inspirations in writing the wonderful 'Stairway' lyrics.

It was such a unique concept that it could only have been created by Led Zeppelin, which is the ultimate compliment.

'Misty Mountain Top', which opens side two, 'is a tune we sometimes play at concerts,' said Page, 'while "Four Sticks" is a riff tune which Bonzo literally played with four sticks – two in each hand tearing along like mad. John Paul added in some Moog synthesiser in a small section as well.'

Despite intense competition, the lilting airs of 'Going to California' represent another stand-out classic. 'If we roll up somewhere with amps and guitars, then we make electric music. But if we roll up to the farm with acoustic guitars, then that's something else and that's when the acoustic stuff gets written.' Plant admitted in 1974 that 'Going to California' had in fact been dedicated secretly to the Canadian-born folk singer/songwriter, Joni Mitchell. 'It's hard to say which single Led Zeppelin track pleases me most now,' said Percy, 'since there are so many moods to a day. "Going to California" is a really nice song. It's so simple and the lyrics just fell right out of my mouth. When you're in love with Joni Mitchell, you've really got to write about it now and again. For a mellow mood, I'd probably name "Going to California" as my favourite Zeppelin song.'

The odd cynic suggested that the track was the band's lament for the touring lifestyle in LA where they invariably raised hell pursuing beautiful young women.

The fourth album closes on a stewing down-home funk feel with an old impending-doom 1928 blues tune called 'When the Levee Breaks'. 'It's an old Memphis Minnie number with Kansas Joe McCoy connections,' Plant said. 'I think the drums on it are incredible. There's a secret to it that we just stumbled across really; and that was by using only one microphone for the drums. The revelation of finding that one mike could do more than about thirty-five in a typical studio set the mood for it, really. It was enthusiasm unlimited. We really wanted to get something like the drum sound on those early Presley records.'

More recently John Paul Jones elaborated on the style of recording which produced such timeless Led Zeppelin moments as 'When the Levee Breaks'. 'We used to try everything. Basically if you're a guitar-bass-drums band, you've got to come up with something a bit different each time so all the tracks don't sound the same. We used to have amps everywhere – in rooms, up stairwells, in bathrooms, outside the building. One of the advantages of not working in a studio was that in an old house, you could always find an old cupboard to stick a guitar amp in. Working at Headley Grange, it was the special sound we achieved that wrote the song of "When the Levee Breaks".

'We'd been working on another song and there was a lot of leakage from the drums, so we moved Bonzo's drums out into the hall where there's a big stairwell about thirty or forty feet high. We set up a mike on the first floor, about ten feet up, and another on the second floor, about twenty feet up. We didn't even bother with a bass drum mike. Bonzo started playing and we said, "Jesus, will you listen to that sound." Then we started the riff and that's how the song came about – through experimentation.'

Summing up the new project, Jonesy gave it his own deft touch of dry humour: 'No one ever compared us to Black Sabbath after this record.'

'By the fourth album we collectively agreed on what the visual aspect should be – total anonymity. It said forget everything from the past – this album is moving towards the future. Just listen to the music,' said Jimmy Page.

The untitled and unadorned fourth album was finally released on 8 November 1971, several months overdue and almost thirteen months to the day since the release of *Led Zeppelin III*. *Billboard* gave the album an excellent review in the 20 November issue, predicting (not exactly surprisingly) that it would rise to the top. But unlike its two predecessors, the fourth LP never did reach the number one position on US charts. It did, however, ultimately remain on the charts longer than any previous Led Zeppelin album (eventually becoming their biggest seller). It galloped on to the Top-200 chart at number 36 on 27 November, moving up to number eight and then number three. From there it moved to number two, where it stayed for five weeks, held out by – of all things – Carole King's *Tapestry*. In the long run, though, Led Zeppelin's fourth album would outsell almost every other rock album ever released.

A single from the album wasn't released until 2 December. In its Christmas issue, *Billboard* gave 'Black Dog' a Special Merit Spotlight, below thirteen other higher-rated singles. 'Raucous rocker cut down in time (to 3.35) from the smash LP should make a heavy Hot-100 chart dent,' noted the reviewer. 'Black Dog' hit the chart at number 67 that same week, and continued upwards, eventually reaching number 15 on 19 February. Its total chart run was eleven weeks, not exactly spectacular – AM radio in America was still nervous about the Led Zeppelin phenomenon which was taking longer to blow over than they'd foolishly estimated.

The band was definitely not delighted about the release of 'Black Dog'; again it had been a question of Atlantic US convincing the lads that it was a necessary move to ensure larger LP sales in the American market. Atlantic vice president and general manager, Jerry Greenberg, assured Peter Grant that a second single from the album, 'Rock and Roll', undoubtedly could be bulldozed into the top ten. *Billboard* gave it a Pop Pick Single review under five other records, and 'Rock and Roll' went on to the pop charts on 18 March at number 77. It had a seven-week chart stay but only climbed to the number 47 position. Jerry Greenberg wrote Grant and the band an apology but said that he felt from the AM airplay thus gained, an additional couple of hundred thousand albums had been sold.

Shortly thereafter Greenberg launched what would be the most ardent pressure campaign ever conducted by Atlantic to convince a highly sceptical Led Zeppelin to release another of the fourth album tracks as a single. This time they wanted 'Stairway to Heaven' out. In his private letter to Peter Grant about the chart quandary of 'Rock and Roll', Greenberg duly noted, 'For your information, stations are now telling us that "Stairway to Heaven" is the most fantastic cut on the album.' It had taken the blinker-blinded AM stations five long months to arrive at this perceptive conclusion, comment enough on the out-of-touch tastes of most North American AM hit programmers.

On 18 April, Grant wrote back tersely to Greenberg, 'I must stress that in no way will I consider releasing "Stairway to Heaven" at this stage in time.' Greenberg was no quitter, however, no matter how lost his cause was.

On 27 July he urgently cabled Grant's London office, 'KHJ in LA and KLIP in Dallas also added "Stairway to Heaven" as Hitbound – unbelievable pressure to release this as a single – won't you please reconsider. Advance orders on the single 100,000 – Regards Greenberg.'

But Grant, with the unswerving support of the group, remained adamant, and rightly so. Observed Phil Carson from the other side of the Atlantic, 'Once again history proved that Peter Grant was right. There had already been two singles off the album, but Atlantic US wanted to revitalise the fourth album prior to the release of the new one, plus the upcoming tour. It was a natural enough move. A lot of AM stations did programme "Stairway" but it didn't come out as a single – so people just bought the album as if it were a single. Which added at least half a million copies to the total sale of the album.' The 'Stairway' album, as it had grown to be called by rock media, stayed on the charts the first time around for 39 weeks, dropping off briefly and then returning in the autumn of 1972. By May 1975, the album was still in the top 60 after more than three years on the chart.

More significant, however, is the fact that in countless polls by radio stations and magazines around the world, 'Stairway to Heaven' has been consistently voted by the public as their all-time favourite rock song. Even if the band had never spent a single second in a recording studio again, their fame and unparalleled place in rock history was secured for all time by the enormous achievements of this one amazing song.

Overall critical response to the fourth album had been more favourable than in the past, but it still left a lot to be desired – at least in my view. 'Originally there were quite a few people picking up on this album,' said Page, 'and giving it a good review. But there were also the usuals who gave it a good slam-off, particularly in England. In fact, you might even call it a major slamming. To many of them "Stairway" was just there – they virtually ignored it.'

For a sampling of critical opinion, consider the following comments: 'Not their best or their worst' *Melody Maker*; 'By far their best album to date' *Disc*; 'Maybe not their best LP' *Record Mirror*; 'It smashes everything Zeppelin has done before into the ground' *Sounds*; 'Has twice as much pure sound as *Led Zeppelin II' PRM*; 'Frankly the quality of this album surprised me' *Crawdaddy*; '*Led Zeppelin IV* is the miracle album of all time' *Ringsman*. Even Led Zeppelin's old enemies at *Rolling Stone* were moved to make their first bow towards the band's avalanching popularity by admitting this album was 'not bad for a pack of Limey lemon squeezers'.

It's not difficult to understand why the band had become so distressed at the petty swiping by rock media, especially in the case of an album representing such milestone artistic development. They felt the fourth album deserved considerably more than the mixed bag of media drivel which drifted into their London headquarters. On the surface however − with the steadfast urging of Peter Grant who knew a trap when he saw one − the Led Zeppelin camp endeavoured to adopt an attitude of simply not caring about the knockers. The simple fact remained that the group *was* proud of the album, no matter what any egghead might write about it. Plant and Page, particularly, felt that it was a turning point in the band's career.

'It doesn't relate to anything we've done before,' Plant observed. 'It was that much longer getting finished than the third one, and so it's that much different. To me, our music is going from strength to strength. Now we're all picking up on something else − playing different instruments. Now that we've got the time − with at least six months between albums − we can sit down and think about things a lot longer than we could before.'

Topping 'Stairway' on any future album seemed a futile and pointless enterprise. But the same thing had been said about 'Dazed and Confused' and 'Whole Lotta Love', and the band had moved on to even more meaningful heights. With the fourth album, a whole new set of standards had been demonstrated and only a band of Led Zeppelin's capabilities could even begin to ponder the next chapter.

7 Holy Houses and Overflowing Audiences

T HE FOURTH ALBUM'S spectacular artistic and commercial success gave Led Zeppelin members what they needed most at this juncture – the time to take time. Not only in the development of the fifth album, but in gaining some sort of realistic perspective on the past three years of music, mayhem and magic. A sense of a looming crossroads seemed to be forming in the mists of the imminent future, and the band was perpetually excited at the prospects. It was a distinctly *up* period.

Initially – fresh on the high of the 'Stairway' triumph – they'd wanted to combine the airy, free-floating style of the third and fourth album with the sheer power and fury of the first two. But they didn't want to manipulate their muse, just for the sake of bowing to any outside pressures and/or deadlines. Already they had about twenty new studio rhythm tracks in the can, and scores of live cuts including never-before recorded chestnuts.

Although they were road-weary, early in 1972 they decided to lay down a few tunes at the odd random session, just to see what might emerge. It was a relative luxury to a group used to fighting tight deadlines. It fitted in with a new, looser recording policy which they'd agreed on just before the fourth album had been released. 'We just record on and off all the time,' Page explained. 'Every now and again we say, 'All right, let's go in and see what we can do.' Every session seems to be a relative statement on what you are at that point.'

The songs were coming together and evolving in a different manner too, now that Page and Jones had set up their own home studios where they were continually working up ideas and riffs. Plant was now father to two young children, and when life with them permitted, was poring through dusty old books on Celtic history and ancient civilisations. He was totally fascinated by his exploration of the centuries of conflict between the Celts and Saxons along the Welsh border, not far from his home town. 'The Battle of Evermore' had been a splendid evocation of his feelings about his common ancestry. 'You don't have to have too much of an imagination or a library full of books if you live there,' he claimed. 'It's still there. On a murky October evening, with the watery sun looking down on those hills over some old castle and unto the river, you have to be a real bimbo not to flash occasionally. Remember, I wasn't living in London. There you can be a fashion victim, but you can't feel like your average working man's Celt.'

Although Atlantic was eagerly pushing for an autumn 1972 fifth album release, the group refused to rush. The album would be ready when it was ready. They played Britain in a leisurely manner (for them) and then travelled to the other side of the planet for a series of successful dates in Australia and New Zealand – their one and only tour of that region.

In the early summer, they arranged to rent Stargroves, a country estate owned by Mick Jagger, where the Rolling Stones' mobile recording truck was in residence. 'When we first went down there,' Page said, 'we had no set ideas. We just recorded the ideas each one of us had at that particular time. It was simply a matter of getting together and letting it come out. I don't think we've ever had any shortages of material or stagnant periods. I've been writing a lot at home and I can try things out in my own studio setup. Lately I've been experimenting with chords a lot more and with unusual voicings. There are several ways in which material comes into the band – but it's always there.'

'The sound in Mick's place,' commented Plant, 'wasn't as good recording-wise as we'd been able to get in that weird place, Headley Grange, which we'd used for the previous album. That was a bit of a deterrent. Nevertheless we did get quite a bit done – the immediate stuff that gets laid down right away, even on some occasions with the vocals.'

Other tracks were captured on tape at the Electric Ladyland Studios in New York and at their old South London haunt, Olympic Sound in Barnes. Barnes, as I discovered on a visit to the studios on a damp April midnight, is a quiet little suburb complete with village green and a tranquil pond. Inside Olympic the pulsating whine of heavy rock filled the corridors – in studio one, England's hot new singles sensation Slade were putting the finishing touches to an album with obvious Led Zeppelin leanings. It sounded similar enough to push open the control room door and ask for Jimmy Page, who'd kindly extended an invitation to drop in and check things out.

Apologetically stumbling out of the Slade session, we were pointed in the direction of the other main studio which had recently been equipped with sixteen-track facilities prompting Led Zeppelin's return from the rural privacies of Headley Grange and Stargroves. As we opened the door below the buzzing red light, the shriek of Jimmy Page's guitar was easily recognisable. He was overdubbing a guitar part on a rhythm track, and doing our best to blend into the background – I was acutely aware of Jimmy's dislike of having anyone around when he recorded guitar tracks – we slithered into seats inside the darkened control room.

Pagey was in a small studio while John Paul Jones was sitting back beside the engineer in the control room. It didn't take long to feel a prevailing tension in the air – from his curt comments over the intercom, it became clear the sound Jimmy wanted wasn't forthcoming. The average Led Zeppelin fan would have had trouble recognising their guitar hero – he'd cut off most of his hair and the beard was also gone. By his own debonair standards, Pagey was looking relatively conservative in a dark red brushed-denim suit, a red embroidered shirt and brown sneakers.

It was an unforgettable scene. A giant Scully sixteen-track tape machine and a filing-cabinet-sized pile of Dolby noise reduction units were bathed in a green aura in one corner. In another corner, a roadie was boiling up a pot of tea. An unidentified person was leaning over the control board hustling bookings for the Stones' mobile studio to anyone who cared to listen.

After about fifteen minutes of fruitless experimentation, Page came into the control room, extending a quiet greeting. 'Hi man, I've got laryngitis – some latent deadly infection.' He went over to the tape operator and asked him to put up two of the new tracks for my benefit. In due course a tune called 'Dancing Days' came sparkling through the huge studio monitors – a cement-clouting sock-rocker with an infectious guitar riff. It was hard to remain cool in the presence of such persuasive power – one felt impelled to leap up and bounce around the room.

'Dancing Days' thundered to a climax and I was impressed. There was no comment from either Page or John Paul Jones, who were adrift in a sea of frustration. The second track was titled 'Slush' and it too rearranged the molecules of the control-room air as it slid through the tape playback heads. Without being asked, I conveyed my enthusiasm to the two Led Zeppelin members, and they appeared pleased if still distracted. It was April, and Page was (far too optimistically, as it turned out) looking towards a June release – delays such as the guitar sound problems on this evening only increased the deadline pressures.

Page went away to make arrangements to test some new guitars and amps the following morning, while manager Peter Grant expounded on the success of the recent Pacific tour. When Page returned, a roadie gave him a phone number concerning a rare guitar he'd been tracking down. He chatted quietly on the phone for a couple of minutes then suddenly hung up. 'Some dozy bloody bird,' he muttered. 'It must have been a wrong number.'

Facing the early hours of an unproductive studio session, Pagey decided to pack it in – it was a 90-minute drive back to his Pangbourne home. 'Well, see you later man,' he whispered, 'sorry there wasn't that much happening tonight. But that's how it goes.'

In parting I enquired about the health of Robert Plant. 'Oh Robert's all right – he's just had a baby. It's a boy. He's up in the wilds of Worcestershire now with his old lady,' Page related, drawing a wave of guffaws from the assemblage. Robert and Maureen had named their son Karac, after the Celtic hero Caractacus who'd waged a fierce and heroic battle against the Roman invasion in AD 43. When Caractacus was captured and taken back to Rome in chains, emperor Claudius was sufficiently impressed by his defiant courage to spare his life.

The following month engineer Eddie Kramer flew in from New York to work on further sessions at Stargroves. 'They were great, inspiring, wonderful,' Kramer reported. 'They were so confident, and so happy with what was going on. The general feeling was excellent.' Kramer particularly enjoyed working with John Bonham on those sessions. 'He was the easiest drummer I ever recorded. I had him in a room to himself, playing inside the bay window of a big conservatory with only three mikes on the drums. His sound was so great that it facilitated a monumental drum sound on record. Bonzo sounded that way because he hit the drums harder than anyone I'd ever met. He had this bricklayer's ability to bang the drum immensely hard. Yet he had a very light touch. In many ways he was the key to Led Zeppelin. You could work fast with him. The only reason Zep ever did retakes were the extremely tricky time sequences of most of the songs. Once Bonzo mastered his part, everything else would fall into place.'

Later in the summer, the group set off on their eighth tour of North America. Almost every gig sold out well in advance: the punters knew that Led Zeppelin above all delivered on stage. The set was now pushing two and a half hours, kicking off with 'Rock and Roll' and winding up with 'Whole Lotta Love'. Their stamina and endurance (both at playing during and after the show) were absolutely amazing to those who travelled on the road with them. Not only that, it was obvious to all that the band really did *enjoy* performing. Said Plant, 'I think that what we're doing now is what each one of us wants to do. I suppose people expect us to be a lot more arrogant than we are. There seems to be a label that's associated with music that's intense. Artists are expected to stand there looking as if they're stoned out of their minds. If I ever was to go out of my mind, I'm sure I wouldn't just stand there. So it's like a big play act and we mustn't act, otherwise we'll run away with ourselves like Jim Morrison did.

'Anyway it isn't just a teenybopper thing with swinging the mike around the place. There's something else going on. Even numbers that we've been doing for years can get changed every night. All sorts of different things can go down from any one of us before we finally get into the riff of a song. I'm sure the audience knows that it isn't just a contrived thing.'

By summer 1972 John Paul Jones in particular was really stretching out on stage and playing a variety of keyboard instruments including electric piano, organ and mellotron. 'I'd get bored playing bass guitar all the time,' he explained. 'I'm playing more and more organ now on stage and I want to concentrate on it even more. I don't mind being in the background. I wouldn't like to be out front playing like Jimmy. To be any sort of artist, you have to be a born exhibitionist. And I am, but not over anyone else in the business. I believe you should do what you have to do and if I'm bass – rather than try to play lead on bass and push myself – I prefer to put down a good solid bass line.'

As always – through thick and thin – Bonzo Bonham was having a ball behind the drums – and he was breaking fewer skins than in the old days when he could ill afford replacement costs. 'I really like to yell out when I'm playing,' he informed me. 'I yell like a bear to give it a boost. I like our act to be like a thunderstorm. But I haven't broken a skin in three tours. You can hit a drum hard if you take a short stab at it, and the skin will break easily. But if you let the stick just naturally come down, it looks as though you're hitting it much harder than you really are. I only let it drop with the force of my arm coming down. That snare skin has been on there for three tours.'

Bonham didn't hide his admiration for Page's ability. 'To me he's a great guitarist in so many fields. He's not just a group guitarist who plugs in and plays electric guitar. He's got interests in so many kinds of music. So many guitarists won't play anything but twelve-bar blues and they think that's it. Blues has to be pure, I suppose, but there are other things too. Some of the greatest musicians in the world have never played blues.'

For Bonzo himself, the joy of playing usually overcame the rigours of touring, although he had been known to go berserk out of frustration at being away from the home hearth. 'Sometimes it gets to be a bit wearing but that's only because I'm married with kids at home. I've never gotten pissed off with the actual touring. I enjoy playing – I could play every night. It's just the being away that gets you down sometimes.'

Nor was Pagey discouraged, despite his long history of low resistance to illness. 'Playing with these people has been fantastic,' he glowed. 'I've never played with such good musicians before in a group and I'm sure that we've all improved within ourselves.'

Broken guitar strings caused by climate variations can be changed, but it's hard to replace a voice. 'It can be difficult,' Plant concurred. 'You get off an air-conditioned plane into staggering heat, then into an air-conditioned car and then back into the heat – then into the air-conditioned hotel. That can affect your voice, especially in dry places where there's no humidity like Arizona and Texas. I almost got nodes on my vocal cords in Texas but what can you do? All singers have to worry about that, but you still can't restrain yourself. You can't walk out on stage and say, "Okay chaps, you'll have to change keys tonight because I can't cope." All the different ranges I reach come to me on stage because those things always come to you at your highest point. It just happens.'

Giving it all you've got every time was the Led Zeppelin credo – the show must go on regardless. When John Paul Jones came down with the flu in October 1972 during Zep's hugely successful second tour of Japan, the ever-ready Phil Carson filled in on bass and went down in performance history. There weren't many of us who got the chance to play on stage with Led Zeppelin.

Returning to England from the Far East, the lads finished off the fifth album and prepared for their most extensive-ever tour of the British Isles in November. Before it began, they carefully reconsidered the repertoire in their stage act. It was now running over three hours, unknown in contemporary rock. 'We really had to be quite mercenary,' Page explained, 'because the last American tour got really silly. There was something like twenty-eight dates in thirty days and we were playing an average of three hours per night – sometimes more than that. It was really doing us in. Now we'll have things from every LP, all the important tracks. It's really difficult because we did want it to just keep on growing but it became impossible time-wise. You can't introduce four or five new numbers without dropping something.'

Just to confound the cacophony of British critics, the entire 24-date UK concert tour was sold out in only four hours. 'A lot of artists give the little places a miss,' said Page, 'but we wanted to play for everybody.' Their strangest memory of the tour was their gig in the Welsh town of Aberystwyth, near the Bron-Y-Aur farm. 'It's a seaside resort,' Page said, 'and the main structure probably hasn't changed in the past two hundred years. We felt fairly warm vibes about the whole place and decided it would be a gas to play there. We booked this corporation-type venue which only held about eight hundred people which was a real folly, I suppose, but we wanted to play there anyhow. The audience was aghast – it was probably the first rock concert ever held there. As it turned out, the people had to sit down. They were regimented in these rows of seats. They were probably thinking "My God, what are we doing here?" After a while, we were thinking the same thing. The audience seemed really uptight about it. It's the first and only time it's ever happened to us. It was quite funny – you really need to have something like that. It's good to have a gig that strange and a bit un-nerving. But only one.'

The other significant event surrounding this low-key tour (by US standards) was the band's appointment of B.P. 'Beep' Fallon as personal British publicist. Led Zeppelin hadn't used a press agent since its pre-first-album days (so much for the critics' claim that the group had manipulated the music media on its way to the top) when former Beatles' publicist, Bill Harry (through a Mickie Most connection) did a few weeks of rudimentary promotion work. Fallon, who'd been associated with Marc Bolan and T. Rex, was handling publicity for the group, Silverhead (whose members included guitarist Robbie Blunt – later to be involved in Robert Plant's post-Zeppelin solo career – and singer, Michael des Barres) when he landed the gig representing Led Zeppelin. Actually the essential thrust of Fallon's brief was to keep the press away from the band – apart from the odd carefully considered exception. This arrangement was a distinct change from the previous Led Zeppelin office norm, where as a matter of policy media calls requesting interviews were totally ignored.

During the British tour, Fallon took the Zep party to a Silverhead gig in Birmingham. Later they all adjourned to Plant's place for an all-night jam session. Silverhead singer, Michael des Barres, was particularly entranced by Jimmy Page, and provides an interesting perspective on the period. 'Both Beep Fallon and Jimmy were very much alike,' Michael observed. 'They were both visionary imps. And they were in love with what I was in love with in rock and roll . . . the atmosphere of it all. It had nothing to do with the songs or the lyrics. The only really important thing was the right earring, the right album cover, and looking right getting off the plane and climbing out of the limo. That and being the most stoned person in the room. The vibe was everything and it still is. The attitude was everything.

'Jimmy was *incredible* because he was the classic rock star with the moated castle, the velvet clothes, the fabulous cars that he couldn't drive and the eighty thousand rare guitars. And, like an idiot, I was dabbling with the Aleister Crowley thing at the time. I used to go down to see Jimmy at Plumpton Place and he'd pull out Crowley's robes, Crowley's tarot deck, all of the Crowley gear that he'd collected. I thought, "This is great!" It was all so twisted and debauched, their whole thing. That's what Jimmy represented to me. I don't know what I represented to Jimmy. I always thought that Jimmy liked me because I happened to say "Rimbaud" at the right time.'

The fifth's album release date pushed back until spring, the band set about making some special plans for the next North American concert adventure, the ninth. It was decided to tie in the album release with the tour, but more notably, Grant and the band were giving serious consideration to the appointment of an American publicist, something they'd always vetoed in the past.

Led Zeppelin finally made themselves more accessible to a still-suspicious media. Commented Page, 'We just decided to do some interviews this time because I was curious to see what sort of questions people would ask after five years of Zeppelin.' Added Plant, 'The only way we could get through after so much silence was to get a liaison who would tell people that we were ready to talk and that we weren't going to throw anyone out of a window. We felt we warranted the coverage; we'd been complacent about publicity for so long.' Page added, 'One writer's opening question to me was, "Why

Robert Plant in 1975. *(Bob Gruen/Star File)*

Jimmy Page performing on violin bow guitar. *(Joe Sia/Star File)*

Robert Plant, as he typically appeared onstage. *(Bob Gruen/Star File)*

The way they were, Jimmy Page and Robert Plant. (*Joe Sia/Star File*)

Zeppelin at Madison Square Garden, 1977. *(Chuck Pulin/Star File)*

John Paul Jones as he appeared onstage in the early 1970s.
(Bob Gruen/Star File)

Jimmy Page taking a break. *(Vinnie Zuffante/Star File)*

Guitar great Les Paul with Jimmy Page. *(Vinnie Zuffante/Star File)*

are you giving me this interview in the first place, Mr Page?" They all seemed so shocked.'

The group also planned to institute some major changes in their on-stage act and the presentation thereof. The actual set line-up was rearranged, mainly to accommodate John Paul Jones's increasing use of assorted keyboard instruments. 'The main thing,' Page said, 'is that we want to go out there with a bit of fire, as opposed to warming up gradually. It just seemed to us that we hadn't been hard-hitting enough in the past. Changing a programme is a devil of a job because everyone in the audience wants to hear something different – that's the way the world's made up. We're very fortunate in that people are prepared to listen to whatever we want to do, without going berserk about the old favourites. They don't yell out for the chorus of "Whole Lotta Love" before we finish our second number. Obviously – if we're going to play a three-hour show – we're gonna play "Whole Lotta Love".'

Another significant change was their decision to use a more sophisticated lightshow. 'It's nothing phenomenal,' Page said, 'but it's just that we've never really had any lights before, so we thought it might be fun and add a little extra atmosphere. We'd been content to let the music speak for itself.' Added Plant, 'We felt that the denim jean trip had been there for a long time. We thought we'd see how far we can take what we wanted to take, so we just started going out on a limb. We've got some amazing ideas . . . they fit perfectly with the mood of the new songs and the excitement of the old ones.'

They also added an eight-foot revolving reflecting disc adjacent to the drum kit, suspended two mirrored balls from which to reflect spotlights above the stage, stocked up on dry-ice blowers for simulated fog, and several exploding cannon contraptions. Said Plant, 'At the end of "Stairway" we'll use those mirrored balls to spin light all ways, along with the revolving disc which is covered with broken glass. When you put the spotlights on all of this, the light beams everywhere and it should be like being in the middle of a diamond.' In the closing moments of each performance, they planned to turn the huge brass gong into a flaming Catherine wheel, set alight by Bonzo's tympani sticks. We were becoming more aware of the band's keen sense of drama.

The tour was scheduled to open on 4 May. The fifth album had been delayed with the usual jacket problems. 'They just couldn't get it right at the printers,' Pagey moaned. 'The colours were so different from what we had anticipated. The basic thing is a photograph in a collage and then some hand painting. We had to compromise because the sky started to look like an ad for Max Factor lipstick. And the children looked as if they'd been turned purple from the cold.'

Houses of the Holy hit the street on 28 March. The only obvious connection between 'Stairway to Heaven' and the new album was the infusion of Celtic mysticism in Plant's lyrics. First introduced in earlier milestones such as 'Thank You', 'Ramble On', 'Going to California' and 'The Battle of Evermore', the romantic influence comes through again clearly in 'The Rain Song' and 'No Quarter' in particular. Along with the hot rockers 'Houses' displayed a certain studied gentility, glimpses of green fields and ancient stone walls, a new maturity underpinned by stunning instrumental virtuosity.

'There are a lot of reflections of the seasons and the weather and the country,' Page agreed. And mysticism? 'Yes, well that has been present from the second album onwards,' he said, 'mainly because it was something that we did well and it pointed in a specific direction. "The Rain Song" was sort of a little infatuation that I had. I had quite an experience and the result is in those vocals and in the lyrics.'

'The Song Remains the Same', on the other hand, took inspiration from the band's other great composing source – its touring. 'It was about five one morning at Stargroves,' Plant said, 'and I'd always wanted to do a song in the style of the Elvis impersonators like Ral Donner who I love. The old C, A Minor, F and G chord sequence stuff, just like the Ricky Nelson records. Jimmy started playing a sequence like that and Jonesy put in a sort of blue-beat bass line and Bonzo did a straight drum thing – it sounded great.

'Every time I sing the song, I picture the fact that I've been round and round the world and at the root of it all, there's a common denominator for everybody. The common denominator is just what makes it good or bad – whether it's Led Zeppelin or Alice Cooper. I am proud of the lyrics – somebody pushed my pen for me, I think. There are a lot of catalysts which really bring out these sorts of things – working with the group on the road, living where I live, having the friends I've got, my children, my animals.

' "D'Yer Mak'er" was another one that just came together straight away at Stargroves, even the creamy vocals. Other times we would have backing track tapes worked out and somebody would cry out "we've got no bloody lyrics". Some of the tapes would be quite intricate and I couldn't sing along instantly. So I had to take them away and listen on my own. Then a week later I'd come back with "Over the

Hills" or "The Crunge". "The Crunge" was amazing because Bonzo and I were just going to go over to the studio and talk Black Country stuff through the whole thing. Then it just evolved when I was at the end of my tether.'

'The Crunge' had started out as a tribute to James Brown with echoes of Otis Redding. 'Bonzo and I were both James Brown freaks,' Jones said. 'We used to play his records all the time on the tour plane. It wasn't terribly cool to listen to James Brown then, especially around the FM underground stations, where they didn't really like black music at all, which was a real shame. But on stage we'd get into funk grooves quite a lot. Bonzo incidentally had very broad listening tastes. When we weren't listening to James Brown or Otis Redding, he might be listening to Joni Mitchell or Crosby, Stills, Nash & Young. Bonzo was a great lover of songs.'

The title of 'D'Yer Mak'er' comes from a traditional Cockney joke where a fellow says to a friend, 'My wife just went on vacation.' 'Jamaica?' enquires the friend. 'No, she went of her own accord."

Several other Stargroves tracks were considered unsuitable for the fifth album (including, strangely enough, its title song) and were set aside for later use. This includes 'Black Country Woman' and 'The Rover' and several untitled rhythm tracks.

Plant provided a thoughtful perspective on the fifth album in a 1990 interview. '*Houses of the Holy* was really a very inspired time. The material is very much to the point − it's very focused and strong. I think "The Crunge" was great. "The Rain Song" was really good. There was a lot of imagination − I much prefer it to the fourth album. It's much more varied and it has a flippance to it with "D'Yer Mak'er" which showed up later in the *In Through the Out Door* album with stuff like "Hot Dog", and "Candy Store Rock" on *Presence* which represented me trying to be Ral Donner or Elvis or whatever.

'I think it was a very successful time and on tracks like "D'Yer Mak'er" we were going for an ultimate drum sound. There was a record by Dee Dee Warwick called "Foolish Fool" [1969, Mercury Records] which had been a minor hit in Detroit. We tried to get the drums to sound the same as on her record. She was Dionne Warwick's sister, and hopefully still is. *Houses* was a great record and we were really proud of it. It was a great time. Plus it was quite smug that we'd done "Houses of the Holy" as a song but didn't release it until *Physical Graffiti*. It was one of those usual twig English schoolboy tricks.'

Two weeks after *Houses of the Holy* came out, *Billboard* reviewed it *under* the Jackson 5's eminently forgettable *Skywriter* LP. 'The heavy beat boys of British rock have produced a standard package of intense rock material utilising their staunchest abilities to praise the beat and bury the melody. One recalls the era of psychedelic music on several of the tracks and a sense of parody in the tune "D'Yer Mak'er", with its recall of 1950s music and splitting syllables.'

Such patronising putdowns aside, *Houses of the Holy* roared into the charts that same week at number 85, while the fourth album moved up to number 120 after 72 weeks. *Houses* went to number 10 second week, then hit number one after the tour started, 12 May, knocking off no less a perennial personage than Elvis (with whom the band would become acquainted before much longer). The following week *Houses* held on to number one, ahead of the Beatles with their first monumental greatest hits collections, *Beatles 1967–70* and *Beatles 1962–66*, at numbers two and three respectively.

The first single from *Houses of the Holy* came out in May and it was an unexpected choice – 'Over the Hills and Far Away', a fascinating track but hardly typical Top-40 fodder. On 2 June, *Billboard* declared (under reviews of singles by the Osmonds, Vicki Lawrence, Johnny Nash and Gladys Knight), 'A Spanish classical guitar flavoured solo begins this fine production. The lengthy intro sets the stage for Jimmy Page's [sic] vocal which works in concert with the guitar sound. Then the whole explosive force of the band breaks in and the mood changes with rock and fuzz sounds.'

'Over the Hills' reached the Hot-100 chart on 23 June at number 87 but the uncompromising nature of the track restricted airplay and therefore any real chart success. Atlantic persevered with the possibility of AM exposure, not that the album really needed it. Early in October they issued a cut which many observers felt had been the most obvious first choice, the biting parody of popdom, 'D'Yer Mak'er'. It became the band's most successful single since 'Whole Lotta Love', remaining on the charts for sixteen weeks and peaking at number twenty. The fourth album meanwhile – aided by a series of box office sensations on the tour – kept on climbing for the second time and reached the Top-20.

It was intriguing to check out the media response to *Houses of the Holy* – once again the poison pens had attacked it with swords flailing and critical sensibilites sadly lacking. Admittedly of all the Led Zeppelin albums this one resists the most superficial understanding or even appreciation. Page once cannily observed, 'It usually takes people a year to really catch up to our albums.' But despite its density and diversity, the pasting the fifth album received in the press seems totally unjustified. Samples: 'This album seems to have less guts than earlier Led Zeppelin material' *South Wales Echo*; 'Awful' *PRM*; 'For the most part, mediocre' *Rock*; 'It would appear that the boys have calmed down' *Circus*; and 'They've been going downhill ever since the first perfect outing' *Charleston Gazette*.

One of the genuine surprises in the *Houses of the Holy* clipping collection at the Led Zeppelin London headquarters was the ridiculous reaction of an old supporter, *Melody Maker*'s Christ Welch, who stated tartly, 'The lack of firm direction is all too apparent. The writing seems to be a compromise between more spaced-out ideas and heavy riffs without ever getting to grips with either.'

The *Rolling Stone* review approximated what the group had cynically expected: 'Beck Bogert and Appice, Black Sabbath, the Groundhogs, Robin Trower – the list is long and they all fare musically better than the Zep because they stick to what they do best. Page and friends should similarly realise their limitations and get back to playing the blues-rock that moves mountains. Until they do, Led Zeppelin will remain a Limp Blimp.' To which *Playboy* magazine hollered, 'The blimp's a long way from limp.'

Many media people appeared to be missing the point and there was no better example of the malady than the response to 'D'Yer Mak'er'. Although the track had obviously been recorded tongue-in-cheek for spontaneous amusement, several critics seized on the song as a sure sign that Led Zeppelin's creativity was buckling at the seams. Some even assumed it was a supremely serious Led Zeppelin attempt to duplicate or re-create the reggae sound, which demonstrates the profound depth of media ignorance.

'It's a cod pop tune that is not worthy of them,' wailed Chris Welch. *Rolling Stone* really tore into it, stating the band 'shows little understanding of what reggae is about – [the song is] obnoxiously heavy-handed and totally devoid of the native form's sensibilities.'

The group was literally astounded at the reaction to their joke and wasted no time in saying so. 'It's just a send-up,' retorted Page, 'and if people can't suss that out on a superficial level, then obviously you can't expect them to understand anything else on the album. It beats me – but I don't give a damn. Obviously it's not reggae. I personally see it as more of a 1950s thing – that's how it started out anyway, just a laugh.'

None of it mattered really – a flea gnashing its teeth on the hide of a rhinoceros – as the band prepared for the largest American tour of its career. It would cover 33 cities from May to July, with the customary halfway break. Concert receipts alone were expected to top $4.5 million, and Peter Grant revealed to the London *Financial Times* that the band would gross $30 million during that year. It would be the biggest American tour by a British act in the history of rock.

To maintain the pace – and facilitate tiring travel schedules and public airport scrutiny – Peter Grant chartered a converted Boeing 720B jet called the Starship (it was owned by a former producer of *The Monkees* TV series). Revamped into a 40-seat luxury liner, the Starship boasted a bar, video screens, bedrooms with fake fireplaces, showers, lounge chairs, and an organ. It certainly wasn't cheap to charter but it enabled the camp to set up base at a preferred hotel in one city while commuting daily to concerts in nearby cities.

Just before *Houses of the Holy* reached the holiest position on the charts in mid-May, Led Zeppelin launched the 1973 extravaganza at the Atlanta Braves stadium – the same hallowed turf which the Beatles had plundered almost eight years earlier. The Liverpool lads had drawn 33,000 fans, the largest crowd ever in that venue or at any other concert in the history of the state of Georgia. A few hours before Led Zeppelin's performance, Pagey slipped into the empty stadium to check out the vibe. 'It was quite incredible,' he said. 'There was all this equipment – even more than they'd used at Woodstock – on a huge great stage. And I looked around the huge arena and I thought, "My God, there's only four of us and all of these people are coming just to see us." It tended to make one feel a bit nervy.'

Page returned to the hotel as people began to file into the stadium. By the time the band hit the stage in nervous splendour, a total of 49,236 raging fans were crammed into its length and breadth for a total gate gross of $246,180. 'They were really warm in Atlanta,' Page noted later, 'and obviously we react to the warmth of the audience.'

Peter Grant, while flabbergasted, took it in his stride. He had even greater glories flying in the vapour trail of his stimulated brain. He escorted newly appointed American publicist, Danny Goldberg, to the upper deck of the stadium. As the band promenaded through a sizzling set Grant pointed to traffic on the nearby freeway and briefed his new promo man, 'Those are the people I want you to reach for us.' Not that they could've found room in the stadium anyway. Then and later, Goldberg's services were superfluous. A band of this enormous stature clearly didn't really need any publicising.

Led Zeppelin had shattered the Beatles' crowd record at the same venue with 16,000 bums to spare – admittedly aided by the unprecedented decision by stadium officials to allow grass field seating in addition to the stands. Atlanta's Mayor Sam Cassell was among the audience and probably hit the nail right on the head when he was reported to have stated, 'This is the biggest thing to hit Atlanta since the premiere of *Gone With the Wind*.' Atlanta was only a passing portent of what would continue to unfold as the world's most popular rock band underlined its mass market, mainstream appeal – with or without a publicist.

Next night the band moved on to Tampa, Florida, where they obliterated the Beatles' all-time concert attendance and gate gross records. In 1965, 55,000 screaming fans had paid $301,000 to catch the stars of Beatlemania at Shea Stadium in New York. In Tampa, a city of less than half a million, a capacity crowd of 56,800 punters paid out $309,000 (at less than six bucks a ticket) to experience Led Zeppelin. It was the largest concert attendance for a single group in the history of the United States, proof yet again of the band's domination of the live rock scene.

Promoters claims that an additional 6,000 gate crashers had obtained entry to the grounds. Local police estimated the crowd *outside* the stadium at one point reached as high as 90,000 with eager but ticketless fans gathering. During the memorable concert 700 doves were released and the audience responded by lighting thousands upon thousands of matches and lighters, which Page described as 'like a galaxy'. Some 10,000 tickets to the Tampa concert had been sold in Miami, a three and a half hour drive distant, and Miami Beach Mayor Chuck Hall offered the group the keys to his city – a remarkable turnaround for a council which not long before had considered banning rock concerts altogether.

Sound quality at the Tampa concert was reported to be excellent from most vantage points in the stadium. 'We used four systems of 3,000 watts each, which is more equipment than they used at Woodstock,' Plant proclaimed proudly. 'I tried it out before the concert – alone in the empty stadium – and it sounded like the hammer of the gods.'

The next day Plant admitted, 'It was a real surprise. Tampa is the last place you'd expect to see nigh on 60,000 people. I think it was the biggest thrill I've ever had. There were just the four of us and then all those people as far as the eye could see. People were on rooftops miles away.' Those who witnessed the event would never forget it. Pagey told one reporter, 'We were almost out of our minds at the reception we got.' The *Tampa Times* described it as 'the biggest boogie since Woodstock'.

The *Financial Times* took pains – in view of its economically literate readership – to indicate that the band didn't pocket *all* the box office receipts. Pointing out expenses were 'vast', the paper detailed that it cost $14,000 for stage construction, $7,500 for the sound system copies at $50 per man, plus a staff of road crew, private plane rental and assorted trucking costs. Led Zeppelin certainly didn't stint on essential costs but that historic performance on the Tampa Stadium went down in pop annals as three of the most lucrative hours in show-biz history.

The group and its entourage of 30 sound and lighting men, stagehands, security guards and roadies, packed up and moved on to Jacksonville, where long-time Led Zeppelin booster, Lisa Robinson, raved, 'There were no intermissions, no waiting, no tuning up, no bullshit. Just music. Just gorgeous rock and roll at its most desperate.'

The highly motivated band kept on rocking and the box office records kept on rolling and tumbling. In Texas (where Pagey was reportedly impressed in a big way by the fact that rich local groupies hired their own private plane to follow the Starship across the skies), the band sold out two successive nights at the Dallas Memorial Auditorium (10,000 people) and the Fort Worth Convention Centre (13,500). Danny Goldberg's mandatory press release pointed out that no other artist(s) in history had sold out both venues back-to-back, the two cities being a mere 30-minute drive apart.

In New Orleans – where the entourage frolicked with drag queens – Atlantic hosted a grand reception for the band featuring soul food and the *crème de la crème* of local rock legends, artists the band worshipped such as Ernie K. Doe, Professor Longhair, Frankie Ford, the Meters Snooks Eaglin and Allen Toussaint.

It was triumph upon triumph – a calvacade of amazing ups for the band, dancing high on the waves of rock history it was making. Robert Plant let slip to Lisa Robinson, 'I like to think that people go away knowing that we're pretty raunchy and we really do a lot of the things that people say we do. This is what we're getting over – it's the *goodness*. It's not the power, revolution, put your fists in the air. I like them to go away feeling the way you do after a good chick, satisfied and exhausted. Some nights I just look out there and I want to fuck the whole first row.'

In San Francisco – long a Led Zeppelin stronghold – the band drew 49,034 patrons to Kezar Stadium for a gross of $325,000, beating the attendance record for California set by Grand Funk Railroad two years earlier with 45,000 people. In Los Angeles, some 36,000 tickets for two gigs at the Forum were snapped up within two hours, easily beating a previous record held by the Rolling Stones. In the course of less than a week, Led Zeppelin had played to more than 100,000 Californians and history had again been made. Great copy for the media, but what really mattered was the power and pull of the Led Zeppelin live show.

The only mishap was an accidental injury to Page's right hand on a fence at LA Airport. 'It was a strained tendon,' he said, 'but it was in that area that's crucial for playing guitar. It was such a stupid thing really, but in five gigs, I fucked it up for five weeks. I had to have all manner of treatment and injections. Think about it this way – after playing gigs for a solid month, I was only allowed to play for ten minutes a day and even then the injury wasn't improving. It was a totally horrifying experience, but somehow it all fell together.'

The first leg of the tour zoomed to a close in LA on 3 June, 'a magic gig' in Plant's words. The time had obviously arrived for some royal raving. Hollywood has always – rather too gleefully – expected the worst from a Led Zeppelin visit and this time around, that's precisely what was provided by tour manager Richard Cole and his coked-out cohorts. The band's reputation as hell-raising loonies had been growing as rapidly as their album sales. Looning, of course, is an ancient diversion for men on the march (even Caesar's centurions are believed to have indulged from time to time). Now in the rock era it's generally recognised as a pent-up pressure-releasing activity which British rock groups have honed down to a fine art. In the 1970s, it grew into such oneupmanship that many American hotel chains made special arrangements for certain groups to be housed in rooms due for re-decorating. It saved the costs of dismantling them for the renovators.

Phil Carson had a ready explanation. 'It's all pretty harmless really – just like schoolboy pranks. Some people may find it difficult to understand but high spirits build up in a group on the road. So the idea is just to embarrass someone innocently. But of course that becomes increasingly difficult because people tend to get less and less easily embarrassed as time goes by. Gone are the days when nicking someone's swimming trunks at the rooftop pool could cause embarrassment. I mean, you just get out of the pool and walk around until you get your trunks back. Now elaborate schemes are sometimes engineered, but often they're difficult to relate later – you had to have been there. It's all relative you know. Room service trays and TV sets have a habit of disappearing out of hotel windows and they're not really worth even talking about. That's normal procedure.'

This time around, the Led Zeppelin camp turned the entire ninth floor of the Continental Hyatt House on Sunset Strip into a rock and roll palace. Even by the band's standards, it was a monumental mayhem exercise presided over by Richard Cole. 'You know how it is, Yorke,' Peter Grant laughingly bellowed to me over a bracket of female giggles on the phone from palace headquarters. 'We always like to put on something a little special for the LA crowd. Come on down here, ya cunt!' Summoning up all my powers of restraint (no mean endeavour in those liberal days of youthful excess) I declined the passionate invitation and set plans to team up with the band at the Madison Square Garden, New York, finale of the 1973 tour.

LA music papers reported the lads were 'in good destructive form' and had allegedly heaved a table off the balcony of their suite as a reprisal against someone who said they couldn't toss liquor glasses down into an open Lincoln convertible in the parking lot. Hearing that Page wanted to try out a new model Japanese motorcycle, Richard Cole obtained one and rode it back to the hotel, through the lobby, into the elevator and along the top floor corridor to Pagey's suite. 'It was all quite straightforward,' insisted Phil Carson. There were even scooter and wheelchair races, and cricket matches, along that war zone corridor.

Ever conscious of the media beat-up they'd received from the Fleet Street gang, Grant and the band agreed to allow a handful of selected London journos to fly out at various points in the tour in order for the British public to get some sense of the extraordinary American success of Led Zeppelin. It was a calculated gamble but it would pay off in ways that perhaps even Grant hadn't foreseen. The London *Sun*'s pop culture 'colour' writer, Australian-born Bob Hart, was selected to compile a 'looning report'. His on-the-spot Hollywood piece is regarded as a classic. 'Led Zeppelin, the wild men of rock, have their own particular ways of escaping from the rigours of exhausting tours. There is a lurid tale of a young lady who is said to have been whipped with a live octopus. John Paul Jones later told me, 'I don't think that's entirely true. As far as I can remember, it was a dead shark!'

The lurid and nearly legendary Led Zeppelin Shark Episode dates back to 1969 when the band was staying at the harbourside Edgewater Inn in Seattle. The year earlier, on tour with singer Terry Reid and supporting the Moody Blues, Richard Cole had discovered that it was possible to rent tackle and bait in the lobby and do a spot of fishing from your room window. What you did with your catch was up to you – Cole took that a bit too literally. There have been a myriad of reports about precisely what did take place during the infamous Shark Episode – I've heard several varying first-hand accounts. In his most recent rendition of the terrible tale, instigator/angler Richard Cole swears, 'The *true* shark story was that it wasn't even a shark. It was a red snapper and the chick happened to be a fucking redheaded broad with a ginger pussy. Bonzo was in the room, but I did it. Mark Stein of the Vanilla Fudge filmed the whole thing. And she *loved* it. It was like "You'd like a bit of fucking, eh? Let's see if *your* red snapper likes *this* red snapper. It was the nose of the fish, and that girl must have come twenty times. I'm not saying the chick wasn't drunk . . . or that any of us weren't drunk. But it was nothing malicious or harmful, no way! No one was ever hurt. She might have been hit by a shark a few times for disobeying orders, but she didn't get hurt.'

Three years later, Led Zeppelin returned to the Edgewater in Seattle and tossed all of their TV sets into the sea. Settling up for room and damage, the hotel manager mentioned that *he'd* always wanted to heave a TV out of a window himself. Peter Grant looked him up and down, peeled off a $500 bill and guffawed, 'Have one on us!'

According to Bob Hart, now doubling as a columnist and marketing director with a Brisbane, Australia daily paper, not all of the touring hi-jinks were quite so harmless or innocent. 'That 1973 Starship tour was an absolutely amazing occasion, probably the peak of the entire looning period,' he recalled recently. 'I flew in with a journo from the London *Times* and what we found waiting for us in LA was pretty extraordinary. We saw a great deal that we *couldn't* write about – the world wasn't ready for those things back in those days.

'The band's behaviour was quite remarkable. I had the feeling that some of the stuff was staged for our benefit. They had the right instincts in terms of publicity. They realised that if they could become notorious, they could cross over from being a great rock and roll band to being the biggest band in the history of mankind. I think that someone at Atlantic convinced Grant that a little notoriety wouldn't be a totally bad thing. They knew in those days that we couldn't write about the illegal stuff, but that wasn't my game, anyway. I was writing about the humour of the situation and some of it was incredibly and outrageously funny.

'However we were appalled by a lot of the things we saw. It was mainly driven by cocaine. Led Zeppelin was a band of great wealth, even at this point, but also a band of incredible decadence. I think that degree of decadence had a lot to do with the amount of coke that was going down. I saw quantities of coke on that tour that were truly remarkable. There was an English girl I'll call Jane who travelled on the tour and she was the coke lady. This was so that nobody ever carried or touched coke. You'd just call for Jane and she'd apply the business. In fact it was one of my favourite little moments of decadence – watching Jane's little routine.

'When she was summoned, she would apply the coke with the little finger of her right hand. Then she would follow that up with a little touch of cherry snuff from Smith's Snuff Shop on the Charing Cross Road in London . . . this being to eliminate the nasty medicinal odour. Then as a final touch, she'd dab the nostrils with a little touch of Dom Perignon 1966. It was the signature drink of the tour.

'I was a bit of a wine enthusiast even then – I was in awe of this vintage. But they weren't: they used to shake it up and squirt it in people's faces. And they'd drink it with orange juice. It was a high-end champagne, the equivalent of a hundred dollars a bottle, and they went through it by the caseload.

'A lot of the wild behaviour was instigated by Richard Cole, the roadies and the entourage, but some of the time, there was direct involvement of the band. They were a real contrast in characters. Bonham was obviously one extreme, but Jimmy and Robert weren't opposed to what was going on. They had a slightly more elevated approach. Bonzo was the animal of the team, the typical drummer. At the other end fo the spectrum you had John Paul Jones and he was extraordinary. While all of this activity was going on along the ninth floor, Jones had a deal where he didn't even stay on the same floor as the rest of the band. There had to be at least two floors between them. He'd sit up in his room playing little medieval reed instruments.

'The way they treated some of the girls was quite appalling. Certainly the girls were predatory, they were into it and they weren't innocent. It was the era of the Sunset Strip groupie, impossibly thin and pretty and talented little girls, most of them about fourteen or fifteen. The girls would be camped at the hotel. They'd come up in the lift and be snatched out and treated fairly abominably for half an hour. Then the security guards would be called to come and throw them out. There was a lot of abuse of people, not necessarily by the band itself. In fact, usually not. But it was happening.'

As it turned out, the hotel antics were just a warm-up for the grand slam of Hollywood gross-out decadence. Phil Carson picks up the pieces: 'It was Bonzo's birthday and a big party was organised by the owner of a local radio station [KROQ's Gary Bookasta]. When we arrived, the porno film *Deep Throat* was showing in a video machine (both being rare items in a typical 1973 LA household). It was *that* sort of scene. Later on George Harrison (then riding the charts with "Give Me Love, Give Me Peace on Earth") tottered in with his [ex] wife, Patti Boyd. When the time came for Bonzo to cut this giant birthday cake they'd made for him, George rushed over and lifted off the top tier and tossed it at Bonzo. John wasn't having any of that of course, so he picked up the second tier and heaved it after a fast-disappearing Harrison. It caught him right between the shoulders, a beautiful shot. Not long afterwards, Bonzo heaved George in the pool and Patti Boyd followed. Everybody but Peter Grant ended up in the pool. It was all innocent fun and anyway, the Beatles had been into that sort of thing themselves for the past ten years.' When George and Patti left the party wrapped in blankets, George said he hadn't had so much fun in years.

George did a bit of hanging out backstage at Led Zeppelin gigs (where he was always royally welcomed) and was reported to have asked a roadie about the opening act and the intermission. Told that Led Zeppelin used neither device, Harrison is supposed to have retorted, 'Fuck me, when the Beatles toured we were on for twenty-five minutes and could get off in fifteen!'

And so the rampage unfolded. Led Zeppelin's looning tales from that 1973 tour could sustain a volume or two. It was just that sort of tour. A bit wilder (and to some, a bit wickeder) than any before. By the band or anyone. 'Mild barbarians was how we were once described,' Page grinned, tongue-in-cheek, 'and I really can't deny it.'

But it was the music that really counted (no matter how barbaric the offstage behaviour) and in this arena it can't be denied that Led Zeppelin excelled. Excelled beyond all expectation. 'The quality of their playing,' Bob Hart said, 'was mind-boggling. The San Francisco gig at Kezar Stadium was really a peak in my mind.

'We flew up in a small jet from LA about mid-afternoon. It was a very interesting flight in a lot of ways. Backstage was an incredible scene. There were huge barbecues burning – it was the best backstage area setup I'd ever seen and this was only the outer backstage area. We were quickly shown into another backstage area at the end. We wandered up to promoter Bill Graham's office and he showed the guys to another little room where there was a table bearing a large pile of a certain white substance. It was mind-boggling.

'The band allowed me to stand on stage while they played and it was an absolutely amazing experience. There were almost 50,000 people there – but no violence of any kind. It was 'Frisco in 1973 – the audience were out of their trees. They'd been sitting out there for two hours listening to Roy Harper, an extraordinary choice as opening act. The audience was bored shitless, half-asleep, stoned out of their minds, ready to rock. They were painted, tattooed, naked, God knows what.

'I don't know why Led Zeppelin had Roy Harper there – he's totally nuts. It was hard to tell just what San Francisco thought of this eccentric Englishman – sitting on a chair, playing acoustic guitar in front of 50,000 people and singing songs about cricket! When Zeppelin came on, it was a tremendous gig, literally awesome, one of the finest performances I'd ever seen. The sense of the occasion was just incredible from the stage. I think people tend to forget the impact of John Bonham. That drive and that incredible attack that he gave them. He was almost knocking people over in the first five rows with his ferocity. He was in an absolute lather on stage – you could have driven a nail between his shoulder blades and he wouldn't have known.'

Bob Hart's report for the *Sun* was edited down, and much of his positive comments about their music were discarded in favour of the more tabloid-appealing tales of their decadence. As a result, Bob Hart never found himself again invited on tour with Led Zeppelin. But his exclusive reporting of the Shark Episode had assured his immortality in the field of rock and roll reporting.

When part one of the 1973 madness finally drew to a sanity-saving close, the band took a month off to rest in Hawaii. By 6 July, they were back into it again, refreshed and rejuvenated. They blasted off part two in Chicago, then moved on through the mid-West. In Pittsburgh they drew 38,000 delighted fans, eclipsing Alice Cooper's record of the year before.

And thus the most dramatically successful tour of North America by any rock act since the Beatles eventually tornadoed to an end with three consecutive evenings of Led Zeppelin at Madison Square Garden in New York City. All 80,000 tickets had been sold weeks earlier. On the plane down to the Big Apple from Toronto, I read in *Rolling Stone* that Robert Plant had said, 'Sometimes me and Pagey have been tempted to stop all the loud stuff and do an Incredible String Band kind of thing, believe it or not.' The comment was exceedingly anti-climactic, but the concerts would be absolutely electric. It was indeed the very peak of Led Zeppelin's performing career.

I'd held back my run at joining the 1973 Starship tour until the finale. As increasingly enthusiastic reports flooded in from all over the continent, I knew that I wasn't going to be disappointed. When Peter Grant finally decided that this tour should be captured on celluloid for posterity, there were only a few days left. Back in England and given three days' notice, director Joe Massot scurried up a crew and headed for Manhattan. The filming saga (which would subsequently provide most of the concert footage for *The Song Remains the Same*) only added to the overall drama of the New York wind-down.

Arriving at La Guardia airport, I found the Big Apple abuzz with Zep-mania. The lobby of the Drake Hotel on Madison Avenue was jammed with people, most of them clutching cameras. Shown up to my room in the Led Zeppelin party, I quickly joined the entourage and watched the lads finally gearing down at the conclusion of the largest rock touring crusade of all time. Their energy was in subconscious overdrive: like hyped-up marathon runners, they were storming to the finish line of this mammoth ordeal which they both loved and hated. Just completing the course would be a major achievement – the real celebrations would come later back in England.

Hard living doesn't take long to inflict its toll, particularly when life is lived with the coke-fuelled tenacity and unbridled passion that had dominated this 33-city rampage. But for all the atmosphere of a supercharged locomotive thundering down on its final destination, the air was also filled with a more delicate feeling of anti-climax. Everyone knew it had to stop soon – or their bodies would collapse under the strain.

In the next day or two, I had abundant cause to ponder how they'd even managed to endure and survive the rampant ravages (self-induced and otherwise) of the past few weeks. It was absolutely extraordinary. The centre of the Led Zeppelin camp – for part-time insiders such as myself plus sundry other hangers-on – was tour manager Richard

Cole's suite. It resembled a scene from a Fellini movie, a true bonfire of Manhattan music vanities, a gathering of assorted adventurers attempting to gain access to the inner sanctum of Led Zeppelin. Hustling was on the horn this steamy summer afternoon on Madison, where the hustle had been honed down to a minor art form during the course of this century by countless ad agencies. Something, everything, seemed so appropriate – the setting, the sensibilities, the sequence of events, the scene at large.

The rock and roll sultan, England's most outrageous reprobate, Richard Cole, was a shadow of his usual ebullient self. Encamped in his own private suite – his inner bedroom the 'special' backstage area in this hotel scenario – Cole was guzzling Burmese beer, racing here and there like a cut snake, stroking the odd journalist or disc jockey before shuffling them on down the line and back out of the goddamn hotel, pecking the odd pair of pretty lips, entertaining special fans, fire-eaters, intructing members of the road crew, handling requests of every imaginable kind. Publicity flacks and music-biz phonies fluttered about, vainly trying to appear essential to the event, plastic floss floating from their frostly lips.

Considering the context, old King Cole was coping rather well, despite the obvious signs of advanced fatigue. The phone never stopped ringing. The person nearest the phone – becoming an instant part of the action – would answer, suss out the caller and relay a message to Cole who would bellow his response from across the room, or from his adjacent bedroom where he would periodically repair for the odd knee trembler.

'No, sorry, we don't wanna buy any fuckin' antique cars . . . no, tell her we don't want any fuckin' chicks tonight, no matter how fuckin' well weird they are . . . no, I don't have the faintest fuckin' idea where John Paul Jones might be . . . no, sorry but we've got no spare tickets for the gig tonight, not even for the press – tell him he should've checked earlier, the dumb cunt . . . no, Robert Plant *definitely* can't do a live phone interview now with a New York FM station – he's fuckin' well exhausted and he'll be flat out playing the gig tonight . . . no, Jimmy Page doesn't want to buy Aleister Crowley's last fuckin' will and testament . . . no, we don't want a fuckin' drag queen parade after the show tonight . . . no, we do *not* need any blow . . . no, we haven't heard of any more death threats on Jimmy . . . no, we don't have any fuckin' backstage passes for a chick with a fuckin' trick pussy – tell her to call up again on the next tour . . . no, Jimmy isn't looking for super-pure smack . . . no, we can't leave any fuckin' tickets for George Harrison because we know he's gone back to fuckin' England last week . . . no, we don't need a psychic magician to open the show tonight . . . no, the lads can't write a song for anybody . . . yes, we'd love Ronnie Hawkins and his wife to come to the concert tonight as our guests – tell him to pick up the tickets from the hotel reception after six p.m. . . . no, we can't possibly do a benefit for the orphans of Mongolia – the boys are so fucked they're about to drop – tell 'em to write to us at the office in London . . . no, Peter Grant won't do an interview with the *Daily News* or any other fuckin' newspaper . . . no, tell them to talk to Danny fuckin' Goldberg if they can find him . . . no, we don't want to go to a fuckin' fag party after the show – aw fuck, leave the bloody phone off the fuckin' hook, I've just about had it for one bloody afternoon, fuckin' hell.'

All this and more in the tiny time capsule of fifteen frantic minutes. From past experience, I could feel Cole's wick of patience burning shorter. Suddenly he came stumbling out of his room and demanded that a roadie clear the suite – he needed time alone to get his act together, take care of details for the final performance of a tour which had cemented his own reputation as a looner and hell-raiser. 'Not you, darling,' he interjected into the room evacuation, 'I wanna talk to you about something.' Cole finally managed to prune his guests by about 50 per cent, leaving only staff personnel and very special friends, who beamed at the privilege. Finally sinking back into the chintz sofa for some rare light relief, Cole muttered, 'Jesus fuckin' Christ, I've never seen so many bloody people to take care of in my whole fuckin' life. We've already got six limos lined up to get us to the gig and someone says we need more. Where are all these fuckin' people coming from? What the fuckin' hell is happening?'

A light tap on the door and Jimmy Page enters, white and waif-like, clearly physically shattered. I'd never seen him look so gaunt or forlorn. 'We're all terribly worn out,' he sighs, shaking my hand and sinking into the sofa with a groan. 'To tell you the truth, I went past the point of no return physically quite a while back. But now I think I've gone past the mental point, too. I've only kept going by functioning automatically. You know, someone asked me the other day – I don't remember where it was – about what songs we were doing on stage now, and I just couldn't remember, I really couldn't. It seems like so long since we've had a break – in fact I simply can't remember when we were *not* working. We've kept up a ridiculous pace. Plus I had all these problems with my hand. I was really terrified that I wouldn't be able to get it together when we resumed the second part of the tour. It was touch and go right up until the last moment.' I sympathised with Jimmy and told him so. He nodded grimly. When he turned to talk to Richard Cole, I examined his condition more closely. It was easy to see that he wasn't joking about exceeding the point of no return.

He was in a drugged stupor. If – as singer Michael des Barres had claimed – Jimmy aspired to be the most stoned person in the room, he was definitely well out in front of a formidable field this particular afternoon. For whatever reasons. Death threats, physical pain and mental exhaustion – plus the substances utilised to overcome all three – had reduced Pagey to a shell of himself. He was clearly in no shape to undertake the in-depth interview we'd been planning for several weeks and I didn't even raise the subject. We rapped briefly about the book I was planning and then Jimmy drifted off in a medicinal daze back to his quarters.

Down the hall in Robert Plant's dimly lit clothes-strewn room, a different set of pressures were manifesting themselves in a most awkward manner. While I sat chatting with Plant and promo flack Danny Goldberg, Robert's wife Maureen called from back home in England, where Bob Hart's riot-at-the-LA Hyatt account of Led Zeppelin's touring activities in the *Sun* had just hit the street and had raised some unexpected hackles. 'No darling,' insisted Percy, '*of course* we don't chase little girls after the gigs, not even in LA. That's just the sort of bullshit they made up to make their story more interesting. You know I wouldn't be doing any of that nonsense,' Robert claimed, digging his way out of a distressing dilemma. It appeared that this notion of notoriety might be a two-edged sword.

As Robert continued to steadfastly proclaim his innocence and strict adherence to his marriage vows, Goldberg nervously fumbled about. Not only had the Bob Hart piece invoked the present irritating call, but Danny seemed to suspect that *this* domestic dispute between Robert and Maureen might also be headed towards the tabloid printing presses. One of those 'Wife-of-Top-Rock-Sex-Symbol-Accuses-Him-of-Being-Unfaithful-on-Tour' nonsense exposés. I acted insulted.

'Ritchie's all right – stop worrying,' Plant told Goldberg when he finally extricated himself from his accusers. 'He's been one of us from the bloody beginning. He's not going to write any shit like that. Bloody Bob Hart has really stirred up the wives though – you better warn the other lads about it.' Goldberg took off and Robert endeavoured to locate the 'right blouse' for the evening's proceedings. Time to move on.

The fleet of six black limousines tooled off from the Drake Hotel to the Garden at seven sharp. En route to the finale of the 1973 tour, Peter Grant told band members of the mysterious theft from their safety deposit box in the hotel safe of $203,000 in cash – receipts from their share of the New York gigs and the largest safety deposit box grab in Manhattan history. While the band sat around their backstage dressing room, Richard Cole remained at the Drake making sure that an expected FBI search of all Led Zeppelin rooms wouldn't turn up any illegal substances.

Looking back on it, Plant remarked, 'It was all so ridiculous, really. Jimmy and I just laughed about it. I remember Bonzo did go a bit berserk. "What the fuck is this losing-the-money thing then?" he said. But for Jimmy and I, somehow it all made sense. There was nothing else you could do but laugh really. Other people not as well endowed as ourselves might draw the conclusion that we're mad. But we just laughed. The big drag of it all was the flipout with the media pouring into our bedrooms and taking pictures and asking questions and everything. That sort of reminded us of being knifed or something, and lying in your room getting your last breath while some guy is trying to get it on film or into a newspaper. That part of it was ghastly.'

Commented John Bonham, 'The problem is that if we say we aren't upset about losing the money, they'll think we have millions to throw away. And if we say we do care about it, they'll say the money is all we care about.' 'It had reached the point,' Page said, 'where we really couldn't care too much. If the tour had been a bummer, then that would have been the last straw. But it wasn't. We heard about it just before we went on stage and I seem to remember we played a very good gig that night.'

Richard Cole was interrogated by the FBI and was even subjected to a lie detector test, which he passed to camp astonishment. Later a hotel employee resigned under a cloud but the money was never recovered. The FBI investigation did manage to put a dampener on that night's end-of-tour festivities, and even Jane the coke lady was transferred to the wardrobe department until the heat was off.

In the Led Zeppelin dressing room a quiet calm prevailed against the muffled roar of 20,000 odd souls stamping and cheering for the show to begin. Just prior to showtime, Grant joined Page, Plant and

Bonham in the backstage toilet area before we all strode out towards the stage area. Richard Cole had now rejoined the troupe, and armed with a torch, he guided me across the stage to a spot in the scaffolding, less than a yard above the boards. Handing me a couple of large joints, he cracked, 'There you are, ya cunt, you've got the best fuckin' seat in the house, and you'll probably end up in the fuckin' movie.' He wasn't wrong.

Igniting an almighty roar from the audience, the lads ran on stage and launched into an absolutely sensational performance. Despite their exhaustion, the robbery and Jimmy's injured hand, they literally tore it out of themselves. The obstacles only strengthened their resolve. To the ultimate delight of 20,000 raging supporters, Zeppelin probed the entire spectrum of their music form – a touch of Elvis, a base of Howlin' Wolf, some rhythm from Chuck Berry, a splash of Cream's gutbucket white blues, a wisp of the Buffalo Springfield, a sampling of the Byrds, some Muddy Waters's raunch, a spark from the Hendrix fire, more than a little of the magic of the Beatles, much more soaring raw energy than the Stones, the down-home laments of Robert Johnson, all mixed and shaken in unison in a crucible of their own creation. The band proved yet again that their unique and intense rapport with the audience represented one of the strongest bondings in the history of rock music.

A frenetic version of 'Whole Lotta Love' brought the house down. Behind the stage the roaring thunder of the fired-up audience put a smile on everyone's face. Flash guns popped, movie cameras whirred away under their artificial lights. A line of well-wishers painted their praises while security men hovered. Atlantic president Ahmet Ertegun stood off to one side, positively beaming with a I-knew-it-all-along grin from ear to ear. Peter Grant looked ecstatic too. Even Pagey, worn down but not quite overdone, presented a satisfied grin. We were all adrift in an ocean of adjectives.

Ten minutes after 'Whole Lotta Love' had thundered to a colossal climax, the stamping and cheering and encore calls continued unabated. Word spread backstage that the encore was imminent. Robert Plant, a towel draped over his shoulder, a bottle of wine in his hand and a raging smile across his face, wandered over and offered me a taste of the Blue Nun. We toasted the evening's success, the end of the tour, the fabulous achievements of this amazing band.

How long, I wondered, could they maintain this astronomical peak? Year after year, album after album, tour after tour, their following had continued to grow, just as their music had evolved. But it had to level out soon, this degree of never-ending growth couldn't possibly be sustained.

As the lads gathered together to ascend the stage stairs for that final tour encore, Plant – as if to read my mind – handed me the Blue Nun for safekeeping and whispered, 'We may be fucked now but we've got a bunch of new songs written and we can't wait to start recording them. We'll just have to see if we can top the other ones.'

8 On the Wings of a Swan Song
Plucking Out *Physical Graffiti*

ITH LED ZEPPELIN'S CAREER-LONG TRADITION of creative independence, it was inevitable that the band and Peter Grant would eventually form their own record label. The band had always fought for total creative control in the studio and the concert stage: their new records were delivered in the form of finished masters and jacket artwork, and the distributor had only to press the discs, print the jackets, promote the product and ship large quantities of every release to record stores in every corner of the globe. The circumstances were ideal for Led Zeppelin to own and operate their own label, but they would undertake the task with characteristic differences.

After taking a fairly long break over the winter of 1973 to 1974, initial steps were begun in the spring for the launching of the Led Zeppelin record label. As soon as the rumours started creaking out in the media, Robert Plant endeavoured to make it clear that the new label would be a legitimate and dedicated rock and roll exercise, with the accent on talent. It wouldn't, he insisted, be some sort of rock star plaything or ego exercise. 'The label obviously isn't going to be like the "Yeah, we'll have a label, far out heavy trip, man" and just putting yourself on it sort of trip. This label won't be just Led Zeppelin, that's for sure. It's too much effort to do as an ego trip and a waste of time really. I haven't got to build myself up on my own label for Chrissake!

'We're going to work with people we've known and liked, and people we will know and will like. It's an outlet for people we admire and want to help. There are so many possible things that we can play around with, people we can help that we haven't been able to help before. People like Roy Harper, who's so good and whose records haven't even been put out in America. People there have yet to discover the genius of the man who set fire to the pavilion at the Blackpool Cricket Ground.

'In trying to come up with a name for the label, we went through the usual ones like Slut and Slag, the ones that twist off your tongue right away – all the names one would normally associate with us on tour in America. But that's not really how we want to be remembered. Better to have something really nice.' Other names that surfaced in creative discussions included Stairway, DeLuxe, Eclipse, Zeppelin and finally, Swan Song, which was arrived at by accident, or an uncommon, for some, twist of fate.

Jimmy Page duly informed New York pro-Led Zeppelin scribe, Lisa Robinson, 'I had a long acoustic guitar instrumental with just sparse vocal sections – the song was about twenty minutes long and the vocal was about six minutes. The whole thing was quite epic really – almost semi-classical I suppose. I'd worked on bits of it and we were recording with the mobile truck and there was no title for it. Someone shouted out, "Swan Song"! The whole thing stopped and we said what a great name for an LP. All the vibes started and suddenly it was out of the LP and on to the record label name.

'I think that Swan Song is a good name for a record label because if you don't have success on Swan Song – well, then, you shouldn't have signed up with them. I'm not personally involved with the business side of it because I'm so involved with the production of the records that I don't have time to worry about it or even take a look at it.'

The actual Swan Song logo was inspired by a painting called 'Evening, Fall of Day' by William Rimner, which is in the Boston Museum of Fine Art. Robert Plant summed it all up, 'The name "Led Zeppelin" means failure, and "Swan Song" means a last gasp – so why not name our record label that?'

Never one to downplay the chart potential of proven big names, Atlantic's Phil Carson was super-positive right from the start. 'Obviously it will be a winning label,' he smirked. 'Apart from being a very clever manager, Peter Grant is such a brilliant talent man. Just run through the people he's been involved with. I was only thinking the other day how Peter had been telling me back in June 1973 about a girl group he'd seen on some local TV show in the American South. They were called the Pointer Sisters and Peter reckoned they were fantastic. On the strength of his rap, I tried to sign them but they'd already been snapped up by Blue Thumb. Peter had seen their potential, he does have a knack of seeing things coming. Not forgetting that Jimmy Page will be supervising the production of the material. It's *got* to be a winning label.'

Swan Song was launched in America in May with special receptions in New York and Los Angeles. The label's first release (Led Zeppelin didn't want to be the first act on their new label) was no great risk – it was a powerfully commercial début album by a new supergroup, Bad Company, comprising former members of highly rated British late 1960s bands: Free, Mott the Hoople and King Crimson. The album *Bad Co.* and its obvious hit single, 'Can't Get Enough', tore to the upper levels of the charts, and Swan Song was off and soaring. Once again a Led Zeppelin-related activity had turned to gold.

Within twelve months of its formation, Swan Song's New York office was able to report with reasonable justification, 'Swan Song is currently one of the hottest labels in the business. In addition to the new Led Zeppelin album, Swan Song has three other albums in the charts – the Pretty Things' *Silk Torpedo*, Maggie Bell's *Suicide Sal* and Bad Company's *Bad Co.* A new Bad Company album, *Straight Shooter*, is scheduled for release later this month. It is believed that no other label started by a rock group has ever had four albums on the charts at the same time. Combined with the Led Zeppelin albums, this makes nine albums on the charts for the young Swan Song organisation. Swan Song is owned by the members of Led Zeppelin and their manager Peter Grant. In the United States it is run [sic] by vice president Danny Goldberg and attorney and administrator, Steve Weiss.'

For a group accustomed to maintaining the lowest of personal profiles, Led Zeppelin members wasted no time in emerging from their shells. They appeared to delight in bathing in the spotlight of Swan Song's success with artists other than themselves. They were in fact intensely proud of the label's success. In a sense, it provided a somewhat world-weary superstar band who'd seen and done it all (in every sense of the words) with a timely shot of fresh incentive and clearer *raison d'être*.

Led Zeppelin's ability to win gold and platinum awards around the globe was commonplace achievement, although the band didn't take it for granted. But having *another* of their Swan Song artists reach gold or platinum popularity levels was an entirely new trip. It gave the lads a new lease on life at a crucial point in their existence. Even Jimmy Page – who'd been ready to check into a sanitorium at the end of the 1973 American tour – was bubbling with fresh enthusiasm.

Being the least ravaged (by far) from the staggering rigours of the previous tour, John Paul Jones was the first Led Zeppelin member to return to the live stage when he appeared at a free Hyde Park London concert in August 1974, with Roy Harper, Dave Gilmour of Pink Floyd and Steve Broughton of the highly regarded Edgar Broughton Band. The following month Jimmy Page journeyed to America with Peter Grant to fly the Swan Song flag at a Bad Company concert. After Bad Company ripped through their set-closer, 'The Stealer', Pagey joined them on stage for a royal workout on 'Rock Me Baby'. At the end of their tour, Grant surprised Bad Company members in Boston with four gold discs for their début album (which by now had reached number one Stateside).

Grant was on a managerial merry-go-round but he juggled careers exceedingly well at this point in time at least. Apart from attending to Led Zeppelin, Grant was looking after Bad Company (who were blowing America apart) and Maggie Bell, the funky singer regarded by some as Britain's answer to Janis Joplin. The massively proportioned Grant had a deep personal attachment to Maggie Bell – he'd managed her band, Stone the Crows, when her boyfriend, guitarist Les Harvey, had been electrocuted while playing a gig in the Welsh town of Swansea on 3 May 1972. Maggie had collapsed after the accident which reportedly prompted the stout-hearted and heavy-fisted Grant to break down in tears, the first time Led Zeppelin insiders had been witness to such an unexpected event.

Page and John Paul Jones, along with Duster Bennett, joined Bad Company for their encore at the Rainbow Theatre in London a few days before Christmas. Obviously the usually retiring Page had unleashed a new lease of public life in the success of Swan Song stablemates, Bad Company, and it looked good on him.

Shortly before Bad Company's London triumph, all four Led Zeppelin members participated in the most bizarre label launch in British recording history – a freakish Hallowe'en night party featuring naked women and strippers dressed as nuns held deep underground in Chislehurst Caves to introduce the new Swan Song label and its first UK release, the Pretty Things' *Silk Torpedo* album. Everybody got roaring drunk and the shrewdly organised launch drew rare rave acclaim from the music press.

Far and away the most significant project in the infancy of Swan Song was the recording of Led Zeppelin's sixth album (the first to be released under the Swan Song banner), which would be titled *Physical Graffiti*. Studio sessions had begun back in late 1973, but the right mood hadn't fallen into place and the project was temporarily postponed. Serious sessions had resumed at the Headley Grange mobile studio in February 1974.

Jimmy Page predicted at that time, 'The next one will still have complex songs and it'll probably have an acoustic guitar piece based on a solo I used to do with the Yardbirds during a song called "White Summer". But I think most of the album will get back to something some people think we've been drifting away from – straightforward rock and roll.' Page even hinted that he might contribute a few lines of his own lyrics, an area of creativity that in the past he had studiously avoided. 'I can see bits of what way I'm going now musically coming out in particular chords and things. I'm just not getting it out as quickly as I ought to be. There's so much to come through and I'm only just scraping the top.'

Robert Plant reported on studio developments a few weeks later. 'In three weeks we managed to spend at least three days a week recording – between various calamities, the Roy Harper gig we did at the Rainbow Theatre on Valentine's Day, highs and lows and all. We got eight tracks off – a lot of them are really raunchy, real belters with live vocals.

'You have to understand that we never plan out an album. Some musicians are capable of sitting down methodically, but we're not like that. Our music is an excitement thing. It has to be impromptu. It drops out of your mind – falls out of your head on to the floor and you pick it up as it bounces. That's how we work. But what can you expect? We hire a recording truck and trudge off to some shitty old house in the country. The last thing you'd expect is for the music to fall right into place. We even spent one night down there sitting around drinking ourselves under the table and telling each other how good we were. It was a good time and the album has some real belters. And we've got a good title for it. It has a reference to lyrics and is related to one of the songs. But it's got a nice extra twist in there.'

With a total of fifteen tracks, *Physical Graffiti* clearly offered fans a fairly broad cross-section of the band's influence at this mid-point in the 1970s. 'In the Light', which launched the second of the two albums, had a definite Indian feel in its intro. 'It's my CIA connection,' Page noted later, 'part Celtic, part Indian, part Arabic. That was played in a guitar tuning very close to the standard Indian sitar tuning but then again it's like a mishmash really because it's sort of pseudo-Indian and pseudo-Arabic as well, so that what comes out still has a sort of Western feel, in the combination, the fusion.'

Early on, however, it was obvious that the likely centrepiece of the new album would be an epic track originally titled 'Driving to Kashmir'.

The fabulous riff of the song first appeared on Pagey's home studio tapes, and had initially been part of a 'guitar-cycle' that he'd been messing around with for years. That same cycle also produced 'White Summer', 'Black Mountain Side' and the unreleased 'Swan Song'. The lyrical inspiration came from the long road from Goulimine to Tan-tan in southern Morocco, the area once called the Spanish Sahara. 'The whole inspiration came from the fact that the road went on and on and on,' Plant recently reminisced. 'It was a single track road which cut neatly through the desert. Two miles to the east and west were ridges of sandrock. It basically looked like you were driving down a channel, this dilapidated road, and there was seemingly no end to it. "Oh let the sun beat down upon my face, stars to fill my dreams . . ." – it's one of my favourites. That and "In the Light" and two or three others really were the finest moments. But "Kashmir" in particular. It was so positive, lyrically.

'I remember at the time there were a lot of musicians who were really insensitive about their audience's interpretation of their work. You'd get all this negativity coming out, as if to be mysterious or dark is to be negative. Mystery is not about darkness. It's about intrigue. There's a fine line in between, of course. Not even a fine line – it's a gossamer thread. How on earth do you want to purport yourself? I believed that it had to be light. Lyrically, you have to stand by your words! There was a lot of gloom purported by guys who went back and took off their stage clothes and played golf. I wanted whatever I was saying to represent what I was doing. But "Kashmir" was tremendous for the mood. A lot of that was down to Bonzo, what he played. Page and I couldn't have done it without Bonzo's *thrift*. He was a real thrifty player. It was what he didn't do that made it work.'

Pagey added, 'I had this idea to combine orchestra and mellotron and have them duplicate the guitar parts. Jonesy improvised whole sections with the mellotron and added the final ascending riff, whereby the song fades.'

Fifteen years down the long and winding road, all three Led Zeppelin members consider 'Kashmir' to be *the* quintessential Led Zeppelin recording. 'It's all there,' says John Paul Jones, 'all the elements that defined the band.'

The inevitable hassles with getting the complicated jacket artwork compled to the group's satisfaction forced the album to be delayed from its originally scheduled July 1974 release until 24 February, 1975. These unfortunate and frustrating delays, however, didn't have a detrimental effect on universal public reaction to *Physical Graffiti* – indeed, much to the contrary. Despite being a double album with a suggested list price of \$11.98, *Physical Graffiti* was greeted with the most overwhelming sales response accorded *any* album thus far in the 1970s. Twenty-three months after *Houses of the Holy*, Led Zeppelin had rocketed back to the top of the album charts with incredible vinyl vengeance.

Physical Graffiti thundered on to the *Billboard* LP chart at number 3, slamming into the number one berth the following week. By now it was widely accepted that Led Zeppelin was an enormously popular act, but the *Physical Graffiti* sales were absolutely phenomenal by any yardstick. On 24 March, Swan Song issued a press statement which summed up the current action quite conclusively. 'Led Zeppelin's new album *Physical Graffiti* is number one on all three music trades, *Billboard*, *Cashbox* and *Record World*, as well as in England, Australia and several other countries around the world. In an even more extraordinary development, all five previous Led Zeppelin albums all went back on the *Billboard* charts with bullets this week at the following positions: *Led Zeppelin* – number 83, *Led Zeppelin II* – 104, *Led Zeppelin III* – 124, *Led Zeppelin IV* – 116, *Houses of the Holy* – 92. No other artist in rock history has ever had six albums on the charts at the same time.

'Furthermore, two weeks is the fastest that any album has ever gone to number one. Both *Billboard* (where the album went to number three the first week) and *Record World* (where it débuted at number five) announced that *Physical Graffiti* had the highest first-week chart number in their history.'

Atlantic revealed that advance shipments on the album were in excess of two million units, making it double platinum prior to release, with a total retail gross sale of more than \$10 million. 'No album in Atlantic history has ever generated so many immediate sales,' crowed label president, Jerry Greenberg. Within two months, *Physical Graffiti* became the biggest album in the group's career to date, aided in no uncertain fashion by another immensely successful North American tour.

Melody Maker described *Physical Graffiti* as 'pure genius . . . a superbly performed mixture of styles and influences that encompasses not only all aspects of Led Zeppelin's career so far but also much of rock as a whole'. For once the usual nagging negative reviews were at a minimum – indeed it seemed that at least, Led Zeppelin's total domination of the mid-1970s rock scene and multi-platinum popularity had frightened off the usual ignorant hack reviews. Seven years and six albums into their career and it was no longer hip for media members to slag them off and put them down. The mere fact of their unprecedented musical evolution (from, say, 'Communication Breakdown' to 'Kashmir') necessitated their being taken rather seriously. It was about time.

On 11 and 12 January, the band warmed up for their ninth North American extravaganza with two European dates in Rotterdam and Brussels, and then plunged into the first leg of the 33-date schedule in freezing Minneapolis on 18 January, continuing through to New York's Nassau Coliseum on 14 February. The band, ever the professional perfectionists, had to overcome early difficulties when Robert came down with the flu and – far worse – Jimmy injured his finger in a railway carriage door while travelling to London for pre-tour rehearsals. These setbacks would have probably acted as a deterrent to a lesser band, but somehow Led Zeppelin took it in their stride and continued in their usual robust and vigorous style. Page's injury did force the substitution of 'Dazed and Confused' with 'How Many More Times' in the early part of the schedule.

The band had already decided to incorporate several *Physical Graffiti* tracks in the 1975 concert repertoire including 'Kashmir', 'In My Time of Dying' and 'Trampled Underfoot'.

The logistics of organisation on the tour were nothing short of staggering – indeed they provide an inside look at the state-of-the-art live sound of a superstar rock band in the mid-1970s. While band members, Peter Grant, and an assortment of key personnel, press and hangers-on were whisked from city to city on the chartered Starship jet, three 45-foot tractor trailers were needed to transport 44 roadies and the vast amount of equipment which included – among other sundry items – 184 loudspeakers, 172 lights, a dry-ice smoke machine, laser apparatus, five 28-foot-high light towers and slide projectors. The sound system, boasting 24,000 watts of power, thrust out some 120 decibels and was reported to be worth over $250,000. The lighting system cost another $300,000. Peter Grant told me the pre-concert sound and light costs amounted to $11,500. Led Zeppelin never skimped on essentials in their efforts to please the punters, and there can't be many people who ever went away disappointed from a Led Zeppelin live event. Indeed most people were convinced beyond all doubt that in 1975 they had mounted the most exciting and entertaining live show in rock history. The Rolling Stones seemed tame by comparison.

The street vibe on the magnificence of the new concert set spread like wildfire – in New York, 120,000 tickets for six shows were all gone in 36 hours. The lads had never been hotter, and despite John Bonham's contracting a nagging stomach disorder just as Percy recovered from the flu, they were savouring every majestic moment. And to show that they had not lost their keen – if bent – sense of humour throughout the obstacles, Peter Grant arranged for Linda Lovelace, immortalised by her performances in *Deep Throat*, to introduce the three final concerts of the second leg of the tour in LA.

Equally, if not more thrilling for the band, was the long-awaited opportunity to meet the ultimate rock legend, Elvis Presley. Robert Plant picked up the memorable story: 'Jerry Weintraub was operating as our agent at the time, and he was based in Vegas and was Presley's agent as well. The King demanded to know who these guys were who were selling tickets faster than he was. We'd been to see *him* already once or twice, just sat in the audience and mopped our dewy eyes and struggled out at the end with the rest of the mere mortals.

'We were told that if we wanted to meet Elvis, he was opposite the Forum in Inglewood. We were summoned to the top floor of the hotel and when we got out of the elevator it was the usual thing – security, a couple of girls very well blessed in the upper chest region, ha ha ha. So we scuttled down the corridor into this suite which was filling up slowly. The door at the end kept opening as someone was checking the room out – that was very funny to us, being big, fucking cynical English tin-pot gods. And when it was suitably full, Elvis came in. He came over to us and the four of us and him talked for a couple of hours. We all stood in a circle and discussed this whole phenomenon, this lunacy.

'You'd have to go a long way to find someone with a better idea of what it was all about,' Plant observed. 'He was very focused. You know when you have a friend who always gets too drunk at the wrong time but you still love him? I think he looked on a few of his aides like that, but he owed them the loyalty. So occasionally he had a tired glance around. Beyond that, his sharp humour and idea of where he was coming from was very different to what you now read. He knew what was going on, but he didn't know anything particularly about the contemporary rock situation. He'd met Elton John and didn't know who he was – somebody told him he was a comedian: I guess he didn't listen to progressive rock: he still listened to the blues. Once we were at a gig of his and he stopped the show. He said, "Wait a minute, guys, we're doing this all wrong. We got Led Zeppelin here tonight, so let's do it right." And he started placing "Reconsider Baby", the Lowell Fulson song. My throat? I was hurling the tears back down with my adam's apple as a dam to stop myself blarting like a fool. He was beautiful.'

Early in March, Led Zeppelin announced that it would bring its spectacular American stadium show to Britain (the first Led Zeppelin concerts on home soil in more than two years) for three major shows at London's Earl's Court Arena on 23 to 25 May. The British promoter, Mel Bush, was inundated with over 100,000 write-in requests for tickets, and a further two concerts were added to satisfy the unprecedented demand on 17 and 18 May.

To report that this string of London homecoming dates was an absolutely stunning success would still understate the surging levels of British popularity Led Zeppelin had attained in their two-year official absence. Quite simply, the band devastated the 85,000 enthusiasts who attended the five concerts. Even their old enigma – the ever-sceptical media – were totally blown away by their sheer concert brilliance, musical capabilities and big-show staging. Accolades poured into Peter Grant's office by the barrowful – the press demonstrated that they'd finally got a fix on Led Zeppelin's phenomenal power and rapport with the public. Gone were the typical snide attacks and the seething resentment that Led Zeppelin had allegedly deserted their homeland to grovel to the North Americans for big bucks. At last this unique phenomenon was being accepted at face value. A *Sounds* reviewer wrote a typical comment, 'This gig is scarred on my brain for life.'

Fleet Street virtually went berserk in their sudden discovery of Led Zeppelin – almost seven years after the band's launching, the straight press had suddenly figured out what was happening. Ludicrous as it may have seemed to members of the public, the daily papers had at last opened their blinkered vision to the realities of what had been so clearly obvious for years: Led Zeppelin was easily the biggest act in 1970s rock and roll. The *Daily Mail* hailed them as new 'rock gods'; to the *Sun*, they were the 'new' superstar band; and the *Observer* pondered the obvious in a colour-supplement piece headed: 'Led Zeppelin – Bigger than the Beatles?" One couldn't help but wonder where these commentators had been for the past five years. So much for the wisdom of the Fourth Estate, floundering in the quagmire of its own sickly ignorance.

Perhaps they'd been turned on to Led Zeppelin by the revelation that President Ford's teenage children regarded them as their favourite band.

After the spectacular London success, members of the group took some well-deserved rest from the spotlight, chuckling to themselves about their overnight success with the British press. Jimmy and Robert took off for Morocco, while the two Johns headed to the country to be with their families.

In the music scene, speculation began to build about the likelihood of a new album. There were rumours of a live album, a Jimmy Page soundtrack from a film, and other tales too numerous or nonsensical to detail. In their newly found position as the foremost superstars of 1970s rock, Zep faced a world clamouring for more record product. The demand was phenomenal, but the inherent organisational details alone posed formidable obstacles.

Atlantic's Phil Carson – whose duties included daily liaison between Swan Song and its distributor – was at pains to point out how unlikely it would be for the band's album productivity to exceed one project a year, no matter how heavy the demand. 'It's a very major project every time,' Carson explained. 'You have to start off with at least a million units in America, and another million spread around the world. If one country ships records ahead of another one, there's always big problems. That's why it can take so long to organise a Zeppelin release. You have to get all that timing together up front and sometimes that can be a problem in itself.'

Jimmy Page said, 'The main problem is because we're working so much. I'm sure people think we sit on our arses all day long but we don't. I haven't stopped for three years. I haven't had a real holiday since the group started. We do a lot of working abroad, too. We can't seem to find the time to increase the album supply.'

Much of it had to do with the machinations of their muse, and finding the inspiration for new songs. Robert Plant offered some observations in recent years that cast illumination on that area of their creativity. 'The majority of the stuff Jimmy and I wrote was in a room with the other two, so it wasn't cloistered – us in the corner and getting all the publishing. Some of the great stuff came from Bonzo taking hold of the whole thing and making it work from the drums point of view. It was all riffs and rhythm tracks, not la-la songs. I would have to try and weave the vocal in amongst it all, and it was very hard. Each song was experimentation, though there were simple things like

"Down by the Seaside" [from *Physical Graffiti*] or "Going to California" [from the fourth album] where you'd sit down and it would come out naturally.'

Summing up the *Physical Graffiti* blockbuster, Plant noted, 'Jimmy is the man who is the music. He goes away to his house and works on it a lot and then brings it to the band in its skeletal state. Slowly everybody brings their personality into it. This new flower sort of grows out of it. "Ten Years Gone" was painstakingly pieced together from sections he'd written. After the tremendous concentration on a song like that, we'll play anything to loosen up. Out of that came "Trampled Underfoot" and "Custard Pie". Before you know it, you've got something that moves.'

Provoking the absolute amount of satisfaction out of the present had long been a band credo – and that is what kept the ball rolling. As Plant revealed at the time, 'As long as we can continue making albums with as much pleasure as this new one has been – when you can sit back and listen to a playback of a new song and then jump in the air with glee from the sheer joy of it – there's just nothing else I'd rather do. When that becomes painful, then I suppose I'll chuck it in.'

But neither Robert Plant, nor any of the other band members, had any idea of what pain Fate held in store for their immediate creative future as the lads settled in to enjoy some of the serenity and solitude of an English summer in their rural retreats – and as they travelled privately seeking other styles of musical inspiration. It wouldn't be long before events began to unfold as unpredictable as one could possibly imagine. In the cold light of hindsight, it can be seen that the first Zep era had ended and a new kind of existence was about to unfold.

9   Troubled Times Saved by a Definite Presence of Mind

I N THE AFTERMATH of the tide-turning London concerts in May 1975, the Led Zeppelin members took a well-deserved breather. But it wouldn't be long before they were once again on the move, this time a result of circumstances rather than choice. The choke-hold of the Labour government's revised tax laws on the super-rich forced the band to relocate temporarily in the mountains above the delightful Swiss lakeside resort of Montreux in June. From now on, the amount of time they could physically spend on British soil each year was limited by the edict of tax laws, which would have seen a staggering 95 per cent of songwriting royalties gobbled up by the Exchequer.

From the new Montreux base (handy to the Swiss-based Atlantic consultant, Claude Nobs, a long-time friend and confidante of the band) each member and his family took off on vacation to try and forget the multitude of problems that accompanied high finance – and their intense desire not to hand it over to any tax man. Peter Grant had long since set up a chain of off-shore companies to funnel the immense Led Zeppelin wealth away from the prying eyes of the tax department.

Robert led his family off towards Morocco, where they were joined three weeks later by Jimmy. They drove into the vast expanses of the Sahara but were forced to turn back from a looming war zone. Returning to Montreux via Spain and France, they made plans for a North American autumn tour after further holidaying. Jimmy talked of setting up camp in Cairo to record with Egyptian musicians, or perhaps in New Delhi. Meantime he travelled to Sicily to check out an old Aleister Crowley haunt, a farmhouse and abbey, which he'd been told was up for sale. Then he continued on to London for some editing supervision on the forthcoming film project.

Reuniting with his girlfriend Charlotte and their daughter Scarlet, Page planned to link up with the Plant family for a mid-summer holiday on the Greek island of Rhodes. Robert and Maureen Plant and their two children had left Montreux for Rhodes with Maureen's sister and her husband. They had rented cars on 4 August to leisurely explore the inspiring ruins of antiquity when disaster struck.

Maureen was driving with Robert in the passenger seat and the children in the back with Jimmy's daughter. The car skidded on the narrow road and Maureen lost control. It plunged over the precipice and slammed into a tree.

Plant glanced at his unconscious wife and assumed she was dead. His children were hurt too but Scarlet Page seemed unharmed. Plant himself had a fractured elbow and a severely damaged ankle. It was a horrible scene.

No ambulance was available in this remote part of Rhodes and it was several hours before the family reached a local hospital on the back of a farmer's open fruit truck. 'I was lying here in some pain,' Plant said, 'trying to get cockroaches off the bed and the guy next to me, this drunken soldier, started singing "The Ocean" from *Houses of the Holy*.'

Back in London, panic set in. Grant, in tax exile with his family in the South of France, couldn't be reached. Richard Cole was told by Charlotte Martin, on the phone from Greece, that Maureen was dying and desperately needed blood of a type not available locally. Calling up Harley Street specialists, Cole eventually arranged a private jet belonging to Robert McAlpine of McAlpine Aviation.

Flying out to Rhodes with two London specialists and a supply of blood, Cole was concerned about how he would be able to spirit the Plant family out of the country. The local car rental outlet had claimed that Maureen was drunk when the accident took place (an allegation she denied utterly), and money-hungry lawyers were gathering at the scene. Unable to persuade Swan Song's accountant to provide cash without Peter Grant's signature, the angry Cole organised funds to be sent to Rhodes by Claude Nobs in Montreux.

Finally the private jet airlifted the injured to Rome, and they made their way back to London. Maureen would spend many weeks in hospital with a fractured skull, and a broken leg and pelvis. 'If we hadn't had the money available to fly to England right away for the best medical treatment, I'm certain my wife wouldn't be alive now,' Plant later commented, adding that he too 'was lucky to be alive'.

He wasn't so lucky to be on British soil. If he stayed any longer under the new laws, his residency would be affected and he would be liable for a fortune in current taxes. Cole – the only member of the camp who could afford to remain in England – quickly arranged for Plant to be flown to the nearby tax-free haven of Jersey. Because of his ankle injuries, Percy had to be hoisted into the cabin with a fork lift. It was an outrageous scenario.

Quickly the other band members and Peter Grant gathered in Jersey and announced the postponement of the North American tour. It was then decided to take a working vacation in California while Robert recuperated from the untimely accident. They checked into the traditional haunt, the Continental 'Riot' House, but somehow the vibe wasn't right and they rented beach houses at Malibu, where Plant watched the movie stars stroll by. Spurred on by a get-well telegram from Elvis, Robert undertook the odd bout of lyric writing.

Despite their absence and the saddlebag of doubts raised by Robert's immobility, the band's popularity zoomed on unabated. Late in September it was revealed that Led Zeppelin 'in an unprecedented feat' had swept seven first prizes and placed in nine other categories in the annual *Melody Maker* music poll. Readers voted them international band of the year, and also named them top group in the international live act category. Jimmy Page was named the world's top guitarist, while Robert Plant took the honours as best male vocalist in both British and international categories. *Physical Graffiti* was selected best album. According to *Melody Maker*, seven first-place awards was the most that any band had ever received.

The band was also placed second in the British band section and third in the British live act category. Jimmy Page and Robert Plant were named the world's number two composers. Bass player John Paul Jones placed third internationally and was ranked eighth for his keyboard skills. John Bonham was honoured as runner-up in the international drumming section. 'Trampled Underfoot' finished second in the international single category, and Jimmy Page captured second place as the finest producer and arranger on the world scene. Summed up Swan Song, 'Led Zeppelin's sweep of the *Melody Maker* awards climaxes the most successful year in their seven-year career.'

Widespread doubt still lingered over how long it would take for Plant to fully recuperate from the August accident, and it wasn't until 13 November that the band released the following information: '. . . while Robert Plant's ankle has healed substantially . . . he still is unable to perform and no Led Zeppelin tour anywhere in the world is currently scheduled. Another medical report on Plant's ankle is expected in February – but under no circumstances would any Zeppelin tour be scheduled before the summer [1976] and no plans or arrangements of any kind will be made until Plant's ankle is fully healed. The cast on Plant's right ankle has been removed but he still cannot put any weight on it. Plant's left elbow, which was also fractured, is almost completely healed now, and he was seen throughout the summer at various concerts in LA and was universally considered to be in very good spirits.'

The announcement also revealed that the band would be spending the month of November in Munich, Germany, at the Musicland Studios, preparing a new album for release early in 1976. They'd been rehearsing on and off for several weeks at the SIR Studios in Hollywood and despite the presence of mellowing white powders, the musical reunion had been hot, even with Robert panting out the vocals from his wheelchair. Surely, one presumed, the accident and its aftermath would have some inspirational impact on the lyrics for the seventh album.

Stopping off in Manhattan en route to Germany (any further residence in America meant they would face US taxes), Robert had progressed out of his wheelchair and was walking with a cane. He was optimistic enough to tell Lisa Robinson, 'I've had time to see. Before I was always bowled over with the sheer impetuousness of everything we did, of what we are, and what was created around it. That was knocked off course, the fulcrum was tilted a little. I had to sort of think everything anew, instead of just being allowed to go on with the rampaging. So it turns out that the new lyrics all come from the period of contemplation where I was wondering "Christ, is it all through? Is it ended?" And as such the album is full of energy, because of that primal fight within me to get back.'

Right from the start, it was apparent that the new album would hark back in style and approach to their very first adventure in the studio. The most obvious comparison is that both the début and seventh LPs were recorded very quickly, under unusual and highly charged circumstances. As Page would conclude upon its release, 'I think *Presence* was a highly under-rated record. *Presence* was pure anxiety and emotion. I mean, we didn't know whether we'd ever be able to play in the same way again. It might have been a very dramatic change, if the worst had happened to Robert. *Presence* is our best in terms of uninterrupted emotion. The whole thing took three weeks and a bit.'

The studio was located in the basement of the Arabella Hotel where the band stayed and it was a full-on, unrelenting around-the-clock workload. Musicland was a busy studio in that era, and Led Zeppelin were lucky to squeeze in a couple of weeks before the Rolling Stones hit town to record their next album. There would be no sitting around pondering their phenomenon. And they'd wisely come prepared. 'Those sessions,' Jimmy reflected, 'were the ultimate test of that whole lifestyle. I mean, that was eighteen hours a day at real intensity every day. You just plunge in and you don't start thinking about three meals a day.

'I think *Presence* is my favourite album, or at least the one which, when I think back on the sessions, I consider the most fulfilling. But maybe that's a rather bad yardstick to use for what one's favourite album is. Every record had its moments.'

Later Page was even more enthusiastic. 'The general urgency and the pent-up "whoa" was in all of us. The mechanism was perfectly oiled. We started steaming in rehearsals. We did a lot of old rock and roll numbers just to loosen up a bit. "For Your Life" was made up in the studio, on the spot. I particularly enjoyed the guitar playing on the blues things. The solos never had that colouring before. I was so happy about it – especially since I have to warm up to solo. I get nervous about that kind of guitar playing. But that's the way I can really concentrate. I'm usually at my best when I'm really exhausted or under pressure or both. When you're exhausted all you want to know about is what you have to do. The golden question is why was this done so fast, and why the others take so long? The fact is that this one we lived all the way through – under circumstances that were extremely frustrating. We weren't sure about Robert, weren't sure what was going to happen. Everyone managed to pull it all in . . . it was great.'

Still unable to put weight on his ankle, Plant was forced to record his vocal parts from a wheelchair, certainly something of a come-down for the frontman in the world's wildest rock band.

Page was especially pleased with his work on the album opener, 'Achilles' Last Stand', a ten-minute opus utilising textured layers of harmonised guitars. 'As with "Stairway to Heaven", I did all those guitars on it. I just built them up. That was the beginning of my building up harmonised guitars properly. "Ten Years Gone" from *Physical Graffiti* was an extension of that, and then "Achilles' Last Stand" is like the essential flow of it really, because there was no more time to think the things out. I just had to more or less lay it down on the first track and harmonise on the second track.

'It was really fast working on *Presence*. I did all the guitar overdubs for that track in one night. There were only two sequences. I don't think that the rest of the band, apart from Robert, could see what I was going to do with it. I wanted to give each section its own identity, and I think it came off really good. I didn't think I'd be able to do it in one night. But I was so into it that my mind was working properly for a change. It sort of crystallised and everything was just pouring out. I was very happy with the guitar on that album as far as the maturity of the playing goes.

'*Presence* was very good for me. It was just good for everything really, even though it was a very anxious point and the anxiety shows, group-wise. I guess the solo in "Achilles' Last Stand" is in the same tradition as the solo from "Stairway to Heaven". It is on that level to me.'

Pagey was still ardently pro the *Presence* project when he re-mastered the best-of-Led-Zeppelin CD boxed set in 1990. Noting that all of the tracks had benefited from the re-equalisation project, he singled out 'Achilles' Last Stand' as sounding 'absolutely fantastic', adding, 'To me it sounds phenomenal. It's a number which I think was missed by a lot of people really. *Presence* wasn't necessarily a wide-selling album. It was pretty well received from people I've spoken to, but it didn't sell in the volumes of the previous albums.'

A pity, because *Presence* was a superb album, one of the band's very finest. Much of its strength and attack came from the pervading anxiety but the time pressures also exercised a relentless under-surge. It was urgent and hungry and often impromptu. There wasn't even time (or inspiration) for the project to be given a working title. 'What happened was the jacket designer said, "When I think of the group, I always think of power and force. There's a definite *presence* there." That was it,' said Page. 'He wanted to call it "Obelisk". To me, it was more important what was *behind* the obelisk. The cover is very tongue-in-cheek to be quite honest. Sort of a joke on *2001* – I think it's quite amusing.'

After the recording and mixing eighteen-day marathon was complete, the band returned to the friendly tax-free shores of Jersey where on 10 December they played a few old favourites for 350 residents at a local pub. It was an auspicious occasion for band-watchers: Plant performed his vocals perched on a stool. Back in his own farmhouse kitchen near Kidderminster on the first day of the New Year [1976], Percy Plant managed to make his way across the room unaided – it was the first time he'd walked since the accident four months earlier. His sense of humour hadn't deserted him as he quipped,

'One small step for man, one giant leap for six nights at Madison Square Garden.'

Plant also offered his retrospective on the *Presence* sessions. 'The album is full of energy because of that sort of primal flight within me, to get back, to get better. There is a lot of determination on the album – fist-banging on the table!'

Initially Zep had hoped to have *Presence* in the stores by March, but the usual jacket hassles delayed the release by a month and it finally hit the streets on 6 April. Amazingly – despite the band's many traumas of recent times – *Presence* racked up the largest advance orders in British recording history, and thundered onto the UK LP charts at number one, breaking all records for Led Zeppelin or any other band, including the Beatles. In America *Presence* hit the *Billboard* charts at number 24, exploding to number one the following week. Even for Led Zeppelin, this represented a considerable triumph but ultimately the album didn't sell in the vast quantities of its mega-platinum predecessors. But its immediate acceptance was a boost to the band's somewhat confused spirits.

Jimmy Page, in particular, was endeavouring to reorganise his personal life, which friends privately claimed was in a shambles. Later he would admit that right after the release of *Presence* he was intensely involved in getting things together on the homefront. 'Well, as far as I was concerned, it was a case of sorting out a year's problems in say a month, and not finding the whole process as simple as that. I mean, suddenly I had time to look around and I became aware of certain people who'd been taking *incredible* advantage of me in the year I'd been away.'

Page's involvement with women over the previous twelve months had been a comedy of confusion (to an outsider), and a few hearts had been broken in the process. Despite all of the ravishing fillies he'd frollicked with while touring America (a subject worthy of its own volume), he was also active on home territory. When part-time Stones member Ron Wood brought his foxy blonde wife, Chrissie, down to Page's Plumpton Place for a visit, the guitarist reportedly disappeared with her for several days. Jimmy's girlfriend, Charlotte Martin, was so miffed she moved out and set up camp at Page's Kensington occult book store. Ron Wood took it in his stride – on the phone one day, he asked Jimmy, 'How's *our* bird?' Page later installed Chrissie Wood at the London residence he'd bought from actor Richard Harris, a unique and surreal mansion called Tower House.

Eventually Page re-united with Charlotte, the mother of their daughter, Scarlet. In a rare burst of candour concerning his private life, Page admitted, 'The troubles – well, for a start, Charlotte's been very ill but that's something one doesn't need to get into really, only that . . . if you've been with someone for a long time and they get ill, then you immediately have that responsibility. I don't really need to say any more.'

Behind his back, associates often wondered how Pagey managed to maintain his harem at arm's length. And it kept on increasing as fresh talent arrived on the scene and was invariably entranced by the simmering decadence of the Page lifestyle. Jimmy always had a peculiar knack of charming the feminine gender. Apparently he was also a deft juggler!

In September, Page and John Bonham took a short trip to Montreux to record a 'total percussion track' produced by Jimmy with additional synthesised effects. Page was confident the track was 'certain to be included' on the next album. In fact, it didn't surface until the 1982 album, *Coda*, under the title of 'Bonzo's Montreux'.

Upon his return from Switzerland, one of the most difficult and annoying periods of Page's professional life unfolded before him. He was confronted by an ugly article which *New Musical Express* summed up as 'possibly the most snide vitriolic attack to appear in a musical periodical in recent years'. Page had been working with filmmaker Kenneth Anger since 1974 on the soundtrack for the movie *Lucifer Rising*. But tiring of the slow progress rate and his inability to reach Jimmy – even though Anger was installed in the basement of the Page London residence, Tower House, working with an expensive German film editing table which the band had loaned him – the filmmaker finally hit the panic button and took his alleged dilemma public.

'The selfishness and inconsideraton were appalling,' raged Anger. 'It was like rapping on inch-thick plate glass. Jimmy had more or less turned into an undisciplined, rich dilettante, at least as far as magic and any serious belief in Aleister Crowley's work was concerned. Page has only composed twenty-eight minutes of music in three years' work on the project. The way he has been behaving is totally contradictory to the teachings of Crowley and the ethos of the film.'

Noting that Crowley too had been very fond of narcotic powders such as cocaine and heroin, Anger insisted that Crowley was able to handle the abuse because of his strong mountaineering constitution. Whereas to Anger, Page seemed wasted and so spaced out he couldn't communicate. 'He couldn't handle it,' said Anger emphatically. It was Anger's accusation that Page was 'having an affair with the White Lady' and was unable to get his act together that really hit the guitarist below the belt.

Forced to also go public with his side of the headlined feud, Page told *New Musical Express*, 'I must start by saying that I've lost a hell of a lot of respect for Anger. The level of pure bitchiness that he was working on . . . at one point, he was writing silly little letters to everybody he thought I knew, so that they would naturally bring it up in conversation when they saw me. This whole thing about "Anger's Curse" – it was just those silly letters. God, it was all so pathetic. I mean, I've got to get my side across now because it's just gone too far.

'He's implying that he received nothing from me, which is totally untrue. I gave him everything in plenty of time.' Page stated further that he and manager Peter Grant had assisted Anger by providing a screening/editing facility in London, and that Grant was in fact considering investing funds for Anger to complete *Lucifer's Rising*.

'Then one day this whole thing just blew up,' a wounded and insulted Page continued. 'And that's all I know about it. This bitchiness is just an extension of Anger's *Hollywood Babylon*. Now whether he thought in his mind that he was indebted to me somehow and that he felt he had to get me off his back, I don't know. I mean I didn't start hassling. I just wanted to see the bloke finish the bloody film. Its whole history is so absurd anyway. I just assumed it was unfinished because he was such a perfectionist and he's always ended up going over his budgets. All I can say is: Anger's time was all that was needed to finish that film. Nothing else!

'I had a lot of respect for him. As an occultist he was definitely in the vanguard. I just don't know what he's playing at. I'm totally bemused and really disgusted. It's truly pathetic. He is powerless – totally. The only damage he can do is with his tongue.

'So much of this year has been taken up with petty little time-consuming things. It's not been a static period so much as an unsatisfying one. There have been so many niggling little things to take care of – things so petty people would never believe that Jimmy Page, rock guitarist, would need to involve himself with them.'

But the damage had been done. Anger's claims of Page's hard drug abuse would achieve folklore status. And they would linger on well into the 1980s, despite Page's claims to have kicked the habit.

His personal aggravations aside, Page and the other Led Zeppelin members had something special in the wings on the edge of completion. There would be no live appearances by Zeppelin in 1976, but they were almost ready to unleash the next best thing – a full-length concert movie of the world's most dynamic rock band in action.

The odd personal struggle on the home front wouldn't prevent this project coming to fruition.

10 The Song Will and Still Remains the Same

'We are working on a film. I don't know if it will ever be shown but we filmed the Albert Hall concert in London.'
Jimmy Page, February 1970

WITH THOSE WORDS, Jimmy Page communicated the early desire of Led Zeppelin to capture the heart and soul of their unique concert performance on celluloid for pop posterity in an age before the avalanche of rock videos. And although it would take almost seven years to reach fruition, *The Song Remains the Same* ultimately would turn out to be well worth the long wait for the band's millions of fans.

The key characters in the evolution of the movie (apart from the group and Peter Grant) would be Joe Massot and Peter Clifton. Massot, a visionary music filmmaker, saw Zeppelin promenading on the concert stage for the first time at the Bath Festival in 1972. The event, which drew 150,000 people, also featured the talents of the Byrds, Santana, the Jefferson Airplane, Dr John, Country Joe and the Fish, Frank Zappa and the Flock. Grant had turned down a reported $250,000 for gigs in Boston and New Haven that same weekend because they were anxious to make a profound imprint on the British market similar to their spectacular invasion of North America.

Although deeply impressed by Led Zeppelin's fevered performance, he had no premonition that they would eventually become the focal point of what may in time prove to be the most important project in his career. 'I'd gone along to the gig at the invitation of Charlotte Martin, Jimmy's lady, and she told me to stand up on the stage to watch it all go down,' Massot explained.

Grant as usual had insisted on presenting the band in the best possible light and circumstances. 'Peter wanted Led Zeppelin to go on right at sunset,' said Massot, 'and to make sure of it, he physically removed the other group's equipment from the stage.' Concerned that encores by the Flock might meander past what promised to be a beautiful sunset, Grant had the plug pulled on their set and basically elbowed the Flock off the stage. As a result, when Led Zeppelin soared into 'Immigrant Song', the sun was sinking into the arms of the hills. 'So the band did go on at sunset, and it was a truly amazing experience. With the sun setting behind Robert's hair, the whole gig took on another dimension. The group always felt that Bath was the real beginning for them in Britain — they'd sold a lot of records and played many concerts before then but Bath represented everything falling into place. They'd perfected their trip when they hit Bath and that particular sunset.'

'We knew that Bath was going to be a crucial thing,' recalled Robert Plant. 'We went on and we knew that the next two or three hours were going to be the ones, as far as holding our heads high. You can go to the States and earn incredible bread but that's not what it's all about. I think we weren't really into it until the acoustic number ["That's the Way"] when we all had a chance to sit down and take a look around. Then it was like clockwork — we looked at each other and we heard it was sounding good, and we looked down and everybody else was grooving too.'

Prior to that memorable Somerset sunset, Massot had gained considerable dexterity in the welding together of rock music and film. He worked himself up the hard way: toiling on documentaries, features, shorts, some films of Cuba in the early 1960s before Castro gained control. After he became attracted to rock music as a mass art form, he made *Zachariah* with Country Joe and the Fish, the first electric Western featuring rock and roll. Then came *Wonderwall*, an esoteric video adventure put together with George Harrison. Massot liked the potential of fusing rock and celluloid, an attitude that instantly set him apart from most of the film industry.

'The essence of all film is movement and tempo and rhythm,' he said. 'Rock music is the same — it's fast and I think ideal for film treatment. There's no point in having static movement in a film, and that's the last thing you'd get with rock music.'

After moving to Berkshire, Massot began visiting Jimmy and Charlotte at Plumpton Place and in the early summer of 1973, he discussed with Page the prospect of producing a Led Zeppelin movie. Unlike the myriad of film makers who have inundated the band's offices with screenplay plans over the years, Massot had a different kind of vision.

'I wanted to represent each one of them as individuals and then incorporate those four sections into a film structure. I told Jimmy I didn't think there was any point in making another *Woodstock* or *Bangla Desh* type of film. They were 16 mm documentaries, almost in a home movie style. Even *Let It Be* fell into that category. There hadn't been a film making any sort of statement about the rock lifestyle since Dick Lester did *A Hard Day's Night* and *Help!*. I felt Jimmy was in the same frame of mind about it. He said he didn't want another *Woodstock*. He felt the need for something different as well.

Having struck a responsive chord with Page, Massot eagerly sat back in his Hampstead house in London to await the verdict. When the guitarist did get back to him a few days later, it wasn't good news. 'It was just too much of a last-minute thing,' said Massot, 'because they were just about to leave on the American tour. Jimmy said they probably wouldn't make a film of the tour and he was sorry but he had to say no for the time being.'

Massot had then turned his other talents to other pursuits when out of the blue he received a call from Peter Grant, on the road somewhere in the States. 'Peter called me on 15 July and said, "Come on over, we want to make the film." It was quite a surprise.' Massot quickly scrambled around for a crew and left Heathrow the next day with three cameramen, two sound men and a couple of assistants. Filming began on 18 July, and the film crew followed the band through Baltimore, Pittsburgh, Boston and then the three-day stint at Madison Square Garden in New York. 'All the music segments were filmed in New York,' says Massot, 'and we wanted it to be first-class footage so we shot it in 35 mm rather than 16 mm.'

Right from the start (sudden as it may have been), Led Zeppelin didn't approach the production in the usual fashion. Instead of spending weeks trying to convince rock-reluctant distributors to put up the production money, the band and Grant decided to finance it themselves. To them, it followed logically that films could be produced independently in much the same fashion as Led Zeppelin produced its records. And after all, it wasn't exactly a huge gamble − anything involved with portraying the image of the band was hardly likely to lose money.

The cost of the American tour footage alone came to more than $85,000, said Massot, and at least as much again was required for the sequence shooting of dramatic situations back in Britain. 'We defnitely didn't want just a concert film – we wanted to show them as individuals,' Massot explained. 'But we didn't want it to be in the traditional way with interviews. They felt that they'd like to come up with a more symbolic representation of themselves [harking back to the fourth album jacket, in a sense]. In a phrase, these are sequence films of *them*.

'All of the individual sequences were to be integrated into the group's music and concerts. Now the basis of the concert footage is movement – because they perform with extraordinary movement, not just on stage but within themselves. Led Zeppelin are a very mobile group. So their individual stories had to have themes of movement as well. I felt this was the key to combining the two. To me the film really took on a lot more interest as I started to do each of the separate stories, because this is where their real characters started to come forth.'

John Paul Jones remembered the circumstances a trifle differently in an exclusive 1991 interview. 'No, the individual sequences weren't originally planned,' he insisted. 'They only happened because there were giant holes in the concert footage. It was actually meant to be a concert movie. And so a couple of days in advance, I'm suddenly told that a film crew was coming down to my house to shoot a sequence, and what was I going to do? That's the amount of planning that went into it.'

In the early days of 1975 (with the film still immersed in a lengthy post-production process), Joe Massot invited me to a very private preview of some early edited segments at his Hampstead house. Before rolling the projector, he elaborated upon each segment in his own words. They provide many significant insights into the *raison d'être* for the film's stylised sequences.

'Robert Plant decided to do a Welsh legend with a character perhpas similar to King Arthur,' Massot explained. 'He overcomes all of his adversaries with the sword given him by a fair young lady. The deed done, he returns to the lady who rewards him with gold. Then he leaves her and he's on his own again. Robert felt it really was him, and that he *is* on his own and alone. Robert wrote the story himself and there's duelling, horses, castles, green glades, the whole works.'

All of Plant's segment was shot in Wales against a backdrop of superb summer scenery. There's a definite feel of the muddled Middle Ages right from the outset when Robert drifts across the waters under sail in a wooden boat bedecked with colourful pennants. His white cape flowing, he leaps ashore and as he strides along a deserted beach, he meets a beautiful young lady (played by his wife Maureen) who gives him a sword which he willingly accepts. He proceeds through the gloriously green woods to moated Raglan Castle on horseback and then scales the walls and does battle with the local louts. The victorious hero then wanders through the forest, contorted with wide-angled lenses and tinted with special filters. Upon his return, the lady rewards him and he kisses her passionately. Then it's back on to the sturdy steed and a wistful gallop along a distant ridge, superbly filmed by the same cameraman who shot *Lawrence of Arabia*. All of this delightful video rhythm to the tune of 'The Rain Song' and 'The Song Remains the Same', supreme choices for any film subject but especially powerful herein.

'Jimmy's film was rather strange,' said Massot, in an avalanche of understatement. 'Jimmy felt that he wanted to say something about time and the passage thereof. There's a mountain out the back of his place, Boleskine House, on the shores of Loch Ness in Scotland. So Jimmy decided that he would climb it and act out a symbolical tale about a young man fighting his way to the top to meet with the old man of the mountain at the summit, Father Time in symbolism. Jimmy plays both parts in the film. He insisted that his segment be shot on the night of a full moon. It was quite difficult lighting the mountain at night – we actually had to build special scaffolds on the side of it to put cameras on and mount arc lamps. It was a weekend and overtime for the crew but Jimmy wanted it to be right.'

Page's portion opens with a cinema verité sequence outside Madison Square Garden in New York. Plant is bobbing up and down across the stage like a rooster strutting in his barnyard – Page fingers the guitar chords as though he's playing an old harp. The whole feeling is incredibly sensual – even the reflections from the special stage lights become twisted, gaping orifices. Then out comes the violin bow and the maestro begins to stroke his instrument. Sonic sensory stimulation. The song is 'Dazed and Confused', sounding more potent and powerful than ever in its extended live rendition. A cut to the full moon, edging behind a cloud. Against the noise of electronic chaos, a young man begins to ascend a steep hill. The trees come alive with light – it is enormously eerie. At the top of the hill stands Old Father Time, the full moon glowing behind his flowing hair. The perfect part for a fully flown Capricorn.

'John Bonham chose to be real, simply himself,' said Massot. 'He's sort of a teddy boy – playing snooker, riding hot rods, a whole exercise in energy and power. He drives a nitrogen-fuelled dragster at 240 mph on a quarter-mile track [Bonzo was filmed at Santa Pod raceway at the controls of an AA Fuueler]. The sequence ties in nicely with his drum solo which is pure power and energy.'

The inside of a pool hall unfolds on the screen. The camera moves to the concert stage where Plant introduces 'Moby Dick'. Then John and his wife Pat are strolling along an oil-stained concrete track through the fields to a yard full of cars. The action continues to move, tearing around country lanes in a hot rod, stunts on a motor bike, hands-only solo at the concert, riding a bike tractor attached to a plough, pneumatic drills and construction scenes, backstage with the three other band members as they take a mid-way breather while Bonzo hammers out his solo. Unofficially intermission. Then it's back at the raceway where Bonzo's ready to burn in a demonic-looking dragster. He dons the safety helmet as flames belch out of the exhausts. Smoke and fire shimmer across the track as the machine roars off and tears into the distance at terrifying speed. Back in the concert, Plant announces, 'One hundred and thirty pounds of glory – John Bonham!!'

'John Paul Jones,' said Massot, 'decided to do an allegorical and symbolic horror tale about how one man and a bunch of masked riders terrify villagers, rape women and act horribly. Eventually the man returns home on his horse expecting a continuation of the violence. But when he gets there, he takes off his mask and settles down peacefully with his wife and family – completely the opposite of what you've anticipated.'

John Paul appears in top hat and wig and velvet suit with lace cuffs. The Puritan father-figure takes a little snuff and plays an old organ in a wood-panelled room. Visions of Mozart at the keyboards. A horse comes riding into view – through the graveyard and inside an ancient church. The rape of a lady. Four men wearing hideous masks stride out of a windmill and leap upon their trusty steeds. They tear around the countryside terrifying local villagers with their acts of violence. Then John Paul is seen galloping back to his manor house. The stout wooden door opens to his knock. Inside he takes off his hat and mask. Dogs and children appear along with a beautiful lady (his wife Maureen) in a grey velvet dress with pink frills. She rushes forward and embraces him. The servants gather round, grinning from ear to ear. The master is home, back from the wars.

John Paul provided a rationale of his sequence in a 1991 conversation. 'Originally I was going to try and get permission to use some scenes from an old Disney movie called *Doctor Sin*. It had a group of horsemen riding across marshes in skeleton suits − it was exactly what I had in mind. Then we'd cut out of that into my opening the door of the house. Somehow I thought that would be quite easy and quite quick to put together. But Disney wouldn't let me use the clips and so I had to quickly hire horses and a few friends and start riding around the countryside in the middle of the night. The whole thing turned out to be like the Horse of the Year Show. Plus I had this awful wig that they wouldn't let me cut. That was rather embarrassing.'

As to published reports that Jones had become infuriated with the crew and sent them packing, John Paul said, 'No, that's just not true. It was all over quite mercifully quickly as best I recall.'

'Originally we made two separate films of Peter Grant,' Joe Massot remembered. 'One where he is an antique collector fooling around with vintage cars and driving one around with his wife beside him. Then he's just lying around on a bed fooling with his kids and playing with a cat. It was a very warm film.

'The other film, in which Peter plays a gangster in the Al Capone style, has him tearing around in a Pierce Arrow 1928 gangster car in clothes of that period. They pull up at this house and machine gun it. Richard Cole is dressed up as one of his henchmen armed with the machine gun. I would say it's a stylised dream sequence. But Peter himself is still uncertain about it. He feels the film might make him look a fool. I don't think it does myself.' Eventually Grant agreed to the gangster portrayal which in retrospect seems a wise decision.

Summing up one mid-1970s winter afternoon, Massot reflected, 'Basically I feel the film is very real . . . the various sequences come from within them. They created each of the stories to say something about themselves. It's just them and that's as honest as you can get.'

Not totally unpredictably, Joe Massot's intense and quite dedicated involvement with *The Song Remains the Same* came to a sudden and quite bitter end shortly after this meeting. A replacement director, an expatriate Australian named Peter Clifton (who'd forged his reputation with a visionary ABC TV series *Now Time*, put together in London for the down-under market, plus a film entitled *Summertime '68 − The Beat Goes On*) was hurriedly brought in by Peter Grant to complete the project. The band was relatively tight-lipped about the reasons behind this unexpected change, but later Jimmy Page would observe, 'I don't really want to pass any comment there. In retrospect, it was possibly okay. I think a lot of things did go over Massot's head. He hadn't grasped the essence. But then again, maybe he had and we were just too impatient, certainly in the early days, and we became very annoyed at the screw-ups.

Clearly one of the problems originating from the original New York concert shoot was a series of crucial missing medium and long shots in vital songs, which forced editors to essentially focus on Jimmy and Robert. Page said, 'With three cameramen on the job, there were certainly a lack of distance shots.' Perhaps the long, drawn-out post-production process contributed to a sense of irritation within the band – it was after all three years from live shoot to silver screen. And three years in the life of, say, a Jimmy Page can be a long, long time.

Massot, steering clear of any emotional media battles with the band over what they had begun to view as a soured project, avoided any comment. But he certainly was distressed over the ultimate outcome of his strong emotional attachment to the project he'd more-or-less initiated. As he well knew however, Peter Grant and Jimmy Page were demanding masters, and not easy-going artists to work with on a creative level. More than a few people who've endeavoured to work with Grant and/or Page on various projects through the years privately attest to their erratic and unpredictable nature, their inexplicable mood swings, their lack of regard for normal business courtesies, compounded by frequent bouts of paranoia. 'These guys,' insisted one who preferred to remain unnamed, 'never did follow any of the rules. They just did what they wanted and damn the consequences. It was a sort of siege mentality.'

I can only add that there wasn't a great deal of difference between the early edited sequences I had watched so keenly at Massot's Hampstead home editing room and the final big-screen product. From Joe Massot's point of view, it had been a truly depressing conclusion to what had first been conceived on such a treacherously high and idealistic plane. Pity.

19 October 1976 was set as the New York world première for the launching of the long-awaited *The Song Remains the Same*. The band flew in from London for the special occasion, and received standing ovations from the audience. Among the celebrities attending the launch party were Mick Jagger, Roberta Flack, Mick Ronson, Bad Company's Simon Kirke, Rick Derringer and a pregnant Carly Simon. Both the movie and the after-show event drew warm praise from *Melody Maker*'s Chris Charlesworth. Rather astonishing since the same writer had

allegedly been attacked by a drunken Richard Cole and thrown out of a New York nightclub. Charlesworth reportedly was granted two apology calls in three days from a grieving Robert over the incident.

Proceeding nonetheless, a forgiving Charlesworth wrote, 'There is a sequence that says more about the rock business in five minutes than anything previously reproduced in film or book over the past twenty years.' He concluded, '. . . three years in the making, *The Song Remains the Same* is a classy, and surely enormously successful, film.'

It's worth reflecting on the Swan Song press release (not issued by Danny Goldberg – he'd been dumped by Peter Grant in the spring) proclaiming the film's release. It likely demonstrates how Zeppelin in 1976 hoped the movie might be viewed by an all too cynical media.

'*The Song Remains the Same* captures the being and the essence of the four people who make Led Zeppelin the most exciting and durable of rock groups. A film directed by Peter Clifton and Joe Massot, produced by Swan Song Inc. with Peter Grant as Executive Producer, the Warner Bros. movie has taken three painstakingly precise years of work to reach the cinema. Incorporating live concert footage, fantasy sequences, backstage glimpses of the band and a personal view of them at ease at home, *The Song Remains the Same* is a rare and human look at four rock musicians. It was their idea, their project totally, and it is their special way of giving their millions of fans what they have been clamouring for – a personal and private tour of Led Zeppelin. *The Song Remains the Same* reveals the members of Led Zeppelin as they really are, and for the first time, the world has a front row seat on Led Zeppelin.'

Such a mundane press statement does little to communicate the actual creativity and adventure of the film. It was set to open in New York on 20 October, followed two days later by openings in LA, San Francisco, Chicago, Toronto, Dallas, Boston and Atlanta, all super-strong Led Zeppelin markets.

A double album of the soundtrack was simultaneously released on Swan Song featuring the established concert classics included in the film: 'Rock and Roll', 'Celebration Day', 'Rain Song', 'Dazed and Confused', 'No Quarter', 'Stairway to Heaven', 'Moby Dick', 'Whole Lotta Love' and the title song. 'The Song Remains the Same', of course, was the hot rock, international-outlook classic which kicked off *Houses of the Holy*. Originally its melody had been saddled with the working title of 'The Campaign', and it finally surfaced as the backing track for Robert's 'Song Remains the Same' lyrics.

The album shipped platinum in America and also topped the UK charts by mid-way through November. But critics once again were far from kind to the live album. Many took exception to the fact that it had taken until 1976 to release a film of a 1973 concert. Some media observers implied none too subtly that both the album and the movie – plus the band – were outdated, a fairly radical statement. Reviewing in *Rolling Stone*, Dave Marsh poured it on. 'Far from being a monument to Zeppelin's stardom, *The Song Remains the Same* is a tribute to their rapaciousness and inconsideration. While Led Zeppelin's music remains worthy of respect (even if their best songs are behind them), their sense of themselves merits only contempt.'

The wrath of the critics once again had no influence on chart movement as Atlantic proudly announced the film had 'gotten to the number thirteen spot on the *Variety* top-gross [film] charts, a remarkable feat considering the fact it was only running in seven theatres in seven cities.'

By 21 November, *The Song Remains the Same* was screening in a further 57 cities as it gathered national momentum. It was a reasonable box office success, and even its distributor, Warner Brothers, was surprised by the extent of its American acceptance. An interview with Jack Schonfeld, assistant to the general sales manager of Warners, in mid-1977 revealed the bottom-line story on the *Song Remains the Same* project. 'Oh boy,' he crowed, 'this film has been very, very successful. It's done $3 million in film rentals and another $9 million-plus in box office percentages. So it's well over the $10 million mark and those are real figures – that's not bullshit.

'My guess is that the film cost the band around $750,000 to produce, so you can see how well the project has done for them. We honestly didn't think we'd do half that business. It's been phenomenal for that kind of movie. It's been in *Variety*'s Top Ten and I think it could only be regarded as a spectacular success . . . I don't think that even the Rolling Stones went anywhere near that. There's no doubt that Led Zeppelin is the only act that could draw in these quantities. They certainly have maintained their position at the top of the rock pile. Plus the picture is still performing. It's still a very active property. Everyone is really pleased.'

It's difficult to track down final figures at this point in time, but the film was released on home video through Warner in 1991.

Probably because of the extended delays between its performance and the public release, Led Zeppelin members have always had artistic reservations about the merit of the movie. After British critics gave the film a right slagging, Page came to its defence, sort of: 'It's not a great film, just a reasonably honest statement of where we were at a particular time. That's all it can be, really.'

Later Page elaborated on certain aspects he felt had to be taken into account in any true appreciation of the project. 'There's a lot of points to be weighed up,' he said carefully. 'It's a musical, yes, but it's also a documentary. For example, the robbery [on the final day of filming, Led Zeppelin's hotel safety deposit box was mysteriously robbed of $203,000]. You've got to take that into account, and, for example, the fact that when we were onstage playing that gig, half the band actually knew about the robbery and the other half didn't know. So the playing isn't totally . . . you know, plus it was right at the end of a long tour.

'At first we weren't going to put anything about the robbery in the film, but then again, it is relevant.' Page was at pains to point out that only three concerts of a huge US tour were actually filmed [because of Grant's belated decision to fly over the Joe Massot film crew] and it wasn't a film of the entire tour. 'As regards the actual gig that was used in the film,' he noted, 'it wasn't a terribly good night and it wasn't terribly bad. It certainly wasn't a magic one – but it wasn't tragic.'

Shortly after the film was released, Page said, 'It's still very difficult to view it even now. I'd like to see it in a year's time, just to see how it stands up. Because it's extremely relevant to the band, because simply – for us – it sums up a certain era. In a nutshell, the film sums up the era when the band finished its set with "Whole Lotta Love". I know that *The Song Remains the Same* was a live album, but it wasn't the *best* performances necessarily. It was just the ones that happened to have celluloid to match up with. There are loads of howling guitar mistakes on there. Normally one would have been inclined to cut them out, but you can't do that when it's a soundtrack. It's an honest album in its own way, but a chronological live album is something I've always wnted to get together.'

While the world flocked into movie theatres to experience *The Song Remains the Same*, Led Zeppelin members were secretly involved in strenuous rehearsal sessions at an old movie theatre owned by Emerson, Lake and Palmer in suburban London. Even before the momentous announcement of a return to the live stage was torpedoed to the media in early February, the band was getting its new concert act together.

Looking back from a 1991 perspective, John Paul Jones was

reluctant to dismiss the movie as a failed project. 'Well, I'm embarrassed to watch it now, of course, as one is. But maybe it provided a bit of an inner look at the band members. I suppose it was a bit of a ground-breaker. There wasn't much of anything else around like it. We just wanted to do a concert movie. Some people didn't like it. Some people hated the band. There'll always be people who slag you off. I don't really worry about it.'

The band members were also checking out some of the protagonists of the highly touted punk scene – turning out after rehearsals to gigs by the Damned (described by Page as 'fantastic'), Eater and Generation X.

Robert Plant had now recovered from the ankle injury sustained in the car accident, and it was grandly announced that the eleventh North American tour would begin in Dallas on 27 February with British shows to follow later in the summer. However Plant came down with tonsillitis and the tour was postponed to an April Fool's Day kick-off in Dallas.

The band's equipment had previously been shipped to America for the original February start, and so the lads were stuck in London with time on their hands. It was rather anti-climactic all round, but band spirits lifted in mid-February with the results of major US and British music polls. For the fourth consecutive year, the band cut a swathe through the honours roll – gaining five first places in both *Creem* and *Circus* magazine polls for 1976, and six firsts in the *New Musical Express* line-up. Over 40,000 ballots were cast in the *Circus* readers' poll declaring Led Zeppelin the year's best group. Jimmy Page topped Jeff Beck and Queen's Brian May to maintain his position as best guitarist. Robert Plant was voted number one male vocalist, and the best songwriting award went to Page and Plant over their much poppier contemporaries, Elton John and Bernie Taupin. Jimmy Page won the top spot as producer of the year. Led Zeppelin were voted the year's foremost live act, which was remarkable considering that Plant's ankle injury had prevented the band from performing live for two long years. John Bonham took second place as best drummer and bassist John Paul Jones ranked second in his field.

The readers of *Creem* voted Jimmy Page best guitarist and most valuable player. Robert Plant came in as top male vocalist, while *The Song Remains the Same* was awarded the number one movie slot. According to *Creem* readers, the 'biggest disappointment of the year' was no Led Zeppelin tour. The group also captured two second prizes – best LP cover for *Presence*, and best songwriters.

The *New Musical Express* poll selected the group as the year's top band. Jimmy Page and Robert Plant completed the sweep, grabbing top honours as guitarist and vocalists respectively. John Bonham was voted best drummer, while *The Song Remains the Same* grabbed the number one album award, and took the top prize for best cover design. Jimmy Page was also voted the second most wonderful human being of the year, following right after Johnny Rotten of the Sex Pistols, a most unusual coupling.

After what seemed to band members like an interminable wait, they finally set forth in late March for the long-awaited – and keenly anticipated – return to the boards. Each member of the band experienced some stage nerves after the two-year break from public performing, but none more so than Robert Plant, who admitted to *Melody Maker* editor, Ray Coleman, who had flown over to cover this eleventh American rampage, 'I was really at home with the idea of playing. The only thing I didn't know about was whether I was going to be able to pace myself out, with this foot problem. For the first two or three gigs, I was really measuring every move I made, to find out if I'd gone too far or whatever.

'I was petrified at the first gig in Dallas. Since the Earl's Court gigs in London, all this horrendous physical hoo-hah had taken place and for the ten minutes before I walked up those stage steps in Dallas, I was cold with fright. Supposing I couldn't move around the stage properly, because my right foot is permanently enlarged now? It was killing for the first two gigs. I had to be virtually carried back on one foot. But once I'd got it used to the concussive knocks of stage work, it was okay and now I've paced myself so I can work without anyone, hopefully realising that I have this thing to live with.

'The thing is I don't really know what I'm doing with my body when I'm playing and I just throw myself around the stage instinctively. But Dallas was the worry: I constantly thought about what would happen if the foot wouldn't take it. Yet when I walked up the steps to the stage, all the premonitions and anxieties washed away and the exhilaration took over. I thought, "Ah, it's been *so long*!" I just loved being back up there. I was a loony again.'

The other major source of potential distress for the band was the absence of a new album's fresh material to be highlighted on the 1977 'Led Zep Returns' extravaganza. The band had always prided itself on taking risks with new material in its concert repertoire, but this time out they were – in Plant's wistful words – 'trading on past glories'. Predictably a large majority of concert-goers were simply delighted to hear the band rejuvenating well-known songs, but in the early stages, the band was reticent about the lack of *new* glories. Perhaps they underestimated likely public reaction to the return of their splendid acoustic set (which hadn't been done in North America for seven years) and the live début of unexpected tunes such as 'The Battle of Evermore', which had been rejected in the past because the band felt it couldn't be accurately reproduced without the presence of singer Sandy Denny, who'd been featured on the original track.

'To begin with, people *were* a little bit restless,' Robert eventually admitted mid-way through the tour. 'They didn't know what the hell was going on. They kept looking at us, presumably thinking, "Are they really *that* old?" But because of the way in which we've taken up the challenge of re-working our old material – and introducing some unlikely aspects of it into our stage work – we've gone a stage further again.

'For the first few concerts, we would look at each other on stage rather sheepishly. But suddenly it burst through after six gigs so that by the time we got to places like St Louis, it had taken on another level of control, rather than merely trotting out the old favourites.'

The basic repertoire for the 1977 tour was fairly predictable – the set, which sometimes stretched to three dazzling hours – opened up with 'The Song Remains the Same', followed by 'Nobody's Fault But Mine', gearing down to 'Since I've Been Loving You', 'No Quarter' (featuring an extended keyboard solo by John Paul Jones, climaxing with his robust rendition of the classic 1962 rock piano instrumental, 'Nut Rocker', by B. Bumble and the Stingers), 'Achilles' Last Stand', 'Ten Years Gone', 'In My Time of Dying', 'The Wanton Song', 'Kashmir', 'Out on the Tiles' (with Bonzo's crowd-busting twenty-minute drum celebration), 'Moby Dick' and the closer, 'Stairway to Heven', with an encore medley of 'Whole Lotta Love' and 'Rock and Roll'.

The acoustic set, introduced midway through each performance, offered 'The Battle of Evermore', 'Bron-Y-Aur Stomp', 'Black Country Woman' and 'Going to California'. It was a simply amazing show, superbly paced and usually executed in grand style. As an exercise in summing up their seven-album career, it was an impeccable and indeed unforgettable set.

Associates close to the band had been quietly concerned about the pre-tour vibe shortly before the Dallas start. There was a prevailing feeling that this tour wouldn't be like many of the previous crusades. Peter Grant, the man responsible for maintaining high spirits on the road in all senses of that seductive state, was bummed out because his wife had left him, allegedly for one of his farm workers. Jimmy Page appeared in a rather weak state and there was an over-abundance of heroin in the entourage.

'It's funny, but I hated that last tour,' claimed Richard Cole. 'You could feel it . . . something very bad. It was all the drugs, I suppose. It wasn't the same.' Jimmy Page was reported to have observed in Chicago that he 'can't just play safe. Dancing on the edge of the precipice – you've gotta live like that. Better to live one day as a lion than a thousand years as a lamb.' Pagey also noted, 'Led Zeppelin is a stag party that never ends. This is no last tour. We're here and we'll always come back. It would be a criminal act to break up this band.'

The entire tour was sold out within days of its announcement. It provides an adequate re-evaluation of the extent of Led Zeppelin popularity to run through the attendance numbers on the first leg of the tour – Dallas (10,000), Oklahoma (15,000), Chicago (76,000 over four nights), Minneapolis (40,000), St Louis (20,000), Indianapolis (16,000), Cincinatti (40,000), Atlanta (17,500), Louisville (17,000), Cleveland (36,000) and Pontiac, Michigan (76,229).

The Pontiac date was a recordbreaker by any definition, a stunning climax to the first leg. 'On Saturday 30 April,' proclaimed Swan Song, 'Led Zeppelin set a new world's record for the largest paid attendance at a single-artist performance in history. 76,229 people filled the Silverdome Stadium in Pontiac to rock and roll with the British supergroup – the previous record had been set by the Who on 6 December, 1975, with 75,962 in attendance at the Silverdome. Zeppelin's gross for the evening, $792,361.50, was also a record breaker (the Who grossed $604,952). Even more remarkable, the Zeppelin show was sold out in one day over the counter at the stadium box office, while it took the Who ten days to sell their tickets by mail order.'

Pontiac was a massive occasion for the audience, but not necessarily for the entertainers. John Paul Jones didn't have particularly fond memories when asked in 1991 about the gig. 'It was awful. It felt like a sound check in the dark. The audience was so far away – there was nothing coming back. You couldn't see them or even hardly hear them.

And it was cold. It was everything you'd expect to be the worst of a huge gig.'

Although the band had dropped 'Dazed and Confused' from the set, one close friend said it was still the essential state of play in Jimmy Page's lifestyle. Pagey had long talked of visiting Crowley's old haunt of Cairo, and when the tour broke for a two-week rest period, he finally took the plunge. He told friends he'd been watching a TV programme one night on the many mysteries of the pyramids. During an old newsreel segment, a Zeppelin was shown flying over the ancient stone piles. It convinced Page that it was time to head for Cairo.

The news distressed me. On the last occasion that I'd spoken to Jimi Hendrix in September 1970 (in what fate would determine to be his final media conversation), he too had been leaving America bound for Egypt. His destination was further up the Nile, to Memphis, where a dream had told him he would meet his maker.

Despite my premonitions, Pagey survived his four-day sojourn in the ancient Egyptian capital, and returned to blaze on 18 May his guitar magic at Birmingham, Alabama (19,000), following through with Baton Rouge (18,000), Houston (18,000), Fort Worth (17,000), Washington (78,000 over four nights), Greenboro (16,000), New York (120,000 over six nights), San Diego (18,000), Los Angeles (120,000 over six nights), and after a short break, Seattle (65,000), Tempe, Arizona (14,000) and San Francisco (110,000 over two nights). The Bill Graham-promoted dates in the Oakland Stadium made a pile of money for all concerned, but they were marred by a widely publicised incident in which Peter Grant, Led Zeppelin security man John Bindon, John Bonham and Richard Cole were involved in a violent altercation with security staff employed by Graham.

By all accounts, a security man had shoved Peter Grant's young son Warren. Seeing this happen, John Bonham went over and kicked the guard. Upon hearing about the incident, Peter Grant and Led Zeppelin's head security man, John Bindon, took the offending guard into a trailer where they kicked the shit out of him until he needed hospitalisation while Richard Cole was supposed to have stood guard outside. Another Graham security guard was roughed up by Cole.

The next night Led Zeppelin played the second of their Oakland shows but the vibes backstage were black and ugly. Bill Graham – who could boast a tempestuous relationship with Peter Grant over the years – stated flatly, 'I could never in good conscience book Led Zeppelin again.'

Packing up the next morning for the trip to New Orleans on their Caesar's Chariot jet hired from the Caesar's Palace gambling organisation, Richard Cole glanced out of the window and saw police SWAT teams surrounding the hotel.

Minutes after Cole had flushed the cocaine supply, he was arrested along with Grant, Bonham and Bindon. They were charged with assault and allowed bail of $250 each.

The incident bummed out the tour, which still had seven SRO concerts set to unfold, including New Orleans (80,000), Chicago (36,000), Buffalo (66,000), Pittsburgh (32,000) and Philadelphia (the 95,000 outdoor tour closer at JFK Stadium).

With a six-day break before the New Orleans Superdome performance which would break their own recently set Pontiac one-act attendance record, John Paul Jones took his family on a Californian camping holiday. Grant and Page stayed in San Francisco, and Plant, Bonham and Cole flew the tour jet on to New Orleans.

As they checked into the Royal Orleans hotel, Robert was advised that the switchboard had his wife on the phone from England with an urgent call. It would be two hours before he would reappear with the horrifying news that his five-year-old son, Karac, was dead. Only months before, Plant had told a reporter, 'We call him Baby Austin after that Bionic Man. He knows no fear, has no anticipation of danger. I envy him.'

On 26 July, Karac had come down with a violent respiratory virus. When his condition worsened the next morning, an ambulance was called but Karac Plant died before reaching the Kidderminster Hospital.

In a state of absolute shock, Robert flew back to Birmingham with John Bonham, to be with his wife Maureen. He was met at the airport by his father who told the assembled media precisely what they wanted to hear in terms of banner headlines. 'All this success and fame, what is it worth? It doesn't mean much when you compare it to the love of a family.'

11 Stage Two: Coming Back In Through the Out Door

FOLLOWING THE TRAGIC, HEART-BREAKING DEATH of Karac Plant, the boy named so passionately after a heroic Celtic general, Led Zeppelin's career momentum ground to a silent heartfelt halt as the three other band members tried – hopelessly and helplessly – to ease Robert's profound grief.

As *People* magazine would later less-than-tactfully conclude, 'While Plant mourned, Led Zeppelin cancelled dates and went spiralling down a stairway of depression.' It wasn't *quite* that grim but the spirit in the band's camp for many moons remained subdued and often sullen. Robert would ultimately admit, 'We did nothing for a year and a half. I tinkered on the village piano and grew so obese drinking beer that nobody knew who I was.' Grief wears many masks.

The death of long-time inspirational idol Elvis Presley on 16 August of a barbiturate overdose added to their unified pain – this band, not socially inclined to spend time together, always drew instinctively closer in the peaks and troughs of good and bad times.

The mood wasn't improved the following month when John Bonham's car spun out of control near his home in Cutnall Green and Bonzo suffered three broken ribs.

And as if the pervasive lingering pain of Karac's death wasn't sufficiently daunting, a sudden spate of Led Zeppelin breaking-up rumours in the British pop tabloids brought added pressure. It was certainly not the right time to deal with this rubbish, but the stories became so prevalent that rock's ultimate recluse, Jimmy Page, was forced to leave the secure confines of his moated manor house in Sussex to journey up to London and face the accusers. The idea of even having to do it appalled him, but the situation had gotten out of hand and was threatening their confused future.

The thrust of his dialogue was, 'No, there is no question of us splitting up. I *know* Robert wants to work again – he'll start working at his own pace to begin with, but I know he wants to work again.' To *Melody Maker*'s usually sympathetic Chris Welch, Page conceded, 'I've got to say to you right now that there are areas that are bloody touchy. You see, I've never known a family to have such bad luck as Robert's and it's really awful. The worst thing is not being able to do anything . . . a feeling of helplessness really.'

Page particularly (and often vitriotically in comments to friends) resented media slurs and inferences that the band had been cursed by alleged bad karma, and was invariably bound – through Page's own involvement with the occult – to suffer grievously a series of continuing mishaps, accidents and tragedies. 'It's [karma] just the wrong term to ever use, and how somebody could write that down, knowing the full facts about what has happened, I don't know. It shocks me. The whole concept of the band is entertainment. I don't see any link between that and karma, and yet I've seen it written a few times about us, like "yet another incident in Zeppelin's karma – John Paul Jones has a broken hand". It's nonsense – that was years back. It's all crap. This thing about karma really bothers me. Where's the clue? Why are they using that term? It's a horrible, tasteless thing to say.'

Jimmy was confounded, and close to devastated. His overall opinion of the media had long since totally soured, and he found the karma contributions right over the top. And he was distinctly unimpressed by the tasteless timing of the flurry of Led Zeppelin break-up stories, all coming within weeks of the devastating death of Karac Plant. 'So much rubbish has been written about us lately,' Page complained. 'There was one thing about me joining the Stones, and it even got to the point of them asking Mick Jagger if Robert was joining them. I thought, "This is getting *really* silly". There were some rumours that Zeppelin was breaking up, all this sort of crap, and for some reason I just can't understand, it just keeps going on.

'In fact, I've been very busy for the past few months, but unless you're being monitored all the time, people think you're doing nothing. Actually I've finally got my studio set up at home. It's taken me fifteen years to turn it into a reality. Now it's all together. The console was installed last Janury and it's taken me all this time to sort out the acoustics.'

As Christmas 1977 crept into view, Page was privately absorbed at Plumpton Place in his home studio, none-too-anxiously awaiting Robert Plant's return to their ranks. To friends, Pagey was positive that it would eventually happen. But for now, the group had decided that there would be no serious consideration of any future Led Zeppelin activities as long as Plant wished to remain in mourning, so to speak, with his family.

Even the usually uplifting news that the band had once again swept the leading American and British music polls appeared to have little impact on the five wounded spirits. Zep took out five first places, including best group in *Circus* magazine's Shure Music Awards poll, four first prizes in *Melody Maker*'s poll, while Jimmy Page was named best guitarist in the *New Musical Express* and *Guitar Player* polls. The readers of *Circus* voted Plant best male vocalist by a margin of two to one, topping Queen's Freddie Mercury. Jimmy Page took the honours as top guitarist and producer, and Page/Plant were again named best songwriters. In addition, John Bonham was again voted third best drummer and John Paul Jones placed third in the bass division.

In Britain's prestigious *Melody Maker* poll, the sweep was repeated as Led Zeppelin were voted best group; Page and Plant best guitarist and producer, and vocalist, respectively. The 9 January 1979 Swan Song proclamation also trumpeted the fact that 1977 had been the year in which Led Zeppelin had established themselves as the world's primo concert draw, setting the world's number one and two box office gross records – at the Oakland Stadium where on 23 and 24 July, they played before 115,000 people, grossing $1,322,500; and for their six nights at New York's Madison Square Garden (7–14 June) which grossed $1,146,367.50. Big big buckaroos.

The Oakland dates, no matter what the gross, drew mixed emotional feelings from band members, especially the following month when Bonham, Grant, Cole and Binden were found guilty of assault charges, but given suspended sentences and one- or two-year probations. Promoter Bill Graham was reported to be furious at the outcome.

The band continued to lie low until May, when they reassembled – for the first time since Karac's sudden death and the abrupt cancellation of the US tour the previous July – for a month-long series of encouraging rehearsal sessions at the rented Clearwell Castle in the Forest of Dean near the Welsh border. The rehearsals had been hopefully scheduled by Jimmy – with Robert's grudging agreement – to sort through material for a ninth album, and a possible return to the live stage. Obviously it was a period of 'feeling out': an examination of prevailing musical emotions to see if, indeed, the four members *did* want to ride the gravy train any further down the line.

The sessions wound down on a positive note, and Page and Plant then entered a period of serious commitment to writing new songs. There never was any verbalised discussion of quitting or resuming. It was poised in the balance.

Back up the line, at the Wolverly Memorial Hall, the mysterious Melvin Giganticus and the Turd Burglers were joined on stage in July by Robert Plant, an old friend, who nonchalantly tossed off lively versions of 'I Got a Woman', 'Blue Suede Shoes' and other rock and roll favourites. A month later, the emerging Plant was up on the boards again – at the Club Amnesia on the Spanish resort of Ibiza – jamming with Dr Feelgood and the ever-jovial Phil Carson on bass. The manager of the club noted, 'Robert looked in great shape and sounded fantastic.'

September was marked by the notable public appearance of Page, Plant and Jones at the wedding reception for Simon Kirke of Bad Company and Richard Cole. Judging from Robert Plant's duly presented public persona, he was doing fine and friends presumed that Led Zeppelin was far from being history. The other heart-starting news that month was the death of Who drummer, Keith Moon, who overdosed on a drug he was consuming to quit alcohol abuse.

The break-up rumours had finally subsided but fans heard very little from the Led Zeppelin camp for several months. Behind the scenes, a revitalised band was extremely pre-occupied with secret London rehearsals for a bunch of exciting new tunes they'd recently gotten together. With Robert moving into a more positive frame of mind after his time of mourning, the aftermath of the Clearwell Castle musical reunion was that three of the four Zep members (Bonham excluded, for his contributions arose from the studio floor) had been prolifically writing new tunes, riffs and germs of ideas.

The preparations were shrouded in deep secrecy, even to long-time friends. The band wanted its much-speculated return to the scene to be a positive and stunning surprise, as indeed it would turn out to be.

When word of the renewal leaked out in the music tabloids in December (a few weeks before Robert and Maureen Plant celebrated the birth of a son, Logan Romero), the news was quite shattering, particularly to a new wave punk generation all too ready to shrug Led Zeppelin off as ancient dinosaurs. The long lost band were ensconced at the Polar Studios in Stockholm, a facility owned by the Swedish Europop group, Abba. Once again the month of December would bring

Led Zeppelin back to the studio tape machines, a phase of the calendar which had served them so well in the past.

Despite snide comments such as *New Musical Express*'s 'Local rumours have it that the album will be a lo-o-ong time coming,' the ninth album was basically supervised by John Paul Jones and was artfully assembled in a mere no-nonsense three-week period of unrelenting activity. Richard Cole might later describe the Stockholm sessions as 'cold and boring', but there would be no denying the band's prolific productivity under the purposeful direction of Jonesy.

It would be the first time that Jones would be the primary composer of all but one track ['Hot Dog'] on a Led Zeppelin album, and his unique and tasteful keyboard skills are showered throughout the tracks. In an exclusive 1991 interview, Jones admitted that he'd played a much larger production role in the ninth album, which would come to be called – quite sardonically – *In Through the Out Door*. 'In fact, Robert and I wrote quite a few of the songs together. And then Jimmy came along and added things to them later.'

Asked if this had been because Jimmy wasn't really up for it at the time, John Paul reflectively (and quite possibly, respectfully) paused before delivering a diplomatic response. 'I don't know. It just seemed that Robert and I got to rehearsals first.' He laughed a tad too heartily. 'We were left alone quite a lot of the time, along with Bonzo, and so we tended to get on with it, I think. I suppose you could say that *In Through the Out Door* is my album, the way *Presence* was Jimmy's album. Looking back on it now, it's one of my favourites from the band. It's quite a keyboard-driven album as well. That, of course, may have simply been coming around at the time, a different emphasis.'

Peter Grant noted, 'John Paul Jones certainly did pick up the reins of the band with the *In Through the Out Door* album. Some people thought we were fortunate to have a man of his calibre available to be able to take over the studio activities. Jonesy is a musical talent of great exception. People tended to think of him as a bass player but he went far, far beyond that. I'd known him from 1963 when he was a session musician and I was tour manager for Gene Vincent.'

Through the evolution of the Led Zeppelin albums, one sees a definite growth in the use and artistry of keyboard instruments in their songs, and one wonders if this had been a conscious growth in the mind of John Paul Jones. 'There was no master plan for any of it anyway,' he declared recently. 'I suppose I was playing more bass in the beginning, and then I wanted to play more keyboards. As the keyboard technology got better, we used more of them. Obviously in the early days we had the Hammond organ – which we used extensively on the first album, and in the early stage shows – but there weren't even electric pianos when we started.

'As the new keyboards became available, we used them. It was always a problem – in live shows – to integrate a keyboard successfully, especially up against guitars. Keyboards simply don't cut through. There weren't synthesisers in those days. We used the wretched mellotron for string pads and flute stuff.

'But there was never a preconceived plan for me to somehow evolve us into a keyboard band – it merely developed along with the technology.' Sometimes the technical advances could be a long time coming. Asked to describe his Led Zeppelin keyboard set-up, Jonesy insisted it was a 'nightmare'. 'I had a Hammond organ and a mellotron. Ah, that mellotron. There was a tune called "The Rain Song" that would start off on guitar and then move into strings played on the mellotron. I used to approach the song with the greatest trepidation and fear. I wondered what was going to come out when I put my hands on those keys. Would it be anywhere near pitch? Would it be at half-speed? Would it be a string sound or a flute sound?

'It used a system of tape loops and it was totally mechanical with plumbing inside of it and everything. As the gig would heat up, the tapes would start stretching and the motors would slip. I spent my entire technological career trying to replace the mellotron. I went all over the world looking for things to replace it with – right up until 1980 when we actually took a Fairlight on the road with us.'

Sceptics had suggested that the new album by the 'tired and worn out old farts' would be forever in the making – given Pagey's penchant for perfectionism – but they would be radically wrong. Within seven months of the news leaking out of Sweden, *In Through the Out Door* – with a total of six separate album jackets no less – would be opening on the streets. Like the previous studio album *Presence*, the ninth album had been produced secretly on the Continent with a minimum of fuss, unwanted intrusions, the usual rip-roaring ribaldry or – most important – artistic indulgence.

It had been 35 arduous months – for Led Zeppelin and the rock scene at large – since the release of the eighth album, *The Song Remains the Same*, and the public were ardently anxious to hear if indeed it had. With three and a half event-filled years since the last studio album – never had the band allowed so much time to elapse between new original material, but a heartful of personal changes had gone down in the intervening period – enough, one thinks, to totally destabilise just about any other band.

And thus the band's return to a radically altered punk-driven music scene was viewed rather seriously by Led Zeppelin members – it wasn't an undertaking to be taken lightly or timidly. Consequently persistent plans were also being hatched to spring the band back on to the performing stage, where they had ruled so thoroughly through the 1970s. The band's millions of concert fans – starved for so many months – would find a whole new buzz in their existence come August 1979.

The unpredictable Peter Grant had been wined, dined and delighted on the wings of countless promoter proposals for massive outdoor concerts headlining Zeppelin in Britain over the past decade. A handful of this barrel of offers had been deliberated on to the extent that Grant had actually inspected proposed sites and venues. But it wasn't until the early summer of 1979 that the circumstances seemed right and Grant undertook serious negotiations with Freddie Bannister. The veteran entrepreneur was assembling his sixth annual Knebworth Park Festival in the spacious grounds of a stately home near Stevenage in Hertfordshire, an hour north of London.

Finally Grant agreed for Led Zeppelin to headline a diverse talent line-up consisting of (in order of appearance) Fairport Convention, Chas and Dave, Commander Cody, Southside Johnny and the Ashbury Dukes, and Todd Rundgren with Utopia. It would be Led Zeppelin's first British appearance since the triumphant Earl's Court series four years earlier, and it was scheduled to take place on 4 August.

Asked to provide his rationale in making the decision to do the Knebworth comeback shows, Peter Grant unearthed some revelations in an exclusive conversation in 1992. 'One of the biggest factors influencing the decision was that Robert Plant – after he'd lost his son – wasn't keen on continuing in any way. So I had to re-affirm that thing within the four of them that they were still the biggest and the best.

'I told them that we hadn't played in England since 1975, and we had a site that could take 200,000 people. "I think you can fill it for two weekends and this is the proof that you" – mainly Robert – "should continue," I said. That was one of the most important things – deciding to make that approach to them.'

Was it then such a battle persuading Plant to return to Led Zeppelin, I asked Grant. 'Yes, it was a battle,' he said, 'although "battle" perhaps is the wrong word – more a case of convincing him. After what he had went through in losing his son during that last tour, I don't know how the man managed to hold everything together. But he did, and he came through with flying colours. It speaks for itself, and I do want to emphasise that.'

The British music media – never too comfortable with Led Zeppelin's irrefutable international success – was in the murky midst of post-punk fever as the daffodils bloomed in the spring of 1979. When the Led Zeppelin at Knebworth news was announced, the more cynical journos and musicians stupidly seized on it as a long-awaited opportunity to determine if the band really still did mean anything, if their mid-1970s popularity had been sustained during their lengthy absence. In the media, it had become hip to dismiss Zeppelin as old dinosaurs, some far-distant excess from eons back, the diehards of decadence. The pre-occupation with punk – and the natural aspirations of eager young musicians trying to muscle established heavyweights such as Led Zeppelin out of the mainstream – apparently annihilated critical faculties. *New Musical Express*, in a typical bashing piece, reflected, 'The manner in which old superfart Led Zeppelin have consistently presented themselves has made the band's name synonymous with gratuitous excess . . . part of the reason for the venomous loathing directed at the band is not just because they've let themselves down, but also because you know damn well that Jimmy Page at least – like so many of the new punk icons a former art student – certainly knows better.' Similarly, the Clash bass player, Paul Simenon, was reported to have spurted out, 'Led Zeppelin? I don't need to hear the music. All I have to do is look at one of their album covers and I feel like throwing up!'

Feelings ran deep in the dying seasons of the 1970s, and Zeppelin were clearly ripe for the shooting. But to cast them alongside Elton John, the Moody Blues and Pink Floyd as ageing, aching icons of another time with no current relevance was surely misplaced. Led Zeppelin were always separate from the rest of the pack, the run-of-the-mill 1970s supergroups, as they were about to forcefully demonstrate. The cynics suggested that slow ticket sales on Knebworth would be the ultimate measure of the band's current popularity – any box office reluctance would prove the demise of the Led Zeppelin era.

The band's legion of big-mouthed detractors were in for an awful shock. When Knebworth tickets went on sale (without the announcement of any supporting acts), a mind-blowing total of 264,000 were sold within just two days! It was phenomenal. Grant and the band were overjoyed – so much for their alleged slide in popularity and significance. So much for the punk attacks and media bash-ups – the numbers spoke volumes. In reality, the band had never been more popular, as audience reaction to the forthcoming ninth album would shortly prove.

August 4th dawned bright and sunny, setting the stage for what would go down in the annals of rock history as one of the greatest outdoor concerts that Britain had ever experienced. Fans had been gathering in the environs of Knebworth for days prior to the event, and they'd made incredible journeys from as far afield as Ireland, all over Europe, the US, Canada and Japan. A temporary village of tents arose in the fields around the stately mansion. Writing for the *Cleveland Scene*, Rhonda Kiefer coloured in the Knebworth lead-up: 'The concert was the talk of the town; the talk told you that this was *the* social event of the year . . . the obvious place to be. Clearly the festival had become an enormous event, regardless of actual music content, even before it began.'

She went on to describe the backstage scene. 'While waiting for the Big Ones, I noticed how many little children are backstage with their parents and realise how old rock and roll is getting . . . here I am looking at the next rock and roll generation and it's almost 1980! Jimmy Page arrives. Five years ago, I never dreamed I'd see Page dressed any other way except as a magician but he hops out of his limousine wearing a tan suit and looking very sharp. It occurs to me that perhaps Led Zeppelin too have begun to feel the hands of time; that maybe they've become more subdued and laid back in their habits.' The writer also was at pains to point out that Page chainsmokes Marlboros.

Paul Morley, reviewing for *New Musical Express*, worked diligently at setting the musical scene at Knebworth, and also at trying to pigeonhole Led Zeppelin's artistic endeavours. The festival, Morley figured, 'was like a ghost of those simpler, smoother progressive rock days, ironically saved only by the nervous energy and genuine amazed-to-be-there vitality of the accepted Holy Ghosts themselves, Led Zeppelin.

'They are one of the few [progressive rock] groups of that era and that school of thought who can make some sense in the contemporary scheme of things. Perhaps out of curiosity or desperation, they did blend their base heavy rock with all sorts of vague strains and they also attempted to push out the borders of heavy metal by exploring the possibilities of repetition and structure.

'When Led Zeppelin play rock and roll – and "Trampled Underfoot" is a classic example – I can begin to understand why people call them the greatest. They come back faced with ridiculously unfair complications, and all we can say is: "What took you so long?" There is no reason why Led Zeppelin should ever speak again; no one has any right to demand activity. One of the bravest moves of the year must be Zeppelin performing when the blanket of suspicion, cynicism and indeed *HATE* must have been suffocating.'

Just after the sun had set on a splendid day (as per Peter Grant's strict traditional dictum), the band hit the stage at 9.45 p.m. and launched into a sensational three-hour comeback set which included in order of preentation: 'The Song Remains the Same', 'Black Dog', 'Nobody's Fault but Mine', 'Over the Hills and Far Away', 'Misty Mountain Hop', 'Since I've Been Loving You', 'No Quarter', 'Ten Years Gone', 'Hot Dog', 'The Rain Song', 'Kashmir', 'Trampled Underfoot', 'Sick Again', 'Achilles' Last Stand', 'In the Evening', 'Stairway to Heaven' and three glorious encores – 'Rock and Roll', 'Whole Lotta Love' and 'Heartbreaker'. It was a fiercely formidable line-up of old and new repertoire.

New Musical Express reported that the lads 'enjoyed themselves and showed it. This is probably the only reason they've returned. They played erratically and delightedly for over three hours. What was most noticeable was the relative brand new economy, the nervousness and unexpected edgy spontaneity. It would be needlessly cruel not to praise the Zeppelin. For these hours alone they were much more than a stabilised anachronism. They did more than enough not to embarrass themselves. At times they were playing rock and roll of such stinging insistence and convulsive perseverence it wouldn't have mattered how old or processed it was.

'Led Zeppelin didn't do enough to live up to their distorted legend, but tht was surely not what it was about. They didn't do anything that proved the last three years have been a waste of time. No one will ever be so big and trapped again, not because rock and roll is declining, but because the load is being spread. I respect what Led Zeppelin did, and although I may eventually lose that respect, right now I'm on their side. Led Zeppelin at Knebworth were a triumph.'

Wrapping up the Knebworth reunion concert in mere words was a futile exercise – unless you actually *saw* ecstatic fans setting fire to tents, newspapers, pieces of wood and even themselves as they pleaded for encore after encore, you couldn't begin to imagine the raw fervour which the band back on the concert stage had generated. The intensity of it had to be seen to be believed.

Yet some media commentators completely missed the point of the exercise. The Reuters correspondent dashed off a superficial news report (reprinted by newspapers on five continents) which stated, '. . . the general verdict was that they had sounded better before.' Noting that 100,000 of the faithful had shown up (in fact, official attendance was near 140,000) Reuters rambled on, 'Zeppelin performed many of their classics, like a "Whole Lotta Love" [sic], but reliance on the old, along with sketchy performances of some newer material, just reminded fans that music has come a long way since success was measured in volume as much as artistry.' This lamentable report was typical of the sort of rubbish churned out by sundry wire services about the 1970s rock scene.

After the second Knebworth concert by Led Zeppelin a week later on 11 August – which would be the band's final live performance in the 1970s – Robert Plant told a *People* reporter, 'Because we laid off for two years, our directions are fresh.' John Paul Jones, attending the gig with his wife Mo and their three daughters, joked backstage that the new tunes were 'brilliant as ever. It was like the first day that we played together.' Robert Plant neatly summed up the prevailing attitude of the revitalised Zeppelin when he noted, 'It's a case with me of maintaining a very good equilibrium by keeping so tied to my family. With what happened to me, I thought I might not have anything left to give, but I found out I've still got it – from here to the moon!'

Recently asked to recall his reactions to the Knebworth comeback triumph, Peter Grant was momentarily lost for words. 'Well, it was pretty fantastic. It was phenomenal. There were 218,000 people there the first weekend – and I must impress on you that that's a *true* figure, although it's not what was said in the press or by the authorities.

'What I did was have aerial photos taken of the site, and we sent them over to one of those American laboratories that deal with filming the moon and things like that. They can guarantee you a plus or minus two per cent true head-count of a crowd. They counted 218,000 the first weekend and 187,000 the second weekend. The interest was absolutely phenomenal – the post office even had to hire special lorries to carry the postal requests to the promoter's office.'

Perhaps the definitive overview of the spectacular Knebworth gigs was provided by John Paul Jones, quite a few moons down the track. 'What I particularly remember about them was the astonishing amount of people that turned up for it,' he mused. 'I think it was a special occasion for the band. But I'd have to say that I do look back on it with some sadness – because it was really the start of a whole new era for us that never actually got going.'

Advance promo copies of *In Through the Out Door* were delivered to radio stations across America on 20 August, and one million copies saturated the nation's record stores a couple of days later. The first million units were sold in two days, and retail re-orders within five days surged to an additional 700,000 copies. An announcement from Atlantic chronicled the chart statistics in impressive terms. '*In Through the Out Door* has exploded on to the top of the national trade charts, reflecting the phenomenal response which has instantly greeted the LP. The début chart positions are: *Record World* – number one with a bullet, *Cashbox* – number one with a bullet, and *Billboard* – number ten with a bullet. This initial performance makes the LP by far the hottest album in recent memory.'

Within seven days *In Through the Out Door* had become Led Zeppelin's sixth number one album, and its fifth to début on US charts in the top ten. Not a bad start for a veteran band that sceptical pundits had caustically claimed were 'over the hill' and 'out of touch' with contemporary music realities. Not bad at all.

Led Zeppelin mania raged on the airwaves, in the stores and all over bestselling charts as the music industry celebrated the return of its crown princes. With *In Through the Out Door* entrenched at number one on all the charts, earlier albums were refuelled for chart re-entries. On 19 September, Atlantic revealed, '. . . sales of Led Zeppelin's previous LPs are enjoying a substantial upsurge. *Billboard* now lists no less than seven Led Zeppelin albums as bestsellers. All of the chart LPs are bulleted, beginning with *In Through the Out Door* and followed by the fourth album at number 90, *Houses of the Holy* (121), *Physical Graffiti* (161), *Led Zeppelin II* (164), *Song Remains* (174) and the first album (184). Current Led Zeppelin sales are such that retailers report that many of the eight previous LPs are among their hottest records in stock, often outselling many popular new releases.'

Such was the Led Zeppelin influence on American retail records sales that trade mags ran articles claiming the band had saved the entire industry from a severe slump. It was a shot in the arm for rock at a time when it was direly needed, and harked back to the golden days of Elvis Presley in terms of one artist's influence on retail trade at large.

Atlantic executives quietly figured that – apart from the obvious musical supremacy of the band, and the three-year gap in studio product – one of the prime reasons for such an avalanche of sales on *In Through the Out Door* was the elaborately contrived method of packaging. There were in fact six slightly different album sleeves, variations on a theme within a paper bag, and a certain lure for the devoted addict. Said one Atlantic vice president, 'By focusing on the paper bag album cover rather than the inner jacket and sleeve, the "mysterious" quality of the whole package is enhanced, while the appearance of the album as it is displayed in the stores is reinforced. The elaborate packaging concept was designed by Hipgnosis, and it includes the production of six different album sleeves which are inserted into a plain brown bag simply stamped with the group's name, title and tracks. There is also a common inner sleeve which holds the disc itself. The whole package is shrink-wrapped, and therefore the buyer is unable to determine which cover variation he or she has until after the purchase is made.'

The striking concept for the half-a-dozen different sleeves was dreamed up by Peter Grant, Jimmy Page and Hipgnosis. Noted Grant at just prior to its release, 'Atlantic didn't even know until quite recently that there were six different jackets. We had sworn the printers to secrecy.

On 24 October, Atlantic was able to declare, '*Led Zeppelin III* débuted on the *Billboard* pop album chart this week, making a total of nine Led Zeppelin LPs in the Top 200. The nine albums represent the group's entire catalogue. No recording group or artist has had that many LPs on *Billboard*'s charts since Mitch Miller accomplished the feat in 1961.

'Leading the way is Led Zeppelin's latest LP *In Through the Out Door* which has held down the number one spot for the past seven weeks. The album, Led Zeppelin's first studio LP in more than three years, racked up multi-platinum sales in its first week of release. *In Through the Out Door* has generally been credited with spurring an industry-wide "comeback" in the third quarter of 1979. The other eight Led Zeppelin albums have accounted for unit sales in excess of one million units this year. This unprecedented upsurge in sales was a major factor in Atlantic's record-breaking third quarter performance, which saw the label exceed $45 million in gross sales.'

In Canada, WEA reported that *In Through the Out Door* had been certified triple platinum. Public attention appeared to focus on four particular tracks: 'In the Evening', 'Fool in the Rain', 'All My Love' and 'I'm Gonna Crawl'.

'In the Evening', a splendid vehicle for Page's grandiose guitar concepts, arose out of his composing sessions for the aborted *Lucifer Rising* soundtrack. With Robert repeatedly screaming out 'I've got pain' the song had a special redemptive spirit. 'Fool in the Rain', which would subsequently be a Top-20 single from the album, was a certain stand-out. 'Yes, we were pleased with that,' agreed John Paul Jones recently. 'It was very Latin-influenced.'

'All My Love', the touching medium-tempo ballad with soaring synthesisers and lyrics written by Plant in memory of his son, was an across-the-board favourite, almost succeeding in landing Led Zeppelin on adult contemporary soft-rock format radio. 'That one just came from Robert and me really,' Jones recalled. 'We came in one morning and just started playing something and it was written as it went, as it were, right on the spot. Even the lyrics – Robert came out with a few lines and we had it finished quite quickly.'

'I'm Gonna Crawl' opened with a superb and unexpected synthesised aural advanture from John Paul Jones, then moved into a more typical blues setting, painting the way for a fabulous, anguished guitar solo from Page.

Media reaction to the new album was mixed, but on the whole more positive than for any earlier LP. Keith Rathburn, reviewer for the *Cleveland Scene*, observed, 'Rock and roll is this LP's predominating musical force. However the band detours throughout on roads paved with Southern boogie, blues, calypso, country and western, and space rock . . . these are the most pleasurable detours I have ever travelled . . . Overall *In Through the Out Door* appears to be the band's strongest since the fourth album.'

In *Circus*, Shel Kagan opined, 'This one is laid back without a single moment's sacrifice of energy. With an emphasis on ensemble work rather than show-off solos, with no acoustic cuts to tickle your fancy, most of the songs are little masterpieces, each different in its own way. It may boggle the mind that after ten years the song really does remain the same – still fresh and refreshing.' Yet Kagan's seemingly perceptive ears totally missed the point when he took time out to hammer down 'All My Love'. Bleated Kagan, 'This is one song that doesn't work. It's glaringly weak and its position [next to last] gives it away. Seemingly given the least attention, even synthesisers and a pounding, sledge-hammer beat can't save "All My Love". Plant's vocals don't strain or even reach, and there's nothing to distinguish the song from a product of other good rock groups.'

The only other critical comments worthy of reproduction came from the *Montreal Gazette*'s Juan Rodriquez. 'Whereas the band's previous outings had bogged down in their own heaviness, this performance moves forward. The sound is as thick and heavy as ever, but it's more economical and doesn't sacrifice basic rhythm. Jimmy Page's guitar work stings as well as it bleeds.'

Thus Led Zeppelin had survived the 1970s, despite many trials and bitter tribulations. They had brought the decade in with historic supercharged style, ousting the Beatles and the Stones from the top of the album charts, and quickly established themselves as far and away the foremost rock band of the decade. And now they were ending the decade the same way they arrived in it – decisively on top. *In Through the Out Door* had swept the world's popularity charts, and the two classic performances at Knebworth had cemented the band's continuing relevance and drawing power.

The decade was over but the Led Zeppelin melody lingered on. And on and on.

The public heard little of Zeppelin in the early months of the new decade, but behind the scenes, the wheels were grinding as the band turned its thoughts and energies towards the prospect of returning to the road. They felt very up about the Knebworth comeback concerts, and the idea of touring again was not unappealing. They were anxious to prove to the world (and not merely the newly re-converted British audiences) that they were no mere aberrations of the 1970s, and that they were steaming in high gear for the escapist 1980s.

Live rehearsals had resumed, partly in response to the rampant nervous energy surrounding the band and their ardent desire to bounce their act back on the stage boards. They'd been given a new lease on life by the triumph of Knebworth. Insiders advised that at these rehearsals, the lads had never sounded better – 'tight but loose' was how the camp liked to summarise the band's sound during this promising period. In short, the lads seemed to be simply itching to get back, even if John Paul Jones now seemed to be guiding the musical reins.

A few changes were taking place in the wings of the organisation. Peter Grant decided that Richard Cole was no longer sufficiently in control of his actions to handle his gig and he was dismissed. 'He just couldn't handle it, and I was pretty pissed off about the situation,' Grant told me. 'But having known Richard since 1966, I found it really hard to piss him off. In retrospect, I've realised that this was part of the thing that was used against me.'

Ultimately Cole flew out to Rome with a girlfriend in an attempt to break free from his heroin habit. The morning after checking into the Hotel Excelsior, a squad of anti-terrorist police broke down his door and reportedly confiscated two switchblades, three syringes, a spoon, a lemon, and an eighth of an ounce of what police alleged was cocaine. Cole was charged with terrorism and was despatched to a maximum security prison outside Rome where he suffered cold turkey for six months.

Back home in Britain, the scene wasn't all too brilliant either. A nineteen-year-old boy, reported to be 'a friend of the band', overdosed at Jimmy's Sussex manor house, Plumpton Place. In the presence of such negative vibes, Jimmy understandably began looking for a new mansion within commuting distance of London.

But still the band persevered in pursuing its chosen route of getting back on the road. Accordingly on 30 May, Swan Song announced that Led Zeppelin would soon undertake their first European tour since early 1973, which would encompass five countries and thirteen cities – Dortmund, Cologne, Brussels, Rotterdam, Bremen, Hanover, Vienna, Nuremberg, Zurich, Frankfurt, Mannheim, Munich and Berlin.

The first gig on Led Zeppelin's first tour since the death of Karac Plant kicked off in Dortmund, Germany on 17 June and continued through 7 July. One journalist reported that Jimmy's on-stage demeanour was rather erratic – at some concerts, he looked 'weary, unshaven, unsteady and sweaty'. At other gigs, he was in fine form, even introducing numbers himself and leaping high in the air.

Melody Maker despatched Steve Gett to cover the Munich gig, and the subsequent report clearly indicated that he (and the Bavarian audience) had been notably impressed. 'It was one of the most enjoyable gigs I have experienced, and certainly the best this year. Elsewhere "Zeppelin Over Europe 1980" had been a resounding success and in fact, audience response had been so wild in music-loving Vienna that one ecstatic fan had hurled a firecracker at Jimmy Page on stage!'

Gett pointed out that the band had only made three changes in the concert repertoire since the Knebworth gigs ten months earlier: 'No Quarter', with Page's violin bow escapade, had been dropped, and replaced by the rock chestnut, 'Train Kept a Rollin' ' which now opened the set. They'd also added 'All My Love' from the latest album to the stage line-up, and it was proving to be a highlight of the new show.

The Munich appearance also featured a surprise guest in the person of Simon Kirke from Bad Company. 'Following the completion of "Stairway to Heaven", another drum kit was set up on stage between Robert's mike stand and John Paul Jones's keyboards, which naturally bewildered the audience,' related Steve Gett. 'Then after a rendition of "Rock and Roll", Robert introduced Simon Kirke. Together the five musicians delivered an extended version of "Whole Lotta Love". Plant was accompanied by Page on backing vocals [!] and this made a fine ending to the show. When it was over the band quit the stage to tumultuous applause.'

'This is the first tour we've done for three years,' Percy Plant proclaimed from the Munich stage, 'and it's certainly been an interesting sketch! And after this – well, who knows?'

What puzzled *Melody Maker*'s Steve Gett (and many other informed Led Zeppelin observers) was the astonishing lack of British and American music media coverage of the 'Zeppelin Over Europe 1980' tour – an event where the band was proving that it had regained its wings. While Led Zeppelin fever enveloped the Continent, barely a word was forthcoming from UK press. 'There has been no media coverage whatsoever,' Gett complained, 'on Zeppelin's long-awaited return to work. Amazing, when one considers that the band are still by far the most popular outfit in the world.

'En route to Munich, encounters with a number of Led Zeppelin fanatics revealed that the dates have been going extremely well. There seemed to be a feeling of total rejuvenation within the band. The majority of the concerts had sold out and the only minor problem has been the cancellation of the Nuremberg show due to John Bonham's physical exhaustion.'

The Nuremberg show on 27 June was notable by Bonham falling off his drum stool and collapsing after the third song of the show. Virtually nobody realised that summer night in Nuremberg that Bonzo's exceedingly exhausted condition might be a presage of what was soon to come. But Bonham was a tough and resilient mule of a man, who had been pushing assorted substance abuse to the limit and beyond for many a day. He was a true survivor, and it reflected in his post-tour comment, 'Overall, everyone has been dead chuffed with the way this tour's gone.'

After the final European gig in Berlin on 7 July (Page reportedly blew out a planned series of French concerts), the lads flew home to prepare for the third and final segment of their stage one concert comeback plan – first Knebworth, a one-off event; then an extensive European tour; to be followed by the ace in the hole, the North American return. Their spirits were zinging, their hope and ambition revitalised, their anxieties dispelled, their faith in themselves restored as if by magic.

'We felt it was the start of a new era,' John Paul Jones told me recently. 'Punk had come along and shaken everybody up and so everybody came back sort of leaner and meaner. Knebworth was probably the first tentative steps in our rebirth. Obviously there's always an obligation to play some of the older stuff, but something new was beginning to show as we did the European tour. The energy was coming back and the songs were much more streamlined. We could *see* the way it was going to go, given a little time.'

Peter Grant is in complete agreement with musical director John Paul Jones's assessment of the new band spirit evident on the European tour and its rediscovered belief in its 1980s potential. 'That's absolutely right. The lads felt a new avenue was opening up for them. We had Knebworth under our belts, so we knew the magic was still there. On the European tour, we'd gone back to using less lights [instead of 480 lamps, there were only 140] – it was very much back to the basics. Back to the music as opposed to an overpowering presentation.

'The whole thing had snowballed – without any conscious move by the band – into this huge extravaganza of lights, mazes, this effect that effect, explosions, the whole thing. On that final European tour, we'd gone back to a presentation of "Hey this is Led Zeppelin, this is four guys delivering incredibly fantastic and entertaining music'.

And so on 5 September 1980, Swan Song churned out what was – in the circumstances – the most exciting news the New York office had ever sprung on North American media. '*Led Zeppelin. The 1980s. Part One*. Peter Grant announced today that Led Zeppelin will tour in the United States for approximately one month starting the middle of October. Exact dates and information will be announced within the next ten days.'

Peter Grant, predictably enough, was simply ecstatic to be getting his lads back on the road. Always sensitive to personal vibes within the groups, Grant had been reticent about pushing the boys back out there in America until they were well and truly ready. He instinctively knew that the four members had to want to do it themselves, they had to feel the inner burning, and he had patiently awaited for that day to dawn.

Not only that, but Grant had an ever greater obstacle to surmount before he could confirm the tour – a prolonged one-on-one mind duel with Robert Plant to obtain his agreement. The band left this sort of political persuasion task in Grant's hands, for Plant was more likely to listen to Peter than to other band members. It turned out to be a lengthy waiting game.

'We were very excited about the prospects of going to America,' Grant said, 'but there was one big problem – Robert didn't want to tour America. He was totally against America. He just didn't want to go that far away – it all went back to losing his son on that last tour.

'To tell you the truth, Robert didn't agree to go to America until the day we came back from the European tour [8 July]. Right through that tour, the other lads were always saying to me, "When are you going to pull Robert? When are you gonna pin him down that we're going to go back to America?" I just said, "I'll do it, I'll do it."

'I knew that Robert was getting worried about it on that tour – he'd look across at me and wonder why I wasn't saying anything about it. It was the old psychological strategy. As we got off our private plane at Gatwick coming back from Europe and we were walking across the tarmac, Robert looked at me and he said, "All right Gee, but not for longer than thirty days." I said, "Okay, I'll call you in a few days' time." He didn't say anything else but that, "All right, but not for more than thirty days." ' Gee would be delighted to oblige: he believed the new era really had begun.

On 15 September, the North American itinerary was unveiled. The tour would unfold in Montreal on 17 October, and then proceed through Landover, Philadelphia, back to Landover, Cleveland, Detroit, Buffalo, Philadelphia for two more gigs, Pittsburgh, St Paul, and four dates in Chicago winding up on 15 November. A second, West Coast segment of the tour would likely begin early in 1981.

Tickets sold like wildfire as American rock audiences braced themselves for *the* concert event of the early 1980s. Despite the confusion created around the punk rock scene and its derision of rock warhorses from Led Zeppelin down, the band's mystique obviously had survived intact. America began to prepare itself for what we all knew would inevitably be a profoundly moving, quasi-religious experience.

Jarred and jaded by the vagaries and lack of genuine vigour in recent new wave rock, many Americans came to regard the upcoming Led Zeppelin concert events as a spiritual rebirth of rock and roll. The more fanatical followers were working themselves up into a state of delirium, their minds – perhaps unwisely – addicted and enthralled by the delicious prospect of once again climbing that stairway to heaven. It was a superbly tempting offer, but these abundant dreams were about to be dissolved by that ultimate drumbeat of reality.

Ten days after the revelation of the North American tour dates, the band members gathered at Jimmy Page's new mansion in Windsor, a massive old stone mill on the banks of the River Thames. Page had recently acquired the new residence – containing ample space for the essential studio and large rehearsal facilities – from actor Michael Caine for close to £1 million.

On 24 September, a cooler day reflecting the onset of autumn, their spirits – individually and collectively – could hardly have been warmer. Even Jimmy had just been quoted in an updraft of positivity, 'I feel there is a lot more to do simply because this band thrives on a challenge.'

'We were in particularly high spirits that day,' John Paul Jones said recently. 'We'd done just one rehearsal – it was the first-day-fooling-around-rehearsal, you know what I mean. We were in really, really good spirits – ready to get it together, ready to get organised for the full-scale North American tour rehearsals the next day.'

And then it all happened. Rex King had been given the task of chauffeuring John Bonham down to the Windsor rehearsals from his home, Old Hyde Farm near Cutnall Green. Bonzo had reportedly quit doing heroin, but he was taking an anti-anxiety medication called Motival. En route to Windsor, Bonham demanded a stop at a pub where he consumed two ham rolls and four quadruple vodkas.

During the rehearsal, he downed a further 'two or three' large drinks before a band reunion celebration party at Page's new house on Old Mill Lane where Bonzo kept up his imbibing pace, putting away 'a couple of large ones every hour'. Around midnight, he passed out on a sofa and was helped to a bedroom by Page's assistant, Rick Hobbs.

Hobbs left Bonham lying on his side, propped up with pillows, and turned out the lights. When Bonzo hadn't appeared by the next afternoon, Robert Plant's assistant, Benji LeFevre, went in to wake him and found him apparently dead. The ambulance was called but John Bonham, aged 32, had died several hours earlier and was far beyond resuscitation.

Robert Plant immediately headed north to console Pat Bonham and the two children, Jason and Zoe. John Paul Jones returned home to his family – 'we were terribly shocked' is his simple response to inquiries about the band's reaction to the death of Bonham – while while Jimmy remained in Old Mill Lane as a group of fans held a silent vigil outside the ancient stone walls.

The news hit international headlines, some grotesquely tasteless. The *London Evening News* tabloid, under a headline of 'Zeppelin "Black Magic" Mystery' alleged, quoting an unnamed source close to the group, 'It sounds crazy, but Robert Plant and everyone around the band is convinced that Jimmy's dabbling in black magic is responsible in some way for Bonzo's death and for all these other tragedies . . . I think the three remaining members are now a little afraid of what is going to happen next.'

John Bonham's memorial took place two weeks later on 10 October at the Rushock parish church, not far from Old Hyde Farm, the Bonham homestead.

The tiny church was packed, and local musician friends from the Electric Light Orchestra and Wings provided support for Pat Bonham and her children. Bonzo's remains had been cremated soon after his death. Eight local Zep fans watched the proceedings in the pouring rain outside the hall.

Weeks later at the coroner's inquest, a pathologist testified that in the 24 hours before he died, John Bonham had drunk 'forty measures' of vodka which resulted in pulmonary edema – waterlogging of the lungs caused by inhalation of vomit. Page testified that Bonham was 'pretty tipsy' when he arrived for the rehearsal, and noted that it as always hard to tell how drunk Bonzo was because he drank alcohol so often.

The East Berkshire coroner ruled that Bonham's death was accidental, and that traces of the drug Motival found in his body 'in no way' contributed to his death. A close local friend of the late drummer told the media that Bonham 'always looked in great shape, but he always put everything he had into his performance and that's why he always felt tired after playing. I don't understand how his heart took it sometimes.'

Others felt, perhaps uncharitably, that Bonham was a victim of his own extravagant excess, and that his death had been inevitable, sooner or later. Observed journalist Bob Hart, 'When he died, I thought he'd already done five laps to everybody else's two laps. He was probably an old man when he kicked off.'

But John Paul Jones, for one, isn't having any of that slippery theory of inevitability. '*Nothing* is inevitable,' he insisted in 1992. 'Bonzo's death was an accident. It could've happened to anybody. If you get that drunk in an evening and then you sleep face up instead of face down, you're asking for it. It's as simple as that really.'

Nor will Peter Grant give any credence to the Bonzo inevitability theory. 'It's total and utter bullshit. Absolute rubbish. I wasn't down at Windsor for that rehearsal but when I heard about it on the phone, well, phew . . .' he paused. 'I'm not sure of the word to use. I suppose my first thought at the time was "who's going to tell Pat [Bonham] and the children?" It was absolutely shocking for me, beyond words.' Still emotionally scarred by the event, Grant took a long pause before continuing.

'It was nothing unusual for John to have a few drinks on the first day of rehearsals. But not excessively, and there were no drugs involved. It's true that he played like he lived, no doubt about that. He fired on all cylinders, didn't he? But one thing you've always got to remember about Bonzo — over and above his musical talents. He was a fantastic family man and when it came to making an album or doing a tour — no matter how much looning he'd been doing — he was always there for it.

'He was always there for the band, as well as his family. One hundred per cent — a real professional, one of a kind.'

In the long days and longer nights which followed the tragic death of their mate and drummer, the three survivors were tormented souls, hidden away in their rural retreats, existing in some sort of time warp vacuum with flashes of past glories and visions of what might have been — and had seemed, so recently, so entirely possible. A glorious rebirth, fading away at a finish line.

'We were all devastated and really confused,' John Paul Jones admitted afterwards. 'I remember that I didn't want to play again with anybody. Bonzo was my ideal drummer, apart from anything else. They were just very confusing times for all of us. Eventually we got together and we talked about it, but there was no point in going on.'

Asked how Bonham's death had affected him personally, Robert Plant stated, 'Well, he was a very, very, very, very close friend. We'd been together since we were about fifteen years old, playing and sparring. It was a dual set-up. In the days before we made it, we used to play at the Speakeasy in the Band of Joy, and he'd insist that his drums were right on the front of the stage, so that I couldn't stand in front of him. So if anybody was going to notice us, and bring us fame and fortune, he'd have as much of a chance as me.

'So we were very competitively close, and it broke me into little bits really. My affinity to him was probably closer because we were both from the same neck of the woods. We'd gone through the struggles togethre and in fact, we'd continued to struggle together. Really I didn't have a great deal of incentive to carry on at all after he'd gone.'

Plant felt that Page and Jones had identical feelings about the loss of Bonham. 'The only difference would be that Bonzo and I were probably closer on a home situation. But we were all really, really close on the road so it was just one of those things where you had to say, "Right, that's it." If it had happened to anybody else – Jimmy or Jonesy or myself – that would have been it anyway.

'So it was emphatically a case of "no, just forget it". It was unanimous – no, it wasn't even unanimous, there was nothing to say really. That's it.'

Peter Grant recently recounted his perspective on those last spluttering moments of Led Zeppelin. 'There were absolutely never any thoughts of carrying on in any way, it just couldn't have been the same. What happened was the three of them – Jimmy, Robert and Jonesy – went over to Jersey in the Channel Islands to have a discussion of what they were going to do in the future. I had never raised the subject with them.

'When they came back, we arranged to rent a suite at the Savoy in London and we had afternoon tea, just the four of us. They looked at me and said, "What do you think, Gee?" And I said I couldn't see them carrying on as it was, because it couldn't be the same. It was a very emotional moment. They all said, "Thank God you've said that, because that's what we thought while we were away."

'There never was any talking backwards and forwards about what we should do. They'd made their mind up and I'd made my mind up. And it was the same.'

Nothing else could have been expected. And when the news finally filtered out, it arrived in a soft mist of anti-climax. The band's official statement said, 'The loss of our dear friend, and the deep sense of harmony felt by ourselves and our manager, have led us to decide that we could not continue as we were.'

12 Gotta Ramble On —
The Mourning After

Close the doors, put out the light
You know they won't be home tonight
The snow falls hard and don't you know
The winds of Thor are blowing cold
They're wearing steel that's bright and true
They carry news that must get through
They choose the path where no one goes
They hold no quarter,
They ask no quarter.

Walking side by side with death
The devil mocks their every step
The snow drives back the foot that's slow
The dogs of doom are howling more
They carry news that must get through
To build a dream for me and you
They choose the path where no one goes
They hold no quarter, they ask no quarter . . .*

EVEN FOR A BAND THAT HAD EXPERIENCED considerably more than its share of personal grief and that aching agony of tragedy during its lifetime, the loss of John Bonham was a mind-boggling blow that all but crippled the survivors.

The winter of 1980–1981 brought dismal, dark and bone-chilling days and indescribable nights into the lives of Jimmy Page, Robert Plant, John Paul Jones and Peter Grant. Each man struggled with the lingering

---

* © 1973. Lyrics to "No Quarter", written by John Paul Jones, Jimmy Page and Robert Plant, and published by Superhype Publishing/Warner Bros. Music. Lyrics reprinted by permission.

pain in his own way. Each suffered in silence, far from the prying eyes of a morbid media which – to the band – had mined rock bottom with its post mortem black magic allegations.

For each of them, it was a journey through hell. John Paul Jones retreated to the bosom of his family for solace, as did Robert Plant. Jimmy Page and Peter Grant chose a more medicinal route to painlessness.

'We were all devastated and really confused – they were just very confusing times,' John Paul Jones admitted. Peter Grant, too, is commendably candid in a 1991 re-appraisal of that bleak and desolate winter of their discontent.

'It was very difficult for me after we lost John,' Grant recalled early one morning. 'I had what I like to call my "period of blackness" for about four years – it was incredibly difficult. But I found it is absolutely true that what doesn't destroy you, only makes you stronger.'

Despite the official disbanding of Led Zeppelin on 4 December, 1980, the music scene at large would never allow their splendid memory to rest in peace. Repugnant stories continued to circulate that surviving members were auditioning various drummers in a futile effort to replace the late John Bonham. The run of rumours spurted forth like tracer bullets – no matter how stony the silence of the survivors – and gained an irrefutable credibility through their despicable abundance.

Nobody – particularly those breathing the incestuous fumes of vested interest – could accept that the band really had called it a day. Never in rock history had a chart-topping superstar act in its prime quit because of the departure (for whatever reason) of one of its members. To outsiders (and the mainstream media), the band was often viewed as a vulgar money-making machine – they didn't credit its members with the dignity or wisdom to simply walk away from a sure-fire success vehicle guaranteed to gross millions regardless of who was playing the drums. Such a non-monetary-oriented choice of the heart went completely against the grain of the profit-hungry entertainment industry, where numbers invariably bulldoze emotion.

Months dragged by and still the spate of drummer audition stories continued unabated, insulting Bonham's memory and the band's period of mourning. 'The rumours were total bullshit,' Grant said flatly. 'But I can tell you,' he added, a chuckle arising within the memory, 'there were plenty of drummers on the phone to me. Managers were driving me nuts. I think that was a key part of my period of blackness. In the end, come 1982 or 1983, I couldn't face the phone any more. I just couldn't face picking the phone up.

'You wouldn't have believed the pressures that were applied in their own ways by the record company. The corporate side of Atlantic and Warner Communications were absolutely a hundred per cent pressuring me into talking the lads into reforming. They wanted to rush out a live album. I told them that I was sure Jimmy Page – as the producer of the band – would have cupboards full of live tapes. But that wasn't the point. Most acts would have done that, wouldn't they? Sling out a live album and coin it in. But not us – I insisted that we weren't going to do that.

'I must stress, though, that this sort of pressure never came from Ahmet Ertegun. Ahmet was our one true supporter through this difficult period. No matter what the corporate side were pushing, Ahmet told me to do what my gut told me, to go with what you felt. He reminded me that on any of the few occasions I'd gone against my gut reaction, it had always been a goof. I really appreciated Ahmet's support at a time when there was such unbelievable pressure on us to do things that we simply didn't want to know about.'

'It was impossible to continue, really,' Jimmy Page observed. 'Especially in light of what we'd done live, stretching and moving the songs this way and that. At that point in time especially, in the early 1980s, there was no way one wanted to even consider taking on another drummer. For someone to "learn" the things Bonham had done . . . it just wouldn't have been honest. We had a great respect for each other, and that needed to continue . . . in life or death.'

Out of this bewildering blackness, the most icy winter band members had ever known, Page – somewhat surprisingly – was the first to stumble back into working mode. Film director Michael Winner, a neighbour of Jimmy's newly acquired Windsor abode, managed to persuade the grieving guitarist to put together a soundtrack for volume two in his motley collection of *Death Wish* revenge-seekers, a film starring a punch-drunk Charles Bronson and a saucy Jill Ireland.

Although the resulting album could hardly be regarded as Page's first post-Zeppelin solo venture, it did indicate beyond any doubt that the still ambitious guitarist was keen to stretch his wings and diversify beyond the Led Zeppelin trademark. The soundtrack album comprised twelve originals produced by Page utilising such varied players as drummer Dave Mattacks, bassist Dave Paton, pianist Dave Lawson, vocalists Chris Farlow and Gordon Edwards (doubling on keyboards) and the London Philharmonic Orchestra. Page himself performed on acoustic and electric guitars, bass and various synthesisers.

Expertly and often eerily performed and eminently appropriate as the music bed on which to mount a scare movie (no matter how tasteless), Page's original concept for *Death Wish II* was not a particularly commercial endeavour and it didn't fly high on the bestselling charts. Fans who'd expected to hear Page ripping off some flashy guitar solos à la Led Zeppelin wouldn't be enthralled by this adventure, even though its moody and mystery-streaked sequences probably provided some significant indications of directions Led Zeppelin might have ventured upon, had not Bonzo tragically lost his life.

As autumn rolled around again, bringing with it the first anniversary of John Bonham's distressing departure, the work-oriented Page arranged to purchase a Berkshire recording studio, The Sol in Cookham, owned by Elton John's pioneering producer, Gus Dudgeon. Page also contemplated an endorsement of Roland synthesisers, and quietly worked away on mixing tracks for a widely rumoured Led Zeppelin studio swansong.

Asked his outlook on Page's involvement with Michael Winner on *Death Wish II* – a fast-talking filmmaker who would also later hustle Jones into creating a soundtrack movie album – Jones was fairly non-committal. 'I thought it was pretty good,' Jonesy allowed. 'It was nice to see Jimmy working. The movie, of course, was just another Michael Winner movie – they all come out like that. Work is work, really.' Jones, however, found such work possibilities uninteresting and maintained an idyllic existence far removed from the Oxford Street rock and roll hustle with his wife and three daughters in the rural delights of Devon.

Further north, Robert Plant – after an intense in-mourning phase which juxtaposed with the period of grief he'd endured after the death of his son – finally re-emerged in the spring of 1981 with long-time friend, guitarist Robbie Blunt (a nearby resident who'd been associated with Sliverhead and Chicken Shack) as a semi-anonymous singer with local R & B band, the Honeydrippers, playing at various northern nightclubs. Percy had found a belated refuge back in the flames of live performance. It was a development of major significance in the overall post-Zeppelin perspective.

'In the Honeydrippers,' Plant proclaimed in mid-1982, 'with guitarist, Robbie Blunt, we were playing a sort of blues thing – Albert King, Otis Rush, Bobby Darin's "Queen of the Hop". It was great, and Robbie had been with several bands in a more contemporary field. So it was a bit of a relief to get back and sort of bash.

'After a month or so on the road playing this twelve-bar idiom at

Bradford University and never really knowing how it was going, we both decided that perhaps there was more there underneath the surface that we could actually write ourselves. So we sat down and started doing that on a very casual basis since we lived close to each other. It was nothing expected, nothing hoped for – and those are the best circumstances to start anything really.'

Plant also took time out in June to put the overall post-Zeppelin situation into his own perspective. 'Last night I went into a clothes shop and there was a Led Zeppelin track playing and I asked the guy who it was. He said "Led Zeppelin" and I enquired what had happened to them. He said the band was carrying on, and John Bonham's son was going to drum for them. Such piffle.

'So I said I'd learnt from a close source that it wasn't true. And he just said "You wait". He didn't know me from Adam. It's that kind of speculation, all that tittle-tattle stuff. I mean, when things are great they're great. When they are no more, there is no more than that.'

Percy had obviously made the all-important decision to move on and face fresh challenges. 'To be quite honest,' he allowed, 'through thick and thin, you do grow close to people and you do get a certain amount of confidence from working with the same old team – that doesn't have a comparison in a way.

'The only comparison it does have – and I didn't know this until now – is sort of turning around and saying "That was that – now what?" And then finding that there's a totally different stimulation by actually going out there and fishing around in that big wide world you've been away from, as opposed to avoided.'

Plant and Blunt continued working on their songs, and then enlisted the services of a keyboard player named Jezz Woodroffe. 'Jezz had been selling synthesisers and what not, and his affair with rock and roll had been a pretty stormy one. He worked for some of the biggest loonies that you could ever work for,' Plant explained.

'Paul Martinez, the bass player, came along a little later in the day. He arrived out of nowhere. By then a lot of the song structures were already in shape. There was only a couple left to be formulated.' As a result, Plant and Blunt wrote six of the tunes, while two others also involved Jezz Woodroffe. By this point, all that was missing was a percussion player, and Percy decided to enlist the assistance of a couple of old mates, Phil Collins (who ultimately played on six songs) and veteran British percussionist, Cozy Powell.

'Cozy was an old pal, so I called him up,' Plant continued. 'And he said, "Yes squire, great idea . . . I've just got to finish snorkelling," or whatever he was doing, "and I'll be right with you." So he came down to the Rockfield Studio [in Monmouth, Wales], and when he arrived, the numbers were coming along nicely. It was all very measured and very laid back – but it was lacking a drummer. Cozy came along, walked through the door and got on the kit, and bang! He suddenly brought the whole thing to life – the adrenalin suddenly started flowing alike to the power of three.'

Between Cozy Powell and Phil Collins, the pigskins were more than adequately taken care of, and Robert was able to get down to the formidable task of recording his first album without Page, Jones and Bonham. 'When I started I was like this weak-kneed, pale-faced kid,' Plant confessed on a subsequent album promo tour. 'But Phil and Cozy insisted on making it fun. The insecurity of going into the studio without being part of Led Zeppelin was there at the beginning of the sessions, but it gave them an edge. It enhanced them somehow.

'Basically we put the album together in a leisurely fashion. We got together and did a couple of numbers and sort of wandered into the studio and started putting some of them down. We did six tracks in three days – we were dripping with enthusiasm. It took a total of five weeks to record and mix the album and I knew right away it was a good one. I'm up for anything after this.'

'Zeppelin is over,' Plant rather proudly proclaimed on the promo tour. 'And that is both good and bad for me. With Zeppelin I never needed to think about going solo because I had all the freedom I wanted within the band. But I need to write, to sing. That's what I do. And I'm not ready for another band. This is my way of doing something new.'

Robert also revealed that he would eventually return to the performing arena. 'Of course I'll tour again, but we'll wait until there's another album out. I've already got five good ideas ready for the next album – we just have to go back into the studio. This is a group of very good musicians on this album, but they're not really a band. We'd have to add one or two people before going on the road.'

'Plant insisted that it would be unfair to contemplate comparing his début album *Pictures at Eleven* (the title, he explained, 'is about information – as in the news') with Led Zeppelin repertoire. 'The mood is quite different. But Led Zeppelin isn't something I want to throw off – I have no problem with legacies – but this album transcends the heavy rock category.'

Plant claimed not to be worried about possible comparisons with his old associates. 'I was obviously conscious of the fact that I was now without my pals, so I had to be emphatic musically that it was that way. I had to demonstrate that this was basically myself and some new pals . . . new friends in new pools if you like. So I made a distinct effort right the way through to try and think in another idiom. So if there's any similarity between the two, it would be because of my contributions to both efforts. I don't think any of the musicians play comparatively to anything I've done before. The styles are totally different but the mood occasionally has a similarity and that's just me coming through.'

Robert Plant's first self-produced solo album was released worldwide on the Swan Song label through Atlantic on 25 June 1982, in a deal set up by Peter Grant, although he no longer acted as Percy's manager. But briefly emerging from his 'period of blackness' in the aftermath of Bonham's death, Grant set Robert Plant's solo career on course.

'Apart from being the leader of his new band, Robert really wanted to manage hmself, and basically I told him to go ahead and do it,' Grant informed me recently. 'I set up a five-album solo deal for him with Atlantic and I left him to pursue his own directions.'

With the album completed, Plant predictably dropped over and played the tapes to his old partner Jimmy Page for *his* reaction. 'It was very emotional,' Plant admitted. 'We just sat there and I sort of had my hand on his knee. We were just sitting on our own without the aid of other people and just forging ahead, and all I wanted him to do was the same thing.'

Pictures at Eleven met with an immediate positive response. The LP leapt on to the British charts at number ten the first week and rose to number two. In the US, Robert's album stormed on to the album chart on 17 July at number 49, rocketing to number 28 in its second week. *Billboard*'s reviewers obviously presumed the album was going to go all the way. 'Millions of Led Zeppelin fans are going to be happy to hear that though Jimmy Page has gone off to make soundtracks, singer Robert Plant is still keeping the faith. Robbie Blunt is the guitarist here, and the drumming is divided between Phil Collins and Cozy Powell, but right up front are Plant's unique wall-to-wall vocals. The music continues Led Zeppelin's tradition of syncopated big rock/blues. The LP has its slow moments but such tunes as "Worse Than Detroit", "Pledge Pin" and "Mystery Title" provide the Led Zeppelin fan with everything he would want, while the epic "Slow Dance" appears ready to join the pantheon of AOR rock classics.'

The album spent five weeks in the American top ten, reaching number three, and was duly described in Plant's bios through the 1980s as 'a triumphant return to active duty'. Robert took time out around the release to detail some background on the songs. 'I think you can take "Burning Down One Side" as literally as you like – the lyrics are quite self-explanatory really. It's just a case of searching for the old flame.

'I think "Like I've Never Been Gone" is one of the outstanding tracks. It doesn't really reflect on myself – I just couldn't find a title for it. The lyrics were one thing, and when I was singing it – for some reason or other – I just started singing those words on the fade. It's so corny it sounds like something from a Tommy Roe LP.

'I felt the song "Pledge Pin" really cried out for something to come out of left field. To a lot of people, the sax is quite an ordinary instrument – synonomous with a certain style. But I've never had sax on one of my records before, and I thought that the song cried out for something to come wailing out at the end.

' "Slow Dancer" has got a mood about it which has been kicked around for years and years in the camp that I've been in. We used to got to North Africa, Jimmy and I – and I still go there – and I buy lots and lots of Arabian classical music. I really am intrigued and infatuated by music from that part of the world. What I wanted to do was to take that mood and tremendous atmosphere and move it across a few degrees, latitude wise.

' "Mystery Title" is quite a thunderbolt really – lyrically it conjures up the agitation that is inside me . . . the desire to be around long enough in one place to start twiddling my thumbs. I like to always have the smell of some other adventure, even it it's around a corner that I can't quite reach yet.

'It's a great challenge. The situation is obviously something I'd never bargained for – or never really thought about until I was halfway into it. Now being a good way into it, the challenge is really there. It's gonna feel strange but it's gonna be quite exhilarating too. I don't find the challenge frightening. I have no fear. It's just a case of I'm going to have to build new relationships with people and we're going to have to get close and we're going to have to become a good, tightly knit unit. But the makings are already there.'

Asked in 1991 his opinion of Plant's first solo album, John Paul

Jones frankly observed, 'How did I react to it? I felt that maybe he'd go on to greater things.'

Jimmy Page meanwhile – apart from a one-off encore number at a May Foreigner gig in Munich with Robert Plant – was busily wrapping up the mixes on what would be the final Zeppelin album, *Coda*.

The tenth Led Zeppelin album comprised eight tracks: 'We're Gonna Groove', a one-time live show-opener from the second album sessions; 'Poor Tom' out of the Bron-Y-Aur era; a stunning live version of 'I Can't Quit You Baby' from a 1970 soundcheck at London's Royal Albert Hall; 'Walter's Walk' from the 1972 Stargroves sessions; three strong tunes from the Stockholm *In Through the Out Door* project – 'Ozone Baby', 'Darlene' and 'Wearing and Tearing'; and the synthesised drum track that Page and John Bonham had cut in Montreux in 1976 called, aptly enough, 'Bonzo's Montreux'.

In the circumstances of its release *Coda* could only have been an agonising anti-climax. 'There wasn't a lot you could do at that point,' John Paul Jones agreed recently. 'We didn't have a mass of tracks left over – what we did have were certainly good enough to put out on an album. They were good tracks, I think – some of them were recorded around the time punk was really happening. It just turned out they didn't fit on *In Through the Out Door*.

'We often had tracks left over at album sessions but they all got used up in the end. We'd always do more tracks than we needed for each album, and they were usually good tracks or they didn't get recorded at all.

'But yes, it was all a bit of an anti-climax in a way, wasn't it? It could only be that way – no matter how many tracks were left.'

Coda was released 19 November 1982 and entered the American charts at number four the first week. The platinum-plus project enjoyed a year-long run on the charts and capped off a mighty career.

Behind the scenes the atmosphere was somewhat less positive. Jimmy was charged with possession of cocaine late in the year, and Peter Grant was also having trouble keeping his act together.

Explained Peter Grant later about Page's arrest, 'It was a very minor situation really. Here's the real story – Jimmy went out one day in a jacket he hadn't worn for four or five months. It was his mother's birthday and he went to cash some travellers' cheques in the bureau de change. But they wouldn't accept that he was in fact Jimmy Page, so he went outside and called a policeman.

'On the way back in, Jimmy tripped over so they arrested him and found a tiny bit of Charlie in his pocket. It wasn't like he'd been out of it – he'd just spent the afternoon with the accountant.

'Jimmy wasn't sure just what he wanted to do,' Grant told me in 1992. 'The bottom line – if you really want to know the truth of it – I really wasn't up to doing it, anyway. I was in that period of blackness. I'm not too ashamed to admit that I couldn't have handled it. I think the old white powder had taken over by that time.'

As Atlantic Records' key contact on the European side of the Atlantic – and even more particularly, as one of the band's closest and most intimate associates – Phil Carson viewed the insidious infatuation with hard drugs evident in the Led Zeppelin camp with dread and dismay. But he wasn't going to sit back silently and let this self-indulgent side of nature take its natural course without putting up a fight.

'Towards the end of Led Zeppelin's period of being an active band,' Carson admitted in an exclusive interview noted for its candour and genuine concern, 'I became more and more involved with the day-to-day situation of the band's existence.

'I certainly don't want to drop Peter Grant in the shit. But as his problem [with heroin] became more and more, my involvement became greater. I tried to support Peter in every possible way.

'Nobody knows this, but at one point, I arranged to get a leave-of-absence from Atlantic so that I could actually work with Peter on a daily basis to try and re-establish Swan Song in the late 1970s. Unfortunately Peter never made it to any of the meetings. We went looking for offices, we went that far down the road trying to get it back together. But sadly Peter was never able to get himself together to finish it up.

'The consequence was that everybody became disillusioned with Peter at that point, and when John Bonham passed away, that drew the chapter to a complete close in any event.'

Grant says there was no specific incident which brought about his falling out with Page – and in the process – the rest of the Led Zeppelin camp. 'No, the whole thing just fell apart really,' is Grant's summary of the end of the association. Jimmy Page has always refused to comment on the parting of the ways. Likewise Robert Plant, except to state that he still respected Grant and their past association. Private squabbles were never meant to go public.

During early 1983, Robert Plant and his new musical companions were busily putting the final touches to a new group of tunes which would constitute his second solo album, *The Principle of Moments*. Percy claimed he didn't have to think differently in terms of voice projection in writing tunes for the 1980s with band members Robbie Blunt, Paul Martinez and Jezz Woodroffe. 'I'm not trying to do anything at all, I'm not thinking about it' was his testy reply. 'I'm just writing songs, writing lyrics around chords. And writing melodies – I'm concerned with melody.'

Once again Phil Collins joined in the sessions held at Rockfield Studios in Wales, and he played on all but two tracks ('Wreckless Love', and 'Stranger Here . . . Than Over There', which featured Barriemore Barlow). Earlier Plant hadn't been sure about the make-up of a possible touring band, because of the lack of available top-line drummers. 'Phil has his commitments,' Plant said, 'and he has a very successful thing going – he's quite at home where he is. Cozy Powell is in the same kind of situation although he's floating a bit more.'

His burgeoning solo career (plus the release of the fourteenth Genesis album) notwithstanding, Plant was able to convince Collins to join him on a one-off two-month North American tour starting in September, shortly after the release of *The Principle of Moments* on Plant's new Es Paranza label (distributed by Atlantic) and its two eminently AOR radio-friendly minor rock classics, 'Big Log' and 'In the Mood'.

I caught up with "The Principle of Moments" tour at Toronto's Maple Leaf Gardens hockey arena where nigh on 15,000 fans turned out to applaud Robert's return to the concert stage. About an hour before the show kicked off, I sat down in the Hot Stove Lounge for a couple of ales and a lengthy chat with Phil about his surprise involvement in the tour.

'It's all been going very, very nicely,' said a very relaxed Collins, freed from his usual duties and constraints of fronting the show, either as a solo artist or as the lead singer of Genesis. 'The audiences have been really, really good actually. None of us on the stage have heard any Zeppelin shouts and no cries for "Stairway to Heaven".'

That was especially important to Robert, who had publicly avowed – somewhat prematurely one thinks – that he would never sing a Led Zeppelin song live again. 'Robert asked me to join him on tour,' Collins continued, 'We talked about it when I did his first album. He said, "If ever it comes together, if ever we've got enough material to go on the road, will you do it with me?" And I said "Of course," and unfortunately he took me at my word!'

After the obligatory laughs all round, Collins said, 'So here I am. It's great for me because all I've got to do is play the drums. It's a nice turnaround for me – it's a relaxing tour in that respect. I mean, we're flying back to New York after the show tonight – Robert's got this fear of being caught – and we flew in this afternoon. If it was my own gig, I'd be feeling a little harassed. Basically,' Phil quipped, 'I'm just a guy who can't say no. It's good when you get asked by lots of nice people to do good things. I wouldn't have passed this thing up – it's been great fun.'

Collins insisted that he definitely didn't consider spending two months on the road with Robert – away from his own expansive activities – to be a calculated career risk. 'No, this is certainly not the wrong thing for me to be doing. It doesn't matter to me if it's the wrong thing to do if that's how it's perceived. One aspect of it I suppose is that one doesn't want to be too available, or be taken for granted – but I don't think of things like that at all really. Not in making a decision to do something like this.'

During the tour, which was managed by Phil Carson who'd recently left Atlantic to pick up the slack created by Peter Grant's withdrawal from active duty, Robert Plant admitted in interviews that he and Maureen had separated and he was living alone. He was also at pains to deny that – contrary to omnipresent rumour – he secretly held a personal aversion to Jimmy Page's fervent interest in the occult and the philosophy of Aleister Crowley.

'Personally, I've always had a fetish for Wolverhampton Wanderers soccer club [rather than Crowley]' Plant stated. 'I think Page just collected the works of an English eccentric. That was all I was concerned about and that was all I knew. I just know a lot of people have made a lot of money talking a lot of bullshit about an entity that never, ever stood up, and said, "You're wrong." I didn't because there was no need to. Let it roll like crazy.'

When Plant returned from America, he got together in London with Jimmy Page and John Paul Jones to discuss the formal dissolution of Swan Song Records. Both London and New York offices had been closed in the absence of Peter Grant, but the three couldn't reach a decision to shut down the company. Plant is reported to have confided to a friend, 'It's still the same – they still can't make up their minds.'

Perhaps stirred on by the sight of Robert with a platinum album and drawing large appreciative concert crowds in America, Jimmy Page finally emerged from seclusion to play in an all-star benefit put on by multiple sclerosis sufferer, Ronnie Lane (who'd operated the mobile recording studio in which Led Zeppelin used to record) to raise money to buy a machine to assist victims of the crippling disease. The gig took place at the Royal Albert Hall in September, and featured such luminaries as Eric Clapton, Charlie Watts, Bill Wyman, Ian Stewart, Joe Cocker, Steve Winwood, Jeff Beck and Jan Hammer. During his set, Page strapped on the familiar double-necked Gibson guitar and proffered an adventurous instrumental rendition of 'Stairway to Heaven' that brought the house down. As an encore, Page returned to the spotlight with former Yardbirds' associates Eric Clapton and Jeff Beck and they ripped through a tasty version of 'Layla'. While Page was out on stage experiencing the ecstasies of a reluctant hero returning to the site of prior glories, his dressing room was robbed – a more basic aspect of public life that probably wouldn't have happened had the enigmatic and protective Peter Grant been in control.

The success of the London benefit prompted Ronnie Lane to take the ARMS [Action Research into Multiple Sclerosis] show to America for concerts in Dallas, San Francisco, Los Angeles and New York. Steve Winwood, tied up with other commitments, was replaced by former Bad Company lead singer, Paul Rodgers. On the urging of Peter Grant, Page and Rodgers had been playing around with the idea of forming a band so this mini-American schedule would give them the chance to further explore the fruits of a possible union.

To celebrate his return to live touring, Page informed friends he was quitting heroin. In Hollywood, Page reportedly told a long-time female associate that he had been so smacked out for seven years that he couldn't even be bothered to see her. He boasted that it had only taken him four days to break the enduring habit.

Pagey's widely rumoured obsession with the occult may have had more than a little to do with the previous year's revelations about alleged backwards-masking of satanic messages on the recording of 'Stairway to Heaven'. As insidious as these allegations appear in retrospect, they were taken seriously at the time by mainstream media. After a Southern Baptist radio evangelist made outrageous charges on a nationally-syndicated Sunday morning programme, a Californian politician told the state assembly that 'Stairway to Heaven' contained nine Antichrist examples of backwards masking (the recording of secret messages backwards on records), including 'Here's to my sweet Satan' and 'I sing because I live with Satan.'

In response to global wire service stories treating this alleged Satanic worship as if it were the gospel truth, a Swan Song statement observed, with icy contempt, 'Our turntables only play in one direction.' Page himself refused to dignify the allegations by making any comment. A few weeks later, Robert Plant declared, 'negativity of any kind is best to be ignored. Even asking that question [about "Stairway to Heaven"] encourages this kind of negative speculation. How could anyone sing backwards? It's complete bunkum – it can't be done. Only Americans would come up with something that ridiculous. Nobody in Europe would understand the point of doing anything backwards – it's hard enough to do forwards. Why don't people take up swimming or squash if they're bored?'

In 1991, the three surviving performers on 'Stairway to Heaven' offered perspectives on the entire episode:

Jimmy Page: 'Well, I don't pass any comments on them . . .'

Robert Plant: 'I mean, who on earth would have ever thought of doing that in the first place? You've got to have a lot of time on your hands to even consider that people would do that. Especially with "Stairway to Heaven". I mean, we were so proud of that thing, and its intentions are so positive . . . I found it foul, the whole idea . . . but it's very American. Nowhere else in the world has anybody ever considered it, or been concerned or bothered at all about that. I figure if backward-masking really worked, every album in the store would have "Buy this album" hidden on it.'

Jimmy Page: 'You've got it, you've hit the nail on the head. And that's all there is to say about it.'

John Paul Jones: 'Of course it's fatal, you know, because you tend to wind these people up after a while. If you go around saying, "Oh yes, if you play track eight at thirty-six rpm, you'll definitely hear a message," they'll go right home and try it. English bands tend to be more ironic and sarcastic, and once they discovered the average American lack of irony and humour, it's just sitting ducks, really. You just sort of have to go for it.'

By early 1984, Jimmy Page was willing to re-enter the commercial embraces of the contemporary music scene. He performed some guitar parts on a Steve Stills solo album but more significantly, he re-united with Robert Plant and a band of mystery musicians including Jeff Beck and Nile Rodgers in a one-off project produced by Nugetre (Ahmet Ertegun), and the Fabulous Brill Brothers. Five of the tracks cut at these sessions – basically an affectionate tribute to classic R & B tunes

– would be released with no individual credits in an EP entitled 'The Honeydrippers – Volume One' in September 1984. The five titles were Hank Ballard's 'I Get a Thrill', Phil Phillips's 1959 hit 'Sea of Love', 'I Got a Woman' by Ray Charles from 1955, the archetype Phil Spector–Doc Pomus ballad 'Young Boy Blues' originally recorded by Ben E. King, and a steaming version of Roy Brown's 1949 chestnut, 'Rockin' at Midnight'.

The EP was released on Plant's Es Paranza label, and Atlantic rushed out a single coupling 'Rockin' at Midnight' backed with 'Sea of Love'. Conservative America radio flipped the single and started programming the soft and familiar old hit 'Sea of Love' which quickly became a huge success, reaching number three on US charts. It would in fact be the biggest ever chart single featuring Robert Plant vocals, and the former Led Zeppelin lead singer was horrified. Almost overnight he'd gained the vestiges of a crooner.

'It was just something I did for a laugh,' he said. 'It sounds crazy – you just go in to record a song you like. It might have been "Run Run Rudolph" or "Promised Land" or "Masters of War". That day with Ahmet Ertegun, we did "Rockin' at Midnight" and "Sea of Love". "Sea of Love" was an enormous hit, and I was having to avoid people because they were coming up and going, "Great, you've made a great record there – it's great to hear you singing with so much feeling." And I was going, "Oh no, that was supposed to be the B side of 'Rockin' at Midnight'."

'All I wanted was to hear some jump blues on the radio. But radio picked up the B side and we had to withdraw "Rockin' at Midnight" and there I was – a crooner: I was white, clean and neat. By sheer fluke, I was suddenly Conway Twitty's godson. Okay, the string arrangement is good, Page plays a good solo, it's a nice song and all that, but if that was the last thing I ever did – oh dear. After all those years of "Kashmir", "Communication Breakdown", "Wreckless Love" and "Slow Dancer", suddenly "Sea of Love" is the height of my achievement. God.

'I mean, my mum thinks it's great, but she always thought I was really Johnny Mathis anyway. I gave her a copy of the record and I saw her twice afterwards and on the third time, she said she'd played the record. I knew she'd played it straight away because she wanted to know if I'm behaving and if I'm going to meet Prince Charles again. So about the third time I see her, she says, "I played the record. It's, it's, it's nice." Thank you, Mum. White, clean and neat, that's what it is.'

Robert would continue outlining this attitude in a song titled 'White Clean and Neat' on his 1988 album *Now and Zen*. But Ahmet Ertegun clearly wasn't sure what the fuss was about when he observed, 'It's clear that if you do any style very well, there will be an audience for it. Robert sings these songs with love.' But there would be no Volume Two of the Honeydrippers after the damage done to Robert's sense of self-image by "Sea of Love".

Page was also feeling the tremors of damage done when he was picked up by police at a major London railway station and found to be in possession of a small amount of cocaine. He was arrested and charged, and since it was his second cocaine bust in two years, friends feared he might receive a jail sentence. But at the November hearing, the magistrate did little more that slap Pagey's wrist, 'Generally for a second offence of this nature, you should go to prison. But I take the view that if a prison sentence is passed, it may well prevent you from pursuing your profession.' Page was fined £450 – a victory, more than anything else, for the power of the millions of export dollars generated by Page's musical activities during the past two decades.

Getting his act back together a few weeks later, Page noted he'd been 'unemployed too long' and announced plans to team up with Paul Rodgers.

Phil Carson by now had taken over the management reins guiding former band members in their various quests for solo identities and a life after Led Zeppelin. 'In a full-time capacity, I was working for the boys in 1984,' Carson recollected recently in his impressive office where he now directs a substantial quest for 1990s chart success with the Japanese JVC-funded Victory Music Inc. company based in Los Angeles.

'I did the Honeydrippers thing with Robert and then several major tours which wound up at the end of the Shaken and Stirred itinerary. By then I was off into other things,' Carson said.

'My next Led Zeppelin-related involvement was in assisting Jimmy Page to get back into the scene. I got him together with Paul Rodgers for the Ronnie Lane benefit and subsequent American tour. Then we put the Firm together, which I managed and organised.

'There were some really great moments in the Firm. It was a terrific band, but there was a clash of personalities between Paul and Jimmy and it was never possible to make it continue. If I could have kept that group together, they would have been enormous. But it wasn't meant to be.'

Another footnote of positivity arrived from an unexpected source – the drums of John Bonham were once again at the top of the charts. A sampling of two seconds of Bonzo's drumming from *Led Zeppelin II* was programmed on a Fairlight synthesiser and utilised as the bombastic drum track in Frankie Goes to Hollywood's début megahit, 'Relax'.

The mid-1980s were indeed strange and unpredictable times in the lives of former Led Zeppelin members, but 1985 would prove to be a fruitful year for enthusiasts of the band, and one which would be assured of immortality in the annals of rock and roll. Robert Plant took his touring band (now including Little Feat's outstanding Ritchie Hayward on drums, replacing Phil Collins). Although Phil Collins was feverishly active with his red-hot solo journey (not to mention the affairs of Genesis), he would take time out to play another gig later in the year with Robert and a couple of his old pals.

With *Shaken 'n' Stirred*, Plant was determined to produce a true album of the 1980s and he pushed his musicians to the absolute limit, a period which guitarist Robbie Blunt later described as 'a nightmare'. Noted keyboardist Jezz Woodroffe, 'Most of the guitar sound came from the keyboard programs.'

Yet strangely enough, the first single from Robert's third album – a blazing evocative bluesy number called 'Little By Little' – was the track which sounded most like the Zeppelin days of yore. Plant planned to support the album with an extensive summer concert tour, kicking off in Vancouver in early June.

Jimmy Page had by now (at least temporarily) teamed up with vocalist Paul Rodgers and they assembled a band called the Firm incorporating Roy Harper's bass player, Tony Franklin, and drummer Chris Slade who'd played with Manfred Mann and others. The first and only planned album – 'The Firm isn't the sort of thing where you sign five-years contracts or five-album contracts at age forty-one,' Page said wryly, 'I might not even live to forty-six' – was co-produced by Rodgers and Page. It would in fact be Pagey's first rock band album production project since *Presence* was laid down in November 1975.

Explaining the band's name, Page pointed out 'the term "the firm" in England is when all the boys go out together at night, without the wives or girlfriends. It's the old firm, chaps that are all out together.'

Although the announcement of the Firm was slammed by the British music papers, Page recruited Phil Carson to organise a North American concert tour to unfold in the early spring. During the Firm's tour schedule, Page agreed surprisingly to take part in a series of interviews which proved to be as revealing as they were rare. Jimmy admitted that he and Plant weren't on speaking terms, and indeed hadn't communicated since the fateful day the previous summer when the guitarist had overdubbed his part on the Honeydrippers' unsolicited hit, 'Sea of Love'. 'We were great friends,' claimed Page in a rare burst of public candour. 'It was like a marriage – like Lennon and MaCartney was a marriage. When you start off from the beginning and you look back many years later, there are so many milestones. Especially for me and Robert and like "Stairway", people could relate to things you couldn't even have comprehended when you started. I hope people don't take it wrong when I say "like a marriage" but it was.'

In media conversations, Jimmy was blatantly honest about the results of his recent years, if not the circumstances which dictated them. 'The worst thing for me was sitting at home and just worrying like mad, wanting to play because that's the only thing I can do in life, and not knowing how to go about it. I needed to get *The Firm* album released, because I needed to get back in command of the instrument again. So I won't be afraid of it any more. Because I was getting really afraid of it.'

As for the unwritten pages of his future, Jimmy observed, 'All I can say is that it will be extremely eccentric. I think it's about time I did something like that anyway, so people can see what I really am. Is he a wise man or is he a fool? That should be my epitaph.'

Most noticeably, Page wouldn't entertain the prospect of playing with Robert Plant in any context. 'Why?' he demanded, grumpily. 'I mean, he's got his solo career, hasn't he? And I haven't done anything for a long time. I was just sitting around, not doing anything. I guess if he wanted me to play with him, he would have called and asked me.'

A second and even less successful album by the Firm, *Mean Business*, would be released in April 1986.

By early 1985, the rock scene had regained a measure of the crucial conscience which had died with John Lennon four years earlier. The hugely successful Band Aid Christmas recording session in London had stirred up superstar sensibilities in America to the extent that Michael Jackson and Lionel Richie had penned their own charity relief tune called 'We Are the World'.

'After the success of Band Aid, and particularly Bob Geldof,' noted instigator Harry Belafonte, 'it was obvious that USA for Africa was an idea whose time had come. The power of artists is unlimited – more often than not, art is the greatest truth-teller. There are no boundaries on art; its universal power is absolutely awesome.'

A total of 45 top-line recording artists contributed to the Quincy Jones-produced single of 'We Are the World' which topped American charts for four weeks in April. Ultimately the song – and other merchandising spinoffs – raised $47 million for starving people in Africa and the United States.

The next step in the bid to raise world awareness of the African famines through rock music would be simultaneous Live Aid all-star concerts in London and at JFK Stadium in Philadelphia, organised by Bob Geldof. Since Robert Plant had been unable to attend the English Band Aid studio session, he was keen to take part in the widely publicised American concert in Philadelphia on 14 July 1985.

Initially the Live Aid producers suggested that Robert should sing with Eric Clapton, but Plant and tour manager Phil Carson weren't too thrilled by those prospects. As it turned out, they'd been tossing around the seedlings of possibilities with Jimmy Page, whose Firm tour of America was in the process of winding down.

Phil Carson detailed how history would be made through a 1985 one-off reunion of the surviving Led Zeppelin members. 'I was out on the road with Robert Plant managing the "Shaken 'n' Stirred" tour when we got a call from Live Aid organisers wanting us to do a reunion gig as an obvious special highlight of the whole Live Aid event. At first, Robert wanted to do the appearance as the Honeydrippers because Jimmy had also been involved with the project at that point. I spoke to Jimmy and he insisted that we had to do it as Led Zeppelin. I said I thought that was absolutely right. It came together gradually.

'Eventually we convinced Robert that was the way it had to be and then it all came together in typical Led Zeppelin fashion in a last-minute situation. We had enormous trouble with the TV network, ABC – the guy at ABC didn't really understand what he had with a Zeppelin reunion.

'Only two hours of the Live Aid event were used on prime-time TV [in the US]. In typical TV fashion, the guy running the coverage of those two hours came from TV sports, and he just didn't understand what was going on. He might have heard of Eric Clapton, Bob Dylan, and Phil Collins, but I don't think he knew about Led Zeppelin.

'First of all, they wanted to put Zeppelin on in the afternoon segment and I said, "No, that's not the way it's going to be. If they're going to be on at all, they have to be on at around 8 p.m." That's the only time that Zeppelin does things. Eventually,' Carson chuckled, 'we got our way.'

By an amazing series of circumstances, Live Aid organisers were looking down the barrel of what the music world had dreamed of for half a decade – a Led Zeppelin reunion. All that remained was the agreement of John Paul Jones, the only member of the band not to have performed publicly since John Bonham's death. As is his usual demeanour, Jonesy was openminded about the possibilities.

'They called me up,' John Paul recalled recently, 'and told me about the situation and I said, "well, if you're going to do any Zeppelin numbers, I know a Zeppelin bass player." I was into it.'

Back in the States, Phil Carson and the principals juggled the band line-up and finally settled on Jimmy Page, guitars; John Paul Jones, keyboards; Tony Thompson (of Chic and the Power Station), drums; Paul Martinez (from Plant's touring band), bass; and Phil Collins (who'd flown over from London to also do a solo spot), drums. Robert Plant of course was providing the vocals.

More than 100,000 rock fans jammed into the JFK Stadium that afternoon and a flock of journalists reported that most of them claimed to be there expressly to see the Led Zeppelin reunion. Phil Carson organised a formal rehearsal session in the afternoon.

'We had a two-hour rehearsal, which was quite a long one for us,' observed John Paul Jones, who probably had the least to lose if the reunion didn't fire. The re-formed Zeppelin and its additional honorary members spent a fairly nervous afternoon leading up to their scheduled twenty-minute set at 8 p.m., which juxtaposed with the onset of network TV coverage of the Live Aid event (in the Grant manner of timing).

The lads planned to perform three Led Zeppelin signature tunes: 'Rock and Roll', 'Whole Lotta Love' and 'Stairway to Heaven'. When they first appeared on stage, the stadium's inhabitants went absolutely berserk. It was without doubt the greatest tribute ever accorded to a returning supergroup, and indicated the awesome levels of audience intensity which Led Zeppelin was still able to generate, a karma connection which classic rock contemporaries can only marvel at. Even in its new and untested reincarnation, the band possessed a magical mystique beyond all rational reasoning or explanation.

'Were we nervous? Well . . . yes, as you are after a long lay-off. It'd been five years since we'd played together,' recounted John Paul

Jones in 1992. 'But once we got up on stage, it really seemed like a continuation of the last tour [in 1980]. Once we'd looked to the sides of the stage and saw the same faces standing there, and the enormous crowd out in front of us, it felt like being back home again. It felt really good – it *was* really good.'

Asked recently how he felt about the reunion performance of the band he'd inherited, Phil Carson uncharacteristically was a trifle evasive. 'Well, I think that Jimmy Page was let down very badly by his roadie, who actually handed him a completely out of tune guitar on which to play "Stairway to Heaven". Apart from that, the gig was very credible, I thought. Robert did a great job under difficult circumstances, as did John Paul and so did Jimmy. But Pagey wasn't helped by an inadequate roadie.'

During a post-performance interview, Plant said it had been very nice but he had his own career and he played down any suggestions of ongoing Led Zeppelin ventures. At the Live Aid reunion, Plant's performance had sparked the odd suggestion that perhaps he could no longer reach those more difficult notes, and subsequent media comments demonstrated that Percy was probably the least happy with the actual musical contents of the much-vaunted reformation.

'It was horrendous,' Plant observed in 1988. Emotionally, I was eating every word that I had uttered. And I was hoarse. I'd done three gigs on the trot before I got to Live Aid. We rehearsed in the afternoon, and by the time we got onstage, my voice was long gone.

'It was very odd. Everyone was congratulating themselves for being there because that's what they'd always wanted. Yet there are a lot more important things to want than Page and I staggering around in Philadelphia, me hoarse and him out of tune.

'Of course I got a buzz from being onstage with Jimmy again. Every time I play with Jimmy, it's great. Jimmy and I, to be perfectly honest, we've played together for various reasons over the last two years, but we haven't really *gotten* together. We don't go out together, we don't sit around together. Our preoccupations and priorities are quite far apart.

'[When we were in Led Zeppelin] our relationship deteriorated, but this is what we've got now. Live Aid was like having the umbilical cord there for me to see again. Because even if it was just a musical umbilical cord, at least the power was there to wake up certain parts of me. But it also smacked of the shambles and shoddiness that Led Zeppelin could never get away with if we were out touring now.'

Peter Grant was another intimate less than thrilled by what he saw and heard at Live Aid. Sitting on the sobering sidelines, Grant was distinctly unimpressed. 'It was diabolical . . . it was absolutely horrendous' was his brief reaction.

Nor had Grant – the old master music industry manipulator – been impressed with the launching of the Firm. 'I think Jimmy made a mistake,' Grant theorised. 'Although it was originally my idea for Jimmy to work with Paul Rodgers, they did it the wrong way. I feel they went about it the wrong way. They didn't spend long enough doing the album, and it should have been promoted in a much bigger way. There wasn't that thing of importance. There wasn't that sense of urgency which I would have created. It should have been presented as something really big. I would have started speaking out while the album was still being made – stamp that sort of authority and importance on the project. It just came out as Jimmy Page and Paul Rodgers have got a band together called the Firm.

'I don't really think it was Jimmy and Paul's problem. Their job was to create the music and get on with it. But the people surrounding them totally fucked it up. They totally blew it.'

Perhaps sensing the lack of appropriate occasion on stage with the Firm (although the tour drew encouraging audience numbers), Page decided to disband the combination after Live Aid, citing an injury to Paul Rodger's shoulder as the reason. Page did however join Robert Plant's New Jersey show for a less-than-memorable encore later in the month.

Three days after Live Aid, Robert Plant's 'Shaken 'n' Stirred' tour entourage zipped into Toronto for a large outdoor gig at the CNE Stadium. A smiling John Paul Jones was along too – more to catch a wisp of 1980s tour life than to contribute musically. Before the show, he mentioned that his visa into Canada didn't allow him to play. Jimmy, it was said, had remained in New York rather than undertake potentially precarious border crossings.

Jones was in splendid humour, joking about the old days, enquiring about the state-of-the-start concert presentation in these new days, exhibiting a very positive outlook about the still-fresh Live Aid get-together.

Plant was considerably more pensive, pondering perhaps the ramifications of the audience response at Live Aid *vis-à-vis* normal crowd reaction at his solo career gigs, which he'd struggled to build up (and evolve beyond the immense mantle of Led Zeppelin) for the past three years.

Led Zeppelin flashes notwithstanding, an impassive John Paul Jones and I watched as Robert and his band presented an outstanding two-and-a-half-hour performance. For the first of three encores before the 17,000 highly appreciative fans, Robert assuredly revived the Honeydrippers with three New York backing singers and a four-piece horn section. At least on some levels he was at last coming to terms with his past.

'The vocals,' reported the *Toronto Sun*'s Wilder Penfield III, 'were strong and supple, a satisfyingly solid element in the sonic compound. He moved athletically, with no trace of fashionable androgyny. He catered to our intelligence rather than to our lust. He did not pander.' Plant's band, Penfield felt, 'were architects of the most complex instrumental structures in hard rock today.'

Phil Carson talked at length backstage about plans for his new Valentino record label. But there would be no after-show drinks or snorts – true-to-form, Robert and essential staff would cram into limos and head for the airport within minutes of the last encore.

Although I'd been less than sure about the commercial appeal of Robert's third solo album, the crowd response on the "Shaken 'n' Stirred' tour showed that Plant hadn't taken the punters where they didn't want to go. But by the end of this tour, Plant felt that the time had come to end stage one of his post-Zeppelin solo career. Musical morale – shaken itself by the heady direction-clashes which sparked the third album's aggressive rehearsal sessions – had slowly but surely withered this particular aggregation.

'The last gig was Wembley in October 1985,' Robert recalled. 'Robbie Blunt said, "I've had enough." And I said, "Not a minute too soon, old chum." And that was the end really. Robbie is a stunning blues guitarist, but he found *Shaken 'n' Stirred* a little bit of a difficult album. He didn't see the guitarist's role in it. He just wanted to play the blues, whereas I wanted to push the capacity of all the members of the band and just see what we could do.

'It was my ball, so it was my game. He played along with it and did the tour and at the end, he said, "I didn't like the record anyway." And I said, "Then you really don't want the money, do you?" And he said, "I'm not talking to you any more," and he scampered off.

'We didn't talk a lot, because we never got it sorted out at the time. That's crazy really. It's just that some people aren't approachable.

The first month of 1986 found Robert Plant, Jimmy Page, John Paul Jones and Live Aid drummer, Tony Thompson, gathered together near

Bath in England undergoing what might be loosely termed comeback rehearsal sessions. Ever since Live Aid, rumours of a Led Zeppelin reunion had been blizzarding like flakes in a Minnesota snowstorm. Behind the scenes activity might have provided sufficient ammunition for this particular round of rumours.

'We did have a week together,' Plant admitted a couple of years later. 'We took a village hall, just off the motorway near Pater Gabriel's house in Bath, and set up the equipment. Pagey duly arrived, and we plugged in. But as much as he wanted to do it, it wasn't the time for Pagey to do that. He'd just finished the second Firm album, and I think he was a bit confused about what he was doing.

'The interesting thing is that after seven years of being without him and fending for myself, I'm a lot more forthright. When I reach a conclusion, I immediately react to it. Way back in the old days, this might have taken a week of mutual discussion. One person couldn't make the decision for four people.

'There was a little club that we used to go to and Jonesy and I often chose to walk back to the place where we were staying at two in the morning. Pagey wouldn't come out, which is hardly the way to get everything back together again.'

Eventually they strung together a couple of days of decent rehearsals. Tony Thompson was involved in a car accident so one of Robert's roadies played drums. 'We had no new material,' Plant said. 'It was the most bristlingly embarrassing moment, to have all that will and not knowing what to play. Jonesy played keyboards, I played bass a bit. It sounded like David Byrne meets Hüsker Dü, I guess, sounding good and quite odd because of Joney's tendency to play those jolly rollicking keyboards, Jimmy cutting right across the whole thing with these searing, soaring chord mechanisms and me plotting the route on the bass. It was pretty good. And there were two or three things that were very promising.

'But the whole thing dematerialised – no proper drummer, Jimmy's having to change the battery on his wah-wah pedal every one and a half songs. And I said, "I'm going home." Jonesy said "Why?" "Because I can't put up with this." "But you lived with it before." And I said, "Look man, I don't need the money. I'm off."

'For it to succeed in Bath, I would have had to have been far more patient than I have been in years.'

Denying that he had now become more ambitious than Page, Plant summed up quite succinctly, 'Jimmy needs a community workshop, and he needs to put his trust and faith and his vulnerability into someone. We shared something and that's fine. It's just that the way we do things now is different. And I don't know if the two ways of doing it are compatible.'

John Paul Jones saw the tentative Bath rehearsals differently. 'We'd enjoyed playing together at Live Aid in Philadelphia and wanted to play together more. Tony Thompson was invited to England just really to see what would happen. In fact we only played for one day, as that night Tony was involved in a car accident which put him in hospital for several weeks. By then the spirit had gone out of the idea.'

The reticent Jones had only recently returned to active duty himself. Like Jimmy Page, Jones was commissioned by filmmaker Michael Winner to provide a soundtrack for one of his epic schlock vid-violence titles, in this case *Scream for Help* which starred Rachael Kelly, David Brooks, Marie Masters and Rocco Sisto in roles they'd probably prefer to forget.

Always the consummate creator, Jonesy recruited the bankable talent of Jimmy Page and Jon Anderson for the project, and even ventured forth on a couple of vocal tracks himself. Vocalist Madeline Bell and guitarist John Renbourne also contributed their expertise.

'Michael Winner wanted some more music for free – the record company pays for the music and Michael sort of does his thing,' reflected Jones, a trifle awkwardly. He wasn't ready to disassociate himself from the end results of the project, but you can tell that the project came together under notable duress. 'It was an interesting experience,' Jones allowed recently. 'I learned a lot about putting music to film, and even more about directors. It was quite fun to do, and working with interesting people. The difficulty was that Winner wanted a lot of different songs in different styles, so obviously as an album it turned out rather strange.

'In the end, it wasn't quite how I'd envisaged the score. Just as I was starting, I had these ideas for a minimalist, very hard electronic score. Then Michael rang and asked when I was booking the orchestra? I said, "What orchestra?" And he said, "The sixty-piece orchestra we always have in our films, John."

'I said that I really didn't have that sort of thing in mind: I wanted this minimalist electronic thing. He said that he always had an orchestra in his films – "We don't want it to sound like TV, do we?" So we'd started from opposite corners.'

Apart from playing on two of the tracks from Jones's *Scream for*

Help soundtrack, Page had been heavily involved with wrapping up the Firm's second and final album. Asked his feelings about Page's involvement with the Firm, Jones observed, 'Again, it was nice to see Jimmy doing something. I saw the Firm play once and they seemed pretty good. Paul Rodgers always was a good singer.' A fairly non-committal comment, but in the circumstances, not all that unexpected.

Questioned in detail about the evolution of Robert's solo career, Jones agreed that a certain growth and maturity had been evident through the 1980s. Was he impressed by this? 'Yeah, why not?' was his reply. 'But to be honest, I didn't pay an awful lot of attention to his albums.' It didn't seem appropriate to dig any deeper, but it appeared reasonable to assume that Jonesy really hadn't had his socks knocked off by any of the post-Zeppelin solo activities.

'Success breeds many, many things in a person,' said Plant. 'The one most obvious thing I see is the desire to maintain success by repetition – to get some kind of idea that's good, that works, and then hang on to it for ever and ever. It's like drudgery. In that case, you might as well be an accountant, rather than repeating yourself on a really well-established thread of success. I started out as an accountant. Now I'm more of an emotional accountant than a financial one.'

Perhaps with that philosophy in mind, Plant had moved beyond the confines of his first post-Zeppelin band and was laying himself open to the winds of chance and circumstance. While one can't help but admire his free-flowing attitude, such emotional accountancy invites a path of potential pitfalls. To Plant's credit, he made it work for him.

'After I got rid of the last band,' he revealed, 'all the tapes I had sent to me sounded like – well, with no disrespect to Steve Perry and the boys – Journey out-takes. I'd rather cut someone's lawn than sing something like that. And then suddenly this tape came in by the Rest Is History. They were produced by Phil Johnstone and his partner, who called themselves Acts of God.

'I heard the opening line, "A brand new human being, razor sharp, all firm and tan/ All clean, all pure, with a thirty-second attention span" – and instantly thought this wasn't Rod Stewart's new album. The music definitely sounded like it was meant. You'll find it's actually a fast chuggy version of "Kashmir" in places. So getting to know them was great.'

For his fourth solo album, 1988's supremely titled *Now and Zen*, Robert Plant would also obtain the unexpected musical services of his old comrade in 1970s skullduggery, Jimmy Page. 'I just wanted some of that stagger, you know. That kind of panache that he's got. And really, I just wanted my old partner around for a bit. I wanted to see him swaying around, leaning around so his hair was dangling on the floor, and he was only in the control room of the studio. Everybody was going, "God, look at that man play." And I was sitting there proud.'

Plant had a fascinating explanation of how he came up with the title for *Now and Zen*. ' "Wolves" was going to be the title, but in parts of Europe, the image is considered Fascist or right-wing. I'll leave the innuendos and double entendres to Pagey. *Now and Zen* seemed a very realistic title to me. It's flippant, really.

'The *Shaken 'n' Stirred* experience was to me a musical high-point, but it didn't do very much. Somebody pointed out the other day that I could have sold more copies if I'd put a $10 bill inside the shrinkwrap, because trying to find a chorus on that record is an impossibility. It was just me dallying around in another musical department rather than getting down to making some songs that I would enjoy singing.

'After saying goodbye to all those musicians and that grand finale of irritation at the end of the last tour, it's been enlightening to work with Phil Johnstone. He's spent so much time listening to classic American pop that every time I go up a gumtree, every time I take a left turn in the middle of a song that sounds quite pleasant and suddenly do some kind of 6/8, 7/4, 9/16 time-change with Arab chanting, Phil says, "Now, why are you doing that?" I'd say, "I don't know. Maybe it was sounding far too successful." So slowly but surely he pulled me into the idea that a chorus now and again isn't really selling out.

'If you look back at some of the Led Zeppelin stuff, there are lots of hooks and things to hang on to. I always thought that you'd lose your credibility as soon as you started singing something somebody can join in with. I've actually believed that since, I suppose, the conception of *In Through the Out Door*. So working with Phil and all these young guys [guitarist Doug Boyle, Phil Scragg on bass (later replaced by Charlie Jones) and drummer Chris Blackwell] has been such a joyous experience because they've never played outside of bars before. Their honesty and their enthusiasm was so good that it was a Zen-like experience. It was like, God, these guys *really* want to do it. There were none of these thirty-five-year-old menopausal mumblings that I was beginning to get with the last band. It was almost the second summer of love. We were going to call the record *Summer of Love*, but . . .'

Released in February 1988, *Now and Zen* would quickly become the most successful of Plant's four solo albums, not least because of its accessibility through the magic of such super-commercial (but nonetheless uncompromising) tunes as 'Heaven Knows', 'Ship of Fools', 'The Way I Feel' and 'Tall Cool One'. 'I do think *Shaken 'n' Stirred* was a bold move,' Robert reflected in 1990, 'and I was very, very proud of it. But *Shaken 'n' Stirred* was a little lacklustre in comparison to this one. This is far more vital.'

Now and Zen marked the first real and true flowering of Robert Plant's prodigious talents in the post-Led Zeppelin period, and was fertilised by the fact that Plant had finally come to terms with his earlier career. And he wasn't ashamed to admit it. For far too long, Plant – in an understandable desire not to become a caricature of himself, or to join the swarm of formula rock protagonists – had energetically avoided his glorious past.

'I was turned on to what I'd done in the past by people [predominantly the younger musicians he was now working with] saying "That stuff was great." And as soon as my eyes were opened again, Zeppelin was everywhere. Everybody was saying, "It's all over the place," and all this time I was going, "Well, I've never heard of them."

'But I had to do that [renounce Led Zeppelin]. I remember poor old Eric Clapton years and years before, having had this phenomenon with Cream. Every time he tried to play "Layla", people would scream for "Crossroads". I wanted to establish an identity that was far removed from the howling and the mudsharks of the 1970s. So if I go onstage now and sing "Misty Mountain Hop", it's cool because I've given it time in between. I can come out and do it without having traded on it all the way down the line.'

Robert went as far as to utilise computer samples of 'Black Dog' and 'Whole Lotta Love' in his *Now and Zen* track 'Tall Cool One', which also featured live guitar from Jimmy Page. 'Throughout every verse, there's this sonic dive-bomber sound. I played it to Jimmy and he didn't even know what it was. It's the guitar that goes into the middle bit of "Whole Lotta Love". Jimmy thought it was just something we'd written in.

'Then he played the solo on it, and we put all the Zeppelin sample bits on at the end. We played it for Jimmy, and I wish I'd had a camera to catch the expression on his face. It was a look of tiresome wonder. Like "What is he doing, and why is this essential for him? Is he taking the piss out of it?" I'm not taking the piss – I'm showing that his riffs are the mightiest the world has ever heard.'

Jimmy Page also contributed ferocious guitar playing on *Now and Zen*'s first single, 'Heaven Knows', the Phil Johnstone/Dave Barrett composition. The memorable video reflected Robert's quintessential credo that past moments can't be re-created at will. 'That video is great,' Plant enthused, 'because it's a whole bunch of remarkable circumstances and situations tied together only by film and me wearing very silly clothes, very *Now and Zen*. You can see people sitting there going, "What on earth does he mean? Why doesn't he just be David Lee Roth and get on with it?" It's the return of the deep and meaningless.'

Phil Johnstone noted for the record that Robert Plant's new sense of reconciliation with his Led Zeppelin legacy had been a bit of an uphill battle. 'We were working on "White, Clean and Neat" (which Johnstone and Plant wrote in a single afternoon along with "Tall Cool One") and I had this neat riff to go with it. He said, "But aw man, that's *bluesy*." And I said to him, "But that's what you are – you're a blues singer." He'd denied that he's a blues singer for so long.'

Plant finally declared that he'd stopped 'apologising to myself for having this great period of success and fanatical acceptance. It's time to get on and enjoy it now. I want to have a great time instead of making all these excuses.'

Accordingly, when Percy and his new companions hit the road on the 'Non Stop Go' tour (Plant's first North American concerts for three years), in the spring of 1988, he'd included four Led Zeppelin favourites in his on-stage repertoire: 'Misty Mountain Hop', 'Trampled Underfoot', 'The Wanton Song' and 'In the Evening'.

It was a vital step forward for Robert, but he still didn't want to have a bar of 'Stairway to Heaven', the tune fans most wanted to hear brought back to life by any of the former band members. 'I wouldn't dream of doing "Stairway" ', he insisted. 'I actually wouldn't enjoy doing it. I could do it, I suppose, with Page now and again.'

The chance to actually perform 'Stairway to Heaven' again with Pagey and Jonesy (although Robert reportedly didn't agree to its inclusion until about half an hour before the gig) would arrive sooner rather than later with the Atlantic Records 40th anniversary party at Madison Square Garden on 14 May 1988.

Robert would perform twice at this historic event – once with his 'Non Stop Go' touring band and again with the re-united Led Zeppelin, this time including John Bonham's rapidly evolving son, Jason, on drums. The 31-minute set featured 'Kashmir, 'Whole Lotta Love', Misty Morning Hop' and 'Stairway to Heaven'. 'It just came together out of the blue,' explained John Paul Jones, the most affable Led Zeppelin member about suitable reunion performaces. 'They just asked, would we do it, and of course Jason joined us as well.' Jones explained that Jason Bonham's contributions to this appearance had been substantial.

'Jason knows all the Zeppelin stuff backwards,' Jones said. 'He knows it absolutely off by heart. Lyrics, the lot. He even knows the live performances – we were wondering how to get from one particular number to another, I can't remember which one, and Jason was even able to recall a live segue we'd done at Knebworth. It was astonishing, and a great help actually. In the end, I thought the gig turned out to be quite excellent, in the circumstances.'

Orchestrator Phil Carson painted a predictable backstage picture in a recent interview. 'It's true that Jimmy was very uptight about the whole thing. The organisers made the mistake of getting Jimmy there far too early. Jimmy Page never likes to arrive at a show any earlier than about thirty minutes before he has to go on.

'When he got there, he walked into what he thought was *his* dressing room to find that he was sharing it with the group Yes, plus Crosby, Stills and Nash. That didn't help his day. The problem was that it was just poorly co-ordinated on Pagey's behalf on that particular occasion.

'I thought that Jason Bonham played incredibly well. He really kept the whole thing together to an extent. He was flawless. It was a stellar performance, I thought. There were some magic moments in that gig, some truly great moments in "Kashmir" between Jimmy and Robert that I thought were electrifying. But unfortunately Jimmy had a bad day. That happens to any musician and Jimmy was less than fluid on that occasion.'

Jason Bonham's impressive contributions to his dad's old band prompted Phil Carson to urge the young drummer to launch his own band. 'After the Atlantic gig,' Carson noted, 'I said to Jason that I thought it was his time. Basically I made a deal that same day with Jerry Greenberg [involved with Atlantic at the height of Led Zeppelin's career] at WTG-Epic. Then Jason and I went about putting a band together. I only moved on from managing Jason Bonham because of my new record company involvement with JVC. He's got a fabulous future ahead of him.'

Peter Grant was not so enthusiastic about the reunion. 'I was invited to attend Atlantic's fortieth,' he said recently. 'But I didn't go because I thought it was going to be a nightmare. The performance, I thought, was diabolical. It was the worst thing they've done.'

On the other hand, Jason Bonham told me in 1990 that it had been a 'fabulous experience – something I wouldn't have missed for anything'. No doubt bearing in mind Jason's percussion-plus contributions to the Atlantic reunion (and their deep allegiance to his dad), the surviving Led Zeppelin members turned out to stage an impromptu, informal, and much less publicised, third reunion appearance at Jason Bonham's wedding in July 1990.

'The wedding was like a big family thing,' recalled Peter Grant. 'A lot of the kids hadn't seen each other for ages. For instance my two children, Helen and Warren, hadn't seen John Paul Jones's three daughters since Knebworth in 1979. Most of us arrived up there in Worcestershire on the Friday night, and we all stayed at the same hotel until around Sunday lunchtime – all except Robert Plant who stayed at home.

'A couple of local semi-pro bands played at the reception – and since there was a kit there and a few guitars, Jimmy, Robert, Jonesy and Jason Bonham just got up and had a jam. It wasn't planned or anything, and they just did four or five numbers, absolutely impromptu. The whole thing was really nice, a bit of fun and it was good to see everyone again.'

A few weeks after the Atlantic anniversary reunion, Geffen Records released Jimmy Page's first album as a solo artist, entitled *Outrider*. 'It was strange but it was also exciting to be on my own,' Pagey revealed in a rare media chat. 'I went into my studio a little over a year ago with absolutely no material. That's the way I wanted to do it. At first we were just basically jamming and coming up with riffs – the record all came together in the studio.

'Obviously this was going to be a guitar album, but not an entirely instrumental one. On the other hand, if you have the same singer throughout, it sets up certain expectations. So this is quite different from what people might expect. It's a small cast but there are a number of singers involved, which makes for different approaches and textures. All in all, this is the album I wanted to do at this point in time. I wanted to give the overall spectrum of the way I play, but I didn't want to just clone myself. It's a full frontal attack with guitars.'

Among the singers on the album is Robert Plant, performing a songwriting collaboration with Page. 'We collaborated on "The Only

One" – I played on a couple of tracks on his *Now and Zen* album. We're really good mates anyway and when I had this track, I thought this would be perfect for Robert if he wanted to do it. He really enthused about it so I gave his a cassette copy of the tape and he came down with reams of lyrics. We had a great time. I'd call it rock but it's nothing like the norm. You might think, well, what on earth's going on here? It's pretty complex,' said Page.

Other vocalists featured on *Outrider* included Chris Farlow and John Miles, who'd worked with the Alan Parsons Project. Musicians included Durban Laverde, Felix Krish and Tony Franklin on bass, and drummers Barrymore Barlow and (on all but two of the tracks) Jason Bonham.

Jimmy was an ardent admirer of the young Bonham's percussion skills. 'He certainly has the power and approach with his drumming which is just right for me,' Page said. 'Mind you, his father taught him to play; encouraged him virtually from the point he could sit on the drum stool.'

Page liked to reminisce about a soundcheck at Led Zeppelin's final British concert at Knebworth: 'I was on stage concentrating on the guitar and I didn't even realise until I turned around that it was Jason playing the drums: Bonzo was out front checking the balance. And Jason must've been only about ten years old.'

Jimmy had obviously felt the time had come at last to pursue a solo career. 'The time was right,' he said. 'I plucked up the courage to finally do it and I'm sailing my ship on my own.'

But *Outrider* wouldn't be the sort of platinum-plus success Pagey had initially hoped for.

Phil Carson had carefully put together a new recording deal for Jimmy with Geffen Records, only to find himself relieved from management duties two days prior to the signing of the agreement (ending an association of some sixteen years). It was an adequate demonstration of Pagey's personal problems and awareness at that time.

'Pagey just suddenly decided to part company with me a couple of days before the Geffen deal was signed and that was it,' Carson said. 'Unfortunately Jimmy had a medium-sized disaster with his first album and tour, in fact, his début solo album as a rock artist. I think that Jimmy had very poor advice at that point in time.

'Jimmy,' observed Carson with more compassion than malice, 'has made a lot of mistakes in his life and I've really tried to help him with that situation. I even went to a health farm with him for a period of time. But at the end of the day, all the thanks you get for all your dedication is a parting of the ways.

'I'd put it all together for him – the record deal, the group, the whole trip. I even had Jimmy come over on holiday to my place in Ibiza at a time when I knew Jason Bonham was going to be around, and also John Miles. I was just trying to help him back into a working frame of mind. And those guys became his group, the Outrider band, the nucleus of it anyway, and the rest of it is history.'

Carson paused to contemplate the emotional seesaw which accompanies any personal association with Jimmy Page. 'Jimmy is still one of the best guitarists in the world, if not *the* greatest on a good day. But he has to get his personal situation sorted out. Jimmy has to come to terms with the fact that he should act like a human being.'

In 1989, Jason Bonham – now under the 'Discipline and Management' of Phil Carson Associates, surfaced on vinyl for the first time with the album *The Disregard of Timekeeping*, commercially produced by Canadian Bob Ezrim (whose legion of credits included Pink Floyd, Alice Cooper and Kiss).

Bonham's band featured British guitarist Ian Hatton (who'd toured with the Honeydrippers and Robert Plant), John Smithson on keyboards and bass, and a young Canadian vocal find, Daniel MacMaster from Barrie, Ontario. 'First we were going to call the band Jason Bonham, but then I thought simply Bonham, because this is a band. We are all good friends, we play and work like a band, but Bonham is a name I am obviously proud of.' On the strength of a début North American tour – and several highly commercial tunes – *The Disregard of Timekeeping* rapidly went platinum setting the stage for a substantial Zeppelin-influenced career.

'I called my album *The Disregard of Timekeeping* because of dear old Stock-Aitken-Waterman [the British sausage-machine-like hit single producers] who took the bloody heart out of soul and music,' Jason told me. 'I don't normally knock success but these guys took over England [in the 1980s] and they took the heart and soul out of music.

'All their stuff is computerised – it saves a lot of money. You wonder how far they're going to go with this rubbish. I believe that the 1990s audience is going to revolt, and get more into the 1970s – real rock and roll. I'd love that to happen and I think it will.'

1988 also saw the release of John Paul Jones's first entry into rock group production circles. More than a few Led Zeppelin fans were astonished, to say the least, when Jonesy bobbed up as the producer of British band the Mission's second album, *Children*. 'As it happened, they found me,' explained Jones in 1992. 'Their music had been fairly light sonically in the past. Somebody played me some of their songs, and I really liked them. But I thought they needed a bit more weight and drive. They agreed that might be the way to go, and so we did it.'

Mission members claimed the *Children* album was inspired by a thoroughly shattering début American tour which saw one of their members packed off home suffering complete physical and mental exhaustion. 'Yes, I could understand their situation,' Jones said, 'especially since it was their first tour of America, and they all found it a little bit much. I'd also heard some awful stories about them – turning up at the studios drunk, this and that. So I had to read the riot act before we even went into the studio. The one thing I could do in my position was at least pull rank.

'In the end, I was very pleased with that album. They worked very hard and I thought it was a very fine project.' The album ultimately went platinum and went in at number two on the UK charts. Mission vocalist, Wayne Hussey, told me that working with John Paul Jones had been 'a very interesting experience. He's a true professional and I dare say we'd like to work with him again if the opportunity came up.'

One of the likely reasons for the success of the Mission project was that the band had no intentions of trying to sound like a Led Zeppelin clone – an inspiration that afflicted the majority of production proposals put to John Paul Jones through the 1980s (he being perceived theoretically as the most likely former band member to undertake such a task since Page was usually unavailable and Plant clearly didn't want to know).

'I turned down a lot of the metal bands, and many of the corporate rock bands, as it were,' Jones admitted. 'I've had a lot of offers from really run-of-the-mill rock bands, who either wanted to be Zeppelinised or Missionised. Really, that's simply not interesting.

'A lot of people don't seem to understand why I don't do those things. A normal production career would normally include working with those sorts of bands. But to me, the thought of having to spend two or three months listening to that sort of music coming out of the studio monitors, is really a very simple test that most of these offers don't pass.'

And so, as the nonchalant 1990s dawned, the former members of Led Zeppelin were operating in a relatively active mode. John Paul Jones surprised his compatriots by slipping off to Spain to produce a most unusual – and for the English-speaking market, incomprehensible – album. 'It was for a sort of theatre company, with a band attached and they were called La Sura Dels Baus,' Jonesy explained. 'It was sort of industrial flamenco. People like this seem to seek me out. They found me through Peter Gabriel and Brian Eno.

'They wanted to make an album that would end up being part of their show. They have this fantastic live show with all these machines and pyrotechnics, explosions and fire. The shows are unbelievable. It was to be their fifth or sixth big live show and they wanted it to be based around the music.

'So we went up into the mountains near Barcelona for a couple of weeks and recorded the songs – it was quite exciting and used some very different music. The album came out on Virgin in Spain – if you can get a copy, send me one!

'Overall it was a very interesting project using rather interesting people – because they're actors as well as musicians. I find a project like this more interesting than the average band productions.'

Robert Plant and his new pals, headed up by Phil Johnstone, had spent much of the previous twelve months writing and recording the material for a fifth solo album, to be called *Manic Nirvana*. 'I've always wanted to swing from one extreme to another,' Percy pointed out, 'whether it was from "Stairway to Heaven" to "Gallows Pole" to "Black Dog" to "Battle of Evermore" to wherever it is.

'The involvement with other people has always been an encouraging atmosphere to go a little more radically from left to right. So that whatever happened or whatever came up was going to be acceptable [to me] – at least to work on. There's nothing sacrosanct here – if someone writes a song and it's all there, that's fine.

'It isn't that Plant's got to be involved in everything because I love singing other people's songs. New songs that haven't been written: I'll sing anything. This time I'm singing a lot better. I think I'm singing with more confidence and I pushed my range until I could use all the high notes I wanted to use. But at the same time, I wanted to be intimate.

'I see a lot of people of my time – contemporary musicians who've become very successful – get too sloppy. It's like "let's drag it out again". I just wanna make stuff that's pretty vital so I can hold my head up and be proud of it. I think this time it's more relevant than at any other time.

'I think *Now and Zen* was a good record but it probably showed a cowardly side of me in places. I took a couple of options which were a bit soft, and I think this record now reverses those decisions. It's very demonstrative. When you ask me what kind of music is it, well *Manic Nirvana* is a term that my manager [Bill Curbishley] gave to me. He calls me "Manic Nirvana". I think it's just fast bliss. This whole thing is like quickly executed bliss for a second, because music is so [clicking his fingers] . . . then it's gone. This stuff is like "Bang, take some of this", it's fast and it's really happy but also twisted happy, you know.'

The 'Nirvana' song came from an unexpected source. 'You can thank the dressing room facilities in Little Rock, Arkansas,' Plant said. 'We looked at the hotel in Little Rock and decided to stay at the gig instead. We stayed backstage because it was a giggle and much more comfortable. We just sat there for four hours playing mad acoustic rockabilly. "Nirvana" came vomiting out of all that.' Added co-producer, Phil Johnstone, 'Listening to all those old records on Robert's jukebox seems to have paid off. The lion sleeps tonight, can you hear the thunder?'

Manic Nirvana was recorded over 60 days (as opposed to Led Zeppelin's 36 hours) at Olympic Studios in Barnes, London. Released on Es Paranza through Atlantic in March 1990, *Manic Nirvana* wouldn't be as successful as *Now and Zen*, although its uptempo tunes would be well received throughout Plant's most extensive tour since *Led Zeppelin* days.

Some observers found it strange that Percy still maintained a concert presence when it would have been that much easier to sit around the familiar surroundings of his home hearth in the north of England. But Robert had always been a seeker, never content to rest on his laurels (or even be comfortable with his icon status). It appeared he possessed a near paranoid desire to be relevant.

'I still want to bite the mystic biscuit,' he grinned in 1990. 'I want to get right in there and tangle with the deep and meaningless. So I want the show visually to look like a cosmic vacuum − everything and nothing . . . way at the back of far out.

'We'll be touring from March [1990] through to the end of February 1991. It looks a bit of a heavy schedule but I really fancy doing it. We'll arrive in America at the end of June and play through the start of August. Then a break and back in September and October. We'll include a segment called "The Tour That Time Forgot" reaching areas where no commercially aware musical outfit dares to tread. This could be the real icing on the cake.'

The tour wound up back in Britain leading up to Christmas and resulted in a trail of favourable reviews, as witnessed by this typical rave in the *Boston Globe*: 'Plant was finally as comfortable with his past as with his present. He seamlessly pulled from his 25-year history, from yearning Willie Dixon-tone blues to explosive stretches of primal hard rock and arching power ballads that had the crowd in a state of hoarse exhaustion by night's end . . . He brought a fresh, pioneering energy that mocked the notion that he could at all be a nostalgia figure.'

A true indication of the Led Zeppelin camp's open disdain for the *modus operandi* of the music industry can be found in the fact that it would take a few weeks short of ten years for a 'best of' anthology of the band's finest recorded moments to reach the marketplace. And even then, the long-awaited Led Zeppelin collection came about more because of chronic dissatisfaction with existing CD versions of their albums than a desire to toe the industry line and flog out a greatest hits package.

Almost any other band would have shoved out a stream of various oldies collections in the space of a decade, but Led Zeppelin (and primarily Jimmy Page, as the band's erstwhile producer) preferred to wait until the occasion was right.

'Over the years, I had heard the odd ordinary Zeppelin CDs,' John Paul Jones said recently, 'and they'd been most disappointing. We've never been happy with them. They sort of just appeared. So the box set was a good chance to put all that straight.'

Added Page, 'In the past, I'd always been in charge of mastering the records. Some of the CD releases didn't sound at all up to scratch to me – they just didn't sound right. So the box set gave us a really good opportunity to get the sound right on the CDs – improve them by going back to the original studio master tapes wherever possible.'

Apparently the problem was caused by lack of first-generation original master tapes. The engineer responsible for the CD transfers has in fact revealed that most of them were cut from second- and third-generation tapes, and that Atlantic had been concerned that CD versions didn't sound dissimilar to the vinyl variety.

The monumental project took life early in 1990 with John Paul Jones's initial headwork.

'I made up the first list of tracks,' said Jonesy, 'and Jimmy worked from that list. Mostly it was pretty obvious what we should use. You were only limited by how many tracks you could fit on each CD. And then we all inputted and fine-tuned a few old preferences. We were all involved in the final product.

'Jimmy took on the job of remastering the whole thing. He did a lot of work just in finding the tapes. I don't know if various stories about tapes disappearing is true or not. Different things turn up in different places – it was quite a job tracking down those original two-track master tapes.'

Page confirmed that the big master tape search was indeed among the most difficult aspect of this labour of love. 'They were all over the place. It was like a treasure trove trying to find them all but fortunately, we were reasonably successful with that. I had some in my possession, some were in security archives.

'But I guess the hardest part was getting the running order to work across the four CDs – taking tracks from all nine albums and interrelating them and getting them to all feel comfortable. And getting comfortable with them myself.

'Since it was a four-CD package, we were re-presenting the songs in a different form. So it became like an old picture with a new frame. It's really interesting because it sheds new light on everything, I think. The difference between the new versions and the originals is that the clarity is obviously enhanced. I think all the songs benefit from the new re-equalising. It just makes them crisper and there's more space to them. But I think the key to it is the new running order, as well. I think that's the thing people will find most exciting, in that it just sheds new light on it all. I think the reaction will be pretty positive.'

John Paul Jones certainly reacted positively to the final product. 'In a way, it was like rediscovering myself. I hadn't listened to a lot of it for quite a long time. I was one of those people that once I made an album – and apart from playing some of the numbers on stage – I tended *not* to listen to it. It was always a case of looking forward to the next thing.

'So hearing a lot of the tunes with good sonic quality was really quite an exciting thing to do – even for me who had played on them. Even the numbers we'd played live a lot weren't the same as they were recorded, and there were a lot of things I'd simply forgotten about, which was great. It was absolutely uplifing.'

Page concluded, 'Putting the material together, I had a big smile on my face. I love the running order. It's shed new light on things and made them fresh. I think it's an interesting little journey. You don't want to tamper with it, because the music means so much to people. But it's every second of my life over those years.'

It was a scenario destined to invite intense personal re-evaluation, and Page was no exception. 'I realised what an absolutely brilliant textbook it was, and obviously still is. Because of the different areas of music that we touched on, and the different pathways that we were prepared to tread down – sometimes really mosey down, steamroller down – that gave such a wide variety of styles. And you know, pretty much of it was done really very well. There was a lot of soul and depth in it.

'I thought I was in the greatest band in the world. But musically, around that point in time, things were so healthy in so many areas.'

Even Robert Plant, notoriously sensitive about his and the band's relative relevance in the overall scheme of things, would say, 'In real terms, Led Zeppelin is as competitive now as it was in 1980. So it should be heard right. What we did back then was always make sure it sounded *good*. It was time to put Zeppelin, sonically, in their rightful place. For me, it's timeless stuff and needed a million-mile service.'

Even Peter Grant was full of praise over what the lads had done with their legacy in this long-awaited selection of many of their finest recorded moments. 'I thought the package was very much over-priced in England,' Grant laughed at the first mention of the box set. 'I think it's quite a nice thing. I think the packaging is very good. I think Jimmy did a super job in representative track selection.

'Somehow though, I think that some of the tracks have lost whatever it was on vinyl – but this is quite common with tape to CD. I think Jimmy was very astute in the things he added. The new live tracks for example – "Travelling Riverside Blues", always a favourite of mine. When you think that it started off as a mono radio show in 1969, it was a very important inclusion. It was a typical Jimmy Page touch to add something that had never been there before.'

The *Led Zeppelin* four-CD box set collection, released in November 1990, contains 54 tracks including two previously unreleased tunes culled from 1969 BBC broadcasts, a newly produced tribute track, and a song called 'Hey Hey What Can I Do', the little-known B side of US and Japanese versions of the 'Immigrant Song' single from 1970.

The two BBC archive tracks were 'White Summer/Black Mountain Side', Pagey's instrumental extravaganza which dated back to the Yardbirds era, and a stunningly scintillating reworking of Robert Johnson's brilliant 'Travelling Riverside Blues' featuring superb slide guitar riffs from Jimmy Page. Percy Plant had enjoyed a long and emotional attachment to the blues chestnut.

'I was weaned on and drawn into blues when I was a kid, and on 20 June, 1937, in Dallas, "Travelling Riverside Blues" was first recorded by Robert Johnson on Columbia. And it says, "If a man gets personal and wants to have his fun, best come back to Friar's Point mama, and barrelhouse all night long . . ."

'Now the idea of that seemed much better than chartered accountancy. The idea of some troubadour going up and down the Mississippi River, getting off at the landing and playing and really having a good time while being not quite a modern highwayman, not even the bard who goes from court to court and sings the praises of the King and then moves on safely but . . . Just the idea of this guy getting away with it. Now Robert Johnson himself didn't get away with it forever – he was murdered.'

'Travelling Riverside Blues', the BBC's original live mono recording first broadcast on 23 June 1969 for John Peel's *Top Gear* programme and widely bootlegged since, was released by Atlantic as a Radio-Only collectors' item CD single.

'Moby Dick'/'Bonzo's Montreux' is a massively powerful percussion track, a personal and heartfelt tribute to John Bonham which Jimmy produced in the spring of 1990 by putting samples from the *Coda* track over the original 'Moby Dick' workout from *Led Zeppelin II*. 'I had an internal whim that it might work,' Page revealed. 'When I tried it, I felt it was meant to be. It's a fitting tribute to John Bonham and I'm very proud of it.'

That was the extent of unreleased completed Led Zeppelin studio recordings according to Page. 'We didn't have any golden nuggets left, so to speak,' Jimmy said, with, one suspects, considerable regret. 'Everything that was left over since *In Through the Out Door* was completed, everything that was completed before John died, they came out on *Coda*. That was because there'd been so many bootlegs out – we thought it would be a good idea to pull all the studio material out then. There's nothing else left now except live recordings, and I have plenty of them.'

The remaining 50 tracks on the *Led Zeppelin* box set comprise carefully chosen selections from the eight studio albums (the live double album *The Song Remains the Same* being passed over) comprised in this numerical fashion: from *Led Zeppelin I* six tracks out of nine included; *Led Zeppelin II*, six tracks out of nine; *Led Zeppelin III*, seven tracks out of ten; the fourth album, seven tracks out of eight; *Houses of the Holy*, seven tracks out of eight; *Physical Graffiti*, eight tracks out of fifteen; *Presence*, four tracks out of seven; *In Through the Out Door*, four tracks out of seven; and *Coda*, five tracks out of eight.

It says a lot about the immense and intensely relevant catalogue of this unique band that in a 50-song collection of its greatest moments, there wasn't room for as strong a tune as their version of Willie Dixon's immortal 'You Shook Me' from the first album. 'There'll always be complaints,' agreed John Paul Jones, 'and everybody has their favourites. But you can't put everything on. Overall I'm very happy with it. Playing it not long ago, I heard "Your Time Is Gonna Come" for the first time in years. I'd forgotten it, with that huge organ intro. It sounds brilliant now.

'It really does give you a whole new perspective. It's nice to be hearing these songs as we originally heard them when we recorded them.' Vitality revisited, the feeling might be termed. The lads were sufficiently satisfied with the box set to shuffle out for the odd major interview around the time of release, which was a fitting demonstration of its significance to them.

Subsequently Atlantic also marketed a collector's edition of a two-CD, two-cassette release called *Remasters*.*

Remastering of familiar icons of the rock culture can be a bit of a double-edged sword to some acute ears. Deep Purple's Jon Lord told me late in 1990 that he'd listened to the remastered version of 'Stairway to Heaven' and he was disappointed. 'Whereas you might get extra clarity, the re-mastering can make a track sound different, and if you've become accustomed to hearing it one way over a long period, the new clearer version can throw you off.'

Atlantic's Ahmet Ertegun has some pertinent observations about the Led Zeppelin phenomenon, from a musical point of view. 'It is only now, in retrospect,' noted Ahmet, carefully choosing the appropriate words, 'only in the last seven years or so that people have come to realise what a tremendous achievement the Zeppelin body of work represents, and how important it is to the overall history of rock and roll.

'Despite the fact that their first album was sensational and that the band contained players that are now recognised as very, very important

* Track details of *Led Zeppelin*, the four-CD box set, and the *Remasters* two-CD package are contained in the Discography herein.

legend-making musicians, the rock critics didn't take them very seriously. It took the critics a long time to overcome a prejudice that really arose out of what I suppose was a jealousy of the tremendous popularity they achieved so rapidly.

'I can tell you that the first album Peter Grant brought us absolutely bowled myself and Jerry Wexler over because it was so powerful. Naturally we knew that we had a band that was going to be extremely popular on radio and in person. There was an undeniable force and energy and inventiveness which characterised Led Zeppelin's first few albums, and they never let up after that.

'They put it all together – the songwriting, their going back to their real musical roots, the early blues music that they heard when they were kids. They transformed it into major rock and roll work.

'There was an incredible mystique about the band that was created not only by the group but by its management. In his day, Peter Grant was a manager that everybody was in awe of. They were all very concerned about their artistic autonomy – which I was happy to let them have because they were so good, as songwriters, producers and performers.

'Now everybody has recognised how great a drummer Bonzo was, how great a guitar player Jimmy Page is, what a fantastic singer and musician Robert Plant is, and what a great all-round bass and keyboard player is John Paul Jones.

'We never regretted giving Led Zeppelin creative control [an allowance unprecedented in rock circles]. Another artist who also had very much artistic freedom on Atlantic was Ray Charles. It takes artists of that magnitude, of that all-round genius. You've simply *got* to let them have their way to achieve their vision.'

Ahmet Ertegun isn't an enthusiastic supporter of the theory that bands such as the Beatles, and Led Zeppelin's body of musical work, invariably look and sound more impressive with the passage of time because – unlike so many of their contemporaries from the Rolling Stones on down – these acts quit while they were creatively ahead. There was no suffering the indignities and short-term judgements that befall a former top act on that soul-destroying slippery slide back down the stairway to the black bog of obscurity. Led Zeppelin and the Beatles took flight from currency in their prime, goes this notion, and their output simply gets better with maturity.

'I think that this particular group would have continued as long as they remained friends,' said Ertegun. 'But of course the shock of losing Bonzo was so great, not only musically but personally, to the group that they couldn't conceive of working with anyone else. So that was one of the reasons they stopped.

'Let me say this: critics are one thing, right, and the critics didn't like the band – now they realise that Led Zeppelin were one of the greatest bands in the history of rock and roll. But that's not important – what is important is that they are the most imitated band today by young, up-and-coming groups. In other words, people like to measure themselves against the standard, and the standard is Led Zeppelin. Today's young musicians basically fall into one of two groups – either Led Zeppelin or the Rolling Stones. They set the standards.

'Their most popular song was "Stairway to Heaven", and I think that was a landmark recording in the history of rock and roll. I can only say that I consider it a great honour and a privilege having been able to work with them.'

Indicative of how Led Zeppelin is viewed by the crop of hard rock and/or heavy metal bands which have soared aloft and beyond in the wake of their iron-fisted grip on the 1970s rock audience are the comments of Jason Newsted, bass guitarist with mega-platinum monsters, Metallica. 'The best thing one can say about Zeppelin's music is that it's just timeless stuff. It's always so good and holds up to anything that comes out now. They definitely set a standard. It was such a unique thing that so many people have tried to copy over the years, and there's no fucker that can pull it off. There's just no way.

'If it wasn't for them and especially John Paul Jones,' Newsted continued, 'I wouldn't have the kind of weirdo style that I've developed. Jonesy has inspired me profoundly, and he still does. He always has done, for however many, many years I've been listening to them.

'You can still go back and listen to "Immigrant Song" or anything that's got a cool, heavy heavy groove to it. Or anything off the second album. It just goes on and on and on.'

The respect for the unquestionable supremacy of Zeppelin music manifests itself on countless occasions, particularly among the band's contemporaries and the legion of later bands which aspired to follow Led Zeppelin down that venerable old hard rock highway to heavy metal hell. And their well-rewarded admirers willingly arise to salute Led Zeppelin's stature, no matter how expansive their own success.

Take the amiable but acutely intelligent Joe Elliot, frontman of one of the 1990s most mega-successful bands, Def Leppard. This consummately commercial combination sold 15 million copies of its

1987 *Hysteria* album, and 10 million units of its 1983 predecessor *Pyromania* – setting the pace for astronomical album sales figures in the 1990s.

Enquiring if the 33-year-old Elliot had ever imagined or dreamed as a teenager growing up in the undercurrent of Zep-mania through the 1970s that one day he might be part of a band which would surpass the total sales mark of Led Zeppelin's biggest chart monster, the fourth album with its stunning centrepiece, the ultimate cultural icon of the otherwise less-than-memorable 1970s, 'Stairway to Heaven', he responds with rare perception in a hype-ridden profession.

'No, I didn't at all ever think that. In fairness, I think that what they achieved in selling as many copies of the fourth album as they did, is much more of an achievement than what we've done, because when they put that album out [in 1973], they didn't have any hit singles. Their popularity was achieved by word-of-mouth, live work, American FM radio. Just in the way that albums were perceived and received in the 1970s, it was much less commercial than it is now, with much less emphasis on advertisements and all the current hype thing.

'I believe that *Led Zeppelin IV* is at the ten million mark in America which is maybe just a few hundred thousand less than where *Hysteria* is at now. But the way in which Led Zeppelin achieved their ten million American sales would I think be perceived by many people as a more creditable way of getting there than we did,' Elliot observed rather shrewdly.

Asked to name his list of the ten best hard rock albums of all time, Elliot included two Led Zeppelin titles: *Led Zeppelin II* ('for obvious reasons') and *Physical Graffiti*. 'Even just for the "Kashmir" track,' Elliot gushed with genuine admiration. 'This is one of the few double albums that doesn't really have a bad track on it. In fact, it's the only double album that doesn't have a bad track, apart from *Goodbye Yellow Brick Road* by Elton John.

'I wouldn't dream of putting ourselves in the same category as Led Zeppelin yet. Maybe in twenty years somebody else can do it.' Elliot paused to reflect upon the infinite possibilities.

I complimented him for his modesty and honesty in the face of mega numbers, which some might claim is all that ultimately matters. 'That's just the way I feel about it,' continued Elliot, undeterred from his thread of expression. 'It was much harder to sell that amount of records then than it is now, and especially without singles which have been an important part of our route to success. But having said that, the other side of the coin is that there was a lot less competition in those days, and there really was nobody around to touch Led Zeppelin. To be honest, there still isn't.'

With the natural momentum of the box set project behind them, Led Zeppelin members entered 1991 with what appeared to be a fresh sense of purpose, a desire to forge ahead with their individual careers.

John Paul Jones in particular had returned to the ranks of active duty with several projects in hand, including one venture rather close to the heart. 'I've been working on an album with my middle daughter, Jacinda, who's twenty-three,' John Paul revealed mid-year. 'She's an excellent singer/songwriter. A couple of years ago, Cindy started writing some very interesting songs – definitely not run-of-the-mill sort of stuff.

'She had quite a pure voice and originally, she wanted me to help with getting some demos together and that evolved into an album. We've done most of the mixing at Peter Gabriel's Real World Studios near Bath. I think the album sounds very nice. We worked together quite well actually. But it turns out she's a bit like her dad. She let me play bass on a few tracks but you'd get remarks like. "Could you make that line there a little less rocky, Dad." It was quite amusing.'

Asked how Jacinda's perspective on Jonesy's involvement with Led Zeppelin fitted into this unlikely production scenario, he noted, 'Well, she's fairly unaffected by it. The scene in England is probably different to what I supposed it was in America. Although we were quite big in England, it was never the type of situation that it was in America.

'The girls [his three daughters – Tamara, Jacinda, and Kiera] had memories of going to shows and things, but it was really quite a long time ago. They were nine or ten when all that happened, the Knebworth concerts and so on. So family life was relatively unaffected by it all.

'It's quite interesting because now they're beginning to find Led Zeppelin tracks, especially with the box set release. They're starting to play some of the old music again – well, not so much again, but for the first time really for them, and Cindy has been finding some of it quite interesting. As well she should!'

Peter Grant said Jones was talking about his daughter's début album project at Jason Bonham's wedding. 'I'm really looking forward to hearing that,' said Grant, long a firm believer in Jones's expansive potential in the production area. Jacinda had yet to sign a distribution deal for her album, but you can be sure she'll have the benefit of her father's music industry wisdom in putting a career together.

John Paul's other major project for 1991–1992 was a substantial involvement in the huge cultural and commercial Expo show in Seville, Spain. 'I'm the music director and co-ordinator for the Expo and I'm writing a piece for it. I'll be working with computer artists and animators and virtual reality and all that sort of thing. I find it very exciting – it's a very big budget, government-sponsored event.

'I know Peter Gabriel's doing a piece for it, and perhaps Laurie Anderson and a few other people. Again, something like this is more interesting than just producing formula bands.'

Late 1992 witnessed the unveiling of what undoubtedly will come to be recognised as the first and most significant post-Zep John Paul Jones contribution to 90s rock – his orchestral arrangements, tasteful and original, for four songs on the critically acclaimed REM album, *Automatic for the People*. The tracks are 'Drive', 'Everybody Hurts', 'The Sidewinder Sleeps Tonight' and 'Nightswimming', and were recorded in mid-92 at Bobby Brown's Boss Studios in Atlanta.

Comments REM's Peter Buck: 'Led Zeppelin was a great band and I always really liked the string arrangements he did on their records. A bad string arrangement can drown a song in sticky sentimentality, so we were looking for his kind of edginess.'

Not only did Jonesy provide them instinctive edginess, but he also entertained REM members with his well-known dry wit. 'As dry as British humour is,' notes bass player Mike Mills. 'If you take that and really wring it out, you've got John Paul's sense of humour.'

Always the most stable member of the Led Zeppelin camp, John Paul and his wife Maureen recently celebrated their silver wedding anniversary with a 'very pleasant' holiday in the Seychelles in the middle of the Indian Ocean.

In the band's heyday, the Jones family lived in a beautiful manor house in Chorleywood, Hertfordshire, which they'd bought in 1969 for the princely sum of £45,000. Surrounded by sloping lawns and an array of mature trees – and in the words of film-maker Joe Massot 'specifically designed to view sunsets which always seemed to be extra incredible thereabouts' – the richly wood-panelled house was always humming with the sounds of dogs and children and a multitude of keyboards and recording equipment.

'John enjoys his house, his wife, his daughters, his wine and his food,' noted Massot in the mid 1970s. 'Of all of them, I think I like John Paul the most. He's not one to do a lot of speaking out. But when you're working with him, he just keeps going until he'd had enough. When that time comes, he just won't go any further.'

Early in the 1980s, the Jones family moved down to the rather more removed rural delights of Devon, and then relocated to not far from Bath later in 1990. There are strong indications that we'll be hearing much more from John Paul Jones in the 1990s than in the previous decade which he'd primarily devoted to the undoubted joy of helping his three daughters through their teenage years.

Phil Carson, who'd steered the band's relationships at Atlantic, and then taken assorted band members' solo shows on the road, sold up in the UK and moved his family to Palm Springs late in 1990. 'Phil is never going to make it as a manager as long as he has a hole in his arse,' joked Peter Grant. 'He's finally realised that and he's fallen on his feet because one of the big Japanese corporations has asked him to form a record label. He'll be really excellent at that.'

Carson had faithfully served the various derivations of Led Zeppelin members taking to the road through the 1980s, in the absence of the old master himself, enduring his 'period of darkness'.

During the 1980s (and aside from managing and touring various Page and Plant endeavours), Carson had valiantly tried to launch a London-based label called Valentino Records which was long on potential but short on practicability. 'Valentino never really got off the ground because of my other commitments,' Carson is now prepared to admit. 'I had a very successful management company going at the same time, so I had no opportunity to concentrate on the record company activities.

'Now,' he proclaimed with the added advantage of hindsight circa 1992, 'I'm not making *that* error on this occasion with my new label, Victory Music Inc., which is affiliated with the Japanese company, JVC. I've given up all my management responsibilities. I've given up Yes, I've given up Motorhead to Sharon Osbourne, along with Bonham. Plus I'm phasing out of the Bad Company situation and turning that over to Bud Praeger.

'I've had an incredibly successful management career – all of the artists that I've managed have had chart action and generally speaking, all have received gold and platinum records. So management hasn't been a bad thing for me – it's just that I'm more happy running a record company because that's what I do best.'

Asked to explain how his current partnership with JVC came

together, Carson obviously enjoyed spinning the tale of how a former roadmate and fellow *bon vivant* of Led Zeppelin has managed to manoeuvre his talents into bed with the extremely successful but conservative Japanese JVC corporation. While so many others in North America continue to whine and complain about the Japanese corporate enemy, Carson has moved on ahead and joined them. It was a move that he could hardly have cause to regret, and nor, one suspects, will JVC ever wish they hadn't taken a punt on the venture.

'I got to know JVC funnily enough,' recounted Carson, 'through the Firm. I was never happy with the Japanese distributor that WEA Records used – there was just too much product and they didn't seem to be able to work the things they had properly. Whereas the JVC label in Japan was hungry for overseas product, and they did a great job for me on both the Firm albums. Then when I was managing Ronnie Wood, I did a project with JVC involving Bo Diddley which also was a big success.

'Consequently we just started talking when I was in Japan touring Ronnie Wood. They approached me to set up a record label in America, which we've done and I'm very optimistic about our chances. Our first signing was David Bowie with the Tin Machine, we'll have the re-formed Emerson, Lake & Palmer and I've signed three new development acts – an LA band called the Apostles, a group named Tonto Tonto from New York and another LA outfit called Ten Inch Men. I've also put Tommy Aldrich from Whitesnake into a group called the House of Lords. I'm really serious about getting this label off the ground in a big way.

'Rock music is what I know about,' claimed Carson. 'I'll never put out a dance or rap record. I'm into rock and roll. At Atlantic, I signed some of the most important rock bands that they've had. AC/DC is of course the highest-profiled of those, but Twisted Sister did incredibly well for a period of time too and there's been a number of other rock artists I've worked with. Because it's what I know best, it's what I'm going to stick with.'

Carson and Victory Music ultimately will succeed, no matter what, I'm sure. I've been associated with Phil Carson too long not to know that he'll bring home the bacon when it matters. There is an air of certain inevitability about it, a question not of if, but when.

Robert Plant, the most highly profiled and productive Led Zeppelin member during the decade after their dissolution, would spend much of 1991 preparing and recording his sixth solo album with Phil Johnstone and the band which had worked on *Now and Zen* and *Manic Nirvana*. As yet untitled, the album was expected to be released early in 1993 with the possibility of a North American tour shortly thereafter.

Peter Grant offers an interesting perspective on the evolution of Plant's solo career. 'I've sat on the sidelines really, seeing it all go on without having been involved,' Grant reflected, 'but with Robert, I'd have to say that his manager, Bill Curbishley [who also manages the Who] has done a fabulous job in recent times. I think the *Manic Nirvana* album was really good.

'For the next album, I think that Robert needs to get some really strong material together. He did the right thing on *Manic Nirvana* by involving another writer. The thing to remember is that in Led Zeppelin, Robert was the lyric writer. As far as the tunes and the music went, he had nothing to do with it. I think it's important for him to work with other melody writers.'

Robert has always possessed a keen sense of place, and glories in his home turf. Through the 1980s, he continued to live at Jennings Farm at Blakeshall, Wolverly – a property which dates back to 1732, and according to local legend, once hosted a brief visit for tea by Charles I after he'd failed to win the Battle of Worcester.

Located between his hometown of Kidderminster and Worcester, Plant's three acres lie in an area dotted with ancient battlefields, Stone Age remains and fierce Celtic legends. The Georgian farm buildings, authentic and unpretentious, were in near ruins when Plant acquired the property in 1970 for a mere £20,000. With the help of a local friend, Plant delighted in renovating and reconstructing the dwelling, finding a rare form of delight in his simple toils.

'It gives me room to think, to breathe and to live,' Percy declared, shortly after moving in. 'I wake up in the mornings and there are no buses and no traffic. Just the sound of tractors and the odd pheasant hooting in the next field. I'd been around big cities since I first left home and ran away to Walsall. I was pretty fed up with humanity in the big cities. The atmosphere here is so easy-going. I just revel in these country things.'

Plant had purchased the Bron-Y-Aur cottage in South Wales and in 1973, he bought a working Welsh sheep property. 'We've got two hundred sheep and I want to learn the trade,' he reported. 'Wales attracts me more and more. That feeling in the West is always there. But I could never give up singing and just do the farm, full stop. It has to be a balance with singing. I've always got to sing. Even when I go bald, I'll go on singing.'

Jimmy Page was thinking too in more focused fashion about life after Led Zeppelin. With the two-album Firm venture and his one solo album, 1988's *Outrider*, behind him – and his year-long involvement with the Led Zeppelin box set – Page wanted to impact on the 1990s with a vengeance perhaps lacking in his post-Zeppelin track record.

By mid-1991, Page was working with Whitesnake vocalist, David Coverdale, on a secret pending project. 'I suppose it'll be good for an album and tour, but I don't know about their longevity,' observed Peter Grant at the time. Friends found Page's new association with Coverdale quite a surprise, especially since of all the so-called Led Zeppelin clones and imitators which had sprung up in the 1980s, old partner Robert Plant had reserved his most stinging putdowns for the Whitesnake frontman.

In 1988, Plant offered a few observations. 'For you listeners at home [making a grand arm gesture], I'm now doing a David Coverdale. The hair goes back over the shoulder, the arm up there, and I'm – I don't know – pretending to be Howlin' Wolf.

'You can't do it forever, so if it looks good and it sells records for David Geffen, then somebody's got to do it, you know. A lot of people have done. Coverdale's the latest, and he's making a lot of money. Now Page and I get offered everything – women, little boys, money, cocaine, the lot, to just go back and do that again. I passed the vacancy on to Coverdale. He'd spent the last couple of years being Paul Rodgers, so he had to move on. In ten years, he'll be George Michael.

'But I don't mind what David Coverdale is doing, to be perfectly frank, because he's never going to get it right.'

So far Robert Plant has declined to comment on Coverdale's involvement with Page. It should be particularly interesting when he does, but it seemed unlikely that Percy would be providing any supplementary back-up vocals on a Page/Coverdale album project.

Observed Phil Carson, Jimmy's personal manager through much of the 80s, 'It's an interesting name they've chosen, the Last Resort. It's sort of like calling Swan Song Records, Swan Song.

'I do think that Jimmy really does *have* to get this one together because I can't see what else he can do at this point. Mind you, I don't think Jimmy would have chosen to do anything with David Coverdale if he thought there was even a prayer of doing something with Robert

Plant. But Robert carefully closed that door, and that's why I think Jimmy went into this Last Resort situation.'

The news that Jimmy Page, one of the greatest rock guitar heroes of the legendary guitar-ridden 1970s, is linking up with one of the 1980s most obvious poseurs in David Coverdale has been met with considerable scepticism from long-time Page admirers. Def Leppard lead singer, Joe Elliot, on being told of this unlikely development, exclaimed, 'I'm not buying that!' Nor, one suspects, will many of the punters long accustomed to Page's superb contributions to the Led Zeppelin recorded legacy.

Jimmy Page now finds himself caught between the devil and the deep blue sea, no pun intended.

In June 1991, Geffen Records revealed that the unlikely twosome had indeed been rehearsing and writing new material for an album to be released in 1993. Their rhythm section consisted of Bad English bass player Richie Phillips, and Heart drummer Denny Carmassi, but a permanent band line-up for the album and subsequent tour was still being finalised.

Noting the implications of Plant's media feud with David Coverdale, Peter Grant agreed, 'It is very odd. Maybe Jimmy could take Robert on the road and nobody would know the difference with the hair and all – they do look the same. Plus Coverdale's nicked all of Robert's stage moves, so who knows? The fact that both of them are on the Geffen label and they weren't really doing anything makes it a big plus for the label to push the combination along.'

Over the years, Page's involvement with heroin has been a concern to friends and associates. It would normally present a significant stumbling block to most musical careers, yet Page – for all of his oft-described frailty and waif-like physical condition – has proved to be astonishingly resilient and durable. In all probability, he thrives best under pressure – and there can be few more formidable pressures than a physical addiction.

Acknowledging that heroin had first surfaced on the 1973 American tour, Peter Grant – himself a one-time victim of the White Lady – confessed that as Page's closest confidant and friend, he had been alarmed by its presence. 'I was very concerned about it in 1976,' he said. 'It was very tough for Jimmy but he did it. We never missed a concert or anything, never blew out a recording session. He always managed to get it together.'

These days, Jimmy's friends claim he's in good shape. 'I don't see much of Jimmy,' John Paul Jones said recently, 'but to be honest, we never did. We mainly saw each other on the road or in the studios. We were never a band that socialised. But I saw him a couple of months ago and he's in excellent shape, I can assure you.'

Added Peter Grant, 'I saw Jimmy at Jason's wedding in June 1990 and he looked fantastic. We spent a lot of time together at the wedding – we even had breakfast the following morning at 9 a.m., which is unheard of for us.'

Jones is cautiously enthusiastic about Page's professional future. 'He's an excellent musician and he always comes up with interesting ideas. I'm sure he'll continue to do so if he continues playing, which he seems destined to do. He always did like the live aspect of playing – he was always particularly good at that.'

Robert Plant too seemed to feel that Jimmy's future was assured in a professional sense. 'Some day, I really want to write with Jimmy again,' he said in 1990. 'I'd like to see if we can get back to "In My Time of Dying". That would be amazing. But I'm not sure we should call it Led Zeppelin. Once that happens, it becomes something so much bigger.

'Really Led Zeppelin was Jimmy. I was a great foil. He was very much . . . there's a word, not "perpetrator", but definitely he had a premeditated view of the whole thing. Even though with my lyrics and some of my melodies, it took off in directions he mightn't have been ready for . . . a couple of times later on, when I got more confident I might have turned his head around a little . . . but the role was his.

'The *risks* were his. The *risks* made it more memorable. Without Jimmy it would have been no good. When people talk about how good other guitarists are, they're talking about how they play within the accepted structures of contemporary guitar playing, which Pagey plays miles outside of. He plays from somewhere else. I like to think of it as . . . a little left of heaven.'

13 Fifth Zep Member, Peter Grant –
The Distinctly Dickensian
Business Player in the Band

Jimmy Page: 'You can develop a tremendous insecurity if your management isn't totally reliable. I know that money is a dirty word in this business but the fact remains that if you have any measure of record success, you're going to have royalties coming in. Many groups who have been working for years and years end up with nothing because they've been screwed all the way down the line. That sort of thing is heartbreaking. We're very lucky in that respect because we've got Peter Grant, who is like a fifth member of the group.'
Robert Plant: 'Had we not had Peter Grant behind us, we could easily have gone to pieces. As much as the credit goes to us, it goes to old Peter as well because he goes all around the States with us, when he could just sit in the office in London.'

PETER GRANT WAS without question the de facto fifth member of Led Zeppelin. He was an integral part of their unique collective unity, and he was – no matter what his hotly disputed tough guy reputation – the band's conduit to concert promoters, industry executives and the planet at large.

Instead of playing an instrument on stage, Peter Grant played the controls of the endless conniving off stage. He was an absolutely vital cog in their machine, a man who mastered and eventually dictated the incredible intricacies of the twentieth century's most pervasive and profitable entertainment form. As the band's musical vision evolved, so too did Grant's ability to manipulate the sacred status quo of the music industry Establishment. In his way, Grant was as influential through his industry-altering management strategies in the 1970s as Led Zeppelin were in their dramatic musical achievements.

To claim that Led Zeppelin wouldn't have reached their position of pre-eminence without Peter Grant might be going a bit far, but he was a crucial factor in their ascendance. More essential, I would suggest from observation, than the role played by Brian Epstein in the Beatles' phenomenon or most other major acts of the 1970s and 1980s in their assorted managerial relationships.

Grant went far beyond simply being the personal manager of Led Zeppelin. Their growing success was monitored and continually reinforced by Grant's formidable presence, in both the physical and mental senses. He was their minder and mentor, guide and protector. He was the salvation of Jimmy Page's tormented, paranoid soul. He was probably the most successful manager that the rock culture so far has created.

During the first five years of Led Zeppelin's heyday, Peter Grant maintained modest top-floor offices in Oxford Street, London, just across from Woolworths and a stone's throw from Soho Square. It certainly wasn't what one would normally describe as a prestige suite of penthouse offices. Visitors used to literally squeeze in through a small door and ascend to the sixth floor in what had to be one of the tiniest elevators ever installed. Grant is by any definition a large man, and when he was aboard the lift, there was only room for one other, necessarily pencil-thin person.

There were two separate offices, a small reception area, a washroom and a small storage room – none of it lavishly decorated. It was what one might have charitably termed the Charing-Cross-Road-end-of-Oxford-Street-funky. 'Expenses down means profits up' has long been a Peter Grant *modus operandi*, and it's stood him – and his clients – in good stead.

The Oxford Street offices housed most of Grant's music-related activities from 1964, and until 1972, he shared the space with his partner in RAK Music Management, producer Mickie Most (Most's RAK Records ultimately moved to plusher, posher premises off Berkeley Square). It wasn't until the later 1970s that Grant somewhat reluctantly relocated his office operations to trendy King's Road in Chelsea.

In an industry where agreement on just about anything is rare, there's a consensus of opinion that Peter Grant was a tough and demanding wheeler-dealer, but a scrupulous man who stuck by his word and believed in the instinctive integrity of the handshake deal. He would, everyone admits, do just about anything to achieve his ultimate aim – the satisfaction of his clients, in particular Led Zeppelin, and most particularly, Jimmy Page. He would willingly forsake personal ego boosts or publicity in order for his acts to be successful and happy. That might sound like the breath of a cliché, but in Grant's case, it was entirely true. In a sense, he was born to take care of Led Zeppelin, to play a comprehensive and all-encompassing role in their unique career. And he himself was as fiercely independent as the volatile act he represented.

By some yardsticks, Peter Grant's operating methods may be considered unorthodox – yet nothing about the Led Zeppelin phenomenon is either orthodox or normal. Grant's greatest enduring assets were honesty and loyalty, and he had on board immense supplies of both attributes. It's difficult to track down equivalent examples of either in the contemporary music management scene. And those qualities no doubt account for the fact that Grant was involved with the notoriously temperamental Jimmy Page from the mid-1960s until 1983, a long-term and often storm-tossed relationship which speaks volumes for itself.

'I believe that without the artist, none of us would have anything to do,' Grant noted in 1976. 'The biggest mistake a manager can do is to think that the artist works for him. It's not true – it's the other way about. They hire you. In the first seven years of my relationship with Jimmy Page, I never had a management contract with him.'

To close associates, it seemed that Page and Grant had some greater fusion of interests and objectives, something beyond the reach of conventional legal jargon and bindings: such was their apparent watertight connection.

'Peter Grant's an incredibly good manager,' affirmed Atlantic's Phil Carson, not the only band intimate to acquire a measure of his own managerial expertise through the association. 'All of us who dealt with him know that he's scrupulously honest. I don't know his internal business but I did know some of the promoters that he dealt with. A lot of the time, he didn't even have contracts with people because they know that if he says, "Yes, I'm gonna do it," then he will do it. He's a man of his word.'

Asked what else set Peter Grant apart from the run-of-the-mill 1970s manager, Carson quickly replied, 'Vast experience – and I mean vast! Now you're talking about a man who started as a stage manager in variety, and did tours around Britain before rock and roll had even been heard of. He'd been a film extra and he was tour manager for Gene Vincent and Wee Willie Harris. He was into rock and roll when it started and that's how he got all this experience.'

Grant in fact started out in Britain even before the infamous Colonel Tom Parker moved from carnival hustling to handling Elvis Presley.

As suitably befits a journeyman who has seen and enjoyed life from several, separate vantage points, Grant details his own background with a breathless and almost adolescent frankness. 'I had a bad, bad education – it was all mixed up with being evacuated during the war and my circumstances . . . I don't remember father but I have a marvellous mother who I've been able to look after really well . . . when I was thirteen I became a stagehand at the Empire Croydon theatre in London . . . I also tried working in a sheet metal factory but after five weeks, I knew it wasn't right for me . . . then I got a job at Reuters, taking photos around Fleet Street – I ran around to the customers with wet pictures hanging over my arms . . . I was also employed as a waiter.

'Then came National Service in the RAOC – I became a corporal in charge of the dining hall. I enjoyed my time there because it was a very cushy number . . . I worked a season at a holiday camp which was dreadful . . . then I stinted for a time as entertainment manager of a hotel in Jersey . . . then back to London to work in a Soho coffee bar where Tommy Steele was discovered – Mickie Most was a waiter and I was on the door – they paid us ten shillings and a meal each night . . . being doorman at Murray's Cabaret Club was good fun too – I wasn't married and what with me the only man around about forty girls backstage, it was all right.

'I also wrestled as Prince Mario Alassio for about eighteen months when I needed some money . . . then I got into acting – I doubled for Robert Morley and Anthony Quinn and had small parts in the TV series *Dixon of Dock Green* and the Sid James–Tony Hancock series . . . I even played in the box-office breaker *The Guns of Navarone*, but filming's not for me – getting up at 6 a.m. and flogging it down to Pinewood Studios or somewhere: it's too much.'

Exit movies and enter rock and roll. 'I was invited to be British tour manager for several early American rock acts – Gene Vincent, Little Richard, Jerry Lee Lewis and the Everly Brothers. Once in Rome, when police started beating up on Little Richard, I was forced to knock six of them flat on their backs! After that I started managing acts, more by chance than anything else . . . I was finishing off working with an agent and I heard a group in Newcastle called the Alan Price R&B Combo – eventually I managed them and they became the Animals.'

In 1964, Grant and Mickie Most – the waiter/doorman coffee bar team – formed a rock management company under the name of RAK Music Management. 'RAK was chosen as the name of the company,' said Grant, 'but names aren't important in this business. People didn't say, "Let's get in touch with RAK Management" – they said, "Let's go see Peter Grant." It was the same with the late Brian Epstein – who'd ever heard of NEMS, his company? It was always, "Let's contact old Brian."

'I think that people tend to spend too much time and energy on finding names and making their premises swell. Why bother? It's the personal bit that matters. At one point, Mickie Most and myself had three girls working in those Oxford Street offices while we had four albums in the Top-20. At that point, I also managed Jeff Beck and Terry Reid, and I had a business interest in Donovan. So why should I have sweated it out just to look ritzy?'

Grant insists that he never had any definite, clear-cut ambitions to become a rock manager. 'I just kind of came around to it. With all the odd jobs I'd done, it just gravitated that way. You don't just wake up one morning having been a salesman or a dentist, and say, "Hey I'm going to manage groups." You've got to move around the show business scene and that I think I've done.'

It was during such shuffling around, stumbling towards that elusive main chance, that Grant first became associated with the Yardbirds and, more significantly, with Jimmy Page. Page and Grant took an instant liking to each other, but it went much deeper than that. Grant was almost entranced by Page's uniquely professional and no-nonsense approach to what he was doing, and by his intellect and sensitivity. He also liked the way Page had adroitly handled his interests through the 'cloak-and-dagger' days of Jeff Beck blowing out the Yardbirds. He didn't think Pagey was all that bad a guitar player either. Page was especially impressed by Grant's unpretentiousness in an era infamous for its legion of shady characters sheathed in tacky suits with an abundance of gold jewellery and very average cocaine.

Peter Grant, it should be pointed out, was never one to dress up and shimmy off to the office. Probably because of his prolific physical proportions, Grant's normal outfit in the early Led Zeppelin days was cowboy boots, jeans (the largest pair you'd ever seen), colourful open-neck sports shirts set off with large scarves. Later he added a deft 1970s touch with an array of hand-made silver and turquoise bracelets and rings. 'Suits are out of vogue,' he roundly, and rather gleefully, declared towards the end of the 1960s. 'You haven't got to be flash any more. The days when agents and managers wore mohair suits and smoked fat cigars are over. I've got three pairs of trousers and that's all I need. I'm not a prima donna – I'm a working manager. I've hardly got any clothes and what I buy, I usually get in America. There's only one place in London selling clothes in my size. There's no style in this country for big men.'

Nor does Grant – a sort of downtrodden Dickensian character who came good and challenged the world on behalf of the Empire's lords and dukes, not forgetting their fair maidens – claim any keen musical awareness or vision. 'I leave that side to the boys. I'm very much a musical pleb and I just don't get involved in that part of things. I've managed some of the greatest musicians in England but with me, music is purely a feeling. It's not just liking the sound you're hearing – it's a feeling about whether it's got magic or it hasn't. You can't define it in words . . . but it works.'

Grant may not be historically literate in the intricacies of music, but he has a nose for picking winners on the track – he has an enviable flair for knowing who has the overall wherewithal to cut through the music industry bullshit and concentrate on creating chart-breaking art. Jimmy Page was the perfect example. And thus when the Yardbirds disintegrated, it was widely assumed that Grant would hang in with Page, no matter what. His unswerving loyalty – and his eye for the surefire – would surely ensure an on-going relationship.

Peter Grant may not have known music but he knew that inevitably Jimmy Page *would* succeed at what he wanted to do – it was just a matter of time and circumstance. Whether Pagey wanted to resurrect the Yardbirds or form a new combination, Grant was with him, behind him, backing him every inch of the way. Whatever Jimmy wanted to do with his musical prowess was fine with Grant – he simply encouraged Page to pursue his dreams and that – history would show – was all the guitarist needed.

Despite the romantic optimism that Page and Grant shared, success didn't leap upon them overnight. When Led Zeppelin started out in England Grant later liked to boast that they 'couldn't get arrested'. And the first North American tour – partially underwritten by Page himself – wasn't any financial bonanza either. 'At $750 a night you don't make money,' Grant noted flatly. Yet twelve months and several trips to America later, the band and Grant were all halfway to millionaire status. It was a mega-enormous turnaround by any account. ':Of course I knew they would draw well in America,' Grant concedes, 'but I really had no idea how big it would become.'

Bigness invariably creates the dilemma of chancing over-exposure in the heady rush to coin it in. 'Continuous touring is the fastest way to grind any musician into the ground,' Grant astutely observed towards the end of the 1970s. 'One of the keys to Led Zeppelin's longevity is that their appearances were well-spaced, preventing over-exposure. After the release of the second album with the hit "Whole Lotta Love", the obvious thing would have been to go straight into big places like Madison Square Garden, but we didn't. We went and played all the secondary markets like Charleston. And then we stayed away for fourteen months before we came back.'

Once superstar success arrived in the lap of the band, Grant and Page *did* know how to handle it. Hard work and luck had – in their common view – succeeded for them and they were both avidly determined to maintain a steady diet of the former to increase the chances of the latter. 'Zep's early assault on America was truly incredible,' affirms Mark London, songwriter ['To Sir With Love' by Lulu], producer, manager and partner with Peter Grant in a separate group of music enterprises. 'Led Zeppelin worked hard and they realised that they were in show business,' London pointed out. 'They're laying down sweat for people and to me, that's what counts. I believe that honourable people appreciate what you do for them.'

Accordingly Grant and Mark London operated on a handshake deal – 'There's no paper because we trust each other and that's our bond,' said London – in Colour Me Gone, a management-production-publishing holding company based on the King's Road in Chelsea. Subsidiary publishing affiliates included What's In It For Me Music and Mediocre Music. 'We like those sort of putdown names,' said London. Led Zeppelin's original group publishing company, an ASCAP affiliate, was called Superhype Music.

'I first met Peter Grant in 1965,' explained London, a self-confessed honourable hustler who grew up in Montreal, 'when I went into their Dean Street offices to play some song demos for Mickie Most. I became friends with Peter and we went into business in 1969. Peter handled the business side while I put together the music side.'

London unhesitatingly painted a grim portrait of the music industry at large, but insisted that Colour Me Gone was no run-of-the-mill set-up. 'There are a lot of managers around but only a very few good ones,' London said. 'And there are very few trips that work out for both parties – artists *and* managers. There's a lot of talk of managers ripping artists off, but very few people talk about how management often gets ripped off by the artists. In this business, you do tend to get fucked a lot of times. But when something does work out, that feeling overcomes all the fuckings that have come your way before. There's just this incredible feeling you get with success . . . it's just unreal.

'Peter Grant is exceptionally good in business dealings. You've got to be rational with record companies, for instance. You can't just go in and rip them off for ridiculous amounts of money unless you really can deliver. The terrible thing with this business is that there's a hell of a lot of fucking rip-offs.

'What I most admire about Peter is his tremendous loyalty to his acts. He always puts the act first, no matter what. For example, there was a very good relationship between Peter and Led Zeppelin, and myself and Maggie Bell. I discovered Maggie and the band [Stone the Crows] up in Scotland. I called up Peter and he said "get cracking". We brought them down to London the next day, made the demo tapes that evening, and I flew to New York with them the next morning to meet with Peter. I played him the demos and he said, "Let's go". And that was it. All sorts of management offers roll in for Peter. But we were a small management company and we wanted to keep it that way. We turned down about twenty acts a year.'

The secret formula? 'Management,' London shrewdly stated, 'is basically a channelling force, simply choosing the right route to take. In launching a new act, over-exposure can be a big problem. The bread is there to be made but only afterwards – firstly it's a question of establishing the act. You've got to pick and choose the gigs, and bugger the monetary return at the start. In the end, no matter how much preparation, the band and its album have to go out there and do it themselves.'

There is a further crucial aspect in the management equation. 'We never had anything to do with touching an act's money,' London swears. 'It all goes straight to the accountants, then they pay the act and they pay us. Money has been a source of contention for a lot of artists and managers in the past, but not with us.'

Peter Grant himself readily admitted that the music business is a tough racket. 'If you can survive in this line of work, then you can survive in the jungle' is how he expresses his overview. 'I know I'm thought of as a rough character at times, but it's horses for courses. If someone's being rough with you, then you've gotta be rough back. What makes me really angry is people who let you down. There's no question that this is the most competitive field around.'

Managing the world's most successful rock act had heaps of financial satisfaction but few other pleasant or soothing qualities. A day never passed without countless hustlers trying to horn in on the band's action, breathlessly tossing in hot ideas, concepts and concert ideas for them to undertake. Everyone with an eye for a quick get-rich scheme had ideas for Led Zeppelin, but first they had to convince Peter Grant. And he of all managers was no sucker for flimsy pipedreams or pie-in-the-sky ventures. Plus the typical hustler had to surmount the larger problem that Grant rarely dealt with people he didn't already know and trust. The immense loyalty he felt for his acts also extended to his business dealings – 'I stick with the people who've done a really great job with me, even if someone comes along and tries to offer me more,' Grant said.

In the early part of the 1970s, you could spend a couple of hours in Peter Grant's office on any afternoon and invariably, there'd be phone calls from Japan, California, Australia, Germany, France and New York enquiring about future booking possibilities. A standard reply was proffered to all promoters – call back later: next month, next year or whatever. It was exceedingly rare for Grant's long-time secretary, Carole Brown, to accept any messages from unsolicited callers. 'Oh no,' she would tell the legion of persistent callers, 'you'll just have to call back. We don't take messages. You'll have to call again. Try tomorrow. No, I don't know when Mr Grant will be in the office.' And so it went, day after day, and Carole Brown merely shrugged it off as the prime part of her relationship with Grant.

This stonewall attitude of detached nonchalance worked effectively against would-be Led Zeppelin infiltrators, but it proved annoying for some industry associates and contacts who were unable to come to terms with Grant's basic *modus operandi*. He talks to people when he's ready, and you just have to grin and bear it and await his decision to speak with you. It can require a reservoir of patience. 'Peter had a great knack of locking himself away completely from things,' observed Mark London. 'He just gets out in the country and locks himself away, and nobody but Led Zeppelin members can reach him.' London agreed that this tactic has frequently been frustrating for those urgently attempting to gain Grant's attention.

Joe Massot, the respected film director who spent a lot of time working intimately with Grant and the group on *The Song Remains the Same* project, carefully commented, 'I don't think Peter means to be so callous with people at times. At home in the country he was another person playing with his children, who just adored him. He was not at all pretentious in his home life and he really was a warm family man.

'At his office, he could have this other side of him take over at times. He'd sometimes bellow at you. And when Peter Grant shouts at you, it's damn hard to answer back. He has this big powerful presence and he can really intimidate you with his own power. He has this strength and force about him.'

A reflective Massot continued, 'I think it's fair to say that there tended to be a lack of communication at times within the organisation. That's probably because they all live separately and only come together occasionally. They really only want to communicate with you when it's about Led Zeppelin. They were a lot more difficult to work with than Country Joe McDonald or the Grateful Dead or even George Harrison, all of whom I've made films with. But I must admit that personally I was allowed more creative freedom while working with Led Zeppelin. And that is very important.'

Invariably concert promoters represented the sector of the music industry which squawked the loudest about Grant's apparent insularity. But if Grant had made himself freely available to respond to their endless avalanche of proposals, he would have done nothing else. Promoters constantly bombarded the office with performance offers – but the lads toured when they were ready to tour and Grant wasn't prepared to debate the wisdom of their wishes with would-be promoters operating with different time priorities.

Keenly aware of the band's drawing power, in effect Peter Grant would ensure his music industry immortality by instituting several vital, and indeed drastically overdue changes in the concert promotion status quo. Back in the financially flimsy 1950s and 1960s, hit artists were hired by cunning concert promoters for a fixed flat fee, regardless of how many punters turned up at the gigs. For an up-and-coming band, this fee was a form of stop-gap insurance; if the public didn't turn out in sufficient numbers for whatever reason, the act lost nothing but prestige. On the other hand, when people *did* flock to an event in large numbers, the promoter creamed off the lion's share of the box office receipts.

In his earlier days, Peter Grant witnessed much more of the latter category of concert eventualities – while artists often struggled, promoters all too often walked away with a bagful of money. And thus when Led Zeppelin became a potent drawing card in America, Grant instituted some new rules in the way the game was played, much to the dismay of the established concert promoters. He ceased scheduling Led Zeppelin through his original agent, Premier Talent, and the band began booking its own concerts, usually in tandem with trusted local or package promoters.

Instead of the traditional flat fee against a percentage of the gate, Grant turned the applecart upside down. After fixed expenses (including advertising, venue rental security et al), the promoter would be assigned a minor percentage of net profits, depending on the individual production effort. Grant appraised each show on its merits – with promoters receiving anything from one to ten per cent of the net profits, like it or lump it. With Led Zeppelin, the promoters always came away with a fistful of rewards, but now it didn't come close to what they'd once been able to eke out of a top act's drawing power.

By 1972, Zep was able to regularly gross between $75,000 and $200,000 per concert, so promoters received a hefty remuneration for a couple of weeks' work and enormous glory. With that sort of money on the line, they had no choice but to accept (albeit bitterly) Grant's terms which had turned the tables on the 1960s status quo.

Grant cited 'definite mystique' as one of the key reasons that the band were able to draw huge concert attendances with low-key promotion campaigns, often costing next to nothing. 'We've never actually set out to pre-plan an image,' Grant emphasised in 1976. 'It's always been an element of surprise with Led Zeppelin. Sort of like first they're there and then they're gone. It's not just a concert, it's an event. We sold 120,000 tickets in New York for three nights at Madison Square Garden and three nights at the Nassau Coliseum, and we never took a page ad in the *New York Times*. I think it was mentioned on the radio a couple of times. In Detroit, where we played for two nights, advertising costs were zero. One disc jockey mentioned the band was playing and within an hour, there were two thousand people waiting out in front of the hall. The tickets hadn't even been printed. What does image matter (as compared with the Stones or the Beatles) – it doesn't matter.'

Journalist Bob Hart is quick to acknowledge Grant's efforts in securing appropriate remuneration for creative performing talent, even if he does have some slight reservations about Peter's legendary heavy methods. 'There's no doubt at all about what Peter Grant did to even up the balance in the concert business. He may have gone a little too far but he put the artist back on a profitable footing. He introduced the ninety-per-cent-to-the-act game and nobody thought he was serious.

'Grant did a fantastic job of making rock music a boom industry in the 1970s for the British. Although I don't think they were quite ready to hand him any government export achievement awards. None of this however meant that a person had to behave like an asshole.'

In later years, money – once publicly flaunted as an example of their unprecedented success – became almost a taboo subject in the Led Zeppelin camp. Partly because of a sceptical media's predictable over-reaction to the extent of the band's monetary success, and also because of a prevailing band paranoia about their incredible ability to earn such vast amounts so quickly, there evolved a marked reticence for the camp to disucss the enormous earnings, which easily surpassed any act in rock history including the Beatles and the Stones. In the early days, Grant used to announce an overall group earnings figure for each tour (at one point, he even revealed to the *Financial Times* in 1973 that the band was set to make $30 million that year), but since 1973 – when Led Zeppelin began receiving $200,000 and more for some large performances – key numerical statistics became very hard to come by. This probably originated out of a desire to avoid the ever-roving eye of the British tax man – even though much of the band's fortunes were shrewdly stashed in offshore corporate tax shelters.

In 1992, Peter Grant still maintained an air of vagueness about the extent of Zeppelin earnings, but the band's dominance in album sales is reflected by a major story in a September 1992 issue of *Billboard*. They reported a triple platinum US certificate for the four-CD boxed set, a staggering three million sales. 'Led Zeppelin,' noted *Billboard*'s Paul Grein, 'dominated the gold and platinum certifications in August [1992] in much the same way that it dominated rock and roll throughout the 1970s.'

Led Zeppelin II was certified as sixfold platinum in the US, and *Led Zeppelin III* at three million. Their ten multi-platinum albums have sold more than 45 million copies in the US alone. Only the Beatles (aided by a string of 48 hit singles) have sold more albums . . . the Moptops' album total in the US was set at 56 million.

Led Zeppelin's privacy and peace of mind were relatively easy to secure back at home in Britain, but maintaining that acutely desired state on the road in America was a totally different story. If Peter Grant did tend to act rough and tough in the American trenches, perhaps there were good reasons for it. There were several heart-stopping occasions when Grant had guns pulled on him, and he even resorted to hiring a squad of special bodyguards to protect Jimmy Page after murder threats were received. Touring in the South was always fraught with the nauseating smell of impending trouble, and in the beginning, some of the promoters were somewhat less than financially stable. I readily recall advancing the sum of $2,000 to the Toronto Rock Pile club owners to cover Led Zeppelin advance payments for a gig in early 1969 – I recovered the money the next day from door proceeds. Never for a moment did I think the funds were at risk.

Band members long boasted that Peter Grant accompanied them on all tours, which, Page noted, 'was something very few managers would ever consider doing.' In all likelihood, the band wouldn't have been able to tour without him – his presence was perpetually required to deflect pressure away from Led Zeppelin members. If you had wanted to contact any of the band for any reason, even drug supplies, you first had to get the green light from Grant, usually through Richard Cole. It was a long, lonely haul to the top if you were hoping to hit on the Led Zeppelin camp. Idol insulation is what it's all about, especially since the horrifying street murder of John Lennon.

In the early 1970s, Grant never missed a gig, unless there was a very bizarre reason preventing his presence. As a rare example, there was a period of a year when Grant couldn't cross the border into Canada because of an outstanding assault charge. During an earlier gig in Vancouver, the ever-vigilant Grant had his attention drawn to a man at the side of the stage operating a portable tape recorder. The concert had already begun but ignoring the jet-like roar from the bank of speakers, Grant loped over and without even a bellow of warning, smashed the machine with his giant fist and roughed up its operator in the process.

When it was revealed that the man was in fact an official of the Canadian Scientific Pollution and Environmental Control Society sent to the concert to monitor noise levels for a special government study, Grant discreetly withdrew himself across the border. Later both the Society and the official withdrew all claims and charges.

Grant has long been hysterically hypersensitive to the point of waging personal war against those who would seek to illegally capture Zep's aural and visual images on tape at concerts. 'It's got to stop,' he once roared in a fit of passionate protest. He declared that during the 1972 Bath rock festival, he threw a bucket of water into a video tape machine which was illegally filming the stage show. The band had regularly vented its rage about the proliferation of bootleg albums and videos which they considered a fan ripoff. Yet despite Grant's eternal battle against the pirates, a feast of live Led Zeppelin bootleg albums have surfaced over the years.

In 1979, Grant pointed out, 'It [bootlegging] is a concern, not in loss of sales and revenue, but in the rip-offs the kids suffer. The pressings are usually of terrible quality with lots of surface noise. But I think kids have wised up to it — the bootleg business isn't as big as it was.' Nonetheless the band must have lost several millions in unpaid royalties over the years for illegal recordings of their live concerts.

Did such a constant barrage of pirateers and crooked promoters justify Peter Grant's sometimes heavy-handed attitude of dealing with people he came into contact with? Journalist Bob Hart has his doubts. On his 1973 junket with Led Zeppelin, Hart journeyed back to the San Francisco airport in a limousine from the massive gig at Kazar Stadium where 50,000 ecstatic fans had been supremely entertained. 'I must say that some things that happened around Led Zeppelin were inexplicable. Travelling back from Kazar Stadium, I rode with Peter Grant and two of the band in one limo, while a second limo carried the other two band members. Along the way, our limo somehow got lost and Grant just exploded. He started ripping the carpet off the floor of the limo. While the driver was trying to find his way, Grant kept ripping things out of the limo interior and tossing them out of the window.

'By the time we eventually reached the airport, the back of the limo was virtually stripped. As we pulled up to the plane, Peter shook up a can of beer and squirted in the driver's eyes. Then we made a hasty run for the plane. Even though the band always paid for any damage they caused, I thought it was an amazingly cruel and unnecessary thing to do.'

There can be no doubt that Grant and Page were pitiless in dealing with errant limo drivers. Other limo anecdotes are more in the moderate mould of harmless pranks that were rather more amusing. I recall vividly journeying one evening by sleek black limo from Ottawa to Montreal in Canada with Grant, Page and John Paul Jones in 1971 after a simply stupendous gig at the Civic Centre where 11,000-plus fans had spontaneously held up a mass of flaming matches and lighters for the first time (a show described recently by Jones as a particularly special live career highlight — 'It was brilliant, it caused a real lump in the throat. It was a very emotional time.').

The trip back to Montreal after the gig was also very emotional. On the wings of a couple of serious beverages backstage and a round of impressive Colombian spliffs in the back of the car, we were tooling down the Ontario highway to the adjacent province of Quebec. In the unexpected light of the impromptu audience blaze at the concert, our spirits were suitably high.

As we tore towards the provincial border through the forest blackness, Grant noticed a pursuing police motorcycle with its pull-over strobe light urgently flashing away a few hundred yards behind us. Quickly sussing the situation, Grant asked the driver how far we were from the border. 'Oh, just a mile or so,' was his jovial reply, whereupon Grant whipped out a $100 US bill. 'This is yours, mate, if you can beat the bloody gendarmes to the border crossing,' was the challenge and our driver instantly jammed his foot to the floor.

With Jonesy, Page, Grant and myself enthusiastically urging the driver on in unison, we burned across the border point at around 180 kph and the Ontario provincial speed cop – running out of his jurisdiction as we zoomed into Quebec – faded away into the dim distance. An insignificant prank – light and relatively forgivable diversions for men on the march, it has been tenuously termed. A bit of frivolous fun for these boys on the run, themselves diverting their unsettled generation from getting up to even worse. They were the court jesters and town criers in a kingdom bursting at the seams through injustice, ignorance and environmental suicide. A bit of harmless looning to let frustrations loose . . . at least that's how we justified it.

Another key personage in the Led Zeppelin camp (from the outset until 1979) was Richard Cole, who carried the job of tour manager but was in effect, Peter Grant's overall righthand man. If Grant wasn't on hand, Cole usually ran the show, at least until a fondness for heroin clouded his vision. 'Knebworth was the last thing I did for them,' Cole admitted. 'I was smacked out of my mind on heroin – I couldn't even handle the money or anything.'

Cole started working with Peter Grant in 1968 and was involved with Jeff Beck, the Yardbirds and the New Vaudeville Band. He'd previously worked with Unit 4 + 2, the Searchers, Vanilla Fudge, and the Rascals, and had been a chauffeur for Keith Moon and John Entwhistle of the Who. Perhaps his most widely publicised industry observation to date is, 'You've got to have a few villains in the business, or nothing would get done.'

When Grant and Cole had their parting of the ways, it was extremely bitter. Grant has admitted that he found it 'really hard' to fire Cole, and with the passage of time, Grant's attitude towards his former righthand man has mellowed considerably.

'I hear from Richard when he's in London,' Grant told me recently. 'He's as clean as a new pin nowadays. He holds his AA meetings at the Rainbow on Tuesday afternoons when he's in LA. Now he's working for Ozzie and Sharon Ozbourne's management company – Sharon of course being [veteran UK manager and entrepreneur] Don Arden's daughter. They manage acts like Ozzie, the Quire Boys, and now, Jason Bonham, John's son. Richard Cole is a tour manager for their company.'

Over the years, Grant has been understandably contemptuous of some aspects of the music industry, but he also finds a working man's offbeat humour in its amazing machinations. One of his finest public managerial moments came when he brilliantly declined an invitation for Led Zeppelin to perform at the annual MIDEM music industry conference in Cannes in January 1972. The MIDEM carnival makes such a mockery of the art of music that the band considered it a total farce. They had no desire to be showcased before a motley assembly of the merchants of music. Incredibly, the official invitation from the MIDEM director referred to the band as 'Led Zeppelin and *his* musicians'. In the next issue of the British music trade paper, *Music Week*, Grant reprinted this MIDEM invitation under the banner 'Mr Zeppelin Regrets'. It was a superb and timely statement about the outdated awareness of many still powerful music industry manipulators. Not since the Rolling Stones took out glorious ads in the mid-60s ridiculing Cilla Black's pathetic cover version of the Righteous Brothers' American classic, 'You've Lost That Loving Feeling', had the British music industry tittered at such cheek and audacity. They loved it, not the least because Led Zeppelin were in a position to get away with it.

Grant usually didn't hold music industry executives in high esteem, with the exception of the tuned-in trio which ran Atlantic in the late 1960s – Jerry Wexler and the Ertegun brothers, Nesuhi and Ahmet. 'I think that Ahmet is the best record executive in the business,' Grant said in 1976. 'He's had a great upbringing through the music business and has done a lot for all of the people he's recorded. His personality plays a great influence on the company because he really does care. I think he cares about the artists.

'There are so many record companies that are set up like the civil service, a terribly bureaucratic sort of thing. These companies don't even care about the name of the group. Everything gets reduced to numbers. But not with Ahmet. He really did care – and that concern filtered through the rest of the company. We required that kind of treatment.'

The urbane and immensely experienced Ahmet Ertegun has seen a multitude of music managers come and go through the decades, and his recent reflections on the ability of Peter Grant carry considerable weight.

'Peter Grant,' declared Ahmet in a matter-of-fact manner, 'was one of the most important factors in the development of Led Zeppelin. Because he kept people away from them, he always protected them as best he could. Peter was a great protector of the group.

'Back in the 1970s, Peter and the band maintained a unique relationship like I've never seen between another manager and an act. Unfortunately that relationship did deteriorate as time passed, and then they all decided to go their separate ways and I wished each one of them all the best.

'Of course, we at Atlantic still work with Robert Plant and I regard him as one of the greatest people I've ever worked with.'

Having sold some 50 million Zeppelin albums around the world, Atlantic's enlightened operating policy and philosophy must have paid off in a big way. But despite dealing in millions of dollars, the street-wise and underdog-oriented Grant never forgot the bottom-line dilemma of the average fan. While many greedy late 1970s acts pursued inflation with a vengeance and squeezed every last dime they could out of the American marketplace, Grant was exceedingly conservative about raising ticket prices. 'I would hate to go more than $11,' he said after the Knebworth concerts. 'I'm against jacking the price of tickets up to $12.50, which I understand Elton John and the Stones are charging. Elton draws a much older audience which maybe can afford it. But if a guy of sixteen or seventeen wants to take his girlfriend, you're talking about an expensive night out.'

Away from the bright lights–big city rock scene, Peter Grant traditionally led a completely different life in rural Southern England, cushioned by the substantial Led Zeppelin cashflow. Throughout the 1970s, Grant showed he had no intention of combining or compromising the two profoundly different lifestyles. His manner, too, changed – like the other band members' – when he was away from the considerable temptations of Broadway or LA. In the peaceful ancient haunts of the Sussex countryside, he mellowed.

Up until their divorce in 1976, Grant lived with wife Gloria and their two children, Helen and Warren, in a supremely beautiful fourteenth-century estate known as Horselunges Manor. It was a perfect picture of pre-industrial serenity with its moat, stout hand-hewed wooden beams and inglenooks, a genuine abode of ancient family life. The Grants had lovingly filled its soulful rooms with art nouveau (Peter could boast an impressive collection), antique pub signs, knick-knacks, brasses, even Sarah Bernhardt's bed. Observed Mark London, 'You've only got to go to Peter's house to see what a gentle person he really is. He collected little glass things and stuff like that. He's an exceptionally sensitive person, I think.'

'Of all the Led Zeppelin members,' noted filmmaker Joe Massot in 1975, 'I would think that Peter had the most architecturally-interesting home. It's really an ancient place and incredibly gorgeous. It had a beautiful feeling to it, probably because so many different people had lived in it through the ages. It really feels like it came straight out of Henry VIII.' The property is also a working farm, and the Grants enjoyed a daily fresh milk supply from their own pastures.

Grant was immensely proud of his property, telling a Hollywood reporter in 1976, 'My house is 550 years old and I don't want to leave it. I know it's a material thing, but I just don't want to move to LA or New York.' Accordingly, he hung on to the property until 1988.

After their divorce, Grant – to his eternal credit – took on the considerable task of raising the two children. 'The kids refused to go with Gloria, so I brought them up,' Grant admitted recently with profuse pride. 'Which I've got to tell you – being a rock and roll manager – is quite something.'

His present home can't boast the splendid history of Horselunges Manor, but he's fond of it nonetheless. 'It's a very nice three-living-rooms, five-bedroom detached house with a double garage in Eastbourne, East Sussex,' he laughed heartily. 'It's wonderful really – double glazing, central heating with an easy garden and no £800 a week to run it.'

Peter Grant has always been a large man in the many years I've known him. On a number of occasions, his sheer bulk has intimidated people. But underneath his formidable exterior, he can be a very gentle person with a notably big heart. Over the years, he's topped the 300-pound mark on several weigh-ins. 'I'd always been an active chap,' he once grinned, 'but getting behind a desk in management, and all the lush travelling I have to do, you just pick up the pounds, and with me, they very easily turn into stones.' Towards the end of 1973, Grant managed to trim about 100 pounds from his frame, but at some cost to his mental demeanour, according to associates. 'I can give up smoking tobacco in a flash, but it's damn hard not to eat.'

'I feel better now than I can ever remember – at least for many years anyway,' Grant informed me recently, despite a 'few coronary problems' in 1987. 'I've lost loads of weight – 100 to 110 pounds which is pretty good for me. I'm down to about 200 pounds now which is quite light by my standards,' he laughed.

Grant always manages to convincingly fit in with the society that surrounds him. Noted one friend in the mid 1970s, 'When he wasn't working in the rock scene, Peter lived a typical middle-class Englishman's life in Sussex. He often gave parties with the local vicar in attendance, and all of the Establishment people involved in village life. He plays the host as straight as can be with the village people. He was quite charming.' To some of his rock contemporaries, all this may seem poles distant from top-floor looning at the Continental Riot House on Hollywood's Sunset Strip. But to Peter Grant, it was always just an hour's first-class train ride back to the more lurid delights of London . . . if he desired it.

Grant's only other publicly professed indulgence, besides fine food and antiques, was always automobiles, both contemporary and classic. During the 1970s, he amassed a whole fleet of them, including a Rolls, a gleaming 1927 4½ litre Bentley ('that's the Bentley at the start of my sequence in *The Song Remains the Same* – there's two vintage cars and it's the big open green one'), a two-seater Mercedes, a Jaguar and even a Ford Capri (for domestic shopping trips).

I once unexpectedly encountered Peter – resplendent in motoring cap and goggles – at the well-worn wheel of the meticulously renovated green Bentley, nonchalantly tooling around the lush meadows of Penshurst Place, a stately feudal home near Tunbridge Wells, Kent, partaking in a vintage car rally. There wasn't any long hair or even a pair of jeans in sight throughout the superb gardens of the old pile, and Grant seemed a trifle perturbed that I had stumbled across him on the sweeping panorama of his private turf. Perhaps he was concerned that I might draw the wrong conclusions about the yawning gaps between his private and public personas. He slowed down the Bentley and we exchanged small talk for a few minutes before he and Gloria glided off into the studied magnificence of a sunny summer afternoon.

Reflecting on many past associations with Grant over the years, I would have to conclude that he emerges as a combination of both Arthur and Terry (the two classic leading characters in the acclaimed British TV series, *Minder*) – he's both the minder and the mind. He has the guile and the guts, all wrapped up in one formidable – but immensely likeable – package. For all of his external terminal toughness (more than once I've seen him chew up offending people mercilessly), he's always been a lovable old terroriser. He is an archetypal sociological study in opposites. Perhaps it all revolves round his literally amazing Dickensian background: the staggering struggle he staged to overcome intensely humble origins and achieve a pinnacle as the most successful rock group manager in history.

Most recently, Grant has been working on making a feature film 'based on my life story'. 'Malcolm McLaren [the shrewd manager behind the Sex Pistols and an unusual recording artist in his own right] came to me with the idea about five years ago. We teamed up with a writer named Barry Keefe, who wrote *The Long Good Friday*, but at the time, there wasn't much interest in any rock and roll films from American distributors.

'Then about eighteen months ago, the three of us formed a company to produce the picture. I've been involved heavily with that since again, and expect to continue working on it until it comes out at the end of 1992.' The fascinating film project – plus his plans to also write a book based on his saddlebag of experiences – ensure that we'll be hearing a lot more from Peter Grant before too long.

Since parting company with the surviving Zeppelin members in 1983, it is notable that Grant hasn't been involved in any other management projects. Asked if he might contemplate such a move in the foreseeable future, his reaction is fairly predictable in the circumstances. 'Well,' he eventually allowed, 'I suppose if a really, really exciting band or artist came along, maybe I'd give it some thought.

'But I hasten to add it would have to be something that was tremendously appealing – not just a monetary thing. Things have never been monetary with me anyhow. It'd have to be something that could be really, really good. I'd have to have the same feelings I had when Led Zeppelin first got together – and to be honest, I don't think that will ever come along again. I may be waiting quite a while for it to happen.'

He's long since learned to deal with the distinct and very real possibility that Led Zeppelin was – when all is said and done – a once-in-a-lifetime connection and he could never honestly and seriously entertain the prospect of it happening again. To anybody.

'In my position,' Grant observed slowly and perhaps a little sadly, 'once you've been involved as a manager who helped put the whole band together and all the rest . . . well, there's nothing that can follow that, really.'

14 What Was, What If and What Could Be . . .

John Paul Jones: 'The very thing that Zeppelin was about was that there were absolutely no limits. There was freedom to try anything, to experiment. We all had ideas, and we'd use everything we came across, whether it was folk, country music, blues, Indian, Arabic. All these bands that are now borrowing from Zeppelin haven't figured that out, and because of that, none of them have got it right. None of them have gotten close.'

OVER MANY LONG MONTHS, the pressure had been gradually building. The numbers kept getting larger. And the demand was growing stronger. It was a groundswell that crossed oceans and reached planetary proportions. From Tennessee to Tokyo, from Buffalo to Oslo, from Vancouver to Vienna, the 1990s rock scene kept crying out for a Led Zeppelin reunion.

The rumours had fed on themselves after the Live Aid appearance, and were boosted again by the Atlantic 40th concert with John Bonham's son, Jason, on drums. By the time the box set was released, there were widespread press reports that a re-united Zeppelin – with Jason Bonham on drums – had been offered between $50 million and $170 million to commit themselves to a one-off North American tour.

'Is that my share, or is it the whole band's payment?' joked young Jason when I put the tour theory to him early in 1990. 'The way things are going now, I think a Zeppelin tour would go crazy. The North American market is just so hungry for it. It would make a mockery of the recent tours by the Stones and the Who. It really pisses me off when I read things saying "the world's greatest rock and roll band are back on tour" about the Stones. What bullshit! Everyone knows that the greatest rock and roll band was Led Zeppelin. And I'm not just saying that because my dad was in the band.'

Jason Bonham doesn't deny that he's heard a million rumours about a reunion. 'What do I know? I'm not one of the original members. They count me as a member now but I'm not one of the forerunners. It's up to Mr Page and Mr Plant and Mr Jones and what they decide. If they do decide to get together again, sure I'd play with them, and I'd be proud to. It wouldn't be the real thing but it would be the closest possible thing you could get to it. I always admired how my dad played – just the way he approached the drums in his powerhouse style. It still sends shivers down my spine when I listen to it now. I don't try to rip him off – I just play the way he taught me. And that's the way I play: there's no other way around that.'

It is precisely Jason Bonham's pedigree that provides the present round of reunion rumours with convincing credibility. Agreeing that Jason's credentials were pretty close to impeccable, John Paul Jones says, 'Well, they are. They really. I think he's a brilliant drummer, a really great drummer. But then again, he doesn't need to play with a bunch of old men. He needs to get together with youngsters, as he's done.'

John Paul Jones, not all that surprisingly, is the first of the original Led Zeppelin members to support the concept of a reunion tour, at least philosophically. Asked in mid-1991 his feelings about the prospects of the reunion, Jones stated, 'Well yes, I mean, it wouldn't be a bad thing to do. I'm not at all opposed to it. I always enjoy playing with the band. I don't think I'd want to tour for ever, but it's certainly good fun when you're out on stage together.' Jones also indicated he'd be delighted to share the rhythm section of the stage with Jason Bonham.

Jimmy Page steadfastly refuses to be drawn on the subject for the record but, according to Jones, 'I think Jimmy feels the same as I do about it.'

With Jimmy, Jonesy and Jason not averse to a reunion tour project, that only leaves Robert Plant to be converted to the cause. Thus far, however, Percy has appeared to be a less than willing participant. Perhaps because the passage of time invariably causes more of a decline in vocal abilities (and being able to reach the high notes of youth) than in instrumental talent, Robert traditionally has been reticent about reunion possibilities.

In a 1988 interview, Plant stated rather emphatically, 'I don't think it's a good idea at all. It was a great band and you can't get it together like Deep Purple and take it out there and all look incredibly old and do it like some goosestep thing. I reserve judgement to change my mind in five years' time, but the whole thing about Led Zeppelin was that it was off the wall. It was crazy. It was one of those one-in-a-million combinations.

'Bonzo was the main part of the band. He was the man who made whatever Page and I wrote basically work, by what he held back, by what he didn't do to the tempos. I don't think there's anyone in the world who could replace him.'

Probably not. But it's likely that nobody will ever get as close as Jason Bonham could.

Two years down the track, Robert was still notably cool to the idea of getting back with his old mates. He seemed more concerned with getting on with his present career. Asked if he thought people would even recognise Led Zeppelin if they were still around today, he obnserved, 'Of course not. It couldn't possibly be anything like it was when it stopped. We'd probably be a lounge act now in San Antonio – who knows? I mean, it wouldn't be recognisable, I wouldn't think. Could we play "Black Dog" for a further ten years? I don't think so. Only if it turned out like Dread Zeppelin [the popular American band which proffers reggae reditions of Led Zeppelin nuggets] and then you could enjoy yourself. I mean, we were doing reggae versions of "Stairway to Heaven" when Tortelvis was thin, at sounds checks and stuff like that.'

In another interview, Plant stated firmly, 'For me, it's impossible to consider Led Zeppelin in the present tense. Because if you took Bonzo's drumming away, the band would sound useless. I think apart from the pride in the work that I did in that band, everything is very much in the past tense.'

Other observers couldn't quite cope with the image of a Led Zeppelin in the present tense. Noted journalist and long-time watcher, Bob Hart: 'This wasn't a band that could have gone out there as forty-five-year-old vegetarians, with bottles of Perrier water by the kit, advocating health food and playing "Whole Lotta Love" – I just don't think it would have worked.'

When I relayed that observation to John Paul Jones, he didn't find much relevance in it. 'Maybe. I quite like Perrier water but then again, it's playing "Whole Lotta Love". That's the telling point. Maybe not, but we *could* be hanging around drinking fruit juice and playing something else completely different.'

Nor is Jones sympathetic to contemporary reasoning that a reunion would interfere with Robert's on-going solo career. 'I'm not really sure what Robert thinks about the reunion, but I definitely *don't* think he's got anything to lose. I think it would be quite possible to do the two things – continue his solo career and do a reunion tour.

'So you never know,' were Jones's closing words on the subject. 'It could be a possibility, but the chances are a bit slim, though, I'd think.'

Peter Grant also has a few thoughts on the possible reunion (and don't totally rule out the possibility that Grant may well turn up in some official capacity on such a tour, if and when) that bear consideration. 'It could be a disaster, I think. Live Aid and Atlantic's fortieth anniversary gigs proved that. I think the potential is there for a disaster because Robert is so much into an attitude of "I don't wanna do this – I wanna do that". That would be my fear.

'Musically of course they're such good musicians that they'd be able to put it together. Perhaps even make a new album. But I don't think they would just bow to the dollar, even though unbelievable money is being offered to them.'

Always the entrepreneur, Grant added, 'They could double what the Stones grossed on their last tour. They always could and they still can.' Grant also agreed with the supposition that no band in history has ever rejected such a vast amount of money to reunite.

Asked if he himself would in fact contemplate a return to leading the camel train on a reunion tour, Grant is somewhat pensive. 'I'd have to think very, very carefully about it. I'd have to think about my health and whether I could really believe in it. As you know, we all agreed separately in 1980 that the band couldn't continue because it would never be the same without Bonzo. I really still think that it could never be the same.

'However if Jimmy, for example, came to me and asked me to become involved in a reunion situation, I'd certainly sit down and discuss it with him, and give him the best of my advice – whether I did it or not. I'd have to say it's not out of the question.'

Simon Kirke, leader of the re-formed Bad Company, the Swan Song label's second most successful act in the 1970s, has the odd reservation about the growing prospects of a reunion. 'Well, I don't think they need the money, but it is an awful lot of money,' noted Kirke in 1992. 'Personally I don't think they could do it without John Bonham, but I'm a purist. Jason Bonham is a very good player – if anyone was to replace his dad, it would have to be him. But he doesn't have the seasoning that his dad had when he died. Jason has had a few years of experience and he's very good, but . . . However, a hundred million dollars is a lot of money. If they want to do it, it's fine by me.'

Journalist Bob Hart was at pains to point out that should Led Zeppelin re-unite, it could never be *exactly* the same. In its original form, it was a magic combination – probably no other drummer that ever lived could have driven the band like Bonzo did. They did everything to extremes.

'Maybe their music wouldn't have been as brilliant without those extremes – maybe it forced something extra from them. Maybe without those extreme edges, they'd have been John Denver. There was extreme behaviour in everything they did, including their playing. That's what made it great. Maybe that is some measure of justification for some of the other behaviour.'

Ever the down-to-earth pragmatist, former Page and Plant personal managers through the 1980s, Phil Carson conceded on the reality of reunion prospects, 'They could do it at any time if they really want to do it. There's no time factor involved. They're still the biggest group in the world, and if they ever chose to do it, it'd be a huge success.

'Having said that, I think that Jimmy's project with David Coverdale will certainly put the tin hat on it, and it will defeat any possibility of it coming back together. There's no question that Jimmy was ready to do it but I think the involvement with Coverdale could blow it out.'

It appears appropriate to allocate the last words on reunion prospects to the exemplary vision of Ahmet Ertegun, whose record label took Led Zeppelin music to the world. 'It's really up to them. It's hard for anybody from outside to realise the implications – not that I really consider myself an outsider. The decision clearly must come from the three surviving members of the group. If anybody tries to impose anything on them, it won't work. It has to come from them.'

Asked if Atlantic would wish to release a new album of Led Zeppelin originals in a reunion context, Ahmet Ertegun leaves no room for doubt. 'I don't think there's anybody in the world who wouldn't want to have them back.'

'I know lots of bands that stopped and are now forgotten,' insisted John Paul Jones, 'because there was never much there in the first place. As for the good bands, the ones that made very strong musical contributions, well I just don't know. Rock and roll is still quite young. We're still the first generation of old rock and rollers, as it were. So nobody's quite sure what happens. There are no rules yet, no precedents.

'It's difficult to theorise. In other fields of music, composers generally mature as they get older. Obviously in the area of dance you get to a point where physically it's difficult to get any better. In rock and roll, you're so tied down by the media and record companies and back catalogue and the whole nostalgia thing. Understandably people want to hear what they always remembered that you did. Then if you try different things, you tend to be hated by everybody.

'So all that works against you which is a shame, because as I was saying, if you were a serious composer, your maturity would be looked forward to by all and sundry. Rock and rollers aren't really allowed to mature in any way.'

Regardless of whether the Zep members do unite for one last North American concert fling – and no matter how successful such a reunion might be – their current feelings about the band's achievements, its ultimate legacy, its uniqueness, will always be valid and relevant.

These comments are in essence the final words on this staggering success story, which in all likelihood will never be equalled or repeated, being completely and utterly in a class of its own.

To instigator Jimmy Page, the most satisfying aspect, 'the most rewarding part of it is having been part of music which stood up and stood the test of time. Every musician hopes that their music will hold up, let alone having been part of a fabulous band as well, in the bargain. It's wonderful.'

For Peter Grant, the band's major contribution was 'what they put down on record, they were able to deliver live. I think that's a very important musical thing.'

With the release of the box set, Robert Plant recalled, 'Muddy Waters said – when, fifteen years ago? – that nobody's got the deep blues any more. Maybe now in this second- or third-generation of Zeppelinisms, people are losing the plot. Maybe people don't feel it the way it was felt originally. But we had it. And that's a hell of a sweeping statement. But we did have something up there, which was not just token cloning or token theft or whatever it was. We had a weave of . . . conspiratorial elegance if you like. In the middle of it all, occasionally, it really did work. And it was wholehearted, and we gave it all a new personality.'

Questioned on how he'd like Led Zeppelin to be remembered, Percy was equally eloquent. 'I'd like to maintain the dignity of the group. I'm very proud that people are so enchanted by it. And I think the way it is now is that whatever it is that people loved, it's not going to be spoiled.

'I think the fact that Led Zeppelin was bold and brave and chaotic and honest in a very loose framework – it *was* honest and it took risks and chances that are no longer possible if you start from scratch. I think it had musical integrity – it captured all of the elements of the kind of wondrous music that we'd been exposed to.

'I think what we did was translate and kick on – it's like we were a filter for all the good things. We filtered it and we begged, borrowed and stole and we made something that was particularly original, by which a lot of other music has been measured.'

John Paul Jones liked to point out that Led Zeppelin 'wasn't a purist band, as you get nowadays, where the entire band listens to the same type of music. Between the blues influences of Robert and the rock and roll influences of Jimmy – who also had strong blues influences – the soul influences of Bonzo and my soul and jazz influences, there seemed to be a common area which was Led Zeppelin. The fusion of all different types of music and interests.'

Looking back on his considerable achievements in expanding the scope of the band, John Paul Jones observed, 'I'm very proud of what we did. It's nice that we are still considered an influence. A lot of surprising people – soul and country musicians – come up to me and say they used to listen to our stuff. You'd get a lot of that "you were a great influence on my playing" sort of thing. That's really very nice. It's no more than really very nice, but I'm proud of what we did.

'We did a lot of good things and a few dud things. But looking back on it . . . it is very interesting. It wasn't something that we could have planned or plotted out, that's for sure.'

> *Leaves are falling all around,*
> *Time I was on my way,*
> *But still I'm much obliged,*
> *Such a pleasant stay;*
> *But now it's time for me to go,*
> *The autumn moon lights my way,*
> *Now I smell the rain, and with it pain,*
> *And it's headed my way . . .*
> *Ah sometimes I grow so tired,*
> *But I know I've got one thing that I've got to do,*
> *Ramble on . . . now's the time, the time is now . . .**

* © 1969 – Lyrics to 'Ramble On', composed by Jimmy Page and Robert Plant and published by Superhype Music, Inc. Lyrics reprinted by permission.

The Led Zeppelin Discography, and Beyond

Following is a list of all albums released by Led Zeppelin, along with a rundown of the various singles and albums to which individual group members officially contributed, either as musicians or as vocalists. There is also a listing of solo endeavours by band members up until July 1991. Release dates apply throughout the world. No singles were released in the UK.

Essential personnel on all Led Zeppelin albums: John Bonham, drums, timpani, keyboards, backing vocal; John Paul Jones, bass, organ, backing vocal; Jimmy Page, electric guitar, acoustic guitar, pedal steel guitar, backing vocal; Robert Plant, lead vocal, harmonica.

Led Zeppelin/Atlantic (US) SD 8216, (UK) K 40031

Released 12 January 1969

Side 1
Good Times Bad Times (Page, Jones, Bonham)
Babe I'm Gonna Leave You (Trad. arr. Page)
You Shook Me (Willie Dixon)
Dazed and Confused (Page)

Side 2
Your Time Is Gonna Come (Page, Jones)
Black Mountain Side (Page
Communication Breakdown (Page, Jones, Bonham)
I Can't Quit You Baby (Willie Dixon)
How Many More Times (Page, Jones, Bonham)

Recorded in November 1968 at Olympic Studios, London. Produced by Jimmy Page, engineered by Glyn Johns.

Led Zeppelin II/Atlantic (US) SD 8236, (UK) K 40037

Released 22 October 1969

Side 1
Whole Lotta Love (Page, Plant, Jones, Bonham)

Side 2
Heartbreaker (Page, Plant, Jones, Bonham)

What Is and What Should Never Be (Page, Plant)
The Lemon Song (Page, Plant, Jones, Bonham)
Thank You (Page, Plant)

Living Loving Maid (She's Just a Woman) (Page, Plant)
Ramble On (Page, Plant)
Moby Dick (Bonham, Jones)
Bring It On Home (Page, Plant)

Recorded between January and August 1969 at various studios. Produced by Jimmy Page and engineered by Edwin Kramer (director), George Chldantz, and Chris Huston.

Led Zeppelin III/Atlantic (US) SD 7201, (UK) K 50002
Released 5 October 1970

Side 1
Immigrant Song (Page, Plant)
Friends (Page, Plant)
Celebration Day (Page, Plant, Jones)
Since I've Been Loving You (Page, Plant, Jones)
Out on the Tiles (Page, Plant, Bonham)

Side 2
Gallows Pole (Trad. arr. Page, Plant)
Tangerine (Page)
That's the Way (Page, Plant)
Bron-Y-Aur Stomp (Page, Plant, Jones)
Hats Off to (Roy) Harper (Trad. arr. Charles Obscure)

Recorded between January and August 1970 at Olympic Sound, London and Ardent Studios, Memphis. Produced by Jimmy Page and engineered by Andrew Johns, London and Terry Manning, Memphis.

The Fourth Led Zeppelin Album/Atlantic (US) SD 7208, (UK) K 50008
Released 8 November 1971

Side 1
Black Dog (Page, Plant, Jones)
Rock and Roll (Page, Plant, Jones, Bonham)
The Battle of Evermore (Page, Plant)
Stairway to Heaven (Page, Plant)

Side 2
Misty Mountain Hop (Page, Plant, Jones)
Four Sticks (Page, Plant)
Going to California (Page, Plant)
When the Levee Breaks (Page, Plant, Jones, Bonham, Memphis Minnie)

Recorded between December 1970 and August 1971 at Island Studios, London; Headley Grange, Hampshire; and Sunset Sound, Los Angeles. Produced by Jimmy Page. Sandy Denny appears on 'The Battle of Evermore' courtesy of Island Records.

Houses of the Holy/Atlantic (US) SD 7255, (UK) K 50014
Released 28 March 1973

Side 1
The Song Remains the Same (Page, Plant)
The Rain Song (Page, Plant)

Side 2
Dancing Days (Page, Plant)
D'Yer Mak'er (Page, Plant, Jones, Bonham)

Over the Hills and Far Away
  (Page, Plant)
The Crunge (Bonham, Jones, Page,
  Plant)

No Quarter (Jones, Page, Plant)
The Ocean (Page, Plant, Jones,
  Bonham)

Recorded between January and August 1972 at Electric Lady Studios, New York and Olympic Studios, London. Produced by Jimmy Page and engineered by Eddie Kramer, George Chkiantz and Keith Harwood.

Physical Graffiti/Swan Song 2SS 200   Released 24 February 1975

Side 1
Custard Pie (Page, Plant)
The Rover (Page, Plant)
In My Time of Dying (Bonham,
  Jones, Page, Plant)

Side 3
In the Light (Jones, Page, Plant)
Bron-Y-Aur (Page)
Down by the Seaside (Page, Plant)
Ten Years Gone (Page, Plant)

Side 2
Houses of the Holy (Page, Plant)
Trampled Underfoot (Jones, Page,
  Plant)
Kashmir (Bonham, Page, Plant)

Side 4
Night Flight (Jones, Page, Plant)
The Wanton Song (Page, Plant)
Boogie with Stu (Bonham, Jones,
  Page, Plant, Stewart, Mrs
  Valens)
Black Country Woman (Page,
  Plant)
Sick Again (Page, Plant)

Recorded between November 1973 and December 1974 at Headley Grange with Ronnie Lane's mobile studio and the Rolling Stones mobile studio, Olympic Studios, Island Studios, Stargroves and Electric Ladyland. Produced by Jimmy Page and engineered by George Chkiantz, Keith Harwood, Andrew Johns, Eddie Kramer and Ron Nevison.

Presence /Swan Song SS 8416   Released 31 March 1976

Side 1
Achilles' Last Stand (Page, Plant)
For Your Life (Page, Plant)
Royal Orleans (Bonham, Jones,
  Page, Plant)

Side 2
Nobody's Fault But Mine (Page,
  Plant)
Candy Store Rock (Page, Plant)
Hots On for Nowhere (Page,
  Plant)
Tea for One (Page, Plant)

Recorded in November 1975 at Musicland Studios, Munich. Produced by Jimmy Page and engineered by Keith Harwood.

The Song Remains the Same/Swan Song 2SS 201

Released 28 September 1976

Side 1
Rock and Roll (Bonham, Jones,
  Page, Plant)

Side 2
Dazed and Confused (Page)

Celebration Day (Jones, Page,
   Plant)
The Song Remains the Same (Page,
   Plant)
Rain Song (Page, Plant)

Side 3
No Quarter (Jones, Page, Plant)
Stairway to Heaven (Page, Plant)

Side 4
Moby Dick (Bonham, Jones, Page)
Whole Lotta Love (Bonham, Jones,
   Page, Plant)

Recorded live in July/August 1973 at Madison Square Garden, New York.
Produced by Jimmy Page and engineered by Eddie Kramer.

In Through the Out Door/Swan Song SSK 59410
Released 15 August 1979

Side 1
In the Evening (Jones, Page, Plant)
South Bound Saurez (Jones, Plant)
Fool in the Rain (Jones, Page,
   Plant)
Hot Dog (Page, Plant)

Side 2
Carouselambra (Jones, Page, Plant)
All My Love (Jones, Plant)
I'm Gonna Crawl (Jones, Page,
   Plant)

Recorded in December 1978 at Polar Music Studios, Stockholm. Produced
by Jimmy Page and engineered by Leif Mases.

Coda/Swan Song 79 00511
Released 19 November 1982

Side 1
We're Gonna Groove (Ben E.
   King, J. Bethea)
Poor Tom (Page, Plant)
I Can't Quit You Baby (Willie
   Dixon)
Walter's Walk (Page, Plant)

Side 2
Ozone Baby (Page, Plant)
Darlene (Bonham, Jones, Page,
   Plant)
Bonzo's Montreux (Bonham)
Wearing and Tearing (Page, Plant)

Produced by Jimmy Page.

Led Zeppelin/Atlantic 7567-82144-2
Released November 1990

Disc 1
Whole Lotta Love (II)
Heartbreaker (II)
Communication Breakdown (first
   album)
Babe I'm Gonna Leave You (first
   album)
What Is and What Should Never
   Be (II)
Thank You (II)

Disc 2
Black Dog (IV)
Over the Hills and Far Away
   (Houses)
Immigrant Song (III)
The Battle of Evermore (IV)
Bron-Y-Aur Stomp (III)
Tangerine (III)
Going to California (IV)
Since I've Been Loving You (III)

I Can't Quit You Baby (Coda)
Dazed and Confused (First album)
Your Time Is Gonna Come (First
  album)
Ramble On (II)
Travelling Riverside Blues (BBC
  broadcast)
Friends (III)
Celebration Day (III)
Hey Hey What Can I Do (B-side
  of Im. Song)
White Summer/Black Mountain
  Side (BBC broadcast)

D'yer Mak'er (Houses)
Gallows Pole (III)
Custard Pie (Physical)
Misty Mountain Hop (IV)
Rock'n'Roll (IV)
The Rain Song (Houses)
Stairway to Heaven (IV)

Disc 3
Kashmir (Physical)
Trampled Underfoot (Physical)
For Your Life (Presence)
No Quarter (Houses)
Dancing Days (Houses)
When the Levee Breaks (IV)
Achilles' Last Stand (Presence)
The Song Remains the Same
  (Houses)
Ten Years Gone (Physical)
In My Time of Dying (Physical)

Disc 4
In the Evening (In Through)
Candy Store Rock (Presence)
The Ocean (Houses)
Ozone Baby (Coda)
Houses of the Holy (Physical
  Graffiti)
Wearing and Tearing (Coda)
Poor Tom (Coda)
Nobody's Fault But Mine
  (Presence)
Fool in the Rain (In Through)
In the Light (Physical)
The Wanton Song (Physical)
Moby Dick/Bonzo's Montreux
  (II/Coda)
I'm Gonna Crawl (In Through)
All My Love (In Through)

Remasters/Atlantic 7567-80415-2 (UK only) Two-CD collection
Released November 1990
but only available until May 1991, and then deleted.

CD1
Communication Breakdown
Babe I'm Gonna Leave You
Good Times Bad Times
Dazed and Confused
Whole Lotta Love
Heartbreaker
Ramble On
Immigrant Song
Celebration Day
Since I've Been Loving You

CD2
The Song Remains the Same
The Rain Song
D'yer Mak'er
No Quarter
Houses of the Holy
Kashmir
Trampled Underfoot
Nobody's Fault But Mine
Achilles' Last Stand
All My Love

Black Dog
Rock and Roll
The Battle of Evermore
Misty Mountain Hop
Stairway to Heaven

In the Evening

POST-ZEPPELIN SOLO VENTURES

Jimmy Page

The Original Soundtrack — Death Wish II/Swan Song XSS 8511
Music by Jimmy Page   Released 1 March 1982

Side 1
Who's to Blame
The Chase
City Sirens*
Jam Sandwich
Carole's Theme
The Release

Side 2
Hotel Rats and Photostats
A Shadow in the City
Jill's Theme
Prelude
Big Band, Sax, and Violence
Hypnotizing Ways (Oh Mamma)

All songs by Jimmy Page except * by Page/Edwards.

The Firm/Atlantic 78 12391   Released March 1985

Side 1
Closer (Page, Rodgers)
Make or Break (Rodgers)
Someone to Love (Page, Rodgers)
Together (Page, Rodgers)
Radioactive (Rodgers)

Side 2
You've Lost that Lovin' Feelin'
    (Mann, Weill, Spector)
Money Can't Buy (Rodgers)
Satisfaction Guaranteed (Page,
    Rodgers)
Midnight Moonlight (Page,
    Rodgers)

Produced by Jimmy Page and Paul Rodgers. Recorded and mixed at The Sol
Studios, Berkshire.

The Firm — Mean Business/Atlantic 78 16281   Released April 1986

Side 1
Fortune Hunter (Page, Rodgers)
Cadillac (Page, Rodgers)
All the King's Horses (Rodgers)
Live in Peace (Rodgers)

Side 2
Tear Down the Walls (Page,
    Rodgers)
Dreaming (Franklin)
Free to Live (Page, Rodgers)
Spirit of Love (Rodgers)

Produced by Jimmy Page, Paul Rodgers and Julian Mendelsohn.

Led Zeppelin

Jimmy Page – Outrider/Geffen 24188-1   Released June 1988

Side 1
Wasting My Time (Page, Miles)
Wanna Make Love (Page, Miles)
Writes of Winter (Page)
The Only One (Page, Plant)
Liquid Mercury (Page)

Side 2
Hummingbird (Leon Russell)
Emerald Eyes (Page)
Prison Blues (Page, Farley)
Blues Anthem (If I Cannot Have
Your Love . . .) (Page, Farlow)

Produced by Jimmy Page. Recorded at The Sol Studios, Berkshire.

The Honeydrippers Volume One/Es Paranza 79 02201
Released September 1984

Side 1
I Get a Thrill (Rudy Toombs)
Sea of Love (Khoury, Baptiste)
I Got a Woman (Ray Charles)

Side 2
Young Boy Blues (Doc Pomus, Phil
Spector)
Rockin' At Midnight (Roy Brown)

(This EP featured both Jimmy Page and Robert Plant in semi-anonymous roles)
Produced by Ahmet Ertegun and the Fabulous Brill Brothers.

John Paul Jones

The Original Soundtrack – Scream for Help/Atlantic 78 01901
Released May 1985

Side 1
Spaghetti Junction (Jones)
Bad Child (Jones, Jones)
Silver Train (Jones, Anderson)
Crackback (Jones, Page)
Here I Am (Jones, Bell)

Side 2
Chilli Sauce (Jones)
Take It or Leave It (Jones, Bell)
Christie (Jones, Jones)
When You Fall in Love (Jones,
Jones)

Produced and arranged by John Paul Jones at Sunday School Studio, Devon.

Robert Plant

Pictures at Eleven/Swan Song XSS 8512   Released June 1982

Side 1
Burning Down One Side (Plant,
Blunt, Woodroffe)
Moonlight in Samosa (Plant, Blunt)
Pledge Pin (Plant, Blunt)
Slow Dancer (Plant, Blunt)

Side 2
Worse than Detroit (Plant, Blunt)
Fat Lip (Plant, Blunt, Woodroffe)
Like I've Never Been Gone (Plant,
Blunt)
Mystery Title (Plant, Blunt)

Produced by Robert Plant and engineered by Pat Moran. Recorded at Rockfield
Studios, Monmouth, Wales.

The Principle of Moments/Es Paranza 79-1011   Released June 1983

Side 1
Other Arms (Plant, Blunt)
In the Mood (Plant, Blunt,
    Martinez)
Messin' with the Mekon (Plant,
    Blunt, Martinez)
Wreckless Love (Plant, Blunt)

Side 2
Thru' with the Two Step (Plant,
    Blunt, Martinez)
Horizontal Departure (Plant,
    Blunt, Martinez, Woodroffe)
Stranger Here . . . Than Over
    There (Plant, Blunt, Martinez,
    Woodroffe)
Big Log (Plant, Blunt, Woodroffe)

Production and quality control by Robert Plant, Benji LeFevre and Pat Moran. Recorded at Rockfield Studios, Monmouth, Wales.

Shaken 'n' Stirred/Es Paranze 79 02651   Released March 1985

Side 1
Little by Little (Plant, Woodroffe)
Doo Doo A Do Do (Plant, Blunt,
    Martinez)
Easily Led (Plant, Martinez,
    Woodroffe)
Sixes and Sevens (Plant, Blunt,
    Martinez, Woodroffe, Hayward)

Side 2
Hip to Hoo (Plant, Blunt,
    Martinez, Woodroffe, Hayward)
Kallalou Kallalou (Plant,
    Woodroffe)
Too Loud (Plant, Blunt, Martinez,
    Woodroffe, Hayward)
Trouble Your Money (Plant,
    Blunt, Martinez)
Pink and Black (Plant, Blunt,
    Martinez, Woodroffe, Hayward)

Produced by Robert Plant, Benji LeFevre and Tim Palmer.

Now and Zen/Es Paranza 90863.1   Released February 1988

Side 1
Heaven Knows (Johnstone, Barrett)
Dance on My Own (Plant,
    Johnstone, Crash)
Tall Cool One (Plant, Johnstone)
The Way I Feel (Plant, Johnstone,
    Boyle)

Side 2
Helen of Troy (Plant, Johnstone)
Billy's Revenge (Plant, Johnstone)
Ship of Fools (Plant, Johnstone)
Why (Plant, Crash)
White, Clean and Neat (Plant,
    Johnstone)

Produced by Tim Palmer, Robert Plant and Phil Johnstone. Recorded at Swanyard Studios and Marcus Studios, London.

Manic Nirvana/Es Paranza 756791336.1   Released March 1990

Side 1
Hurting Kind (Plant, Johnstone,
    Jones, Boyle, Blackwell)

Side 2
Tie Dye on the Highway (Plant,
    Blackwell)

Led Zeppelin

Big Love (Plant, Johnstone, Blackwell)

S S S & Q (Plant, Johnstone, Jones, Boyle, Blackwell)

I Cried (Plant, Johnstone)

Nirvana (Plant, Jones, Boyle)

Your Ma Said You Cried in Your Sleep Last Night (Schiaks, Glazer)

Anniversary (Plant, Johnstone)

Liar's Dance (Plant, Boyle)

Watching You (Plant, Johnstone, Blackwell)

Produced by Robert Plant and Phil Johnstone. Co-produced and engineered by Mark Stent. Recorded at Olympic Studios, London.

MISCELLANEOUS CONTRIBUTIONS

John Bonham
Cause I Love You – Screaming Lord Sutch (album)

John Paul Jones
Singles
'Baja' – John Paul Jones
'Sunshine Superman' – Donovan (bass)
'Mellow Yellow' – Donovan (bass)

'Hurdy Gurdy Man' – Donovan (bass)
'Little Games' – Yardbirds (cello arrangements)
'She's a Rainbow' – Rolling Stones (misc. arrangements)

Albums
Their Satanic Majesties Request – Rolling Stones (misc. arrangements)
Madeline Bell – Madeline Bell (producer)

John Paul Jones also played on literally hundreds of London recording sessions between 1963 and 1968 with an assortment of artists.

Robert Plant
Singles
'You Better Run' – Listen (singer)
'Our Song' – Robert Plant
'What Time is Love?' – KLF (singer)

Albums
Bootleg Him – Alexis Korner (singer on one track, 'Operator')

Jimmy Page
Singles
'Diamonds' – Jet Harris and Tony Meehan (rhythm guitar)
'I Can't Explain' – The Who (rhythm guitar)

Albums
You Really Got Me – The Kinks (snatches of rhythm guitar)
Little Games – Yardbirds (lead and bass guitar)

'You Really Got Me' – The Kinks (tambourine)

'Hurdy Gurdy Man' – Donovan (lead guitar)

'Happenings Ten Years Time Ago' – Yardbirds (dual lead guitar with Jeff Beck) backed with 'Psycho Daisies' (bass guitar)

'Ha Ha Said the Clown' – Yardbirds (lead guitar)

'The Little Indians' – Yardbirds (lead guitar)

'Goodnight Sweet Josephine'/'Think About It' – Yardbirds (lead guitar)

'Baby Please Don't Go' – Them (second guitar)

'She Just Satisfies' – Jimmy Page (all parts except drums)

'With a Little Help from My Friends' – Joe Cocker (lead guitar)

The Yardbirds Live with Jimmy Page at the Anderson Theater – Yardbirds (withdrawn)

Joe Cocker – Joe Cocker (lead and rhythm guitar)

Cause I Love You – Screaming Lord Sutch (lead guitar)

Valentine – Roy Harper (lead guitar)

Album tracks

'Telephone Blues,' 'I'm Your Witch-Doctor,' 'Sittin' on Top of the World' and 'Double Crossing Time' – Eric Clapton (producer)

Film soundtrack

'Stroll On' – Yardbirds for *Blow Up* (dual lead guitar with Jeff Beck)

Jimmy Page also played on many hundreds of London recording sessions between 1963 and 1968.

What follows is a reasonably definitive guide to the mass of Led Zeppelin bootleg recordings floating around the world. This list was compiled with the assistance of *Hot Wacks* magazine, Kitchener, Ontario, Canada. None of these records were released with the co-operation or permission of the band itself, it should be noted.

Absence/Toasted 23921

Comments: Both records are a re-release of 'On Stage in Europe 1975' (ZAP 7867) with a deluxe colour back cover (front is b&w).

Archipelago/ZAP 7885

Comments: A reissue of 'Sin City Social'.

Ballcrusher/Flat 8214

Side 1
Immigrant Song
Heartbreaker

Side 2
That's the Way
The Lemon Song

Led Zeppelin

Since I've Been Loving You	Whole Lotta Love
Black Dog	Communication Breakdown
	Going to California
	Dazed and Confused

Recording: Excellent mono (cover says stereo)
Source: London, England 1972
Comments: Reissued in 1978 with a b&w deluxe cover as TAKRJ 810.

BBC Broadcast/TMOQ 71070

Side 1
Communication Breakdown
Dazed and Confused
Going to California

Side 2
Stairway to Heaven
What Is and What Should Never Be
Medley: Whole Lotta Love; Boogie Woogie; That's Alright My Momma; Stop What's That Sound
Minnesota Blues

Recording: Excellent stereo
Source: 1971 Royal Albert Hall
Comments: Also available on Midnite Recs/Renaissance 2255. Available on Berkeley 2046 as *BBC Concert*.

BBC Broadcast/K&S Records 007

Comments: 200 pressed on red vinyl from original TMOQ plates. Excellent stereo, crackles.

BBC Broadcast/79-037

Comments: Pressed from *BBC Zep* plates with deluxe b&w cover.

BBC Concert

Comments: A colour picturedisc reissue. 1,000 pressed.

BBC Concert/Berkeley 2046

Comments: Same as *BBC Broadcast*.

BBC Zep/CBM

Side 1
Communication Breakdown
Dazed and Confused

Side 2
Going to California
Stairway to Heaven
What Is and What Should Never Be

Recording: Excellent mono
Source: 1971 Royal Albert Hall
Comments: Song separation.

Best of Led Zeppelin Live in Concert/I.C.R. 6

Side 1
Since I've Been Loving You
What Is and What Should Never
  Be
Thank You

Side 2
Whole Lotta Love
Communication Breakdown
Good Times Bad Times
I Saw Her Standing There

Recording: Good stereo.

Blueberry Hill/TMOQ 72002

Side 1
Immigrant Song
Heart Breaker
Dazed and Confused
(26:14)

Side 2
What Is and What Should Never
  Be
Moby Dick
Medley: Communication
  Breakdown; Good Times Bad
  Times; For What It's Worth
(26:53)

Side 3
Since I've Been Loving You
Organ Improvisation
Thank You
Out on the Tiles
Blueberry Hill
(27:00)

Side 4
Bring It On Home
Medley: Whole Lotta Love; Let
  That Boy Boogie Woogie; I'm
  Moving On; Think It Over;
  Lemon Song
(26:46)

Recording: Good and very good stereo
Source: LA Forum 4 September 1970
Comments: Also available on CBM 30/31, Zeppelin Records S2549-52, and Led Records (WCF). On the latter the recording runs into the labels on sides 3 and 4.

Blueberry Hill/X&S Records 009

Comments: 150 pressed on multi-coloured vinyl from original TMOQ plates.

Bonzo's Birthday Party/TMOQ 72007

Side 1
Misty Mountain Hop
The Song Remains the Same

Side 2
Dazed and Confused

Side 3
No Quarter
The Ocean

Side 4
Heartbreaker
Whole Lotta Love

Recording: Excellent mono
Source: Inglewood Forum, Calif., 31 May 1973
Comments: Also available on Berkeley 2006/7 and CBM.

Led Zeppelin

Bonzo's Birthday Party/K&S Records 029

Comments: 200 pressed on blue & black and orange & black discs.

Caution Explosive/WRMB 329

Side 1
Train Kept a Rollin
Thank You
What Is and What Should Never
  Be
Blueberry Hill

Side 2
Bring It On Home
You Shook Me
Bron-Y-Aur

Side 3
Medley: As Long As I Have You;
  Fresh Garbage; Shake
That's the Way
Since I've Been Loving You

Side 4
John Paul Jones Organ
  Improvisation
Medley: Communication
  Breakdown; Good Times Bad
  Times; For What It's Worth; I
  Saw Her Standing There
Encore: Communication
  Breakdown

Recording: Good mono
Source: Winterland, San Francisco 1969 and Los Angeles 1970.

The Destroyer/Smilin' Eero 77-300

Side 1
The Song Remains the Same
  (14:11)
Sick Again; Nobody's Fault But
  Mine (5:56)

Side 2
Since I've Been Loving You (17:24)

Side 3
Guitar Solo; Star Spangled Banner
Achilles' Last Stand (18:21)

Side 4
White Summer; Black Mountain
  Side
Kashmir (15:31)

Side 5
Ten Years Gone (8:56)
Battle of Evermore (5:25)
Going to California (4:19)

Side 6
Black Country Woman
Bron-Y-Aur Stomp (7:00)
Trampled Under Foot (6:19)
Rock N Roll (3:54)

Side 7
Kashmir (17:13)

Side 8
Moby Dick (16:25)

Recording: Excellent stereo
Date: 28 April 1977
Comments: Deluxe box set.

Detroit – Just About Back/King Kong 1046

Side 1
Rock and Roll
Call My Name
Rap
Over the Hills

Side 2
Rap
Song Remains the Same
Cash Me In

Side 3
No Quarter

Side 4
Stairway to Heaven
How Many More Times

Recording: Satisfactory stereo.

Earl's Court/Europe LZL 19775

Side 1
No Quarter (22:00)
Tangerine (5:00)

Side 2
Kashmir (9:06)
Going to California (5:02)
That's the Way (7:43)
Woodstock (5:02)

Comments: European bootleg with full colour deluxe cover and song separation. Also available on IMP 1107. Available as *Kashmir* on Berkeley and *On Stage in Europe* on ZAP 7867.

Earl's Court II/Europe LZL 1977511

Side 1
In My Time of Dying
The Song Remains the Same

Side 2
Trampled Underfoot
Black Dog
Stairway to Heaven

Recording: Very good stereo
Comments: Deluxe colour, song separation.

V½/TMOQ 72019

Side 1
Rock and Roll
Celebration Day
Black Dog
Over the Hills and Far Away
Misty Mountain Hop

Side 2
The Song Remains the Same
The Rain Song
Stairway to Heaven

Side 3
Misty Mountain Hop
Since I've Been Loving You
No Quarter
Recording: Very good stereo
Source: Seattle May 1973

Side 4
The Ocean
Whole Lotta Love
Boogie Woogie

Comments: Also available as *Live in Seattle* and as *On Tour* (Berkeley 2025/2026).

Led Zeppelin

Flying High/White Knight WK21

Side 1
Train Kept A-Rolling
I Can't Quit You
Medley

Side 2
You Shook Me
How Many More Times

Side 3
Baby I'm Gonna Leave You

Side 4
Baby I'm Gonna Leave You (cont.)
Sittin' & Thinking
I Fought My Way Out of the
Darkness

Recording: Good mono
Source: Fillmore West, San Francisco 8 November 1969
Comments: Deluxe colour cover, not Japanese as cover says.

For Badge Holders Only/LZ 1234-Dragonfly Recs.

Side 1
Sick Again
Nobody's Fault But Mine
Over the Hills and Far Away

Side 2
Since I've Been Loving You
Ten Years Gone
The Battle of Evermore

Side 3
Going to California
Black Mountain Side
Kashmir
Trampled Under Foot

Side 4
Stairway to Heaven
Medley: Whole Lotta Love; Rock
N Roll*

Recording: Excellent stereo
Source: LA Forum June 1977
Comments: *introduction & drums Keith Moon.

For Badge Holders Only (Part Two)/LZ 7-Dragonfly Recs.

Side 1
No Quarter

Side 2
No Quarter (cont.)
Black Country Woman

Side 3
Out on the Tiles*
Moby Dick*

Side 4
Star Spangled Banner
Achilles' Last Stand

Recording: Excellent stereo
Source: LA Forum 23 June 1977
Comments: *Keith Moon on drums.

Gone to California/Dittoline Discs S2322

Side 1
Side 2 of 'Blueberry Hill'

Side 2
Side 3 of 'Blueberry Hill'.

Going to California/TMOQ 72004

Side 1
Immigrant Song
Heart Breaker
Since I've Been Loving You
Black Dog

Side 2
Dazed and Confused

Side 3
Stairway to Heaven
That's the Way
Going to California

Side 4
Whole Lotta Love
Boogie Woogie
Hello Mary Lou
Minnesota Blues
Blues Dedicated to Sheryl S.
I Want You Bonny Airport But
    You Shook Me

Recording: Very good stereo
Source: LA Forum September 1971
Comments: Also available on CBM 3713.

Going To California/Berkeley 1973

Side 1
Stairway to Heaven
Going to California

Side 2
Whole Lotta Love
Let That Boy Boogie Woogie
Hello Mary Lou
My Baby Left Me
Whole Lotta Love

Recording: Very good stereo.

Hiawatha Express/ZAP 7980

Side 1
Heartbreaker
Thank You
Minnesota Blues
The Lemon Song
(24:25)

Side 2
Stairway to Heaven
Riverside Blues
Whole Lotta Love
(18:06)

Recording: Excellent stereo
Comments: Live.

In The Evening/Dane Records SX502

Side 1
Trampled Under Foot
Sick Again
Achilles' Last Stand

Side 2
In the Evening
Stairway to Heaven
Whole Lotta Love

Side 3
The Song Remains the Same

Side 4
Over the Hills and Far Away

Led Zeppelin

Celebration Day
Black Dog
Nobody's Fault But Mine

Misty Mountain Hop
Since I've Been Loving You

Recording: Very good stereo
Source: Falkoner Centre, Copenhagen August 1979
Comments: Deluxe colour front cover.

Kashmir/Berkeley 7867

Comments: Reissue of *On Stage in Europe*, deluxe b&w cover.

Knebworth Fair Vol. One/K&S 056

Side 1
Communication Breakdown
I Can't Quit You
Dazed and Confused
What Is and What Should Never
   Be
Communication Breakdown
(22:10)

Side 2
My Rider
Whole Lotta Love
I Can't Quit You*
(18:20)

Side 3
White Summer*
The Song Remains the Same
Celebration Day
(22:05)

Side 4
Black Dog
Nobody's Fault But Mine
Over The Hills and Far Away
Misty Mountain Hop
(23:40)

Recording: Sides 1 and 2 excellent mono (BBC June 1969); *excellent stereo (Montreaux Blues & Jazz Festival 1974); sides 3 and 4 exccellent mono (Knebworth Fair 4 August 1979)
Comments: Deluxe b&w cover.

Knebworth Fair Vol. Two/K&S 057

Side 1
Since I've Been Loving You
The Rain Song
Sick Again
(23:40)

Side 2
White Summer
Black Mountain Side
Kashmir
Trampled Underfoot
(24:00)

Side 3
Guitar and Drum Solo
In the Evening
Stairway to Heaven
(26:30)

Side 4
Rock and Roll
Whole Lotta Love
Heartbreaker
(19:20)

Recording: Excellent mono
Source: 4 August 1979
Comments: Deluxe b&w cover.

Knebworth 79/Phoenix 44787

Side 1
The Song Remains the Same
Celebration Day
Black Dog
Nobody's Fault But Mine

Side 2
Over the Hills and Far Away
Misty Mountain Hop
Since I've Been Loving You
The Rain Song

Side 3
No Quarter

Side 4
Kashmir
Trampled Under Foot

Recording: Good and very good mono.
Comments: Deluxe colour cover.

Knebworth Volume One

Comments: An EP with pic sleeve.

Knebworth Volume Two

Side 1
Hot Dog (3:30) (excellent mono)
Rock 'N' Roll (3:53) (very good
    stereo) (song separation)

Side 2
Achilles' Last Stand (9:27) (very
    good stereo)

Source: 11 August 1979
Comments: B&w pic sleeve.

L.A. Forum/LZ 1234

Comments: A copy of 'Going to California' (TMOQ 72004) with a deluxe
colour cover. 'Immigrant Song' is very good mono, rest is very good stereo.

Led Zeppelin/Joker 3721

Recording: Excellent stereo
Comments: Same as 'Stairway to Heaven', deluxe cover. Supposed 'legitimate'
Italian release.

Led Zeppelin/K&S 074

Side 1
Operator (Robert Plant 1968 with
    A. Korner & S. Miller,
    excellent stereo)
I Can't Quit You
I Gotta Move
Dazed and Confused

Side 2
How Many More Times
Riverside Blues
Communication Breakdown
Whole Lotta Love

Recording: Excellent mono
Source: Last three tracks Top Gear 1969, rest Stockholm 1968
Comments: Song separation.

Led Zeppelin

Live

Comments: Sides 3 and 4 of *Going to California.*

Live at Knebworth 4 August 1979 Part One/Raven LZ4879

Side 1
The Song Remains the Same
Celebration Day
Black Dog
Nobody's Fault But Mine

Side 2
Over the Hills and Far Away
Misty Mountain Hop
Since I've Been Loving You

Side 3
No Quarter
Ten Years Gone

Side 4
Battle of Evermore
In the Evening
Hot Dog (Stairway to Gilligan)
    (original 45, excellent mono)

Recording: Very good mono
Comments: Deluxe b&w cover.

Live at Knebworth 4 August 1979 Part Two/Raven LZ 4879-2

Side 1
Kashmir
Trampled Underfoot

Side 2
The Rain Song
White Summer
Black Mountain Side

Side 3
Stairway to Heaven
Whole Lotta Love
Heartbreaker

Side 4
Rock & Roll
Hot Dog*
Rock & Roll*
Achilles' Last Stand*

Recording: Very good mono
Source: *11 August 1979
Comments: Deluxe b&w cover.

Live at the Chicago Stadium/Digger Productions 2675

Side 1
Rock N Roll (poor)
Sick Again
Over the Hills and Far Away
When The Levee Breaks

Side 2
The Song Remains the Same
The Rain Song
Kashmir
Wanton Song

Side 3
How Many More Times (poor)
Stairway to Heaven

Side 4
Trampled Underfoot
Moby Dick
Black Dog
Communication Breakdown

Recording: Fair mono
Comments: 1975 tour.

Live At The L.A. Forum 9 April 1970/Rubber Dubber 70-007

Side 1
Bring It On Home
That's the Way

Side 2
Bron-Y-Aur
Since I've Been Loving You
Organ Improvisation

Side 3
Thank You
What Is and What Should Never
  Be
Whole Lotta Love; Boogie Mama

Side 4
Boogie Mama (cont.)
The Lemon Song; Whole Lotta
  Love
Medley: Communication
  Breakdown; For What It's
  Worth; She Was Just Seventeen.

Live At The Lyceum In London/Grant Musik Recs.

Side 1
Introductions
Good Times Bad Times;
  Communication Breakdown
I Can't Quit You
Heartbreaker
(15:35)

Side 2
You Shook Me
What Is and What Should Never
  Be
(13:07)

Side 3
Dazed and Confused
(14:58)

Side 4
How Many More Times; Eyesight
  To The Blind; Let That Boy
  Boogie Woogie
(15:28)

Recording: Very good mono
Source: 12 October 1969
Comments: Deluxe red and black cover.

Live In England 1976/TAKRL 918

Comments: A reissue of *On Stage in Europe 1975* with a deluxe b&w cover.

Live In Japan/TAKRL 1966

Side 1
Tangerine
Moby Dick
Celebration Day
Recording: Good stereo.

Side 2
Immigrant Song
Hertbreaker
Stairway to Heaven

Live In Japan '69/TM 1698

Side 1
Communication Breakdown
I Can't Quit You

Side 2
Friends; Smoke Gets in Your Eyes
  (excellent stereo)

Led Zeppelin

You Shook Me
Stairway to Heaven (excellent
   stereo)

Baby I'm Gonna Leave You
Blues (not listed on cover)

Recording: Good mono
Comments: A copy of 'Unburied Dead Zeppo's Grave' with a deluxe green and black cover.

Live In Seattle/TMOQ

Comments: Same as V½. Reissued in 1978 with b&w deluxe cover as TAKRL 2964.

Live On Blueberry Hill/Mushroom Records 3

Comments: A reissue of *Blueberry Hill* on coloured vinyl. Available on CBM 30/31.

London Live/Right Records SX503

Recording: Very good mono
Comments: A copy of *Live at the Lyceum in London* (Grant Musik Recs.) with a deluxe colour front cover.

Montreal 75/Phoenix 44774

Comments: A re-release of *1975 World Tour* (TAKRL 2960) with a deluxe colour cover.

Mudslide/TMOQ 71041

Side 1
Heart Breaker
Thank You
What Is and What Should Never
   Be

Side 2
Communication Breakdown
Ramble On
Since I've Been Loving You
Whole Lotta Love

Recording: Excellent mono
Source: 1971 FM broadcast
Comments: Reissued on Mushroom Recs. 5 on coloured vinyl.

Mudslide/BRR 004

Comments: 200 pressed on red vinyl from original TMOQ plates. Excellent mono.

My Brain Hurts/IMP 1115

Side 1
Over the Hills and Far Away
Misty Mountain Hop
Since I've Been Loving You

Side 2
Dancing Days
The Song Remains the Same
The Rain Song

Bron-Y-Aur   Stand By Me

Recording: Excellent mono
Source: December 1972, Japan
Comments: First pressing on coloured vinyl, song separation.

The 1975 British Tour/LZ 6897

Comments: A copy of *Earl's Court* (excellent mono) and *Earl's Court II* (very
   good mono).

1975 World Tour/TAKRL 2960

Side 1   *Side 2*
Rock N Roll   The Song Remains the Same
Sick Again   The Rain Song
Over the Hills and Far Away   Kashmir
In My Time of Dying   Trampled Under Foot

Side 3   *Side 4*
Dazed and Confused   Stairway to Heaven
                                   Whole Lotta Love
                                   Black Dog
                                   Heartbreaker

Recording: Fair stereo
Source: Montreal Forum 6 February 1975
Comments: Reissued in 1978 with a b&w deluxe cover.

No Quarter

Side 1   *Side 2*
No Quarter   Going to California
                                   That's the Way
                                   Bron-Y-Aur Stomp

Recording: Excellent stereo
Source: Earls Court, London, England, 18 May 1975
Comments: European bootleg with deluxe cover, song separation.

On Blueberry Hill/Abstract Recs.

Comments: Also available as *Blueberry Hill*.

On Stage in Europe 1975/ZAP 7867

Comments: A reissue of *Earl's Court*.

On Tour/Berkeley 2025/2026

Comments: A reissue of *V½*.

Led Zeppelin

On Tour/Black Gold Concerts BG52025

Recording: Very good stereo
Comments: A copy of V ½ (TMOQ 72019) with a deluxe b&w cover. Sides 2 and 3 are reversed on cover.

Performed Live In Seattle/HH Seattle 1-4

Side 1
Rock N Roll
Celebration Day
Black Dog

Side 2
Over the Hills and Far Away
Misty Mountain Hop
Since I've Been Loving You

Side 3
No Quarter
The Song Remains the Same
The Rain Song

Side 4
Stairway to Heaven
The Ocean
Whole Lotta Love

Plant Waves/WRMB 337

Side 1
Rock N Roll
Sick Again
Over the Hills and Far Away
In My Time of Dying

Side 2
Kashmir
Trampled Under Foot
How Many More Times

Side 3
No Quarter
The Song Remains the Same

Side 4
Stairway to Heaven
Whole Lotta Love
Black Dog
Heartbreaker

Recording: Poor mono
Source: Detroit & New York 1975.

Rock N Roll Circus

Comments: See listing under Rock N Roll Circus.

Seattle '73/Phoenix 44772

Comments: A re-release of V ½ (TMOQ 72019) with a deluxe colour cover.

The Second Night/Geiko-Sukui 3ZC-07249

Side 1
The Song Remains the Same
Celebration Day
Black Dog
Nobody's Fault But Mine

Side 2
Over the Hills and Far Away
Misty Mountain Hop
Since I've Been Loving you

Side 3
No Quarter

Side 4
Rain Song

Ten Years Gone
Hot Dog

White Summer; Black Mountain
    Side
Kashmir

Side 5
Trampled Underfoot
Sick Again
Achilles' Last Stand

Side 6
Instrumental
In the Evening
Stairway to Heaven
Whole Lotta Love

Recording: Excellent stereo
Source: Falconer Theater, Copenhagen
Comments: Deluxe b&w cover; song separation.

Sin City Social/K&S Records 001

Side 1
Introduction (:22)
No Quarter (11:51)*
The Song Remains the Same
    (7:56)*

Side 2
I'm Going Down (3:25)**
What Is and What Should Never
    Be (4:23)
Medley: Good Times Bad Times;
    For What It's Worth; I Saw Her
    Standing There (7:19)†
Slick Black Limousine (4:12) (Alice
    Cooper)

Recording: Excellent mono
Source: *Inglewood forum 31 May 1973 and **Inglewood Forum 3 June
1973, †*Best of Led Zeppelin Live in Concert.*

Stairway to Heaven/TMOQ 73017

Side 1
Immigrant Song
Stairway to Heaven
What Is and What Should Never
    Be

Side 2
Whole Lotta Love
Boogie Woogie
Travelin' Momma
That's Alright Now Momma
Minnesota Blues
Little Honey Bee
Lemon Song

Recording: Excellent stereo
Source: LA Forum 25 June 1975
Comments: Also available on HH STH and CBM 1852 (song separation).
In 1978 200 copies were pressed on multi-coloured yellow vinyl from the
original TMOQ plates (excellent mono).

Swiss Made/S 8006

Side 1
Nobody's Fault But Mine
Black Dog

Side 2
Hot Dog
All My Love

Led Zeppelin

In the Evening
The Rain Song

Trampled Under Foot
Since I've Been Loving You

Side 3
Achilles' Last Stand
White Summer
Black Mountain Side
Kashmir

Side 4
Stairway to Heaven
Rock & Roll
Heartbreaker

Recording: Good mono
Source: Zurich, Switzerland 29 June 1979
Comments: Japanese bootleg with deluxe b&w cover.

Unburied Dead Zeppo's Grave/TM 1698

Side 1
Stairway to Heaven (BBC, not
    studio as cover says, excellent
    stereo)
Communication Breakdown
I Can't Quit You

Side 2
Friends; Smoke Gets in Your Eyes
    (excellent stereo)
Baby I'm Gonna Leave You
Blues

Recording: Very good mono
Source: Cover says Winterland but this is a Japanese concert
Comments: Japanese bootleg. Stroll On is listed on the cover but doesn't appear
on the LP.

Three Days After/TMOQ 72016

Side 1
Stairway to Heaven
That's the Way
Bron-Y-Aur

Side 2
Moby Dick

Side 3
Heartbreaker
Whole Lotta Love
I'm Going Down
Boogie Woogie

Side 4
The Ocean
Communication Breakdown
What Is and What Should Never
    Be

Recording: Very good mono.

Trampled Underfoot/JPP 14001

Side 1
Rock and Roll (3:30)
Sick Again (4:00)
Over the Hills and Far Away
    (6:15)
In My Time of Dying (9:50)

Side 2
The Song Remains the Same (6:10)
Rain Song (6:20)
Kashmir (7:50)
Trampled Underfoot (7:10)

Side 3
Dazed and Confused (26:00)

Side 4
Stairway to Heaven (9:45)

Whole Lotta Love (1:15)
Black Dog (4:40)
Heartbreaker (6:40)

Recording: Satisfactory stereo
Source: Madison Square Garden 1975
Comments: Song separation.

White Summer/MARC LZ 76053

Side 1
Train Kept A Rollin'
Since I've Been Loving You
Black Mountain Side
White Summer
Black Mountain Side (Reprise)

Side 2
Dazed and Confused
Communication Breakdown
ABC Song (studio)

Recording: Very good stereo
Source: Hamburg, Germany, 11 March 1970
Comments: Japanese bootleg with deluxe brown cover.

Zeppelin Concert/HH Seattle 1, 2

Side 1
Rock and Roll
Celebration Day
Black Dog
Over the Hills and Far Away
Misty Mountain Hop

Side 2
The Song Remains the Same
What Is and What Should Never
   Be
Whole Lotta Love

LED ZEPPELIN SINGLES RELEASED IN THE US

Communication Breakdown/Good Times Bad Times – Atlantic 2613
Released March 1969

Whole Lotta Love/Living Loving Maid (She's Just a Woman) – Atlantic 2690
Released November 1969

Immigrant Song/Hey Hey What Can I Do – Atlantic 2777
Released November 1970

Black Dog/Misty Mountain Hop – Atlantic 2849
Released December 1971

Rock and Roll/Four Sticks – Atlantic 2865
Released March 1972

Over the Hills and Far Away/Dancing Days – Atlantic 2970
Released April 1973

Led Zeppelin

D'Yer Mak'er/The Crunge — Atlantic 2986

Released November 1973

Trampled Underfoot/Black Country Women — Swan Song SS70102

Released May 1975

Candy Store Rock/Royal Orleans — Swan Song SS70110

Released April 1976

Fool in the Rain/Hot Dog — Swan Song SS71003

Released January 1980

LATEST RELEASES:

Coverdale Page/ Geffen GEFD-24487 Released April 1993

Shake My Tree	Easy Does It
Waiting On You	Take a Look At Yourself
Take Me For a Little While	Don't Leave Me This Way
Pride and Joy	Absolution Blues
Over Now	Whisper a Prayer For The
Feeling Hot	Dying

All Songs written by David Coverdale and Jimmy Page. Produced by Coverdale, Page and (Mike) Fraser. Recorded at various studios.

Fate of Nations/ Atlantic/Esparanza 92264 and Fontana 514 867-2 Released June 1993

Calling To You	If I Were a Carpenter (Tim Hardin)
Down to the Sea	Colours of a Shade
Come Into My Life	Promised Land
I Believe	The Greatest Gift
29 Palms	Great Spirit
Memory Song (Hello Hello)	Network News

Songs written by Plant/Blackwell/Jones/Johnstone/Woods/MacMichael